The Best of SkyLight

Essential Teaching Tools

Edited by

James Bellanca

FOR INFORMATION:

Corwin
A SAGE Company
2455 Teller Road
Thousand Oaks, California 91320
(800) 233-9936
www.corwin.com

SAGE Publications Ltd.
1 Oliver's Yard
55 City Road
London, EC1Y 1SP
United Kingdom

SAGE Publications India Pvt. Ltd.
B 1/I 1 Mohan Cooperative Industrial Area
Mathura Road, New Delhi 110 044
India

SAGE Publications Asia-Pacific Pte. Ltd.
3 Church Street
#10-04 Samsung Hub
Singapore 049483

Printed in the United States of America.

This book is printed on acid-free paper.

LCCN 2001090709
ISBN 978-1-5751-7492-1

Acknowledgments

A heartfelt thanks goes first to all those consultants, authors, students and colleagues who contributed to the development of SkyLight, not only as a business, but especially as a wonderful idea place committed to the implementation of professional development programs that made a difference for so many teachers and children. Foremost among this host of contributors, I must recognize Robin Fogarty whose eye on what would most help teachers improve their work was unflinchingly sharp and caring. Her support, dedication, and insight were essential in making SkyLight the best.

For this book, I wish to thank the SkyLight authors with whom I discussed the possible selections and those who contributed their works. I must also thank Sue Schumer, the acquisitions editor who kept me on task, and Carol Luitjens, President of SkyLight, who seeded the idea for this collection of essential teaching tools.

Not to be forgotten are those who have long stood in the background and were the backbone of SkyLight: my wife, Gerry; Mary Jane Bloethner, SkyLight's "ear to the ground" Director of Client Services; and, especially with this book, Dave Stockman, Bruce Leckie, and Donna Ramirez—who have always made SkyLight books look "best" with their design and layout.

JAMES BELLANCA
Editor
Founder of
SkyLight Professional Development

Contents

Part III: Assessment Tools for Today's Classroom

Introduction

those who Can,
teach Well

Three Lies and Three Truths About Teaching

After thirty-nine years in education, I have identified the three biggest lies I hear about teaching. The first lie is those that can, do and those who can't, teach. The second lie is the only good classroom is the teacher-proof classroom. The third lie is there is no correlation between good teaching and increased student achievement.

There are, I believe, three truths about teaching which counter the three big lies. The first truth is those who can, do teach. The second truth is the best classrooms are led by teachers who are bent on lifelong development in the art and science of teaching. The third is good teaching is the heart and soul of student achievement.

Each of these truths can stand on its own, yet each is linked inextricably to the others. When all is said and done, the most all-encompassing truth about good teaching is that all teachers, given appropriate support and opportunity, can learn the art and science of teaching. While some are born good teachers, most become good through hard work. As teachers develop their teaching talents, students' achievement increases.

Faux Reform Efforts

In the past decade, at every level of the education system, reform has been a watchword. National goals, assessments, and the linkage of education to the economy have driven the new agenda that makes school funding a high priority at both the national and local levels. Unfortunately, there has been a reticence to make these monies pay off in substantive increases in student achievement. The key reform issue is not textbooks, buildings, vouchers, charters, daily or annual schedules, digitized curricula, or standardized tests; it is the quality of classroom instruction.

The key reform issue is the quality of classroom instruction.

The majority of the changes brought about by the current reform efforts have been tangential, random, superficial, and, most sadly, not systemic. Too few reforms get to the heart of the matter. Most reforms scratch the surface: student textbooks are updated; class schedules are put into blocks; the number of standardized tests is increased; mini-schools are chartered; televisions are strapped to every classroom wall; computers are placed in every classroom corner; and grades are changed from letters to numbers and from numbers to letters. In any one district, students in school A get new desks; school B, a new daily schedule; school C, a new reading program. In any one state, students in district A get mini-schools; students in district B get an aligned curriculum. Although districts talk about systemic reform, teachers in school A learn about brain research; teachers in school B have a publisher's workshop on the new math textbook; and teachers in school C are told that they will not have time for an inservice.

Much of the time, educators claim that changes in school practice are made for the benefit of students. However, too many are made for the benefit of adults who work in the school or are made to benefit students in ways other than improving their academic performance in a substantive manner. Thus, schools experience even more random scattering of reforms such as providing assistants to the principal for discipline, scheduling, or daily operations; outsourcing student tutoring programs; placing parent volunteers in the lunchroom; adding district curriculum coordinators and directors; writing new report cards; and organizing study committees to rewrite the curriculum, increase or decrease special education paperwork, and adjust discipline codes. Although no one can deny that such activities are worthwhile, for the most part, few, if any, have significant, measurable impact on the quality of classroom instruction and the improvement of student achievement.

True Reform Efforts

Real reform seeks to improve student academic achievement. The key to increasing student achievement is a significant and systemic effort to improve the quality of teaching. And the key to improving teaching quality is effective school leadership.

Over the years, I have been constantly reminded of the truth in the formula: as the principal goes, so go the teachers; as the teachers go, so go the students. Consider one example.

As the principal goes, so go the teachers; as the teachers go, so go the students.

Principal Yvonne Minor transformed Dyett Middle School (Chicago) from an education pit into a model school where students' achievements in multiple domains of learning were evident. When Yvonne arrived at the modern, well-appointed school, she found graffiti on the walls, students running in and out of the building, significant student and staff absenteeism, discouraged teachers, and rock-bottom tests scores. Furthermore, the district that was being called the worst in the nation by William Bennett.

The start was difficult. After focusing the teachers' attention on the school's low reading scores, Yvonne made fast moves. First, she explained that every teacher was to act as a reading teacher. She also asked that the first two periods of the day be dedicated to reading and writing and that instruction in every subject be centered on reading. She scheduled workshops on how to teach reading more skillfully, found reading tutor volunteers through the city's electric company and a naval base, coached and counseled individual teachers, and started a book reading competition.

Yvonne did not stop there. More volunteers were called in from a neighborhood senior citizen home, the local police station, the high school, and any source she could find. Graffiti was washed away, interior walls were constructed to make more classrooms, and students were kept in their classrooms until the bell rang. Parent volunteers and teachers composed a dress code and monitored the exit doors. Teachers tested students on the subskills of reading and met once a month to review the reading progress of each student.

By year five of Yvonne's principalship, Dyett was a different school. A visitor walking down the hall could look into any classroom and see engaged students. "When I could walk past a room," said Yvonne, "and see students at work or hear them thinking out loud as the teacher engaged them in discussion, I was a happy principal. When I saw glazed eyes or heads down on the desk or students off task, I was not. Happily, as the teachers transferred my expectations to the students, the former became the norm."

Thanks to Yvonne's continuing effort on instructional improvement, visitors in the classroom were not surprised to see changes in every classroom. They might find students working in cooperative groups to analyze a short story. They could view students peer tutoring one another while reviewing vocabulary words. They could happen upon a hands-on science lab in which students were alive with excitement as they complete their measurement experiments. They could witness math students using problem-based learning to measure contour maps. Finally, they might listen in on a guest lecture by a local businessman explaining the importance of mathematics in managing a business.

Where did all this change lead? First, and most importantly, it led to significant positive changes in student performance.

Where did all this change lead? First, and most importantly, it led to significant positive changes in student performance. The teachers, reflecting on the improvement results, took pride in finding ways to continue the progress. In five years time, Dyett's reading scores escalated from the bottom of the district's results to well above the median. For the first time, Dyett students applied to and earned acceptance into the best high schools in the area. In addition, Dyett students began earning seats in high school bands and orchestras, others won science fair awards for the first time, and, as the years progressed, more and more Dyett students moved on to college.

This school is only one example of what can happen when teachers are given the opportunity to develop their teaching talents and skills by a principal leader who focuses on instructional improvement and higher achievement for all. In Seattle (Washington), Indianapolis, Boston, Taunton (Massachusetts), Rockford (Illinois), Norman (Oklahoma), and in cities and towns across the nation, these changes have occurred, not because of educational policy or practice changes that waste effort on tangential improvements, but because they focused on improving instruction as the sine qua non for improving student achievement.

Principles for Improving Classroom Instruction

These example schools and an increasing body of research reaffirms what teachers and principals working together can do to increase achievement. From examples and the research come two basic principles that lead to successful systemic school reform.

Principle 1: Develop Teachers' Content Knowledge

No matter how prestigious the university the novice teacher attended or how high the grades he or she earned in an undergraduate program, novice teachers do not arrive at their first teaching jobs with all the tools they need to teach well. Consider the following example.

Novice teachers do not arrive at their first teaching jobs with all the tools they need to teach well.

A middle school principal was searching for a seventh grade, certified mathematics teacher who would teach pre-algebra to the gifted class, two general classes, and a "basic math" class. (The principal wanted to eventually eliminate the basic math class.) He wanted to hire a certified mathematics teacher, but the district human resource department could not find a certified teacher. Therefore, he decided to look for a candidate who had a sufficient mathematics background, who understood the core concepts of pre-algebra, and who could identify conceptual errors made by students and mediate the corrections. The best he could find was a candidate with high college grades. The candidate had completed a college algebra course, a college trigonometry course, a statistics elective, and a mathematics methods course. Unfortunately, the candidate knew the rules and procedures that he had memorized for his college math courses, but he had little understanding of the core concepts in the middle school curriculum. In the end, the principal determined this candidate was his best option, but he needed advanced studies that would challenge him to learn the "why" of mathematics so needed in the development of middle school students' mathematics abilities.

Teachers must have a thorough knowledge of the course content they will teach. Teachers who have inadequate knowledge of their subjects cannot teach well. Consider the following example.

A consultant who has his undergraduate degree in engineering and a Ph.D. in curriculum and instruction was working with a group of high school teachers. His first step was to visit each of their classrooms and observe algebra lessons. Before class, the first teacher complained, "The kids can't do it. They just aren't bright enough to do algebra." During class, this teacher began the lesson by asking the students, "What is a fraction? Do you know?" A student in the first row responded: "It is when you put a 1 over a 2." "Is that all?" asked the teacher. "No," said the student. "It is anytime you put a one over another number." Additional conversation, mostly supplied by the one student with silent and glazed assent from the others, ended with the statement that "only a one could be above another number because that is what Mr. Smith taught us." Sadly, Mr. Smith, whose credentials were in special education, had no more idea where to take the lesson or how to correct the misunderstanding. Happily, the consultant gave the teacher a series of lessons in how to properly define fractions, how to explain the key attributes of fractions, how to teach the core concept, and how to identify and remediate students' common and predictable misconceptions. With this expanded knowledge of the content of the algebra curriculum and a new understanding of high school students' tendencies to misunderstand certain elements, the teacher was able to develop the students' understanding of fractions. Subsequent discussions between the consultant and the teacher resulted in the teacher changing his belief about what his students could learn. More importantly, student performance in working with fractions improved noticeably.

Teachers must have a thorough knowledge of the course content. Teachers who have inadequate knowledge of their subjects cannot teach well.

Principle 2: Go Beyond Information Dissemination

Information acquisition is the foundation of knowing. However, information acquisition alone is insufficient for learning. Information acquisition may prepare a student for success on a test, especially if she has a good memory. However, as time and new information intervene, the student's memory will diminish. In a classroom where information acquisition is the be-all and end-all of work, learning and memory are mistakenly treated as synonymous functions. Good teaching moves student learning beyond rote memorization of information to developing an understanding and an ability to use information.

To illustrate this point—and to show how a teacher can become trapped in the misconception that information acquisition is sufficient for learning—consider the following example. Since early in my career, I have helped experienced teachers develop their abilities to mediate learning experiences through targeted questioning. I always start by asking how many are familiar with Bloom's taxonomy (1956). Invariably all hands go up. Next I ask how many used the taxonomy to guide their questioning during classroom discussions or on tests. Invariably, one hand in twenty-five goes up. "What then," I ask, "is the reason for your familiarity with the taxonomy?" The reply changes seldom: "In our teacher education class, we had to memorize the levels and key words for the course exam." "So," I add, "when you say, 'I've studied Bloom's taxonomy,' you mean that you studied it for the test and not to use in the classroom? Isn't that ironic?" "Oh, yes," the teachers say, chuckling, "but that's the nature of education methods."

Good teaching moves student learning beyond rote memorization of information to developing an understanding and an ability to use information.

How does this happen? It happens because education methods teachers have low expectations. They believe that memorizing certain ideas is sufficient. Many education professors lack K–12 classroom experience beyond what they had in their own education, and they become defensive about their own ability to go beyond theory. Therefore, they create so-called rigor in their courses by increasing the amount of work that students must memorize. More often than not, when experienced teachers chuckle at the irony of memorizing Bloom's taxonomy, they also describe how their professors made the course really tough by requiring them to memorize long lists of the subwords in each level or write a long research paper reviewing how critics of Bloom saw the taxonomy. The ultimate irony, more than one teacher has volunteered, is that most of what and how they learned in their education classes followed the same pattern: memorize, read others' criticism, and write abstruse papers that were graded more on form than on content.

Experienced teachers recognize that the real rigor in the teaching profession comes from applying ideas and theories, not just memorizing them. Teachers who have worked long and hard in the trenches need information about ideas that work to excite, motivate, and increase student achievement—ideas such as Bloom's taxonomy, cooperative learning, multiple intelligences, and brain-based learning. But simply knowing about these methods is only the first step. Learning how to apply and assess sound theory to meet the day-to-day challenges of improving student performance is the crucial step. The shortcomings attributed to teaching methods come not from the methods themselves, but from the low expectations of professors who seem to have little knowledge about the skilled and appropriate use of these methods.

Learning how to apply and assess sound theory to meet the day-to-day challenges of improving student performance is the crucial step.

Donna Ogle and Robin Fogarty are examples of professional teachers of teachers who are willing and able to create substantive rigor in teacher development. They do so not by having teachers memorize and regurgitate, but by assessing classroom applications which put theory into practice.

Donna Ogle, a pioneer in the study of how prior knowledge impacts the learning of new ideas, does not lock herself into the theoretical ivory tower. She works with teachers to find concrete tools that put this theory into successful practice. As a result, she has developed a strategy, the KWL (Ogle 1986), which has become as valuable and powerful a teaching tool as Rowe's (1969, 1996) wait time, graphic organizers, Johnson and Johnson's (1986, 1987a, 1987b) cooperative learning model, and deBono's (1985, 1986, 1992) PMI. Going beyond asking her graduate and undergraduate students to memorize what the letters mean or beyond assigning them to review the research on using the KWL, Donna emphasizes how these students can use the strategy in their lessons and how they can assess the results.

Robin Fogarty, who has researched learning transfer (1992) and has found that many teachers struggle with how to appropriately use teaching tools, has developed guidelines to help teachers integrate these tools strategically across the curriculum. (See References for a listing of Robin's books.) Robin not only made rules to memorize, but also has shown various ways to think about each strategy's best use. It is through the thinking processes that she identified—the processes mapped out in The Three-Story Intellect (1991)—that has shaped a new and more meaningful understanding of rigor. In place of the superficial definition of rigor promulgated by education professors who focus on review of low-level studies and discussion of abstruse topics, Robin's definition challenges teachers to think deeply enough to develop applications of theory that lead students beyond mere memory into deep understanding and high transfer.

Applying the Principles in the Classroom

What happens when a teacher discovers the rigorous challenge of teaching beyond recall? There are many examples to see and to hear in classrooms led by Robin Fogarty's students who have integrated these principles into their instructional repertoires.

A "Low-Track" Class

One of my favorite examples is Dolores Burns, a high school English teacher. Dolores and I met in her classroom; she had invited me to observe and critique her lessons on Hawthorne's *The Scarlet Letter.* When I entered the room for her first period class, filled with juniors ensconced in the lowest track in that school, I was struck by what I saw: tables with five chairs each, a full wall of student essays about characters in the novel, a visual outline of a twelve-paragraph essay, a wall of pictures showing Puritan New England, and student-created mobiles with thematic quotes from Hawthorne's other works hanging from the ceiling.

I followed the students into the room and took a seat at the back. The students stopped at a shelf unit and pulled out various utensils including scissors, magazines, newsprint, and markers. (Remember, this is not an elementary classroom!) While Dolores took attendance, the students settled into their seats and laid out their tools. Dolores stopped their work long enough to remind them that after thirty minutes they would have to be finished with their "group web collage" of the symbols in the novel. She also explained that she would tell them how to write a twelve-paragraph essay using the group collage. After directing the students back to work, Dolores moved from table to table. At each stop, she reviewed the students' progress, asked questions, encouraged and gave feedback. At the table next to me, she stopped and asked the students to identify one of the symbols. "What is that symbol?" "A bird," answered a student. "A bird?" she feigned. "I don't recall a bird." "Oh, yes. Let me read you the passage on page . . . hmmm . . . 56." After he read the passage, Dolores asked, "And what does it symbolize?" "I know that," added a female student who proceeded to explain how she thought the bird represented Dimmesdale's love. "Good for you," acknowledged Dolores. "You folks are really thinking well. Keep at it."

As she had promised, Dolores called the groups to attention with twenty minutes left in the period. "I am really pleased with the work you have done on the symbols. You did what I asked in making sure you showed how the symbols connected to your characters and where you could find proof in the story. Now we are going to work on putting all your ideas into a paper. You worked together well to gather the research. You helped each other find a lot of good ideas. Now it is time for you each to show me what you have learned and to write your own essay. But first, let's review how you will organize this essay. Let's look at an example on the overhead of what a good paper will look like . . . ."

Dolores concluded the period by using the overhead projector to show a visual map of the twelve-paragraph essay and the rubric by which she would grade their work. She presented several examples of opening paragraphs "to get my interest and give the purpose of your paper." She explained that paragraph twelve should be a "summary of your ideas in which you will tell me what you said in the other paragraphs." Again she showed some examples that she liked and two that she explained were "weak." After answering questions, she showed the model and examples for the middle paragraphs, each one built around one of the symbols from the group chart. After checking for understanding of the writing task and reviewing the rubric, she instructed the groups to put away their tools and to come to the next class ready to start writing one of their middle paragraphs.

An Advanced Placement Class

Dolores' next class period was an advanced placement (AP) English class. They too were studying *The Scarlet Letter*. Dolores began this class with a KWL. First, she asked the students to think individually about what each already knew about the task they were doing. Then, using the KWL chart on the board, she solicited a variety of responses: "We're preparing to write an essay comparing one character from the novel with a current TV character." "We are looking for evidence in the novel that fits our hypothesis." "We are working in teams to help each other do research." "We have to do our own essay to prove the group's thesis."

When she completed the K column, she progressed to the W: "What is it that you *w*ant to know about the task?" Responses included "How long will the paper be?" "Do we do it at home or in class?" "Do we have to footnote the draft?" "Can we . . . ". After recording all the questions, she noted that the paper was to be at least twelve paragraphs long and said, "You can do a draft outline at home, but will write the first draft here and then get feedback from your group using 'Mrs. Potter's questions' " (Bellanca and Fogarty 1991). "No footnotes are needed in the draft, but know your source spot." Dolores concluded the class by reminding them that part of the final assessment would be a graded journal entry, done at home alone and identifying the L, what they had *l*earned about (a) the novel, (b) comparing characters using a Venn diagram, and/or (c) writing a twelve-paragraph comparative essay.

The "Cliff Notes" Approach

In our conversation later that day, Dolores and I discussed how the structure and format of these two classes differed from each other and from how she had taught the novel in previous years. In her first few years, Dolores used what she described as the "Cliff Notes approach." She only taught the novel to her "college bound" class. It was close to the way her own teacher in junior year had done. First, she assigned a chapter to the students. On the following day, she lectured to them. She summarized the events of the chapter and described the what and why of certain events. Some days, she would check their reading comprehension by starting with a quiz. On other days, she would ask factual questions to start a discussion about what happened to whom. To add variety, she added some short lectures on the historic times, the Puritan religion, and the life and works of Hawthorne. "I was the teacher. I had the knowledge and I had to give it to them," she said. "They didn't have the background to analyze the book, I thought. So I was their Cliff's Notes."

When Dolores began teaching the AP class, she added the essay assignment to her basic approach. "I was very comfortable with my style of teaching. I saw no need to worry about their learning styles." She provided the class with a list of background topics before they began to read the novel. To her lectures, Dolores added character analysis, symbolism, historic background, theme, and an overview of the author's style. This was information she felt was important for their "deep understanding" of the novel and its place in American literature.

Making the Transition to Cooperative Learning

When the district offered a class in cooperative learning taught by a highly respected colleague, Dolores decided to sign on for two reasons. First, she needed her required re-certification points; second, she thought she could debunk the whole topic of "changing our methods" which the administration was "pushing." "Did I ever surprise myself!" she said.

My pride was hurt and I got frustrated when the basics kids didn't respond the way I wanted. I decided that I had nothing to lose, so why not try something different?

Dolores took great pride in being an excellent teacher. "I was somebody," she said, "who knew her stuff. I wanted every kid to learn what I was teaching and to love the great literature I loved." In the year she began to work with the AP students "who would do anything you told them," Dolores also was assigned the "basics" whose "bodies were lucky to arrive" in class. They were the reason Dolores gave for trying out some of the Robin Fogarty's ideas. "My pride was hurt and I got frustrated when the basics kids didn't respond the way I wanted. I decided that I had nothing to lose, so why not try something different?" Her first days of cooperative learning were a disaster. The students challenged Dolores' management skills. She found some off task, one or two doing everyone's work, and many not doing anything. "They were great hitchhikers," she explained. With her colleague's coaching, Dolores added graphic organizers, roles, challenge points, and an individual concluding task to her group assignments. She also took some time to do fun team-building tasks such as team names, slogans, and symbols and a trust walk to motivate collaboration. "I couldn't believe I was doing these things in my high school class. I don't think [the students] could either, but it worked. The teams actually became quite competitive with each other.

Best of all, they transferred it to the novel. When they discovered that I wasn't going to talk to them endlessly about the book, they began to build their interest. I almost danced the first time one of the groups backed up their ideas with the perfect quote."

Success with the basics class motivated Dolores to try some of the new techniques with her AP and regular classes. At first, she limited the cooperative work to out-of-class assignments by letting students pick their groups and a research topic to jigsaw (Johnson & Johnson 1987a). Ultimately, she blended the study of the novels in the curriculum with cooperative groups, graphic organizers, discussion structured with second- and third-story questions, portfolios, reflective journals, and a thematic project to integrate the literature studied each semester. "Each unit, I added more and more of what I learned. Some of the stuff flopped. Overall, instead of being the big critique, I became a fan. I couldn't believe the changes in how I taught and how well everything worked. In that first year, my AP class ended up with the highest scores in the school. I felt revitalized and the quality of my students' work got better and better. This year, I decided that all my students would study Hawthorne. I was comfortable enough to use different strategies with each group. However, there were certain elements in my plan, such as using the essay to be a final individual assignment, that would let me assess what each student had learned."

I couldn't believe the changes in how I taught and how well everything worked. My AP class ended up with the highest scores in the school.

The Change Continues . . .

In subsequent visits and conversations with Dolores over the years, I observed her continued growth as a teacher who guided her teaching by the two principles. By no means, is she the only teacher I have seen disprove the three biggest lies about the teaching profession. When I hear someone blithely spout "Those who can't teach . . . ," I challenge them to visit her classroom and to do what she is doing. Two persons have taken me up on that challenge. Both had the same reaction. "Oh, she's not what I meant. She's a born teacher." "No," I retort. "She is not. Let me tell you her story." When I finish the story, I add, "And what she can do now is demonstrate to you that there is a direct relation between how she is teaching and the higher achievement she is getting from all her students."

Firmly believing the third biggest lie about teaching, they challenge me to prove my statement. For that challenge, I smile. "Let's take a look at Dolores' portfolio. Over the years, she has saved the essays that her students write." When they finish reading the samples, they nod their heads. Seeing is believing. Those who can, do teach!

In our classrooms, there are many teachers who prove the biggest lies wrong. These are the teachers who have learned to teach well. Over their years in the profession, they have sought out and added to their repertoires ways to improve how well their students perform. By deepening their own knowledge of what they teach (the content in the curriculum) and by developing their skills in mediating their students' learning experience by using a variety of methods thoughtfully and skillfully, imbedding these methods appropriately into complex and challenging lessons, and assessing the results on a variety of levels, these teachers show by word and deed their belief in their own capability to influence their students' academic performance. They *do* help all children learn.

About this Book . . .

This book is a collection of excerpts from what I believe to be the best of SkyLight's books. Through these excerpts, you will discover keys to teaching well. It is my hope that through this book, you will be encouraged to develop your content knowledge and go beyond information dissemination, therefore striving to teach well so that all students may learn.

Just as it is helpful for students to know the criteria for success before they begin a new unit or lesson, I thought it would be helpful for you, the reader, to know the criteria I used to select the articles in this book.

Having decided to organize the book into three main sections that best "map" the book's theme, "Those who can, teach well," I identified six criteria. (see Introduction, Section 2 for an exposition of each.)

1. The approach (tools methods, strategies, etc.) has a proven track record in educational research.
2. There must be a sound process for developing teachers' appropriate use of the approach.

3. The approach challenges students to use their brains as they learn the assigned curricular content.
4. The approach celebrates and empowers the teachers.
5. The approach celebrates children as thinking individuals learning how to make use of their multiple talents.
6. The approach lends itself to multidimensional lesson designs in highly differentiated classrooms.

When the criteria are taken together, they add up, I believe, to the belief that the most effective teachers are those who are instructional thinkers and problem solvers. There are no formulas. There are no "teacher-proof" recipes. There is only the opportunity for teachers to build a repertoire of sound knowledge and productive strategies that engage students' minds in the very difficult tasks of instruction and assessment. When school districts create the conditions and when "teachers of teachers" model this belief and use the six criteria to guide teachers in their professional development, my experience has shown that classroom teachers and their students can and do make major gains in learning.

The ideas and the tools in this collection are not meant as the "be all and end all" of effective teaching. They do, however, represent, I believe, what has proven most helpful from the SkyLight way. As you study what I have selected, I hope that at the very least you will find one of two benefits: (1) ideas and strategies that confirm and reinforce the successes that you have experienced in your classroom, and/or (2) new ideas that will increase your success in helping all children become the most effective learners they can be.

REFERENCES

Bellanca, J., and Fogarty, R. 1991. *Blueprints for thinking in the cooperative classroom.* Palatine, IL: IRI/SkyLight Training and Publishing.

Bloom, B. 1956. *Taxonomy of educational objectives.* New York: David McKay.

de Bono, E. 1985. *Six thinking hats.* Boston: Little, Brown.

———, E. 1986. *Teaching thinking.* New York: Penguin.

———, E. 1992. *Serious creativity: Using the power for lateral thinking to create new ideas.* New York: HarperCollins.

Fogarty, R. 1990. *Designs for cooperative interactions.* Palatine, IL: IRI/SkyLight Training and Publishing.

———. 1991. *The mindful school: How to integrate the curricula.* Palatine, IL: IRI/SkyLight Training and Publishing.

———. 1992. *The mindful school: How to teach for transfer.* Palatine, IL: IRI/SkyLight Training and Publishing.

———. 1994. *The mindful school: How to teach for metacognitive reflection.* Palatine, IL: IRI/SkyLight Training and Publishing.

———. 1995. *Best practices for the learner-centered classroom.* Palatine, IL: IRI/SkyLight Training and Publishing.

———. 1997a. *Brain-compatible classrooms.* Arlington Heights, IL: IRI/SkyLight Training and Publishing.

———. 1997b. *Problem-based learning and other curriculum models for the multiple intelligences classroom.* Arlington Heights, IL: IRI/SkyLight Training and Publishing.

———. 1999. *How to raise test scores.* Arlington Heights, IL: SkyLight Training and Publishing.

———. 2001a. *Literacy matters: Strategies every teacher can use.* Arlington Heights, IL: SkyLight Training and Publishing.

———. 2001b. *Ten things new teachers need to succeed.* Arlington Heights, IL: SkyLight Training and Publishing.

Fogarty, R. and J. Stoehr. 1995. *Integrating curricula with multiple intelligences: Teams, themes, and threads.* Palatine, IL: IRI/SkyLight Training and Publishing.

Johnson, R.W., and D. Johnson. 1986. *Circles of Learning: Cooperation in the classroom.* Alexandria, VA: Association for Supervision and Curriculum Development.

Johnson, R.W., and D. Johnson. 1987a. *Joining together: Group theory and group skills,* 3d ed. Englewood Cliffs, NJ: Prentice Hall.

Johnson, R.W., and D. Johnson. 1987b. *Learning together and alone: Cooperative, competitive, and individualistic learning.* Englewood Cliffs, NJ: Prentice Hall.

Ogle, D. 1986. K-W-L: A teaching model that develops active reading of expository text. *The Reading Teacher.* 39: 564–571.

Rowe, M.B. 1969. Science, silence, and sanctions. *Science and Children.* 6: 11–13.

• PART I •

Cognitive Tools for Teaching

All teaching is for transfer. All learning is for transfer.

In the two excerpts selected for Part I, Robin Fogarty and Kristen Nelson provide the rationale for teaching and learning in a cyberage school.

Robin begins her essay with a simple, but very complex and meaningful statement: "All teaching is for transfer. All learning is for transfer." Her article probes what transfer is, why teaching and learning for transfer is important, and how to teach for transfer. This seminal piece deserves study and re-study by every teacher who wants to do more than teach for a test.

Kristen's essay expands the underlying principles in teaching for transfer and connects these principles with brain research, multiple intelligences theory, and the Internet as a tool to take teaching and learning into new dimensions. Her excerpt does what individual courses or workshops in each of these areas often fail to do; she bridges across the topics and relates each to the other. Her insights foster many "ah hahs" for the reader.

Transfer, multiple intelligences, brain research, and electronic learning opportunities provide teachers and learners with the understandings they need to keep up with the emerging demands of living in an ever more intellectually and emotionally challenging world. Without these understandings (and others yet to emerge), other tools, strategies, and learning systems do little for the young people in our classrooms. If classroom work focuses on memorizing facts and ideas, students lose out. While rote recall may have benefited our parents and grandparents, today's students need to move beyond memorization. Today's students need to be equipped with the necessary tools not only to pass a test, but to sustain a lifetime of learning in an increasingly challenging world.

REFERENCES

Burke, K. 2000. *What to do with the kid who . . . : Developing cooperation, self-discipline, and responsibility in the classroom,* 2nd ed. Arlington Heights, IL: SkyLight Training and Publishing.

Costa, A.L., J. Bellanca, and R. Fogarty. 1992a. *If minds matter: A foreword to the future. Vol. 1: Rationale for change.* Palatine, IL: IRI/SkyLight Training and Publishing.

———. 1992b. *If minds matter: A foreword to the future. Vol. 2: Designs for change.* Palatine, IL: IRI/SkyLight Training and Publishing.

Fogarty, R. 1992. *The mindful school: How to teach for transfer.* Palatine, IL: IRI/SkyLight Training and Publishing.

———. 1994. *The mindful school: How to teach for metacognitive reflection.* Palatine, IL: IRI/SkyLight Training and Publishing.

———. 1995. *Best practices in the learner-centered classroom: A collection of articles.* Palatine, IL: IRI/SkyLight Training and Publishing.

———. 1997. *Brain-compatible classrooms.* Arlington Heights, IL: IRI/SkyLight Training and Publishing.

Gardner, H. 1983. *Frames of mind: Theory of multiple intelligences.* New York: Basic Books.

———. 1991. *The unschooled mind: How children think and how schools should teach.* New York: Basic Books.

———. 1993. *Multiple intelligences: The theory in practice.* New York: Basic Books.

Lazear, D. 1999. *Eight ways of knowing: Teaching for multiple intelligences,* 3d ed. Arlington Heights, IL: SkyLight Training and Publishing.

———. 1999b. *Eight ways of teaching: The artistry of teaching with multiple intelligences,* 3d ed. Arlington Heights, IL: SkyLight Training and Publishing.

Nelson, K. 2001. *Teaching in the cyberage: Linking the Internet and brain theory.* Arlington Heights, IL: SkyLight Training and Publishing.

Parry, T., and G. Gregory. 1998. *Designing brain-compatible learning.* Arlington Heights, IL: SkyLight Training and Publishing.

Raese, R. 1997. *internet.edu.* Arlington Heights, IL: SkyLight Training and Publishing.

SELECTION 1

Teaching for Transfer

by **Robin Fogarty**

All teaching is for transfer. All learning is for transfer. The mission of the thinking classroom, then, is to extend learning, to bridge the old to the new, and to lead students toward relevant transfer and use across academic content and into life situations.

In our work with teachers in the area of teaching for transfer (Fogarty, Perkins, and Barell 1991), we have found a simple framework to be helpful. As we explore such questions as "Why am I teaching this?" and "Where is the transfer?" with teachers, we introduce this notion:

> There are SOMETHINGS that we SOMEHOW want to use SOMEWHERE.

To clarify this esoteric statement of transfer, the diagram in Figure 1.1 illustrates the somethings, somehows, and somewheres inherent in the transfer of learning.

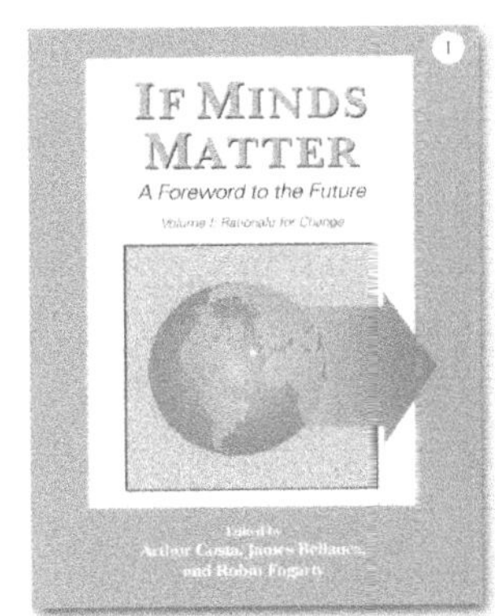

Basically, the diagram illustrates that there are somethings that we want to transfer. These include the more obvious things such as content, knowledge, and skills as well as the more universal things such as principles, concepts, attitudes, and dispositions. As we plan lessons, the identified somethings determine the shape of those lessons. For example, if a targeted something is the attitude of cooperation and teamwork, the lesson will need activity components that require collaboration.

Adapted from *If Minds Matter: Foreword to the Future, Vol. I: Rationale for Change,* by Arthur Costa, James Bellanca, and Robin Fogarty, pp. 211–24. © 1992 by IRI/SkyLight Training and Publishing, Inc.

Teaching for Transfer

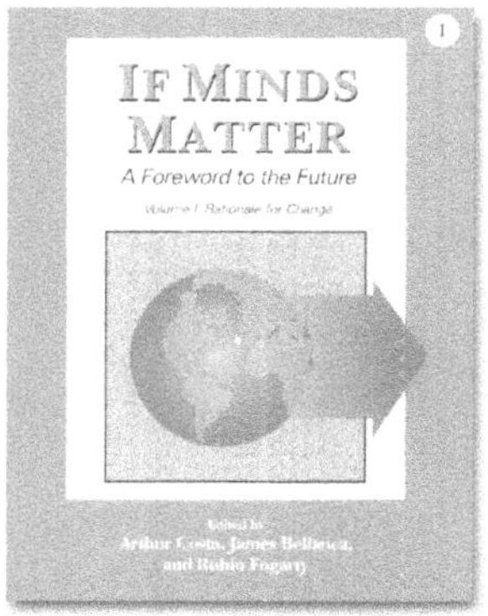

Paralleling this attention to the somethings of a lesson, another consideration illustrated in Figure 1.1 is the somewhere. Exactly where might this something transfer? Within the content? Across other subject matter lessons? Into life situations? Determining the somewheres ahead of time or anticipating future applications also has an impact on the shape of the lesson.

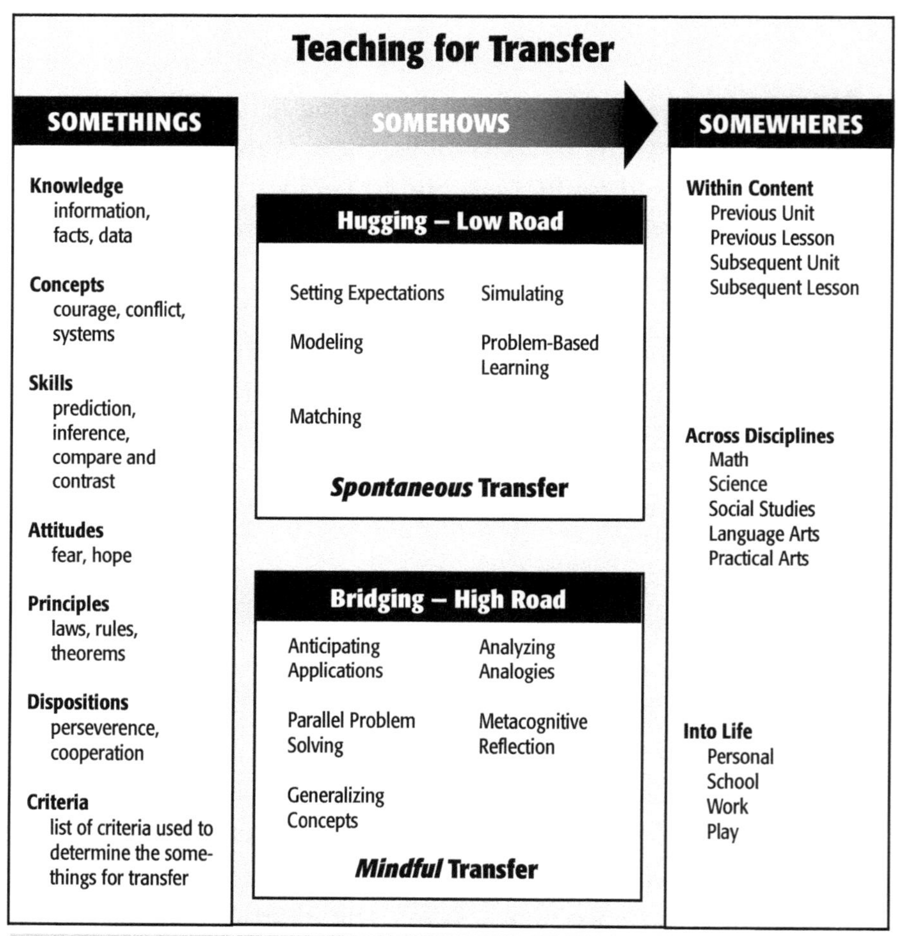

Teaching for Transfer
SOMETHINGS
SOMEHOWS
SOMEWHERES
Knowledge
information, facts, data
Concepts
courage, conflict, systems
Skills
prediction, inference, compare and contrast
Attitudes
fear, hope
Principles
laws, rules, theorems
Dispositions
perseverence, cooperation
Criteria
list of criteria used to determine the somethings for transfer
Hugging – Low Road
Setting Expectations
Simulating
Modeling
Problem-Based Learning
Matching
Spontaneous Transfer
Bridging – High Road
Anticipating Applications
Analyzing Analogies
Parallel Problem Solving
Metacognitive Reflection
Generalizing Concepts
Mindful Transfer
Within Content
Previous Unit
Previous Lesson
Subsequent Unit
Subsequent Lesson
Across Disciplines
Math
Science
Social Studies
Language Arts
Practical Arts
Into Life
Personal
School
Work
Play

Figure 1.1

However, once the somethings are sifted out and the somewheres consciously targeted, the somehows of transfer are the next consideration. The center of the diagram in Figure 1.1 illustrates the somehows, or transfer options, that are available.

These options include both low-road mediation strategies that hug the lesson closely or high-road bridging techniques that require thoughtful application. Either way, through simple hugging strategies, such as setting expectations, modeling, matching, simulating, and using problem-based learning, or through more complex bridging strategies, such as anticipating applications, parallel problem solving, generalizing concepts, analyzing analogies, and cultivating metacognition, explicit mediation fosters the transfer of learning.

The primary focus of this chapter is to describe and illustrate the practical aspects of how to teach for transfer. Therefore, the emphasis is on the somehows or mediation strategies of transfer. However, in order to present a truly practical model of teaching for transfer, some attention must be given to ways of finding the somethings worth teaching and ways to target the somewheres.

The Somethings of Transfer

[Scenario One: Prior to a lesson introducing the Periodic Table of Elements, the teacher deliberately looks for the somethings worth teaching to make the relevance explicit to students for later transfer.]

PHYSICS TEACHER: (He points to a dilapidated and yellowed Periodic Table of Elements hanging above the black lab table. The chart is framed along the bottom with an uneven fringe of frayed threads.) *You will be responsible for knowing the contents of this table. It will serve you well, as you work in this lab.*

TIM: (Eyes rolling up, he thinks to himself, "I'm never gonna use this stuff ever again. What a waste. How am I ever gonna memorize all this?")

PHYSICS TEACHER: *Some of you are probably thinking, "When am I ever gonna use this?"*

TIM: (He sits up with a start, waiting for the punch line.)

PHYSICS TEACHER: *Well, for those of you who are plotting a career using the sciences, it's quite clear that the scientific knowledge contained in the chart will be invaluable to you. But what about those of you who already feel that the sciences will not be a life*

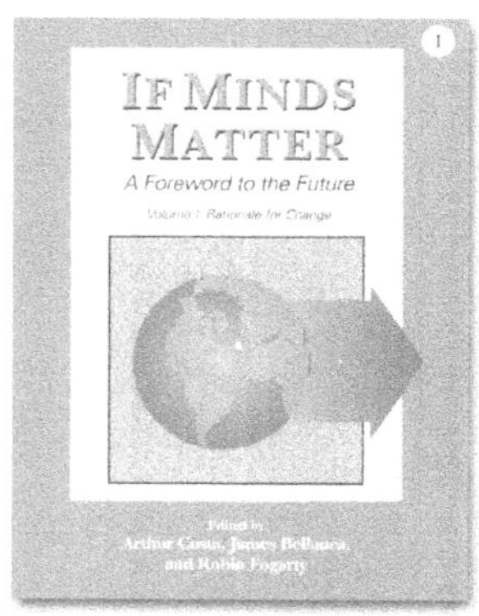

pursuit? Let's talk a little about how learning this table might benefit you in other ways. Let's look at what might transfer for you besides the science content. Any ideas?

RENEE: *I was thinking that maybe the chart itself might serve as a model for gathering information. Grids and matrices are useful tools to organize data. I use them in social studies a lot.*

PHYSICS TEACHER: *That's pretty insightful. How many of you have used a matrix to sort or depict information?* (Three hands go up.) What else?

JOSÉ: *The symbols on the chart remind me of Greek letters and other symbols we use in math. So I guess the idea of decoding symbolic language may be useful in other situations.*

PHYSICS TEACHER: *Quite so! I agree with you. The use of symbols is something we encounter throughout life. Just look at the international road signs. What else?*

ROSA: *Probably because I'm so involved in art, but I think the thing that is most interesting, and maybe most universal in terms of future use of this Periodic Table of Elements, is the pattern in the chart. There are patterns in everything and these patterns help us understand and remember things.*

TIM: (He is now sitting on the edge of his seat.) *Yeah, and I've been thinking, too. Just figuring out how these elements are related to each other might help me see connections in other things. Once I find a way to get this in my head, I'll be able to connect lots of things.*

PHYSICS TEACHER: *I'm amazed at your ingenuity. Great thinking, today. Now, do we agree at least mildly, that this Periodic Table of Elements is worth my teaching and worth your learning?*

Finding the Somethings

Scenario one illustrates that sorting out the somethings worth teaching is a crucial first step for teaching for transfer. In fact, there are three distinct reasons why teachers need to take the time to target the somethings. As never-ending curriculum demands burden already overloaded schedules, teachers find it more and more necessary to sift out the real meat of the curriculum and set curricular priorities. However, in addition to this selection process as a survival tactic, the trend toward more holistic curriculum models of instruction also dictates the need to scrutinize the curriculum for integrating threads. And finally, as illustrated in the scenario, there is a compelling need to emphasize the pieces that have real transfer power, so students can see their relevance.

We can only teach so much. Our time and resources are limited. Yet, we want our students to learn in natural and holistic ways. And of course, we expect them to transfer that learning with ease and frequency. To uncover the sources within our curriculum that provide fertile ground for relevant student transfer, Costa (1991a) says we must "selectively abandon" and "judiciously include" curricular components. It is the work of the skilled teacher to find the somethings worth teaching.

To become good at searching out the somethings, a general framework such as the one illustrated in Figure 1.2 is used. This framework is a guide to use to look for particular knowledge pieces, skills, concepts, attitudes, principles, and dispositions to emphasize explicitly in the lesson for deliberate transfer later. That is to say that each is examined for possible transfer power. By sifting the content through this framework, the real curricular priorities can be sorted out quite easily as the teacher weighs the results against the district philosophy, academic criteria, and student relevance.

SOMETHINGS:______________________________
lesson/unit/topic

Knowledge: information, facts, data (e.g., definitions, dates, statistics)

Skill: social, thinking, organization (e.g., cooperation, prediction, ranking)

Concept: domain specific, universal (e.g., photosynthesis, courage)

Attitude: feelings, tone (e.g., inadequacy, optimism)

Principles: rules, laws, theorems (e.g., Second Law of Thermodynamics, Pythagorean Theorem)

Disposition: behaviors, habits, tendencies (e.g., impulsivity, procedural, humorous)

Figure 1.2

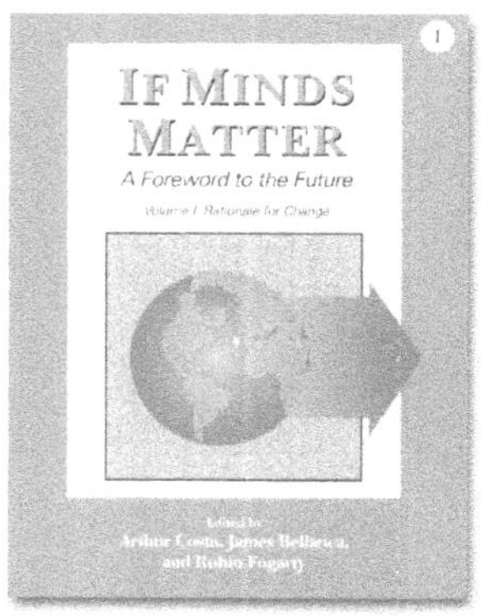

For example, as the teacher examines a unit on the digestive system, a completed frame might look like the one in Figure 1.3. Note the memos on the right side of the chart, which record the teacher's thoughts about how to approach this unit and get the most transfer power from it.

Finding the Somethings: The Digestive System

FIRST PASS	SECOND THOUGHTS
Digestive system search for somethings	*Maybe I should expand the topic to systems in the body or "Your Inner Environment"*
Knowledge: human anatomy, digestive system, vocabulary	*The text is the best resource here, but I will need some library time.*
Skill: diagrams, flow charts, sequencing, use of analogies	*I need to target one major thinking skill—maybe sequencing; can use graphic organizers to illustrate and utilize skill. Using analogies is a possible way to culminate unit.*
Concepts: digestive system, systems, loops, assimilation, environment	*Systems is the universal concept, but I like the idea of "inner environment." Then I could do health, nutrition, substance abuse prevention, and self-esteem—fertile themes.*
Attitudes: value good health, nutritious diet	*This would fit with the expanded concept idea.*
Principles: cause/effect	*Cause and effect could also be the thinking skill focus: more sophisticated than sequencing.*
Dispositions: awareness of bodily functions, whole health and fitness point of view	*Like the idea of connecting this to health/fitness focus.*

SOMETHINGS WITH TRANSFER POTENTIAL

- Inner environment or systems
- Cause/effect
- Self-esteem

NOTE: Use graphic organizers: flow chart, cause/effect circles, decision tree

Figure 1.3

This process of searching for the somethings worth teaching can be done quite painlessly after a few practices. Many of us already do this sort of analysis in our heads as we look at upcoming units. However, the point is to make the process of setting curriculum priorities a deliberate and systematic procedure that precedes the instructional activity in the classroom.

Once we begin this conversation of, What's worth teaching? and Where is the transfer power in this content piece? we can use it to examine past units of study as well. Sometimes it is easier to look back at a lesson or unit just completed and sift out the priority pieces for the next time. Or, it may be easier to work through the priorities in professional dialogue with colleagues.

As a pre-planning strategy or as an evaluation tool, setting curricular priorities—finding the somethings worth teaching—must guide the instructional acts in our schools.

The Somehows of Transfer

[Scenario Two: Using the history chapter on the causes of World War II as the content target, the history teacher also targets the skill of asking good questions as part of the lesson focus. The specific type of questioning that is targeted is metacognitive reflection questions. This scenario illustrates how a history teacher uses a bridging strategy to facilitate meaningful transfer.]

HISTORY TEACHER: *Your assignment involves two parts. Part one is to review the questions at the back of the chapter and, with a partner, categorize them as either "skinny" questions that can be answered directly from the text reading or as "fat" questions that go beyond the given information.*

MELISSA: *Question? Can you give us examples.*

HISTORY TEACHER: *Better yet, let me pose a question. You value it, fat or skinny. Here's one. What were significant battles of World War II?*

MELISSA: *That seems pretty narrow. I think it's a skinny question.*

HISTORY TEACHER: *How about this? Define one of the following statements: Great men make great events or great events make great men.*

MELISSA: *Definitely a fat question. I would have to give lots of supporting evidence—it would turn into a long answer.*

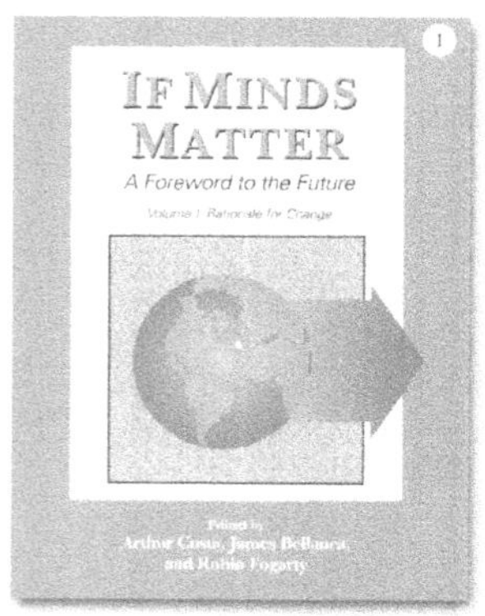

History Teacher: *That's right! You've got the idea. Now, part two of the assignment—I didn't forget!—is to select questions from your list and write your answers to turn in.*

Andrew: *(He waves his hand in the air.)*

History Teacher: *Will this be a fat or skinny question, Andrew?*

Andrew: *Skinny!*

History Teacher: *OK, what's your question?*

Andrew: *How many questions should we answer?*

History Teacher: *You're right, it is skinny. The answer is four! Write answers to two fat and two skinny questions.*

Identifying the Somehows

While the search for the somethings in our curricular content is of primary concern in the instructional process, the main focus of this essay is to present practical strategies to ensure that those somethings, once found, are taught in such a way that the learning "takes" and that the somethings are internalized, applied, and transferred appropriately. This section, which comprises the bulk of the essay, addresses the somehows of teaching for transfer.

Perkins' and Salomon's good shepherd theory of transfer (1988) proposes that to foster transfer of learning, transfer must be "shepherded," or helped along. The somehows are the shepherding or mediating strategies that promote relevant transfer.

In the theory of mediated transfer, two roads to transfer are posited: the low road of near or simple transfer and the high road of far or complex transfer. We may design lessons that "hug" the expected outcome if we are looking for near or somewhat automatic transfer. For example, if we want students to become better writers, we have them write, rather than circle, answers in a multiple choice worksheet model. Alternatively, we may select "bridging" strategies that call for mindful abstractions to encourage far more complex transfer. If we want students to connect the problem solving they do in math class with the problem solving they do in science, we orchestrate a discussion that leads students to generalize about problem solving. In the process, we bridge problem solving in math to problem solving in science.

In fact, we may even map out combinations of both hugging and bridging strategies to deliberately induce transfer. A specific example of combining strategies would be the use of simulations in the driver's education lab (to hug for transfer) as well as an exploration of analogies to sports in a discussion of defensive driving techniques (to bridge for transfer).

Figures 1.4 and 1.5 illustrate ten somehows—five hugging strategies to facilitate new or simple transfer and five bridging strategies to span wide gaps between original learning and remote situations.

Shepherding Strategies: The Somehows of Transfer

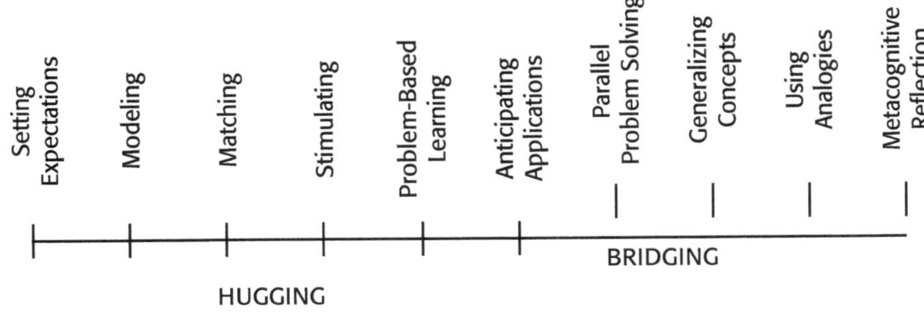

Figure 1.4

Mediating Transfer

HUGGING STRATEGIES

1. *Setting Expectations:* targeting explicit goals
2. *Modeling:* demonstrating, showing
3. *Matching:* engaging in the very performance being developed, practicing
4. *Simulating:* role playing, acting out
5. *Problem-Based Learning:* experiential learning

BRIDGING STRATEGIES

6. *Anticipating Applications:* developing rationale, scouting for relevant uses
7. *Parallel Problem Solving:* moving learning from one context to another
8. *Generalizing Concepts:* extrapolating generic threads
9. *Using Analogies:* comparing, finding similarities
10. *Metacognitive Reflection:* thinking about thinking, planning, monitoring, evaluating

Figure 1.5

Teaching for Transfer

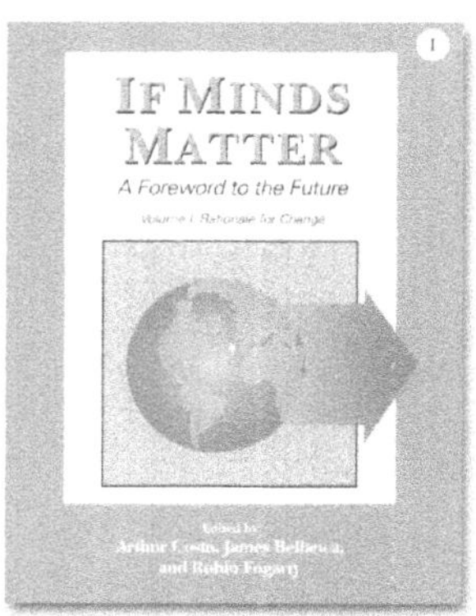

In the discussion of the somehows of transfer, each strategy includes a brief definition and an illustration of its use. In addition, specific examples are cited as practical cues for teacher use.

Setting Expectations—HUGGING

Definition: Talking to students about expectations for transfer to increase the likelihood that transfer occurs; explicitly planning into lessons the questions or tasks that help students connect across content so transfer is more likely to occur.

Example: When studying the skill of detecting bias in social studies, students encourage each other to look for instances of bias in constructing graphs in math class or in point of view pieces in language arts class. Suggest that they look for bias across the curricula and deliberately plant the seed for transfer.

Verbal Cues:

- "What's the big idea?"
- "How does this connect to what you already know?"
- "Where might you use this?"
- "Do you see how this might fit with what we were working with last week?"
- "How is this relevant?"

Modeling—HUGGING

Definition: Demonstrating the desired behavior with a running monologue about what you're doing to emphasize key elements; modeling the behavior for students to adapt; talking about it; making sense of the demonstration.

Example: When asking students to prioritize their homework, the teacher will first create the list of items on the board while talking about prioritizing. For instance: "Here's how I prioritize. Once I have listed all the things I want to do, I find the most urgent items and rank those numbers one, two, and three. Then I find the least important items, things I would like to do, but are not due the next day. I rank those toward the bottom. Then I sort out the middle items. Finally, I take the most important items, or the things that need to be done the soonest, and put them at the top. Now I have prioritized my work."

Verbal Cues:

- "Here's an example."
- "Let me illustrate."
- "Give me a specific instance."
- "Show me."
- "Use this as a prototype."

***Matching*—HUGGING**

Definition: Matching the lesson design to the desired outcome; engaging the student in the very performance you're trying to develop; guiding the targeted behavior; using procedural learning.

Example: If the goal is to get students to take a stand, advocate a position, and support an idea with detail, give them many opportunities to practice that behavior. For example, weave agree/disagree questions throughout a lecturette and have students practice taking a stand as they learn the art of public advocacy.

Verbal Cues:

- "Practice the model."
- "Try it."
- "Duplicate this."
- "Repeat the process."
- "Follow the steps."

***Simulating*—HUGGING**

Definition: Role playing, personifying or simulating the real thing to hug the desired outcome; experiencing the actions and feeling of the actual situation by practicing or pretending.

Example: In driver education classes, have students simulate driving before they drive an actual car; or act out the job interview, taking on the role of the job applicant. Stage the trial of the big bad wolf (from *The Three Little Pigs*) to learn about bias and jury selection.

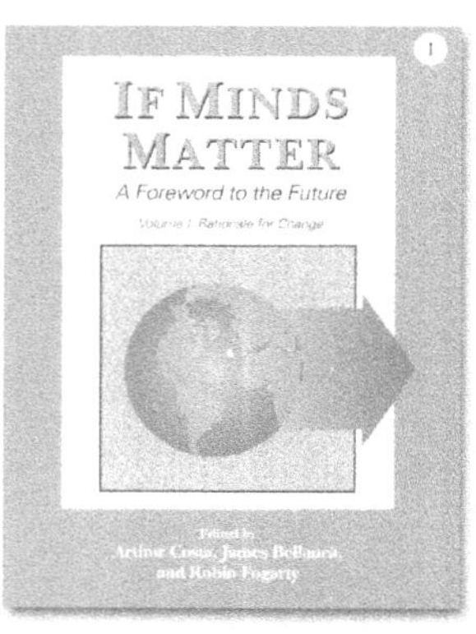

Verbal Cues:

- "Pretend."
- "Put yourself in her place."
- "Imagine."
- "Take his role."
- "How might she think about this?"

Problem-Based Learning—HUGGING

Definition: Placing students in problematic situations; immersing them in the experience in order to pull together relevant information in an inductive teaching method that hugs the target behavior; having students apply their knowledge in the context of the problem, with no "up front" information offered formally.

Example: Construct a situated learning experience from a current newspaper article. For example, in one article a student locker has been searched for drugs. Have students in the class decide if the student's human rights have been violated after gathering and evaluating data.

Verbal Cues:

- "Here's the situation…"
- "What do you need to know?"
- "What can you do?"
- "What is the goal?"
- "How can you accomplish the task?"

Anticipating Applications—BRIDGING

Definition: Thinking about an upcoming opportunity to use the new idea; thinking about an adjustment that will make your application more relevant; targeting future applications or speculating on possible uses.

Example: After working on the division of fractions, guide students to project possible future uses of the skill as you mediate for transfer. Ask students, "How might you use this idea across content or in life?"

Verbal Cues:

- "How might you use this?"
- "What if you adapted it this way?"
- "Do you see any opportunities to try this out?"
- "Can you think of an application?"
- "Have you seen this used somewhere else?"

Parallel Problem Solving—BRIDGING

Definition: Using parallel thinking to ask, Where is this (idea) applicable in my personal life?; taking information and drawing parallels with experiences, with prior information and past knowledge; associating one idea with ideas already known and exploring options and possibilities for the application of an idea.

Example: Have students place a global or historic problem in the context of their personal lives to help them understand the more abstract problem. For example, during the American Revolution the colonists did not want taxes. They were in conflict with the mother country. Ask students, "What do you do when you're in conflict with your mother? She wants you to eat your peas, and you hate peas. What do you do? Boycott? Retreat? Throw a temper tantrum? What strategies do you use? How do these compare to the strategies the colonists used?"

Verbal Cues:

- "Do you see parallels to your own situation?"
- "How is this like your life situation?"
- "Can you relate this to personal issues?"
- "Does this sound familiar?"
- "Do you see any similarities to your own life?"

Generalizing Concepts—BRIDGING

Definition: Asking students to point out elements with general accountability in a given situation; encouraging them to generalize concepts; applying concepts universally.

Example: As students learn geometry, ask them to reflect upon their own problem-solving processes and to generalize

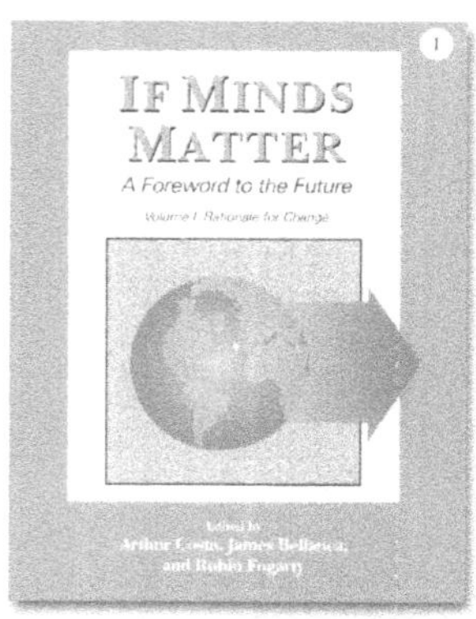

about elements of that process that seem to help. For instance, students might say, "Use a diagram." Then ask, "Is that generally useful in other situations? How? Why? Give me some specific examples."

Verbal Cues:

- "What big ideas can you piece together from this?"
- "What truths seem apparent?"
- "What's the real lesson?"
- "Is there a rule, law, principle here?"
- "Can we say that 'Generally speaking…'?"

Using Analogies—BRIDGING

Definition: Finding likenesses to yield useful transfer; finding and analyzing analogies; comparing; using metaphors and making creative connections.

Example: Have students compare *courage* and *rain.* For example, courage is like the rain. Both can come upon you unexpectedly. Have students discuss how the unexpectedness of a courageous act is similar to the unexpectedness of a summer shower. Analyze this analogy by engaging students in a discussion about courage that elaborates and extends thinking and explicitly forces transfer through comparison. This seemingly difficult exercise is actually a lot of fun. You may be surprised at the connections the students will make!

Verbal Cues:

- "How is *a* like *b*?"
- "*a* is like *b* because both *c*."
- "a : b :: c : d."
- "Compare *a* (abstract) to *b* (concrete)."
- "Find the similarities in *a* and *b*."

Metacognitive Reflection—BRIDGING

Definition: Planning, monitoring, and evaluating one's own thinking; being aware and controlling one's own thinking and behavior; thinking about thinking in tacit, aware, strategic, and reflective ways.

Example: After completing a series of math problems on the associative principle, ask students to think about how they attacked the problems. Ask, "What things were similar problems? What were the stumpers? Were there any elements of this problem that you had encountered before? If so, how did you deal with them?" Have students evaluate their own performance as they think about their thinking strategies and become aware of their own behavior in relation to their learning.

Verbal Cues:

- "What are your aims, goals, and objectives?"
- "Track your steps in this and evaluate your progress."
- "Look back and reflect on your work."
- "Monitor your progress periodically."
- "What would you do the same or differently next time?"

Shepherding the transfer of learning with the selective use of these ten hugging and bridging strategies can easily become an integral part of the instructional design. It is just a matter of consciously targeting transfer as a desired outcome, rather than simply assuming that transfer automatically happens. Once transfer is targeted, the appropriate scaffolding can be provided to carry the transfer.

Although these strategies for mediating transfer comprise only a partial list of the somehows, they represent explicit tools for transfer that we can add to our instructional repertoire. As we become more conscious of teaching for transfer, we will find creative ways to facilitate transfer and continually add these instructional tools to our teacher's tool kit.

The Somewheres of Transfer

[Scenario Three: By asking students to think back to an experience or to project ahead to a possible application, the teacher targets the somewheres for future transfer.]

LITERATURE TEACHER: *In* The Old Man and the Sea, *Hemingway presents an impressive characterization of a man who perseveres*

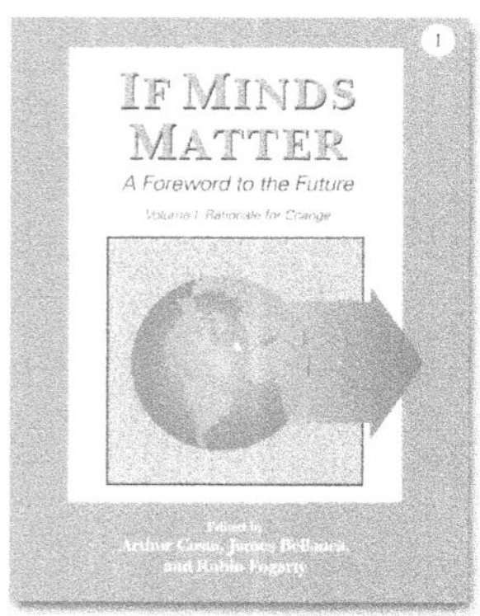

against tremendous odds. Take a moment to think back to a time in your life when you used your willpower to stick to something and see it through. (Allow a minute or two of silence.) *Now, share your stories with a partner.*

DENNIS (TURNING TO LOUISA): *Once when I was really little I climbed a tree and when I was trying to get down I slipped and ended up clutching onto this branch. I had to hold on really tight for a long time while my brother went to get the ladder. It seemed like forever.*

LOUISA: *I remember once when I forced myself to finish my social studies project because it was due the next day. I had to paint this salt and flour relief map. It was a lot of fun when I started, but boy did I get sick of it. That was hard to do, just like the old man's struggle with the marlin.*

LITERATURE TEACHER: *Now, go to your logs and think ahead. Write a sentence or two about how this ability to persevere will help you in another class. For example, when will persevering help you in math class or in the science lab? Be specific. Target an upcoming assignment for another subject area that is going to take lots of willpower and "stick-to-itiveness" to get it done. Try to think about how you can use this persevering attitude in other places. See if you can transfer it to another subject.*

JOSÉ (WRITING IN HIS LOG): *The algebra problems are really hard for me, right now. If I don't give up so easily—if I stick to them longer, like the old man—maybe I can get through them.*

Targeting the Somewheres

The somewheres of transfer are the end targets of the somethings and the somehows. By definition, learning in one situation and using that knowledge in another situation is called transfer. This transfer may occur within the content being taught, across disciplines to other subjects, or into life situations (conversely, of course, life experiences can transfer into school learning, etc.).

To suggest that one would teach something (or learn something) with no expectation for transfer or use is ludicrous. However, in viewing the research, the literature suggests that this transfer of learning, if left alone as in the bo peep and lost sheep theories (Perkins and Salomon 1988), may not occur as spontaneously or as regularly as we want.

However, when the transfer is shepherded, the likelihood for relevant application and use seems to increase quite dramatically. In order to shepherd or mediate for transfer, we use hugging strategies that engage students in the very behavior desired or we use the bridging strategies of mindful abstractions as delineated previously in this chapter.

However, in addition to hugging and bridging, we can provide further, albeit temporary, scaffolding to the learning process by targeting specific somewheres. This additional targeting of the somewheres for transfer, within the same context, across disciplines, or into life situations, is fairly easy to do.

An example of targeting a somewhere for transfer within a similar context is the science teacher who directs students to relate the concept of the life cycle from the plant unit to the metamorphosis of the butterfly in the insect unit. To target a somewhere for transfer across subject areas, the math teacher may suggest that students check their hand calculations on the computer during their technology lab period. Similarly, to target a somewhere into real-life situations, the social studies teacher may cue students to scout the newspapers, magazines, and broadcasts for current illustrations of aggression as an extension of the study of World War II.

Deliberately focusing the learner's attention on possible transfer opportunities is a powerful early-use strategy for promoting the transfer of learning. Over time, of course, less scaffolding is necessary as the learner takes over the task of finding the somewheres for relevant transfer.

Conclusion

In closing, there are somethings that we want somehow to transfer somewhere. Hopefully, this discussion will provide the catalyst to begin the work of teaching not for a test, but for a lifetime.

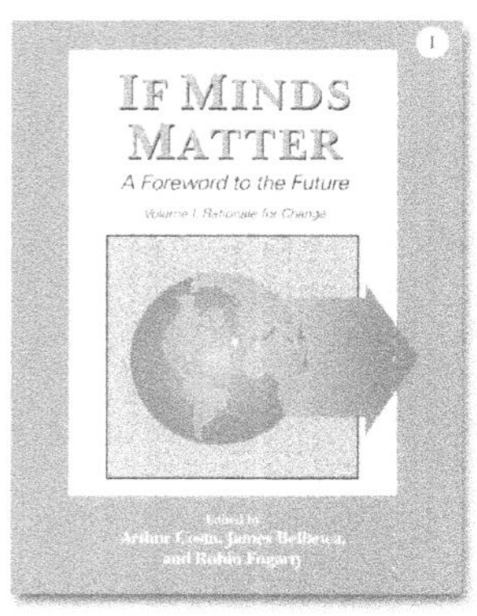

REFERENCES

Bellanca, J., and R. Fogarty. 1990. *Blueprints for thinking in the cooperative classroom.* Palatine, IL: IRI/Skylight Training and Publishing.

Beyer, B. 1987. *Practical strategies for the teaching of thinking.* Boston: Allyn & Bacon.

Brandt, R. 1988, April. On teaching thinking: A conversation with Arthur Costa. *Educational Leadership,* p. 11.

Costa, A. 1991a, Winter. Orchestrating the second wave. *Cogitare,* p. 1.

———. 1991b. The search for intelligent life. In *The school as a home for the mind.* (pp. 19–31). Palatine, IL: IRI/Skylight Training and Publishing.

Costa, A., and R. Garmston. 1985, March. The art of cognitive coaching: Supervision for intelligent teaching. Paper presented at the Annual Conference of the Association for Supervision and Curriculum Development, Chicago.

Cousins, N. 1981. *Human options.* New York: Norton.

Feuerstein, R. 1980. *Instrumental Enrichment.* Baltimore: University Park Press.

Fogarty, R. 1989. *From training to transfer: The role of creativity in the adult learner.* Doctoral dissertation, Loyola University of Chicago.

———. 1991. *The mindful school: How to integrate the curricula.* Palatine, IL: IRI/Skylight Training and Publishing.

Fogarty, R., and J. Bellanca. 1989. *Patterns for thinking: Patterns for transfer.* Palatine, IL: IRI/Skylight Training and Publishing.

Fogarty, R., D. Perkins, and J. Barell. 1991. *The mindful school: How to teach for transfer.* Palatine, IL: IRI/Skylight Training and Publishing.

Fullan, M. 1982. *The meaning of educational change.* New York: Teachers College Press.

Hord, S., and S. Loucks. 1980. *A concerns-based model for delivery of inservice.* CBFM Project—Research and Development Center for Teacher Education, The University of Texas at Austin.

Hunter, M. 1982. *Teach for transfer.* El Segundo, CA: TIP Publications.

Joyce, B. 1986. *Improving America's schools.* New York: Longman.

Joyce, B., and B. Showers. 1980, February. Improving inservice training: The message of research. *Educational Leadership,* p. 380.

———. 1983. *Power in staff development through research and training.* Alexandria, VA: Association for Supervision and Curriculum Development.

Marzano, R., and D. Arredondo. 1986, May. Restructuring schools through the teaching of thinking skills. *Educational Leadership,* p. 23.

Parnes, S. 1975. *Aha! Insights into creative behavior.* Buffalo, NY: D.O.K.

Perkins, D. 1986. *Knowledge as design.* Hillsdale, NJ: Lawrence Erlbaum.

———. 1988, August 6. *Thinking frames.* Paper delivered at ASCD Conference on Approaches to Teaching Thinking, Alexandria, VA.

Perkins, D., and G. Salomon. 1988, September. Teaching for transfer. *Educational Leadership,* pp. 22–32.

———. 1989, January/February. Are cognitive skills context bound? *Educational Researcher,* pp. 16–25.

Polya, G. 1957. *How to solve it.* Princeton, NJ: Doubleday.

Posner, M., and S. Keele. 1973. Skill learning. In R. Travers, (Ed.), *Second handbook of research on teaching.* (pp. 805–31). Chicago: Rand McNally.

Sergiovanni, T. 1987, May. Will we ever have a true profession? *Educational Leadership,* pp. 44–9.

Sternberg, R. 1984, September. How can we teach intelligence? *Educational Leadership,* pp. 38–48.

———. 1986. *Intelligence applied: Understanding and increasing your intellectual skills.* New York: Harcourt Brace Jovanovich.

Tyler, R. 1987, January. The first most significant curriculum events in the twentieth century. *Educational Leadership,* pp. 36–7.

Wittrock, M. 1967. Replacement and nonreplacement strategies in children's problem solving. *Journal of Educational Psychology.* 58(2): 69–74.

SELECTION 2

Connecting Brain-Compatible Learning, Multiple Intelligences, and the Internet

by **Kristen Nelson**

To help teachers design creative and personalized Internet-based lessons, this chapter focuses on concepts that range from brain compatibility research and the multiple intelligences theory to an overview about the Internet. Its purpose is to introduce these concepts as the bases for developing classroom applications.

Brain-Compatible Learning

The 1990s were called the "Decade of the Brain" by many. This is indeed difficult to dispute. Advances in technology in the neurosciences vastly improved how the human brain may be studied. These advances centered on brain-imaging techniques that allow neuroscientists to actually watch the brain at work. For example, the Positron Emission Tomography scan (PET) uses radioactive glucose to gauge blood flow through the brain as various areas are activated. This provides researchers with information about where and how an experience or problem is processed in the brain. Magnetic Resonance Imaging (MRI) looks at chemical differences in the composition of different tissues of the brain. Another familiar and well-used brain imaging technique, the Electroencephalogram (EEG), uses

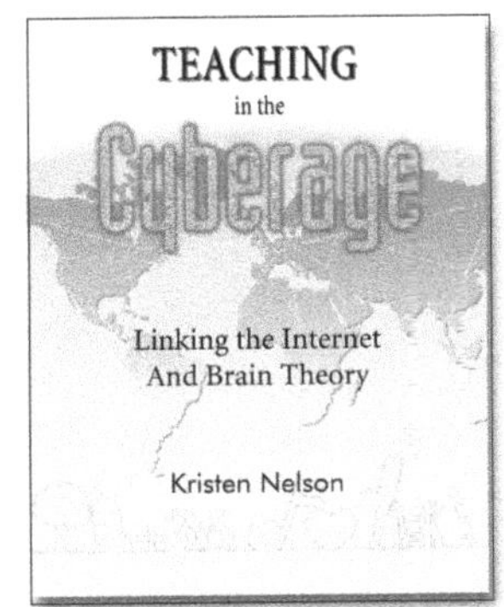

Adapted from *Teaching in the Cyberage: Linking the Internet and Brain Theory,* by Kristen Nelson, pp. 7–22, 27, and 175–77.

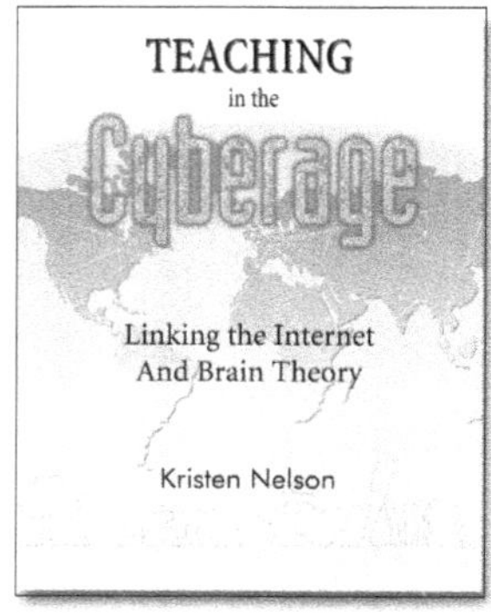

electrical transmissions to study brain patterns. The latest in brain imaging is the functional MRI or fMRI, which allows researchers to monitor brain activity as the person is participating in a cognitive activity.

One of the greatest challenges in education is to use research information gathered through these technologies in practical ways in the classroom to help children learn. This is no easy feat. It is much easier to stay the same course and continue doing things the way they have always been done. Yet, educational pioneers push teachers onward and upward in using new information about the brain. The term *brain compatible* was first used by Leslie Hart in his book, *Human Brain, Human Learning* (1983). He challenged the education community to make teaching and learning more compatible with how the brain learns and processes information. Susan Kovalik expanded on these concepts in her book, *ITI: The Model—Integrated Thematic Instruction* (1993). Writers adding to the wealth of knowledge and ideas on brain-compatible learning include Sylwester (1995), Fogarty (1997), Caine and Caine (1991), and Sousa (1995) to name just a few.

Numerous books and articles are available to educators that relate directly to brain-compatible learning. Yet, educators are still searching for how to relate these ideas to specific curriculum domains. The concepts and ideas of brain-compatible learning are still in their infancy. For the sake of this chapter, an amalgamation of many individuals' work is used to define the major tenets of brain-compatible learning. These are the most important ones for lesson design:

- *Meaning and Relevance:* One of the brain's important jobs is to seek meaning and relevance in everything it does. If a student does not see meaning or relevance in a lesson, his or her brain automatically begins looking for something that has more meaning (possibly slipping a note to a fellow student or sending a spitball across the room to an enemy). Students find meaning and relevance one way or another. Although this seems like a simple concept, it is really one of the most important ones and serves as a foundation for all other brain-compatible learning ideas. Teachers themselves can think of many workshops where they have been bored or maybe even escaped out the back door because what was being taught was perceived to be not relevant or meaningful to them. Seeking meaning and relevance is what drives human learning.

- *Emotions:* Emotions play a central role in learning and memory and therefore are a gateway to learning. The emotional part of the brain is located in the amygdala, which stores emotional information and acts as a file cabinet for all the experiences people have in life. When new information comes in, it travels through the amygdala and, if it has emotional content, is processed, filed, and sorted into memory. Emotional memory is one of the strongest memory systems humans possess.
- *Repetition and Rehearsal:* Learning and memory are reinforced through hearing, seeing, and experiencing the information repeatedly. In order for a student to make sense and meaning of new learning, he or she needs adequate time to process and reprocess it. This continuing reprocessing is critical to the transference of the information from short-term to long-term memory.
- *Prior Knowledge:* New learning builds on past learning and prior knowledge. When students learn new information, they instantly process the information for relevance and relationship to other pieces of information they have already learned. If there is indeed prior knowledge about the subject, the brain is able to more readily store the information in its memory. If there is no prior knowledge, the information can lack meaning and relevance to the learner. Therefore, it is important for teachers to help students link new information to their prior knowledge.
- *Adequate Time:* The brain needs time to process information. It is important for teachers to build time into each lesson for students to process and work with the information and skills they are learning. This can be done by giving students more time to work in an activity, stretching out a lesson's overall time schedule, or allowing for wait time before calling on students for an answer. By providing this time, students are able to rehearse and repeat what they have learned, make connections to prior knowledge, and reflect on their learning.

Connecting Brain-Compatible Learning, Multiple Intelligences, and the Internet

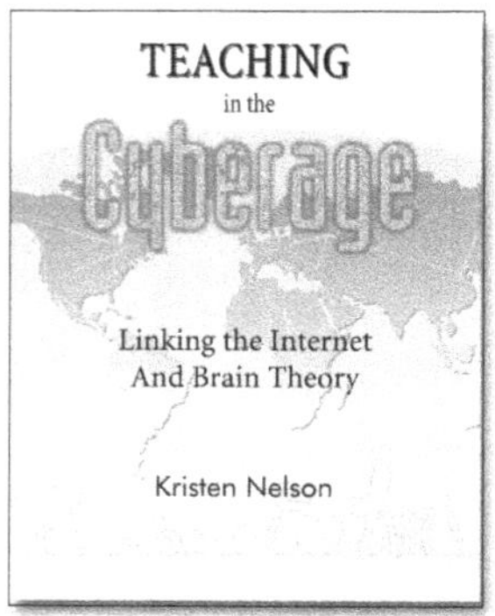

Without adequate time, the new information is unlikely to ever make it into long-term memory storage because of the lack of connection and meaning.

- *Immediate Feedback:* The brain learns best when given feedback during the learning process. This feedback is most powerful when it is given during or immediately after the lesson. The brain is able to use this feedback to make the necessary changes instead of having time to repeatedly practice something incorrectly. Without immediate feedback, the new learning is seen as not relevant and unimportant, hindering new connections and memory storage.
- *Collaboration:* The brain is social by nature and enjoys learning and reflecting on learning with others. Human beings are social creatures, and teachers need to recognize that learning does not take place in a vacuum but in social settings in which the brain has time to process information with others. This is especially true for individuals who are strong in the interpersonal intelligence and rely on their social interactions to process new information.
- *Reflection:* The brain needs time to reflect on what has been learned so that it may store the new information in its memory system for later retrieval. If the brain is unable to reflect on learning, it is difficult, if not impossible, for it to store the information into its long-term memory system. Many adults acknowledge the fact that what they remember long term is information and knowledge that they spent a lot of time working with and reflecting on. By reflecting on learning, the brain is able to scrutinize, observe, sort, synthesize, and connect new information to prior knowledge. During this reflection process, the brain is able to reorganize itself based on new information being learned.
- *Safe and Nurturing Environment:* The brain thrives on a climate of safety, caring, and low stress. This occurs mainly because, when humans are in an environment that is not safe and might contain a high level of stress, their limbic systems are activated. This system, one of the oldest in brain development, uses the emotional part of the brain to activate "flight or fight" responses. If humans feel threatened, the release of

stress hormones such as cortisol may cause interruptions in the processing of information and therefore of the learning process. By being in a safe and nurturing environment, these stress hormones are not released, enabling the brain to concentrate on learning and remembering.

- *Active Learning:* Concepts and information learned must be actively used so that the brain transfers learning from short-term to long-term memory. If students simply sit and listen to information and have no active participation with it, they may quickly forget the information because it lacks meaning and relevancy. This is why many, even teachers, struggle to remember five things they learned in their American history high school class. In contrast, active learning helps students make meaning of new information for themselves. It increases motivation to learn and helps students develop connections with other knowledge and information.
- *Choice:* The brain thrives on choice. Motivation is increased when the learner chooses what to learn instead of learning what others say is important. This empowerment increases meaning and relevancy to the learner, therefore increasing the level of motivation to learn and remember the new information.
- *Pattern Seeking:* The brain is a pattern-seeking machine. It constantly seeks patterns in information and learning experiences and is able to use these patterns to file the new information into its memory system. The brain uses these patterns to make connections that help make sense of new learning, enabling the brain to organize the information in a way that is meaningful.
- *Chunking:* The chunking of information helps the learner organize and retain the information because a set of data is perceived as a single item, just as the reader currently sees *chunking* as one word instead of eight letters. By chunking information, less working memory is used, allowing for more information to be processed at a time. As working memory's capacity is enhanced, the learner is better able to associate chunks of information in a meaningful way.

Connecting Brain-Compatible Learning, Multiple Intelligences, and the Internet

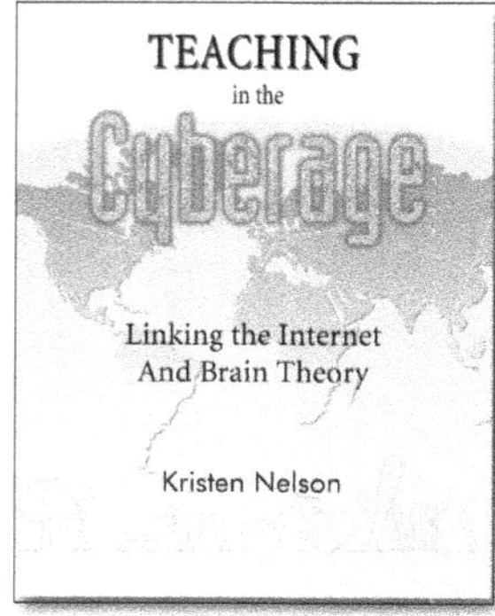

Multiple Intelligences Theory

In addition to information from the brain research community, teachers can improve their understanding of how students learn by examining the theory of multiple intelligences, which was proposed by Dr. Howard Gardner of Harvard University in *Frames of Mind: The Theory of Multiple Intelligences* (1983). Gardner derived his theory from extensive brain research, including interviews, tests, and studies of hundreds of individuals. He studied the cognitive profiles of stroke and accident victims, prodigies, autistic individuals, those with learning disabilities, idiot savants, and people from diverse cultures. He concluded that intelligence is not one fixed trait that dominates all the skills and problem-solving abilities a person possesses. Gardner's theory does not question the existence of a general intelligence but does probe the possibilities of intelligences not covered by a single concept of intelligence. His research suggests that intelligence is centered in many different areas of the brain, which are interconnected, rely on one another, work independently when needed, and can be developed with the right environmental conditions.

Gardner defines an intelligence as comprising three main components: (1) the ability to create an effective product or offer a service that is valuable in one's culture; (2) a set of skills that enables an individual to solve problems encountered in life; and (3) the potential for finding or creating solutions for problems, enabling a person to acquire new knowledge. The intelligences Gardner recognizes include verbal/linguistic, logical/mathematical, visual/spatial, bodily/kinesthetic, musical/rhythmic, interpersonal, intrapersonal, and naturalist. Each intelligence area is demonstrated through specific talents, skills, and interests (see Figure 2.1). The fact that these intelligences can be nurtured and strengthened has a monumental influence on how students can be taught for maximum learning and achievement.

As current brain research continues to provide information that educators never dreamed of knowing, the multiple intelligences theory adds to this wealth of information. Because Gardner continues to research and study possible intelligences,

Multiple Intelligences

INTELLIGENCE	TALENTS, SKILLS, AND INTERESTS	LEARNING ACTIVITIES
Verbal/Linguistic	reading, writing, telling stories, memorizing, thinking in words, oral communication	reading, hearing, and seeing words; speaking; writing; discussing; debating
Logical/Mathematical	working with numbers, doing math, computing, reasoning, logic, problem solving, finding patterns	working with patterns and numbers, classifying, categorizing, working with the abstract
Visual/Spatial	using maps and charts, drawing, completing mazes and puzzles, imagining things, visualizing, building, designing	working with pictures and colors, using mind's eye, drawing and creating visual representations
Bodily/Kinesthetic	participating in athletics, dancing, acting, doing crafts, using tools, possessing hand-eye coordination	touching, moving, processing knowledge through bodily sensations
Musical/Rhythmic	singing, picking up sounds, remembering melodies, playing rhythms, playing an instrument, listening to music	singing, listening to music and melodies, playing rhythm, putting information to song
Interpersonal	understanding people, leading, organizing, communicating, resolving conflicts, joining groups	cooperative learning, sharing, comparing, relating, interviewing, working with peers
Intrapersonal	understanding self, recognizing strengths and weaknesses, setting goals, reflecting	working alone, completing self-paced and independent activities, having own space, reflecting
Naturalist	understanding nature, making distinctions, identifying flora and fauna	working in nature, exploring living things, learning about plants and natural events

Figure 2.1

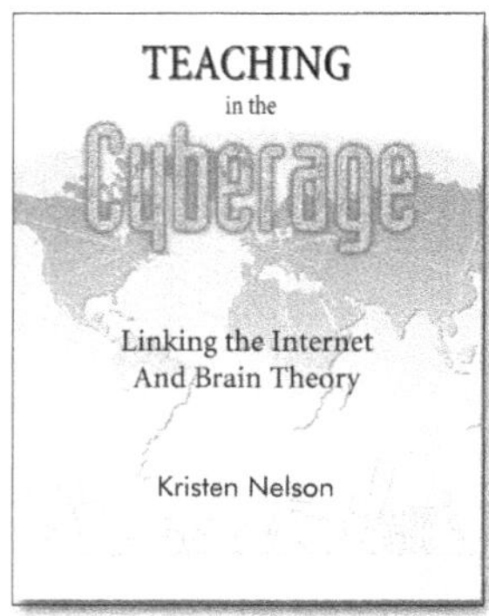

it is important to recognize that this is a *theory in progress.* Although the multiple intelligences theory has powerful implications for the world of education, it is not an educational prescription. There is no one way to use it in the classroom, and there is no one way to use it with the Internet. It is important to remember that research continues to show that when learners are able to use their own particular style of learning and processing information, their motivation, initiative, and results improve (Carbo 1986; Campbell and Campbell 1999).

Through the lens of multiple intelligences, teachers see students as more capable as they demonstrate learning in a multitude of ways. Students are given the opportunity to be acknowledged for their strengths—for what they can do well. This new approach can literally change the way teachers view students—turning an average student into a genius as his or her teacher legitimately acknowledges the amazing ways this child processes information and produces knowledge. This overall teaching philosophy adds to the richness and complexity of a classroom as a wider variety of experiences and ways of thinking and processing information are honored.

At Russell Elementary School in Lexington, Kentucky, the staff chose to move the entire school into an education program based on multiple intelligences. One of the powerful structures they have put in place is the Cycle of Success (Campbell and Campbell 1999). This cycle encourages teachers to teach to students' strengths and personalize education. The cycle of success begins when teachers are trained to observe students' multiple intelligences and learn to perceive each student's strengths. Teachers then personalize instruction for their students, which leads to success. The cycle provides a simple yet powerful way to guarantee students' academic and social success.

The multiple intelligences theory provides a foundation to personalize instruction and recognize student strengths. In discussing the ways his theory relates to education, Gardner recognizes that the multiple intelligences theory can be used in the classroom in the following three ways:

1. to cultivate desired capabilities and talents in students;
2. to approach a concept, subject matter, or discipline in a variety of ways;
3. to personalize education as human differences are taken seriously.

All three of these uses can be fostered and strengthened by integrating the multiple intelligences theory in brain-compatible classrooms with the powerful instructional tool of the Internet.

Many ask if the theory of multiple intelligences really helps students learn better. A simple question without a simple answer, yet the most recent research shows great promise. Linda and Bruce Campbell, in their book *Multiple Intelligences and Student Achievement: Success Stories from Six Schools* (1999), reported that when schools and classrooms implement instructional programs based on the theory of multiple intelligences, achievement scores do indeed show great growth. The six schools the Campbells' studied, ranging from elementary to high schools, went beyond anecdotal stories to show growth on actual standardized tests and classroom-based assessments.

The Internet

As teachers continue to learn more about how the brain works, they are also being challenged to learn about and use the Internet in their instructional practice. The Internet has revolutionized communications like nothing before it. The invention of the telegraph, telephone, radio, and computer set the stage for an integration of powerful communication tools. The Internet is at once a worldwide broadcasting center, a mechanism for disseminating information, and a medium for collaborating between individuals and their computers without regard for geographic location.

The Internet represents a myriad of tools for students. It can function as a library, an encyclopedia, or simply as a replacement for pencil and paper. It can serve as a telephone, deliver mail like a mailman, and act as a file cabinet for

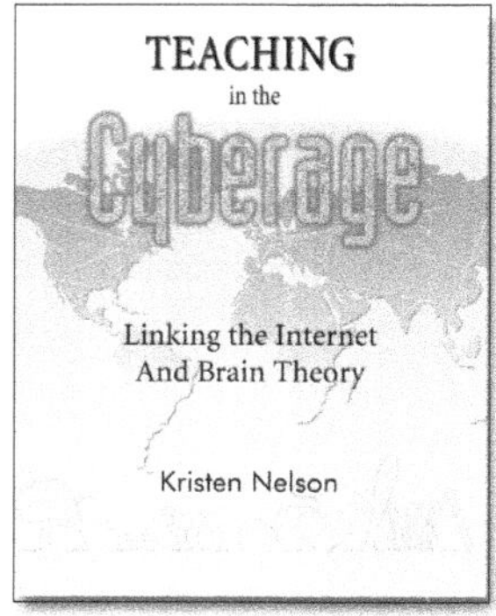

collections of information. Most of all, it can be overwhelming and, at times, frustrating if students are not taught how to navigate this expansive source of information. As students become adept at navigating cyberspace, they need to know what to do with all of the information, knowledge, and personal links that the Internet delivers to their fingertips.

The Internet has slowly trickled into classrooms throughout the United States, and what once seemed unique and rare is now ubiquitous for most teachers and students. Seen as threatening by many educators at one time, the Internet has become a useful and important teacher's aide in many classrooms. The Internet is one of the most powerful and rewarding instructional tools at teachers' fingertips. Within seconds, an entire civilization or country thousands of miles away is delivered to a teacher's desktop. Questions that would have taken hours to answer are not only answered but also expounded upon. Because of its timeliness and currency, the Internet can capture teachable moments. As students' eyes light up with excitement, the Internet can expand a teachable moment with pictures, facts, and human stories that make learning come alive.

The Internet provides a wealth of resources and information that make teaching exciting and new. Just a few of the things that can be found on the Internet include:

- lesson plans
- virtual field trips
- simulations
- facts, figures, and formulas
- exhibits
- collaborative problem-solving activities
- maps
- science fair projects
- seminars for professional development
- songs and stories
- tutorials
- telementors
- book reviews
- historical archives
- information about authors, artists, and others
- collaborative projects
- electronic appearances
- electronic publishing
- experiments

Yet even with all of these Internet additions, educators have quickly realized that the Internet does not necessarily improve education in the classroom. The Internet is merely a tool just as a pencil is a tool. A pencil can be used to write the great American novel, tap a beat on a table, or poke someone in the eye. The Internet is similar. It can be used as a powerful educational tool, but only if it capitalizes on new understandings of how the human brain learns.

One question that has haunted the educational community since the Internet made its way into classrooms is, Does the Internet increase student learning? *Education Week* (*Technology Counts '99* 1999) conducted an exhaustive study in all fifty states of schools' use of technology. The study concluded that when technology was used by *highly trained teachers* who applied it productively, students scored higher on one mathematics exam. But, the study also showed that when computers were not used effectively, student scores on this exam were flat or fell. How students use computers is more important than how often they have access to this technology, researchers reported. Technology should be seen as simply one in an array of classroom tools rather than as the focus of the classroom. Teachers can take this instructional tool and use it with what they know about brain research and the theory of multiple intelligences to make the learning process more powerful, meaningful, and memorable.

Two recent trends in education have been an increased emphasis on standards and high stakes tests and an intense focus on using technology in the instructional process. In his article, "Building the Digital Curriculum," Hoff states, "The need for better links between digital content and curricula is driven by the convergence of two major trends in education—state officials are increasingly prescribing what should be taught in the classroom, through academic standards and high stakes tests; at the same time, they're encouraging greater use of technology" (1999, 51).

At first glance, these two trends might seem adversarial. In the 1999 *Education Week* survey (*Technology Counts '99* 1999), many teachers reported feeling that they did not have enough time to figure out how to use technology in the classroom because they felt pressured to teach to standards and to

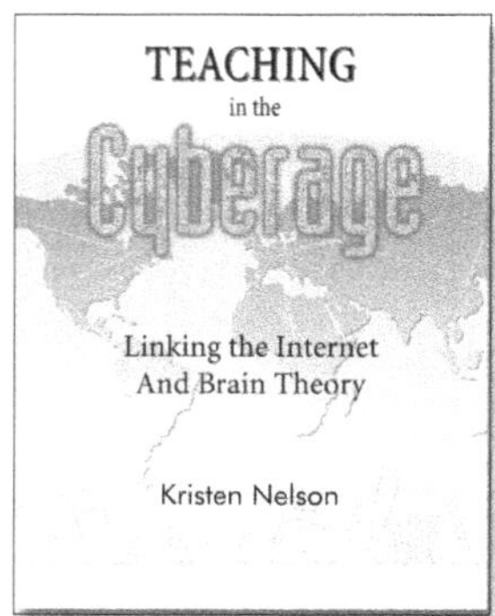

prepare students for exams. Yet teachers who figured out how to use technology for these tasks knew that, after crossing the technology bridge, there was no going back. When technology becomes integrated into the daily curriculum, the power of this tool becomes evident, directly resulting in increased student learning.

The bottom line is that a direct link must be formed between what students need to learn and how the Internet is used in instruction. Many Internet projects and activities are developed without this vital connection—with no direct link to standards and objectives and with no end learning goal. The failure to connect standards and the Internet is understandable. After all, teachers have found it difficult to say no to an Internet activity that, for example, puts a class in communication with a biologist at the South Pole studying penguins even when few, if any, standards or learning objectives relate specifically to penguins.

Some classrooms engage in work that is hands-on without being minds-on. When using the Internet, teachers may find it especially easy to simply require students to experience, rather than *learn* and *understand*. Teachers may feel caught in a "catch 22" situation—they race the calendar to cover material, feeling pressured to "teach by mentioning it" or "teaching by surfing it via the Internet."

Brain-Compatible Learning and the Internet

Figure 2.2 includes the most applicable brain-compatible learning components and how they relate to using the Internet in the classroom. Teachers can improve students' learning if they are aware of this direct link between these concepts and the Internet. The Internet in and of itself is not necessarily brain compatible, but how a teacher uses the Internet in the instruction process can most definitely be compatible with how students' brains work.

As teachers become aware of how brain-compatible learning components can work seamlessly with the Internet, they can design activities and experiences that provide students with powerful learning opportunities. No longer is the Internet a

Relating Brain-Compatible Learning Principles to Internet-Based Activities

Brain-Compatible Principle	Internet Relationship
Meaning and Relevance: The brain seeks meaning and relevance in all it does.	Many Internet activities are problem based and ask students to research relevant and timely issues, collect data, or complete other tasks that relate to real-life issues.
Emotions: Positive emotions are critical to learning and memory; negative emotions hinder the learning process.	The Internet is fun, novel, and students feel in control. Students are stimulated by most Web sites that allow them to hear, see, and do content as they think for themselves.
Repetition and Rehearsal: Learning and memory are reinforced through consistent rehearsal and practice.	The Internet allows students to visit and revisit sites allowing for repetition and rehearsal of information.
Prior Knowledge: New learning is supported by prior knowledge.	Internet links allow learners to start and review basic concepts and build on those with additional links.
Adequate Time: The brain needs time to work with new learning and information.	Some Internet activities make time allowances for person-to-person communication as well as time to access Web sites. This virtual waiting time allows students to learn and reflect.
Immediate Feedback: The brain needs ongoing and consistent feedback during the learning process.	Internet activities can be shared electronically with mentors and classmates to provide immediate feedback. Person-to-person Internet activities also provide this type of feedback.
Collaboration: The brain is social by nature and enjoys learning and reflecting with others.	The Internet provides interpersonal communications and collaboration opportunities via e-mail, chat rooms, and bulletin boards.
Reflection: The brain needs reflection time to process and store new learning.	Internet activities can include a reflection component. Students can also reflect on their learning through e-mail and bulletin boards.
Safe and Nurturing Environment: For academic and social success, the brain needs a climate of safety, caring, and low stress.	With appropriate safety measures (e.g., firewalls, preselected Web sites, student search engines), the Internet provides a virtual environment that is safe and nurtures students' interests.
Active Learning: New learning must be used actively to transfer learning from short-term to long-term memory.	The Internet lends itself to active learning as students participate in collecting and working with information. Active manipulation of data and skills on a site requires students to do something with the information and aids in the transfer to long-term memory.
Choice: By giving students choices, their motivation and learning are increased.	The Internet provides a wide range of choices and selections throughout each site. In addition, Internet activities include giving students choices.
Pattern Seeking: The brain is a pattern-seeking machine and uses these patterns to file new information into its memory.	The Internet provides repetition of information found on different sites and the opportunity to link pieces of information together as different sites are explored.
Chunking: Chunking information helps the brain process new information.	Most Internet sites are designed with information naturally chunked into smaller sections.

Figure 2.2 This list of characteristics compiles knowledge and is based on information from multiple sources including, but not limited to, Sylwester 1995, Sousa 1995, Caine and Caine 1991, and Kovalik 1993.

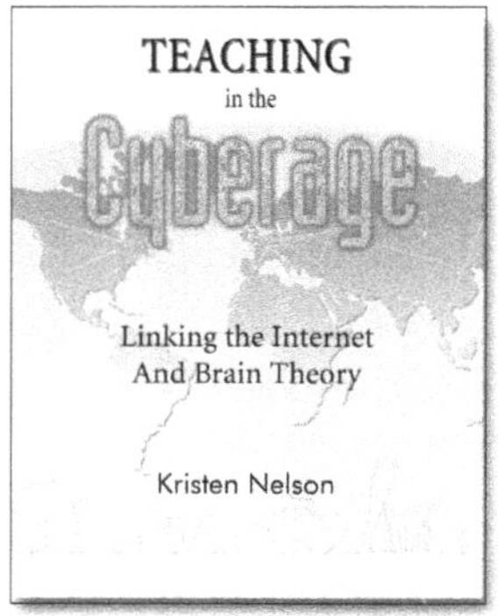

stand-alone educational tool, but it may now take on greater importance as teachers are able to link it with how students' brains learn.

The Internet is also an ideal mechanism for encouraging students to assume responsibility for their own learning. As students find different learning resources on the Internet, they become active participants in their quest for knowledge. Incorporating the Internet into the classroom provides students with more opportunities to structure their own learning. Students can define their learning needs, find information, assess its value, build their own knowledge base, and communicate their discoveries. Finally, the Internet engages students in interactive learning. The Internet turns passive students into active participants—asking students on a regular basis to take information and turn it into knowledge.

Multiple Intelligences and the Internet

Separately, the Internet and the theory of multiple intelligences promise to help students learn more; when integrated, these two educational tools can promote student learning even more. When combined with strong, strategic teaching and the theory of multiple intelligences, the Internet can transform classrooms and create magical moments of learning.

One of the great promises of educational technology is that it will help teachers find individual pathways into students' brains. Recent advances in the quality of Internet projects and activities offer educators a real possibility for providing students with access to knowledge and information. A key to effectively using the Internet lies in recognizing and understanding that all students have different intellectual profiles, and the use of the Internet needs to reflect that knowledge in well-constructed activities and projects.

The Internet provides learning opportunities for students to gain access to information using their multiple intelligences. For example, five years ago a student may have become disengaged and bored while listening to his or her teacher discuss the military strategies behind World War II. Today, this same student can use the Internet to access the same information—

he or she can watch an interactive video, study maps of Europe that show the different military positions, and read firsthand accounts of military action. This type of learning not only engages students but also motivates them to gain a deeper understanding of a concept or event.

Figure 2.3 shows the different types of Internet opportunities available to reinforce the multiple intelligences. It is important to remember that the intelligences do not work in isolation, but instead work together through a variety of tasks. Therefore, many intelligences and Internet activities overlap.

Multiple Intelligences and Internet Opportunities

Intelligence	Internet Opportunities
Verbal/Linguistic	e-mail, chat rooms, listservers, newsgroups, access to libraries, online journals, e-zines, electronic publishing, bulletin boards, and text used in most sites
Logical/ Mathematical	databases, current research, information and data analysis, math and science game sites, scientific simulations, and sequential problem-solving opportunities
Visual/Spatial	virtual tours of museums around the world, virtual reality sites, video bits, three-dimensional representations, clip art, colorful displays, and graphic environments
Bodily/Kinesthetic	centers for health and research, information on athletics and dancing, manipulation skills used for basic keyboarding and games
Musical/Rhythmic	sites highlighting music genres and history, downloading music, sound files in some sites
Interpersonal	telementoring, online discussion groups, travelers' guides, keypals, e-mail communications, working with others on Internet projects
Intrapersonal	personal home pages, personal thoughts and reflections expressed in e-mail, listservers, and discussion groups
Naturalist	electronic field trips, geographical sites, environmental and social action sites

Figure 2.3

Connecting Brain-Compatible Learning, Multiple Intelligences, and the Internet

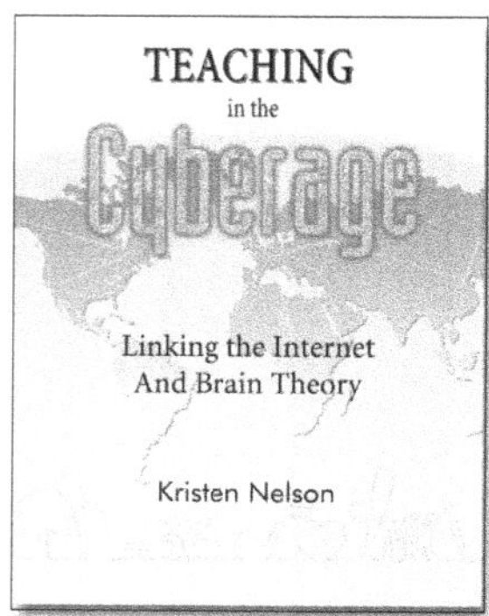

The Internet provides an avenue to strengthen each intelligence as students are asked to participate in activities and projects that foster cognitive and social growth. As teachers design learning experiences that reach out to their students' multiple intelligences through active engagement, student learning becomes more efficient and effective because it is consistent with natural brain operations. The Internet is an incredible tool for reaching all intelligences and reinforcing learning through these neural networks.

The Internet also allows students to take charge of their own learning through direct exploration, expression, and experience. This shifts the student's role from *being taught* to *learning* and the teacher's role from *expert* to *collaborator* or *guide.* As teachers make this important shift and use the theory of multiple intelligences with students, their classrooms increasingly become brain-compatible learning environments. With the growing amount of brain research available, teachers have a wonderful opportunity to integrate brain-compatible learning components and the Internet to provide powerful lessons to students.

By integrating the Internet with ongoing opportunities for engaging students' different intelligences, teachers provide students with learning activities that not only increase the personalization of instruction but also raise students' level of learning and retaining knowledge.

Short- and long-term Internet-based activities or projects provide individual learning opportunities that are tailored for students' growth and academic achievement. Brain-compatible Internet projects provide students with choices, meaningful context, and valuable interactive learning time, helping students make sense of the information they are learning. As students work on individual projects, teachers have time to give immediate feedback on an individual basis, thus reducing the students' natural fear of failure.

Because using the Internet usually requires individuals or small groups to work independently, teachers need to instruct students in the skills of independent work habits. Without the ability to work independently, students reduce the learning and engagement inherent in Internet activities and may become thorns in their teacher's side. The ability to work alone results from intrapersonal intelligence, and teachers can discuss the importance of self-monitoring within this important intelligence area. Teachers can help students strengthen their independent work habits and increase their motivation by setting timelines for the completion of work, by teaching students to self-edit their work, and by taking time to instruct students on how to present their work creatively and professionally. This last point is especially important. Students must be taught—directly and in concrete terms—what an excellent final product includes and what it looks like. Students need to see, experience, and read good examples of final products. By providing these examples, teachers help students set goals for themselves and greatly enhance their quality of work.

When a teacher provides class time for students to work on Internet projects, he or she must set expectations for behavior. Without expectations and appropriate follow-through, independent work on Internet projects simply will not succeed.
The opportunity to develop one of the most important skills students need to learn for today's world—the ability to motivate themselves to complete an independent project—may fall by the wayside. Teachers can set simple expectations: work quietly, be sensitive to other's work habits, ask a peer for help before asking an adult, and visit only Internet sites specified in the activity or allowed by the teacher.

The purpose of this chapter was to lay a foundation of information theory and instructional methods for teachers to apply as they design powerful Internet-based lessons. As teachers learn to keep brain-compatible learning principles and the theory of multiple intelligences in mind, their lessons will have greater depth and more significance in the lives of their students.

Connecting Brain-Compatible Learning, Multiple Intelligences and the Internet

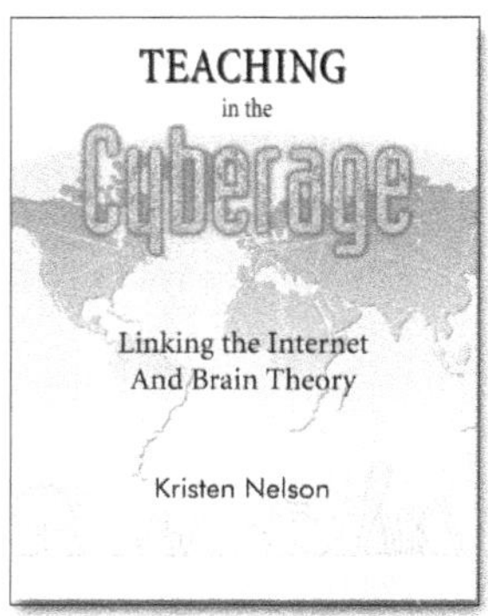

REFERENCES

Caine, R., and G. Caine. 1991. *Making connections: Teaching and the human brain.* Alexandria, VA: Association for Supervision and Curriculum Development.

Campbell, B., and L. Campbell. 1999. *Multiple intelligences and student achievement: Success stories from six schools.* Alexandria, VA: Association for Supervision and Curriculum Development.

Carbo, M. 1986. *Teaching students to read through their individual learning styles.* Englewood Cliffs, NJ: Prentice-Hall.

Fogarty, R. 1997. *Brain-compatible classrooms.* Arlington Heights, IL: SkyLight Training and Publishing.

Gardner, H. 1983. *Frames of mind: The theory of multiple intelligences.* New York: Basic.

Gardner, H. 1993. *Multiple intelligences: The theory in practice.* New York: Basic.

Hart, L. A. 1983. *Human brain, human learning.* Kent, WA: Books for Educators.

Hoff, J. David. 1999. Technology counts '99: Building the digital curriculum. *Education Week.* 19(4): 51–60.

Kovalik, S. 1993. *ITI: The model—Integrated thematic instruction.* Oak Creek, AZ: Books for Educators.

Sousa, D. 1995. *How your brain learns.* Reston, VA: National Association of Secondary School Principals.

Sylwester, R. 1995. *A celebration of neurons: An educator's guide to the human brain.* Alexandria, VA: Association for Supervision and Curriculum Development.

• PART II •

Hands-on Tools for Teaching

Over the past two decades, best practices research has produced a wealth of strategies and structures that have proven worthwhile in the classroom. The best of these strategies transcend specific content. They enable teachers to become creative artists who transform these basic strategies into powerful teaching tools that enrich students' learning experiences. As a teacher designs a strategy into a content-rich lesson, she increases the odds that students will become fully engaged in the curriculum and will increase the quality of their learning experiences.

Strategies such as checking for understanding, 2-4-8, think aloud, think-pair-share, mediated questioning, and structured interactions are the core tools of the effective, strategic teacher.

About Part II

Part II of *The Best of Skylight* begins with three excerpts that feature a selection of instructional strategies that can be applied in any content area. When placed appropriately in a lesson, these strategies motivate students to higher achievement. These essential and basic methods have proven themselves effective with a variety of students regardless of age, in a variety of content areas across the curriculum, and for a variety of purposes. Strategies such as checking for understanding, 2-4-8, think aloud, think-pair-share, mediated questioning, and structured interactions are the core tools of the effective, strategic teacher. "Check for Understanding" by James Bellanca is an activity that can be incorporated in any lesson. This strategy helps the teacher discern if students have understood an explanation or set of instructions. "The New School 'Lecture' " by Robin Fogarty and James Bellanca includes twelve models for cooperative interaction among students. The models include mediated questioning, think-pair-share, wrap around, jigsaw, and others. "Paired-Partner Problem Solving" by James Bellanca is an activity that can be used by teachers when they are teaching students the steps to problem solving.

The second group of articles in Part II provides examples of strategy-rich lessons from a variety of content areas. A practicing classroom teacher designed and used each. These lessons illustrate how a lesson that has been carefully designed with a variety of simple strategies can challenge students at various levels. Bob Kapheim designed his "Create a Creature" lesson for biology students at York High School in Elmhurst, Illinois. He had three purposes: to engage all of the students in his diverse class; to teach students how the classification system works by having them classify; and to teach students the attributes of the insect family. Using a matrix organizer, Bob's lesson guides students through the fun task of inventing a bug. Students classify the bug and create artifacts to identify the bug's key attributes. When Bob's students finish this lesson, they are required to pass a departmental unit exam on animal classification. It was no wonder that Bob's class scores, including those from the low-track, regularly rank at the top of the departmental results.

Two more excerpts round out this group. The "African and Asian Elephants" excerpt is a lesson designed by James Bellanca and Robin Fogarty. "Challenge" features two lessons—Problem-Solving Stories and Heritage Heroes—created by Eleanor Renee Rodriguez and James Bellanca.

The third group of excerpts introduces more complex strategic thinking strategies imbedded into various content areas. In the "Stock Market," Hope Martin illustrates how the National Council of Teachers of Mathematics (NCTM) standards can be used as a framework for teaching. She demonstrates how the teaching of rote procedures can be used as a tool to promote student thinking and to demonstrate connections between classroom mathematics and real-world mathematics. In "Helping Students Become Strategic Readers," Bonnie Burns describes the array of strategies she has found successful in affecting her students' reading comprehension. She also demonstrates how to integrate them into the instructional flow. In "Metacognition," Evelyn Rothstein and Gerry Lauber tap their years of classroom experience to outline how to use writing to promote student thinking across the curriculum. The strategies they selected, including KWL, taxonomy, and sentence starters show how powerful the simple application of instructional strategies can be in a variety of content areas.

The final group of excerpts shows high-level examples of strategic teaching. In "Planning Problem-Based Learning for the Classroom," Diane Ronis outlines a commonsense, how-to-design process. Problem-based learning (PBL) requires the teacher to put into practice a curricular process that uses all of the principles and practices presented in Parts I and II of this book. The proponents of teacher-proof curriculum and instruction do not find this type of teaching to their liking, because PBL celebrates the teacher as a creative designer, a thinker, and a problem solver. The PBL teacher recognizes that the most effective lessons and units stimulate students to think, to transfer, and to probe for deep understanding. Finally, Scott Mandel, in "How to Integrate Virtual Field Trips into the Curriculum," adds another dimension to strategic teaching—the integration of technology into complex and challenging lessons. Understanding the power and the limits of the Internet, Scott details how the strategic teacher can take students beyond the walls of the classroom on virtual field trips. On the Internet, teachers can help students immerse themselves in the author's times, in distant cultures, or in a scientist's lab.

PBL celebrates the teacher as a creative designer, a thinker, and a problem solver.

The SkyLight Way—Best Practices

The strategies explained in Part II are not the only methods that work well. They are, however, representative of a way of teaching and learning that has proven effective for thousands of classroom teachers who have learned in the SkyLight way of instruction.

What is that way? What is the secret of its effect on learning? Why does it work, not only in transforming how teachers teach, but also in how students learn?

There is nothing magical about the SkyLight way. And it is not unique. What SkyLight has done over the years is to gather together those approaches to teaching and learning that met the following criteria.

1. *The approach (tools, methods, strategies, etc.) has a proven track record in educational research.* Valid and reliable research studies indicate that the approach, when correctly applied, has a positive effect on student learning. In the most desirable scenario, research has shown that the approach has a positive and measurable effect on student achievement.

The best example of an approach supported by a significant amount of achievement related data is cooperative learning. Roger and David Johnson (1986, 1987a, 1987b), Robert Slavin (1983, 1990), Sharan and Sharan (1976, 1992), and others, all respected education researchers, conducted hundreds of studies comparing the effectiveness of cooperative learning against the effectiveness of whole class lectures and individualized instruction on achievement. The results were clear. Cooperative learning produced measureably higher achievement results than whole class lectures and individualized instruction. Students in a classroom led by a teacher well prepared in the strategic use of the cooperative learning approach had a better chance of knowing the material or mastering the taught skills than students in classes where the teacher lectured to them or where the teacher provided self-paced worksheets on a topic.

2. *There must be a sound process for developing teachers' appropriate use of the approach.* Two conditions are necessary for a research-proven approach to succeed and survive in classroom implementation: instruction in the method and a hospitable environment in which to apply and adapt the method.

Teachers must receive sufficient instruction in the method, the rationale for the method, and the appropriate use of the method.

First, teachers must receive sufficient instruction in the method, the rationale for the method, and the appropriate use of the method so that they can make thoughtful, strategic application. The more complex the approach, the more necessary it is to have a sound developmental model of teacher preparation. Instruction in the method must include teachers "learning by doing." When teachers learn an active learning strategy such as paired-partner problem solving, think-pair-share, or jigsaw, it is essential that the professional development instructor demonstrate how to use the strategy with the teachers acting as students. Instructors should help the teacher-students identify and overcome the predictable instructional problems and assess trial applications in their classrooms. The professional development instructor is the expert on the approach; the teachers are the experts on their own students. Any preparation for using a complex approach such as cooperative learning must recognize, accept and facilitate the integration of expertise and experience.

Second, after teachers have experienced the approach, understood its critical attributes, assessed how each attribute is used, and learned how to tie the method to a variety of curricular contents, it is important that the school site provide a hospitable environment for using the approach in the classroom. Bruce Joyce and Beverly Showers' (1983) seminal study on peer coaching made clear the elements of such an environment. These elements include scheduled time for teachers to meet for a review of their progress and to observe each other

Cooperative learning, in spite of its extensive research base, was almost obliterated by the superficiality of teacher training and environmental support for the method.

and provide constructive feedback, leadership from the principal, and formative support and coaching from the professional development instructor. Art Costa and Bob Garmston (1994) explain that cognitive coaching is also important. Mary Dietz (2001) encourages principals to use teachers' professional portfolios to help the teachers refine their techniques and strengthen implementation of the method. Most up to date, Arnie Barbknecht and Connie Kieffer (2001) detail proven ways to organize and develop peer coaching as a site-based empowerment tool.

Cooperative learning, in spite of its extensive research base, was almost obliterated by the superficiality of teacher training and environmental support for the method. As educators became aware of the achievement results of cooperative learning, many school districts elected to jump on the bandwagon. Cooperative learning soon became its own worst enemy, not because it was an unworkable strategy, but because too many districts implemented cooperative learning without providing the necessary training programs. Too few teachers received the full range of development support. In too many cases, large school faculties were given a one-hour after school "quickie" workshop or a one-hour institute day "shot in the arm" and told to go forth and use cooperative learning. Others received lectures on how to use cooperative learning and on what the research said, but received no support for installing the practice. In the end, many improperly prepared teachers experienced cooperative learning only as a bad taste in the mouth, a name for a fad, or as a loss of control and interest of their students. Like so many other fads inappropriately and inadequately implemented, these teachers knew instinctively that "this too will pass." With the exception of the Robert Slavin's (1983, 1990) model, cooperative learning became another dead fad by the end of '90s. Like many other methods, it was a victim of poor implementation. However, cooperative learning still remains one of the most research-supported best practices available to teachers who want to make a significant difference in student achievement.

3. *The approach challenges students to use their brains as they learn the assigned curricular content.* All best practices adapted by SkyLight are aligned with the theories discussed in Part I. Although cooperative learning, mediated learning

experiences, and graphic organizers appeared in teachers' repertoires well before Howard Gardner's theory of multiple intelligences (1983) or brain-based learning (Caine and Caine 1991) came to the attention of educators, they each were based solidly in cognitive learning research. Many were influenced by Reuven Feuerstein's (1980) theory of Mediated Learning Experience (MLE) which challenged the conventional belief that intelligence is fixed and could not be changed. In fact, Feuerstein was among the first to promote the belief that all children can learn. Sound educational approaches seek to teach students how to improve their thinking abilities and how to use metacognition (to think about how they think). These approaches provide new and better ways to change the child's capability to know and to learn.

Sound educational approaches teach students how to improve their thinking abilities and how to use metacognition.

4. *The approach celebrates and empowers the teacher.* Some advocates of school reform promulgate the notion that it is best to prohibit teachers from using any instructional tools, curriculum, or assessment approaches that fail the "teacher-proof" standard. "Turn each classroom into a repetitive formula," they argue. "Give teachers a seven-step lesson plan that never varies." "Prescribe each lesson." "Evaluate performance by how closely each lesson uses the seven steps. Take a small bit of information and use the seven steps to drill the facts into each student's memory." "Test to see how many 'got it.' " "Give a grade based on strict percentages that match the bell curve."

There is nothing more demeaning to the professional teacher than being forced into a teacher-proof mold in which she never has the opportunity or the challenge to adapt, adopt, modify, and change curriculum; to select different instructional methods; to solve learning problems with creative approaches; or to think independently. Teachers are celebrated when they are given the challenge and opportunity to teach to their students' varied cognitive needs, styles, and motivations. They are celebrated even more when they are encouraged and supported to add new tools, strategies, and programs to their instructional repertoire. And most of all, teachers are celebrated when they are challenged to use these innovations to help their children grow and learn, not just to regurgitate facts on a test, but to learn how to learn for a lifetime.

When teachers are celebrated, children are challenged to develop in multiple ways. First, they are challenged to learn the

The mind of a child must be the focal point of classroom activity.

content in the curriculum. Second, they are challenged to transfer that knowledge across the curriculum and into life. For example, writing skills used in language arts are also used in mathematics, social studies, art, and science. Third, students learn how to use information to solve problems and gain new insights. Whether students are using paired partners or are immersed in a problem-based investigation, they develop their abilities to live, work, survive, and succeed in a world that is fast-changing and unpredictable. All in all, they become skilled, competent and secure users of their three-story intellects (Bellanca and Fogarty 1991). They know how to gather knowledge skillfully, to develop deep understanding of the core concepts in the curriculum, and to assess its value for transfer.

5. *The approach celebrates children as thinking individuals learning how to make use of their multiple talents.* Early in its existence as a company, SkyLight took its name from the words of Oliver Wendell Holmes. These words matched closely with SkyLight's emerging framework for celebrating all children as thinkers:

> There are one-story intellects, two-story intellects, and three-story intellects with skylights. All fact collectors, who have no aim beyond their facts, are one-story men. Two-story men compare, reason, generalize, using the labors of the fact collectors as well as their own. Three-story men idealize, imagine, predict-their best illumination comes from above, through the skylight.

With the addition of Howard Gardner's (1983) theory of the multiple intelligences to illuminate the sky, Holmes' words took on a new aura at SkyLight. Going beyond the limited notions of learning styles popular at that time, Gardner's theory stretched the understanding of intelligence as an ability to problem solve in a variety of culturally significant ways. His ideas enriched SkyLight's understanding of a high-transfer curriculum centered on developing students' problem-solving capabilities. Because of Gardner's theory, it became clearer than ever that the mind of a child must be the focal point of classroom activity. This focus did not mean brainwashing the child with a set belief system, but it meant developing each child's propensity for learning through curriculum and instruction. This curriculum and instruction must challenge the child to look beyond the third story and through the skylight to explore her multiple intelligences and to develop problem-solving capabilities most suited to her multiple intelligences.

When teachers apply the theory of multiple intelligences in their classrooms, they use methods and processes that develop the children as unique individuals with unique sets of intelligences. This approach truly celebrates each child. When classroom instruction uses a prescribed curriculum that forces children to regurgitate information without opportunities to discover how to think and problem solve, then the classroom not only disrespects the child, but tells him to live a life without distinction.

Problem-based learning also has great potential for creating classrooms that celebrate children. In her excerpt, "Planning Problem-Based Learning for the Classroom," Diane Ronis presents a standards-aligned, problem-based learning scenario that captures the essential value of the problem-based approach. Instead of handing students a plethora of facts to memorize or creating a psuedo-problem as a game, Diane integrates the study of key mathematics and science concepts with higher-order thinking skills, multiple intelligences tasks, and integrated technology. Her assessment rubric illustrates, via benchmarks, that this lesson is based on a true celebration of the child as a unique learner developing unique talents and capabilities.

Curriculum and instruction must challenge the child to explore her multiple intelligences and to develop problem-solving capabilities most suited to her multiple intelligences.

6. *The approach lends itself to multidimensional lesson designs in highly differentiated classrooms.* In the SkyLight model, lessons are more than plans, they are designs. Thus, every tool, strategy, process, or structure included in a lesson should not only positively affect student learning, but should also be applicable in different content areas and should be adaptable to individual, small group, or whole class instruction.

Designing lessons that meet the needs of a diverse population of students in a classroom is a difficult challenge. Even if a teacher only has two students, he must consider how to differentiate instruction. With a classroom of more students, the spectrum becomes more complex. In today's classrooms, factors such as language differences, mainstreaming special needs students, and applying multiple intelligences theory, make the task of differentiating instruction more difficult than ever.

Teachers must begin by developing a repertoire of effective strategies.

Where does the teacher who wants to celebrate these differences begin?

Teachers must begin by developing a repertoire of effective strategies. The criteria described in the first five points provide a guideline for the selection process. Use of these criteria narrow the possibilities for applying approaches. The teacher can also get a jump-start by using the strategies and approaches described in this book.

The Principles in Action

An example of an educator who has developed an amazing facility to design powerful lessons is Sally Berman. A unit of study that I saw Sally teach to a high school chemistry class is an excellent example. Following is the outline of that lesson.

1. Multi-level objectives
   - A. Students will know the mole theory.
   - B. Students will collaborate in making correct calculations of their estimations based on the theory.
   - C. Students will assess the quality of their estimations as they use the theory to make estimates in other areas of science and technology.
2. Instructional strategies
   - A. KWL
   - B. Think-pair-share
   - C. Question web
   - D. Groups of four: lab tasks
   - E. Reflective journals with stem statements
   - F. Concept maps
   - G. Venn diagrams
   - H. Higher-order questions with wait time
   - I. Paired-partner problem solving
   - J. Expectation chart
   - K. Mole models (Students create bean bag moles with unique names such as Molby Dick, Moletel Operator.)
   - L. Mole poems
   - M. Mole history day
   - N. A mole application project
   - O. Mediated learning focus

During one of my observations in the middle of the unit, Sally instructed the class to match up with partners and think of questions they had about mole theory and the calculations they were doing in lab. Each pair agreed on one or two questions. Drawing names from a hat (to ensure a distribution of responses) Sally wrote the questions on a web on the board. When she finished, she asked for students to volunteer part or whole answers to any of the questions. Where there were misunderstandings or disagreements, she facilitated the discussion and moved the factual answers to correctness. She concluded the period by responding to those questions that were not discussed by the students and by asking the students each to write in their journals their responses to the stem: "The most important answers I gathered today were . . . ."

In the lab period that followed, students assembled in groups of four at the lab tables. At each table, name cards identified role assignments. After Sally reviewed the assignment with an expectation chart that showed the rubric for evaluating the day's task, she worked among the groups. She answered questions, checked and corrected calculations, encouraged, and mediated the learning according to the focus she kept in mind for each student.

Sally integrated in her design several tasks that allowed students to develop their multiple intelligences. A closer look at this lesson's content and methodology reveals opportunities for students to develop their naturalist, interpersonal, intrapersonal, verbal/linguistic, logical/mathematical, and visual/spatial intelligences. Sally also added traditional folk dances to celebrate the anniversary of the mole theory, thereby including the musical/rhythmic intelligence and motivating heart-felt involvement.

Throughout the lessons, Sally also imbedded thought-inducing strategies that promoted seeing relationships, analyzing data, solving problems, estimating, reflecting, inventing, and assessing results. Sally engaged students with active learning tasks that included paired-partners, think-pair-share, small group work, and a whole class exercise in constructing a web. By starting with three key, and purposefully ambiguous questions (What is a mole? Why are moles important? How do we find moles?), she challenged students to integrate several content areas (language arts, mathematics, visual arts, science, and social studies) into a comprehensive study of the prescribed content in the chemistry curriculum.

Although there were no student complaints about her multilevel approach, some of her peers initially doubted her. One colleague said, "I can cover mole theory in two class periods and a lab." "What is all this fluff?" asked another. Sally did not respond initially. At the end of the unit when all chemistry students took the departmental exam, students from Sally's four classes, including a wheelchair-bound parapalegic, English as a second language students, and several students repeating chemistry for the second time, dominated the top rankings.

The respect Sally Berman won from her students sprang from the respect she gave them.

Similar to so many successful teachers, Sally is a lifelong learner who pushed herself to learn new and better ways to instruct her students. She never stagnated with a limited repertoire of instructional strategies nor with a shallow understanding of her content. Over the years her repertoire, honed in the fire of the ever-changing classroom, grew larger. Her teaching was not for a test; she wanted to prepare each and every student for a lifetime of learning. The respect she won from her students sprang from the respect she gave them. On her retirement day, the celebration that her students gave her sprang from the way she had celebrated each of them.

REFERENCES

Barbknecht, A. and C.W. Kieffer. 2001. *Peer coaching: The learning team approach.* Arlington Heights, IL: SkyLight Training and Publishing.

Bellanca, J., and R. Fogarty. 1991. *Blueprints for thinking in the cooperative classroom.* Palatine, IL: IRI/SkyLight Training and Publishing.

Berman, S. 1999. *Service learning for the multiple intelligences classroom.* Arlington Heights, IL: SkyLight Training and Publishing.

Caine, R., and G. Caine. 1991. *Making connections: Teaching and the human brain.* Alexandria, VA: Association for Supervision and Curriculum Development.

Costa, A. L., and R. Garmston. 1994. *Cognitive coaching: A foundation for renaissance schools.* Norwood, MA: Christopher Gordon.

Dietz, M. 2001. *Designing the school leader's portfolio.* Arlington Heights, IL: SkyLight Training and Publishing.

Feuerstein, F. 1980. *Instrumental Enrichment.* Baltimore, MD: University Park Press.

Gardner, H. 1983. *Frames of mind: The theory of multiple intelligences.* New York: Basic.

———. 1993. *Multiple intelligences: The theory in practice.* New York: Basic.

Johnson, R. W., and D. Johnson.1986. *Circles of learning: Cooperation in the classroom.* Alexandria, VA: Association for Supervision and Curriculum Development.

———. 1987a. *Joining together: Group theory and group skills,* 3rd ed. Englewood Cliffs, NJ: Prentice Hall.

———. 1987b. *Learning together and alone: Cooperative, competitive, and individualistic learning.* Englewood Cliffs, NJ: Prentice Hall.

Joyce, B., and B. Showers. 1983. *Power in staff development through research and training.* Alexandria, VA: Association for Supervision and Curriculum Development.

Sharan, S., and Y. Sharan. 1976. *Small group teaching.* Englewood Cliffs, NJ: Prentice-Hall.

———. 1992. *Expanding cooperative learning through group investigation.* New York: Teachers College Press.

Slavin, R. 1983. *Cooperative learning.* New York: Longman.

———. 1990. *Cooperative learning: Theory, research, and practice.* Englewood Cliffs, NJ: Prentice-Hall.

Check for Understanding

by **James Bellanca**

Note: The following basic strategy can be incorporated into any subject area lesson.

Activity-at-a-Glance

Purpose

Indicate understanding of a taught concept.

When to Use

Use throughout a lesson or unit or at the end of an explanation or set of instructions to check for student understanding.

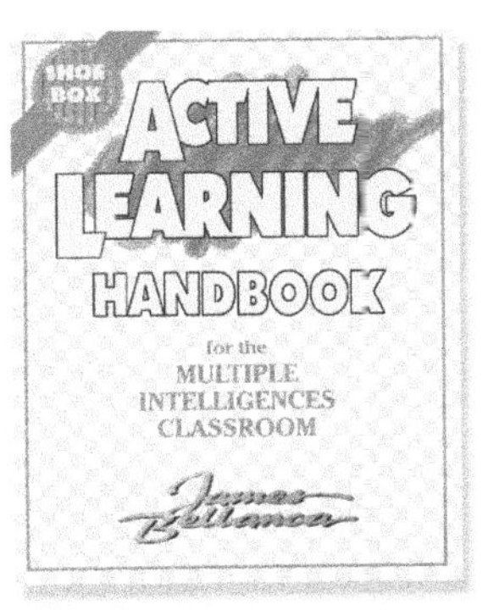

What You'll Need

- No materials necessary

Check for Understanding

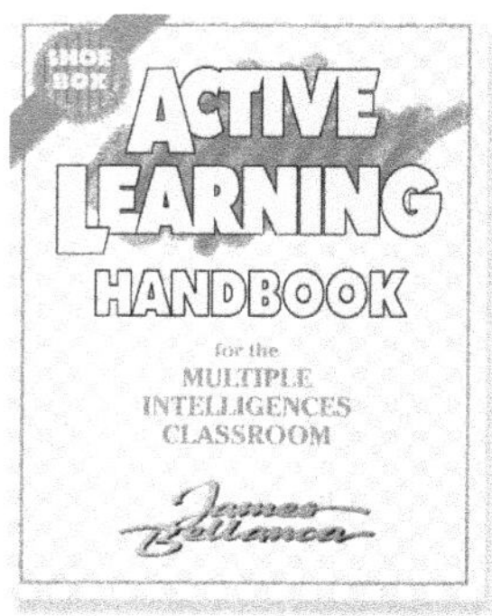

What to Do

1. Present information to students about how to do a new mathematical function [or task from another subject area] and explain rationale.
2. Demonstrate the procedure.
3. At appropriate steps in the procedure, ask students to show understanding by indicating with thumbs up for yes, down for no, or to the side for unsure.
4. Ask students who are signaling uncertainty to tell what they *do* understand so far. Clarify as needed.
5. Ask students who don't understand to pinpoint the spots of confusion. Reteach as needed or call upon another student to coach or explain.
6. Ask students who do understand to explain the procedure to the class.

Variations

1. Give students a cue card with different colors on each side (e.g., red and green) to use instead of their thumbs.
2. Use a think-pair-share check by asking pairs to recite or summarize what was said before calling for a random check.

REFERENCES

Bellanca, J., and R. Fogarty. 1991. *Blueprints for thinking in the cooperative classroom.* Arlington Heights, IL: IRI/SkyLight Training and Publishing.

———. 1993. *Patterns for thinking: Patterns for transfer.* Palatine, IL: IRI/SkyLight Training and Publishing.

Bellanca, J., and R. Fogarty, eds. 1995. *Multiple intelligences: A collection.* Palatine, IL: IRI/SkyLight Training and Publishing.

Bellanca, J., C. Chapman, and E. Swartz. *Multiple assessments for multiple intelligences* (Course Edition). 1997. Arlington Heights, IL: IRI/SkyLight Training and Publishing.

Berman, S. 1995. *A multiple intelligences road to a quality classroom.* Palatine, IL: IRI/SkyLight Training and Publishing.

Brown, A. L., and A. S. Palincsar. 1989. "Guided, cooperative learning and individual knowledge acquisition." In *Knowing, learning, and instruction: Essays in honor of Robert Glasser,* edited by L. B. Resnick. Hillsdale, NJ: Lawrence Erlbaum.

Campbell. L. 1992. *Teaching and learning through multiple intelligences.* Seattle, WA: New Horizons for Learning.

Chapman, C. 1993. *If the shoe fits . . . How to develop multiple intelligences in the classroom.* Palatine, IL: IRI/SkyLight Training and Publishing.

Chapman, C., and L. Freeman. 1996. *Multiple intelligences centers and projects.* Arlington Heights, IL: IRI/SkyLight Training and Publishing.

de Bono, E. 1976. *Teaching thinking.* New York: Penguin.

Feuerstein, R. et al. 1980. *Instrumental enrichment: An intervention program for cognitive modifiability.* Baltimore, MD: Univ. Park Press.

Fogarty, R. 1997. *Problem-based learning and other curriculum models for the multiple intelligences classroom.* Arlington Heights, IL: IRI/SkyLight Training and Publishing.

Fogarty, R., and J. Stoehr. 1995. *Integrating curricula with multiple intelligences: Teams, themes, and threads.* Palatine, IL: IRI/SkyLight Training and Publishing.

Gardner, H. 1983. *Frames of mind: The theory of multiple intelligences.* New York: Basic Books.

———. 1993. *Multiple intelligences: The theory in practice.* New York: HarperCollins.

———. 1995, November. Reflections on multiple intelligences: Myths and messages. *Phi Delta Kappan.*

Lazear, D. 1991. *Seven ways of knowing: Teaching for multiple intelligences.* 2nd ed. Palatine, IL: IRI/SkyLight Training and Publishing.

———. 1991. *Seven ways of teaching: The artistry of teaching with multiple intelligences.* Palatine, IL: IRI/SkyLight Training and Publishing.

———. 1993. *Seven pathways of learning: Teaching students and parents about multiple intelligences.* Tucson, AZ: Zephyr.

Martin, H. 1996. *Multiple intelligences in the mathematics classroom.* Arlington Heights, IL: IRI/SkyLight Training and Publishing.

Murnane, R., and F. Levy. 1996. *Teaching the new basic skills: Principles for educating children to thrive in a changing economy.* New York: Free Press.

Check for Understanding

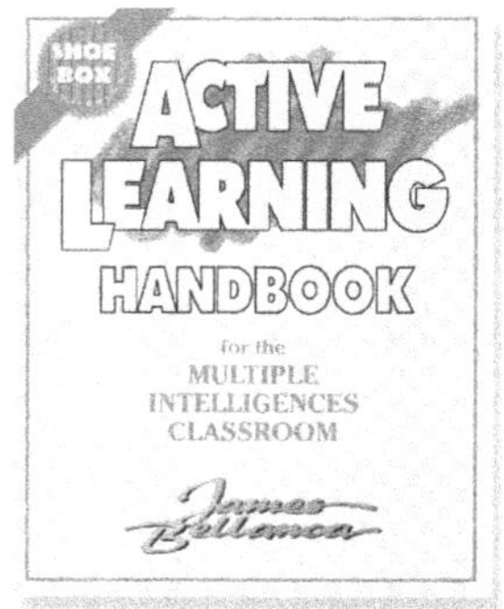

O'Connor, A. T., and S. Callahan-Young. 1994. *Seven windows to a child's world: 100 ideas for the multiple intelligences classroom.* Palatine, IL: IRI/SkyLight Training and Publishing.

Perkins, D., and G. Salomon. 1988, September. Teaching for transfer. *Educational Leadership.* 46: 22–23.

SELECTION 4

The New School "Lecture"

Cooperative Interactions that Engage Student Thinking

by **Robin Fogarty and James Bellanca**

The new "lecture" does not resemble the old lecture very much; in fact, the new "lecture" is really a myriad of interaction patterns. These authentic interaction models take the focus off the lecturer and put it squarely on the learner. From kindergarten classrooms to college lecture halls, educators are moving toward more involving models of instruction. The emergence of the new school "lecture" is unmistakable.

At one end of the spectrum of possibilities for cooperative interactions is the traditional stand-up teaching model. In this model the learner is viewed as a vessel to be filled. At the other end of the spectrum is a total group involvement model called the Human Graph, in which the learners actually move to spots on an imaginary graph that symbolize their position on an issue.

The shift from the most didactic teaching models to more intensely involving models is no easy task for teachers. Just as in any paradigm shift, major philosophical underpinnings are shaken. Yet, the move toward the new school "lecture," with its accent on student interactions, is made easier if seen as a gradual change. Student involvement is designed so that strategies increase student participation by degrees. In this

Adapted from *Best Practices for the Learner-Centered Classroom: A Collection of Articles* by Robin Fogarty, pp. 205–221. © 1995 IRI/Skylight Training and Publishing, Inc. This article is reprinted by permission of the publisher from Davidson & Worsham, *Enhancing Thinking Through Cooperative Learning* (New York: Teachers College Press, © 1992 by Teachers College, Columbia University. All rights reserved.), pp. 84–100.

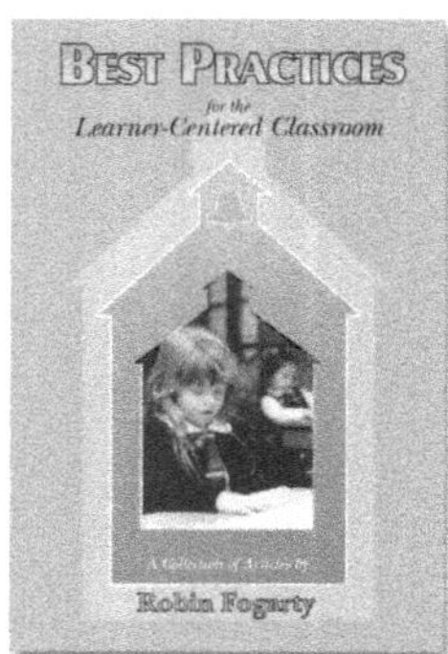

way, teachers and students are able to adjust and adapt to the new model over time.

Surprisingly and almost unfailingly, once the philosophical shift begins, once teachers begin implementing cooperative interactions, the evidence of student motivation becomes so overwhelmingly visible that teachers are encouraged to try more. The momentum builds for both teachers and students, and before long "the new school lecture" becomes the norm in the classroom. By then, the novelty of the models is no longer the challenge. The challenge becomes choosing the most appropriate interactive designs for the target lesson; it is choosing a design in which the final focus rests on the learner, not on the lecturer.

An Overview of Twelve Cooperative Interactions

The many variables that come into play as one is selecting the most appropriate interactive strategy include time, space and facilities, level and behavior of students, number of students, purpose of the lesson, background and experiences of the students, support materials, and teacher expertise.

In the high-content, high-support, high-challenge classroom (see Figure 4.1), the overriding goal is intense student involvement and the subsequent transfer of learning across subject areas and into life situations. High content refers to rigorous disciplines such as the sciences, the humanities, and the arts; high support cites the expectation for cooperative interactions; and high challenge dictates the need for meaningful and thoughtful learner activities. By accumulating a repertoire of interactive strategies and coupling student involvement with information-processing models, the skillful teacher moves learning for all students to new depths. As one surveys the various interactive strategies, it becomes apparent that different strategies are appropriate for different classroom situations.

Twelve basic cooperative interactive models are presented at the end of this chapter. These models can be adapted to meet

The New School Lecture

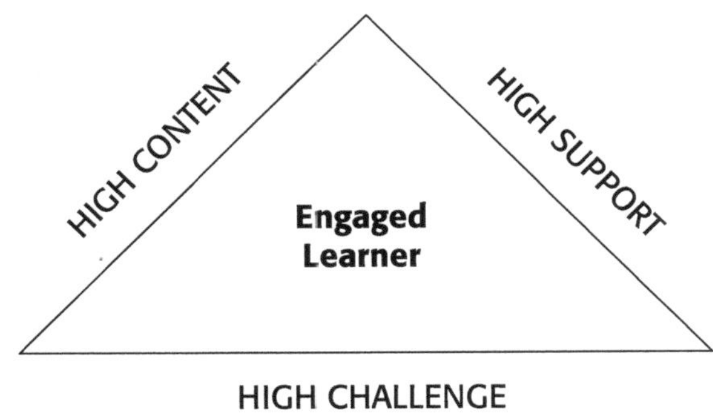

Figure 4.1

less-involving to more-involving teaching goals. For example, the strategies in Model 1, Lecture/Rhetorical Questioning, require minimal learner participation, while Model 8, Cooperative Learning: Groups, or Model 10, Forced Response: Wrap Around, engage the learner intensely due to the very nature and structure of the strategies.

The skillful teacher introduces increasingly engaging interactive models over time. As students become more adept in their social skills, the models are selected strictly for appropriateness. Initially, however, the models are subtly slotted into the lessons to familiarize students with the different interactions and to lead them toward involvement in the learning situation.

Each model included at the end of the chapter indicates the type of interaction, a source, and a lesson description. The prescription suggests when this particular model might be appropriate. A classroom *vignette* provides brief illustrations of the interactions that define the model. The brief *notes* are metacognitive cues or labels that explain the example under scrutiny.

Interactive models work with all levels—elementary, middle, high school, and college. Each of these particular

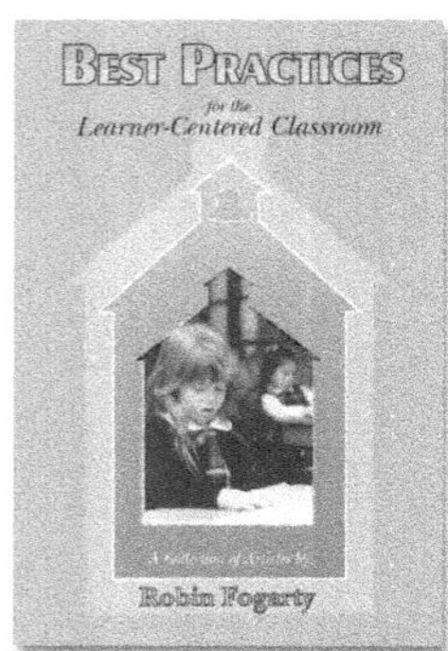

examples features just one of the levels. Adjustments by the instructor are needed to tailor the examples for age, grade, and content appropriateness.

Conclusion

Based on current research and practice, the cooperative interaction designs that distinguish the new school lecture from the traditional seem to offer a positive and optimistic prognosis for future use in our nation's classrooms. By their very nature, cooperative learning strategies create a bubbling-up effect among both students and teachers. They somehow produce an energy that is at once contagious and self-propelling.

Teachers using cooperative interactions in the classroom say the positive effects on student motivation, achievement, and self-concept are so immediately visible and so astonishingly dramatic that the incentives are there for novices to do more. That's why cooperative learning has taken root in schools at the grassroots level.

The designs for thoughtful interactions presented in this chapter provide a vigorous repertoire of instructional strategies. The seasoned practitioner will appropriately select from these strategies as opportunities occur in the instructional arena.

By varying the types of interactions and creating designs or variations on the themes presented, teachers provide a myriad of social and cognitive learning experiences for students. In turn, students reveal both their social skills and their thinking paradigms as they become involved in and responsible for their own learning.

The old lecture, according to John Gould, is "an occasion when you numb one end to benefit the other" (Peter 1977, p. 101). The new school lecture, however, is more like a conversation. In a conversation, as Richard Armour suggests, "it is all right to *hold* the conversation for a time, but you should *let go of* it now and then" (Peter 1977, p. 119). The new school lecture sees the teacher skillfully holding student attention and letting go of center stage, thus inviting thoughtful and engaging student conversations.

Model 1

Source	Type of Interaction
Perhaps "Professor Kingsfield" from The Paper Chase	**Lecture/Rhetorical Questioning**
Description	
Traditional lecture or stand-up teaching in which interaction is a one-way broadcast, punctuated with occasional rhetorical questioning.	
(Suggested) Prescription	**Lesson: Ethics of Medical Technology** **Level: College**
Use with large groups and/or a lot of information; punctuate with rhetorical questions throughout.	Methodology class at a university level in which 200 students attend an hour lecture twice a week as part of a required premed course.
Source	**Type of Interaction**
Lecture Input (or Teacher Talk)	*With the breakthroughs in medical technology, the options for life support systems are increasing at a rapid rate.*
Rhetorical Question	*How do you think that affects us?*
Lecture Input (or Teacher Talk)	*It seems quite straightforward to make a technical decision. But one must consider all the implications of that decision.*
Rhetorical Questions	*Haven't we all faced a dilemma such as this?*

The New School "Lecture"

Cooperative Interactions that Engage Student Thinking

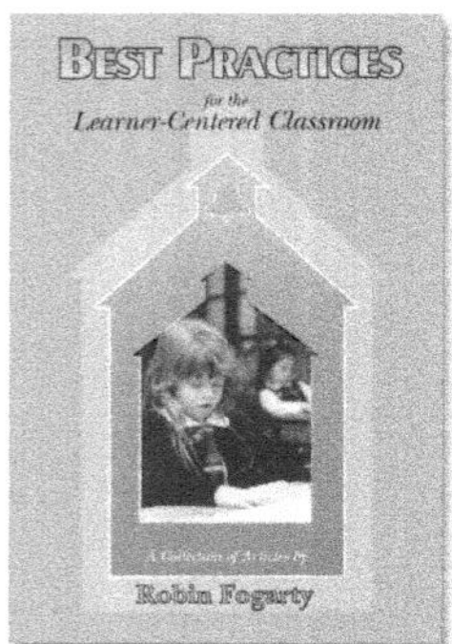

Model 2

Source	Type of Interaction
Hunter, 1983	**Signaling and Direct Questioning: Surveying**
Description	
Traditional lecture format interrupted every five to seven minutes; a posed question that requires a physical signal from students (raised hands) or a single student response that may require some elaboration.	
(Suggested) Prescription	**Lesson: Biology/DNA** **Level: Grade 10**
Use to make lecture slightly more interactive (á la interactive video model) so students are hooked momentarily—at least interacting with a physical response or a one-student in-depth answer.	As the high school biology teacher punctuates his DNA lecture with signaling questions, he deliberately weaves direct questions into the lecture for occasional in-depth student responses.
Notes	**Vignette: Signaling and Direct Questioning**
Signaling	*How many agree? Disagree?*
Direct question	*David, tell us why you agree with the text, why you believe the assumptions are true.*
Student response	*Well, I'm not sure, but I was connecting the idea to . . .*

Model 3

Source	Type of Interaction
Weaver & Cotrell, 1986	**Turn To Your Partner And . . . (TTYPA)**
Description	
An informal strategy used throughout an input sequence in which two students discuss ideas from the lecture.	
(Suggested) Prescription	**Lesson: Down Memory Lane** — **Level: Grade 8**
Use to punctuate a lecture, a film, or a reading. After 7–8 minutes of straight talk, students need to be actively cued and engaged.	This informal, quick interaction, in which students turn to a partner and dialogue briefly on a specifically directed task, is used effectively as students are guided to model both cognition and metacognition in a lesson on thinking.
Notes	**Vignette: TTYPA**
Lecturer	*Metacognition is thinking about your thinking. Let me demonstrate.* *Turn to your partner and recite a piece you know by memory. Then, switch roles and listen to your partner's memorized piece.*
Student 1 response	*Four score and seven years ago . . .*
Student 2 response	*We the people of the United States . . .*
Lecturer	*That's called cognition.* *Now, turn to your partner and tell each other how you learned that piece by heart so well that you could say it today.*
Student 1 response	*I learned by repeating . . .*
Lecturer	*Thinking about how you learned is called metacognition.*

The New School "Lecture"
Cooperative Interactions that Engage Student Thinking

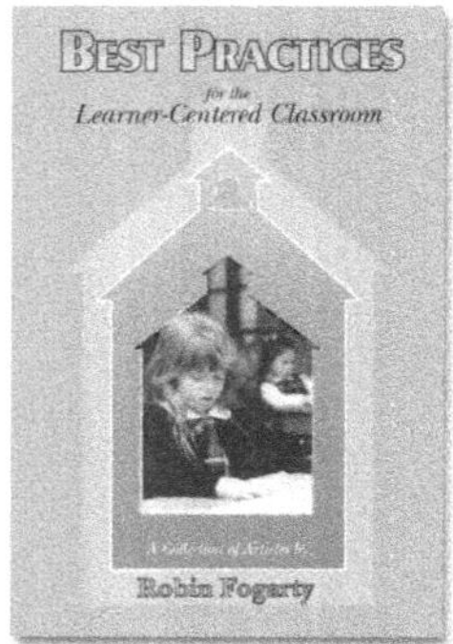

Model 4

Source	Type of Interaction
Bloom & Broder, 1950 Whimbey, 1975	**Paired Partners: Thinking Aloud**
Description	
A problem solver talks his way strategically through a problem. A partner monitors his progress with cues and questions. Both reflect on problem-solving patterns.	
(Suggested) Prescription	**Lesson: Math Problem Solving** — **Level: Grade 6**
Use over time to develop metacognitive, think-aloud tracking of student behaviors.	One partner thinks aloud as he or she solves a problem. The monitor cues the thinking with appropriate questions as the problem solver works systematically through the math calculations.
Notes	**Vignette: Paired Partners**
Teacher	*With partners, solve this story problem using the think-aloud strategy.*
Problem solver (Thinks aloud and says everything that occurs to him or her in a systematic procedure.)	*I'm going to add these two numbers. Then, I'll . . .*
Monitor (Asks leading questions to elicit the inner reasoning.)	*Why are you doing that? Are you expecting a larger number or a smaller number than the original?*
Problem solver (Elaborates and catches another thought for a new strategy.)	*Because the question calls for a total, I'm thinking the number, of course, will be larger and therefore I will add or multiply. Hmm, could I multiply here?*

Model 5

Source	Type of Interaction
Lyman & McTighe, 1988	**Dyads: Think/Pair/Share**
Description	
Partners are cued to think first with the use of wait time. Then pairs of student share their thoughts with each other. After pairing, students may share in the whole class.	

(Suggested) Prescription	Lesson: The Non-Listening Game	Level: Grade 3
Use when formal wait time is needed for student internalization and connection making; use any time thoughtful articulation will help students understand.	To teach the social skill of active listening needed for cooperative interactions, the non-listening game is used. By exaggerating the opposite behavior, students more readily focus on the desired behavior.	

Notes	Vignette: Dyads
Initial activity	Following a partner interaction for which a "listener" is asked to exhibit *non*-listening behaviors to the "speaker," the teacher instructs students:
Think alone	*Think about the things the listener did that signaled no listening.* (Wait 3–10 seconds.)
Pair/share	Listener: *I looked away.* Speaker: *You interrupted me.* Listener: *I felt bad because I knew I wasn't paying attention. It was rude.* Speaker: *I wanted to quit talking to you.*

The New School "Lecture"

Cooperative Interactions that Engage Student Thinking

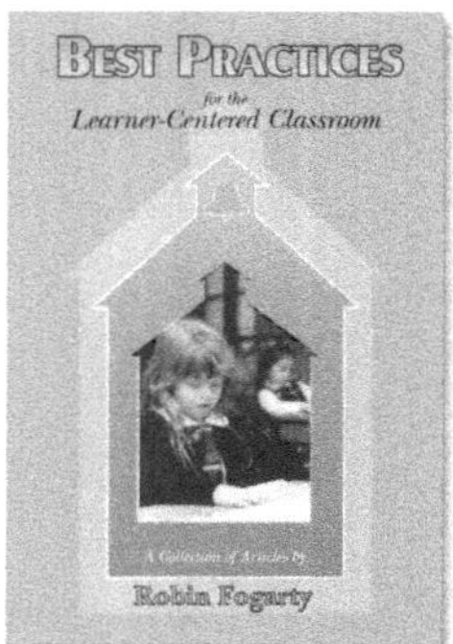

Model 6

Source	Type of Interaction	
Rowe, 1969 Costa, 1986	**Triads: Observer Feedback**	
Description		
Partners practice a designated interaction while a third-party observer records and reports feedback data.		
(Suggested) Prescription	**Lesson: Biology/DNA**	**Level: Grade 10**
Use when partner interactions can be extended or elaborated by objective observer feedback.	To teach students to use higher-order questions, the teacher introduces the concept of fat and skinny questions and then asks student trios to practice their question asking.	
Notes	**Vignette: Triads**	
Teacher targets behavior to look for.	*Observers, I will be noting FAT and Skinny questions. FAT questions will be those that elicit elaborate answers with examples and details. Skinny questions will be those that get "Yes, No, Maybe So" answers.*	
Question asked (Recorded as a FAT question.)	Interviewer: *How do you compare and contrast democracy to socialism?* Interviewee: *Similarities might include ___ while differences include ___.*	
Question asked (Recorded as a Skinny question.)	Interviewer: *Which do you prefer?* Interviewee: *The former!*	
Question asked (Recorded as a FAT question.)	Interviewer: *Imagine justifying your choice. What might you say?*	

Model 7

Source	Type of Interaction	
Fogarty & Opeka, 1988	**2–4–8: Tell/Retell**	
Description		
Partners tell their own stories. Then they retell a partner's story. The pairs double—2–4–8.		
(Suggested) Prescription	**Lesson: Biology/DNA**	**Level: Grade 10**
Use to structure active listening in a partner sharing or for a quick gathering of many ideas.	In a typical primary classroom, "show and tell" time is structured carefully for both speaking and listening skills.	
Notes	**Vignette: 2–4–8**	
2 Partners share show and tell items. (A)(B) 4 A tells B's, B tells A's C tells D's, D tells C's (A)(B) (C)(D) 8 Each tells a new story.	A: *This is my skin from a snake. I found it on the hiking path. It was there in the sunshine. I think the snake wiggled out of it while he was getting a suntan.* B: *I brought my favorite Transformer. My dad couldn't figure it out. I had to help him. It's pretty tricky if you don't know much about them.* A: *"B" brought the Transformer that his dad couldn't figure out.* B: *"A" found a snake's skin while he was hiking.* C: *"D" brought photographs of his birthday party at the pizza place.* D: *"C" forgot her show and tell but she told me about her ride in the rowboat.* A: *"C" forgot hers but she rode in a rowboat.* B: *"D" has pictures of the pizza place* C: *"B" can transform his Transformer.* D: *"A" has the skin of a snake.*	

The New School "Lecture"

Cooperative Interactions that Engage Student Thinking

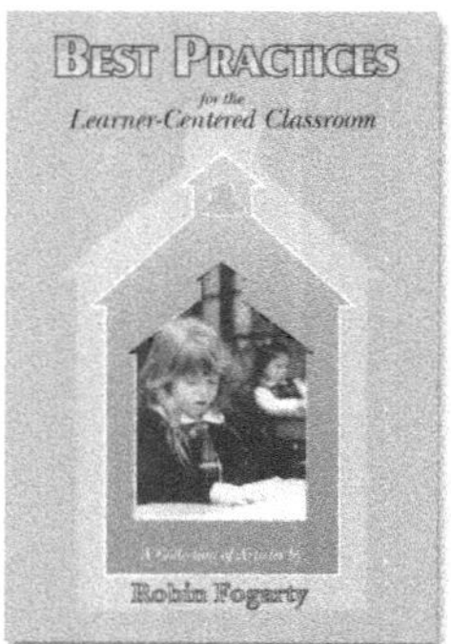

Model 8

Source	Type of Interaction
Johnson & Johnson, 1986 Slavin, 1983 Kagan, 1988	**Cooperative Learning: Groups**
Description	
Three to five learners, heterogeneously grouped for an academic task. Key elements for formal cooperative groups include positive interdependence, individual accountability, group processing, social skills, and face-to-face interactions.	
(Suggested) Prescription	**Lesson: Biology/DNA** **Level: Grade 10**
Use to engage students intensely in the processing activities needed for learning for transfer.	Cooperative groups are used in a Directed Reading Thinking Activity (DRTA) to predict and justify what students think will happen next in a story.
Notes	**Vignette: Cooperative Learning**
Checker checks for understanding (Teacher monitors)	*Does everyone understand? We will use BET.* **B**ase on facts **E**xpress possibilities **T**ender a bet on what we think will happen next in the story entitled "The Dinner Party"
Encourager (Teacher monitors)	Encourages response in turn: • *I think it's a murder mystery because of the title.* • *I think it's about cannibals. There will be a twist.* • *Maybe it's about animals having a tea party. This is from school, you know.*
Encourager (Group consensus)	*Let's write down the cannibal idea because it's so different. What do the rest of you think?*
Recorder	Writes down group answer.

Model 9

Source	Type of Interaction
Fogarty & Bellanca, 1987	**Traveling Clusters: People Search**
Description	
Students are prompted with questions to move about and find someone who . . . . Informal clusters form as students select new partners in their search for answers to the questions.	
(Suggested) Prescription	**Lesson: People Search** — **Level: Grade 12**
Use as ice-breaker, as prelearning strategy to activate prior knowledge or as a review of important concepts prior to a test.	A lesson used as a pre-learning strategy to "stir up" prior knowledge about thinking skills. The cue sheet starts the student interaction.
Notes	**Vignette: Traveling Clusters**
Prompted by sheet	Using: Find Someone Who . . . 1. Can classify friends 2. Can name problem-solving steps 3. 4.
Students move about and talk to each other.	Student A: *I think I can classify friends into four groups.* Student B: *Great. Go ahead.* Student A: *The good, the bad, the ugly, and best friend.* Student B: *Super. Maybe, I can help you with the steps to problem solving. First, decide on the real problem . . .*
Students move on to newly forming clusters of 2, 3, or 4 students.	Student A: *Thanks. Talk to you later.*

The New School "Lecture"

Cooperative Interactions that Engage Student Thinking

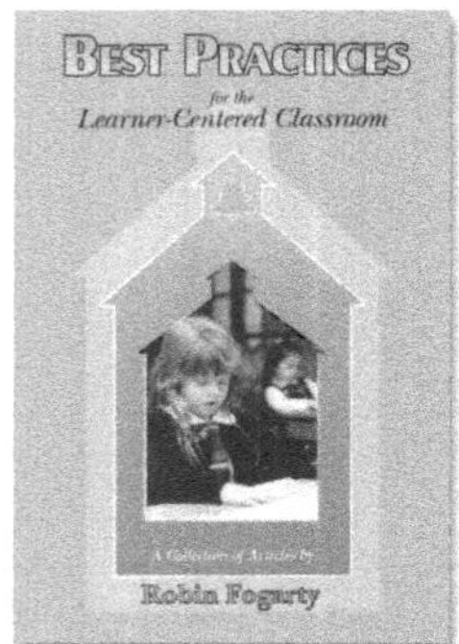

Model 10

Source	Type of Interaction	
Howe & Howe, 1975	**Forced Response: Wrap Around**	
Description		
Round-robin style, students respond in turn to a lead-in statement cued by the teacher.		
(Suggested) Prescription	**Lesson: Analogies**	**Level: Grade 5**
Use to anchor individual thoughts or give a quick reading of the group.	At the close of the lesson, students are asked to compare thinking to an animal. After jotting down some ideas, a verbal wrap around the room is used to share the ideas.	
Notes	**Vignette: Forced Response**	
	Wrapping around the room, each student responds in turn . . .	
Response of student #1	*Thinking is like a frog because it hops around in your mind.*	
Teacher	[Signals next student without judging each response.]	
Student #2	*Thinking is like an elephant because it's heavy on your mind.*	
Teacher	[Nods.]	
Student #3	*Thinking is like a horse because both can throw you.*	
Student #4	*Thinking is like a cat family because it helps to be in a group.*	
Student #5	*Thinking is like a monkey because you can fool around with both.*	
Student #6	*Thinking is like a chicken because both can lay an egg!*	

Model 11

Source	Type of Interaction
Fogarty & Bellanca, 1987	**Total Group Response: Human Graph**
Description	
Students advocate an opinion by standing at designated spots on an imaginary axis. This human graph is a living, breathing graph that can change as students change positions.	
(Suggested) Prescription	**Lesson: Equity** **Level: Grade 9**
Use to take a quick but highly visible reading of the group members' feelings on an issue, idea, or concept.	Used to introduce a unit on equity issues, the teacher structures an agree/disagree statement for sampling "public opinion."
Notes	**Vignette: Total Group Response**
Present graph format	Disagree / Neutral / Agree D C B A A B C D Die for it, Convince others, Believe, Disagree, Agree, Believe, Convince others, Die for it
Teacher cues for graphing interaction	*Indicate how strongly you agree or disagree:* Women are stronger than men.
Students move on graph	D C B A A B C D
Sample reasons from students	*I agree strongly. Think about the pioneer women and the hardships they had to overcome.*

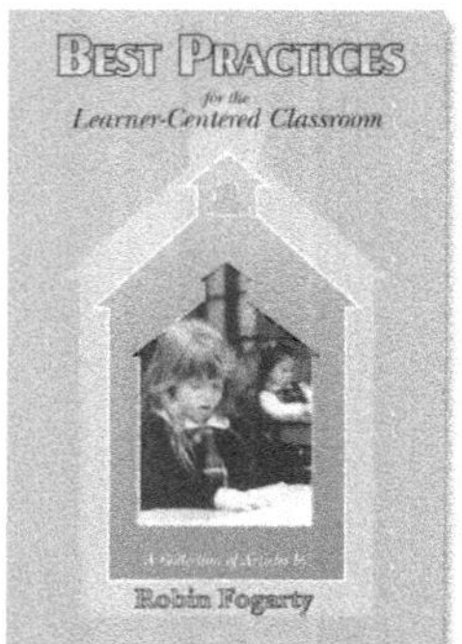

Model 12

Source	Type of Interaction
Aronson, 1978 Sharan & Sharan, 1976	**Group Investigation: The Ultimate Jigsaw**
Description	
Each member has a piece of the puzzle; responsibility is divided; to get the whole picture, or all the information, the separate pieces must be reassembled or synthesized into the completed puzzle by the various group members.	
(Suggested) Prescription	**Lesson: Geographic Regions** **Level: Grade 4**
Use when groups are socially sophisticated or to build individual responsibility within the team.	In a fourth grade classroom, groups of three students are given regions of the United States to investigate and research. The group is ultimately responsible to know all three regions and will "teach each other." Students with the same topic help each other master it before presenting it to their groups.
Notes	**Vignette: Group Investigation**
Teacher	*Ones, take the Eastern seaboard. Twos, research the mid-section of the country. Threes, gather information about the western portion of the United States.*
Student #1	*I'm going to start in the library.*
Student #2	*I need to define my area.*
Student #3	*This is great. I love the West.*

REFERENCES

Aronson, E. 1978. *The jigsaw classroom.* Beverly Hills, CA: Sage Publications.

Bloom, B., and L. Broder. 1950. *Problem solving process of college students.* Chicago: University of Chicago Press.

Clarke, J., R. Wideman, and S. Eadie. 1990. *Together we learn.* Toronto: Prentice-Hall.

Costa, A. 1986. Teaching for intelligent behavior. Unpublished syllabus (3rd ed.).

Dalton, J. 1985. *Adventures in thinking.* Melbourne, Australia: Thomas Nelson Australia.

Fogarty, R., and J. Bellanca. 1987. *Patterns for thinking: Patterns for transfer.* Palatine, IL: IRI/SkyLight Training and Publishing.

Fogarty, R., and K. Opeka. 1988. *Start them thinking.* Palatine, IL: IRI/SkyLight Training and Publishing.

Howe, L., and M. Howe. 1975. *Personalizing education: Values clarification and beyond.* New York: Hart.

Hunter, M. 1983. *Reinforcement.* El Segundo, CA: Tip Publications.

Johnson, R., and D. Johnson. 1986. *Circles of learning: Cooperation in the classroom.* Alexandria, VA: Association for Supervision and Curriculum Development.

Kagan, S. 1988. *Cooperative learning: Resources for teachers.* San Juan Capistrano, CA: Resources for Teachers.

Lyman, F., and J. McTighe. 1988, April. Cueing thinking in the classroom: The promise of theory-embedded tools. *Educational Leadership,* p. 7.

Peter, L. J. 1977. *Peter's quotations: Ideas for our time.* New York: Bantam Books.

Reid, J., P. Forrestal, and J. Cook. 1989. *Small group learning in the classroom.* Scarborough, Australia: Chalkface Press.

Rowe, M. B. 1969. Science, silence and sanctions. *Science and Children.* 6: 11–13.

Sharan, S., and Y. Sharan. 1976. *Small group teaching.* Englewood Cliffs, NJ: Educational Testing Publications.

Slavin, R. E. 1983. *Cooperative learning.* New York: Longman.

Weaver, R., and H. Cotrell. 1986, Summer. Using interactive images in the lecture hall. *Educational Horizons.* 64(4): 180–185.

Whimbey, A., and L. Whimbey. 1975. *Intelligence can be taught.* New York: Innovative Science.

Paired-Partner Problem Solving

by **James Bellanca**

Note: The following basic strategy can be incorporated into any subject area lesson.

Activity-at-a-Glance

Purpose

Apply the mathematical problem-solving process.

When to Use

Use throughout a unit or lesson to help students review the explicit steps necessary for problem solving.

What You'll Need

- No materials necessary

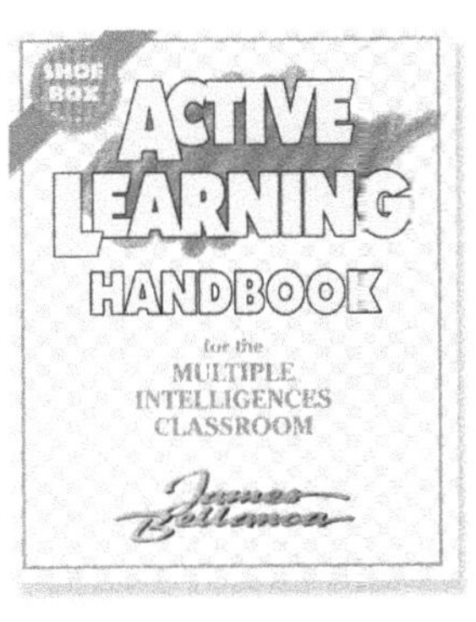

Paired-Partner Problem Solving

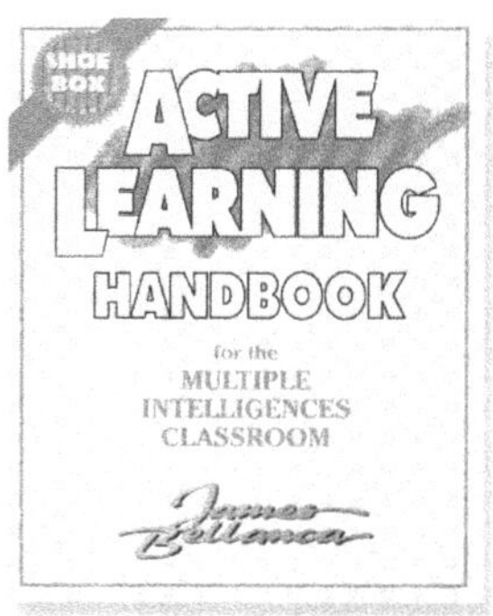

What to Do

1. Review the problem-solving process and check for student ability to follow the steps.
2. Arrange students in pairs and assign two problems to each pair. Explain that one student is to solve problem one, identifying the problem-solving steps as he or she completes them. The other student is to record the first student's thinking.
3. Monitor student work and coach as needed.
4. Instruct students to repeat the process for the second problem but to reverse their roles.
5. Invite two to three pairs to demonstrate their problem-solving steps for the class. Ask questions to mediate accuracy and complete use of the process.
6. Reteach any steps with which students have difficulty. Remix partners, assign two new problems to each pair, and repeat the problem-solving sequence.

Step 1
What is the problem asking me to find out?

How many miles per gallon the car uses

Step 2
My plan

Take the total number of miles the car traveled and divide it by the number of gallons it used.

Variations

1. Use the problem-solving process after the students finish a problem to assess their thinking.
2. Invite pairs of students to create a puzzle by writing the steps to solve a problem and leaving out some steps. Have different pairs try to determine the missing steps.

REFERENCES

Bellanca, J., and R. Fogarty. 1991. *Blueprints for thinking in the cooperative classroom.* Arlington Heights, IL: IRI/SkyLight Training and Publishing.

———. 1993. *Patterns for thinking: Patterns for transfer.* Palatine, IL: IRI/SkyLight Training and Publishing.

Bellanca, J., and R. Fogarty, eds. 1995. *Multiple intelligences: A collection.* Palatine, IL: IRI/SkyLight Training and Publishing.

Bellanca, J., C. Chapman, and E. Swartz. 1997. *Multiple assessments for multiple intelligences* (Course Edition). Arlington Heights, IL: IRI/SkyLight Training and Publishing.

Berman, S. 1995. *A multiple intelligences Road to a quality classroom.* Palatine, IL: IRI/SkyLight Training and Publishing.

Brown, A. L., and A. S. Palincsar. 1989. "Guided, cooperative learning and individual knowledge acquisition." In *Knowing, learning, and instruction: Essays in honor of Robert Glasser,* edited by L. B. Resnick. Hillsdale, NJ: Lawrence Erlbaum.

Campbell. L. 1992. *Teaching and learning through multiple intelligences.* Seattle, WA: New Horizons for Learning.

Chapman, C. 1993. *If the shoe fits . . . How to develop multiple intelligences in the classroom.* Palatine, IL: IRI/SkyLight Training and Publishing.

Chapman, C., and L. Freeman. 1996. *Multiple intelligences centers and projects.* Arlington Heights, IL: IRI/SkyLight Training and Publishing.

de Bono, E. 1976. *Teaching thinking.* New York: Penguin.

Feuerstein, R. et al. 1980. *Instrumental enrichment: An intervention program for cognitive modifiability.* Baltimore, MD: Univ. Park Press.

Fogarty, R. 1997. *Problem-based learning and other curriculum models for the multiple intelligences classroom.* Arlington Heights, IL: IRI/SkyLight Training and Publishing.

Paired-Partner Problem Solving

Fogarty, R., and J. Stoehr. 1995. *Integrating curricula with multiple intelligences: Teams, themes, and threads.* Palatine, IL: IRI/SkyLight Training and Publishing.

Gardner, H. 1983. *Frames of mind: The theory of multiple intelligences.* New York: Basic Books.

———. 1993. *Multiple intelligences: The theory in practice.* New York: HarperCollins, 1993.

———.1995, November. Reflections on multiple intelligences: Myths and messages. *Phi Delta Kappan.*

Lazear, D. 1991. *Seven ways of knowing: Teaching for multiple intelligences.* 2nd ed. Palatine, IL: IRI/SkyLight Training and Publishing.

———. 1991. *Seven ways of teaching: The artistry of teaching with multiple intelligences.* Palatine, IL: IRI/SkyLight Training and Publishing.

———. 1993. *Seven pathways of learning: Teaching students and parents about multiple intelligences.* Tucson, AZ: Zephyr.

Martin, H. 1996. *Multiple intelligences in the mathematics classroom.* Arlington Heights, IL: IRI/SkyLight Training and Publishing.

Murnane, R., and F. Levy. 1996. *Teaching the new basic skills: Principles for educating children to thrive in a changing economy.* New York: Free Press.

O'Connor, A. T., and S. Callahan-Young. 1994. *Seven windows to a child's world: 100 ideas for the multiple intelligences classroom.* Palatine, IL: IRI/SkyLight Training and Publishing.

Perkins, D., and G. Salomon. 1988, September. Teaching for transfer. *Educational Leadership.* 46: 22–23.

SELECTION 6

Create a Creature

A Secondary School Lesson

by **Bob Kapheim**

➤ Setting Up the Scaffolding

Distribute a die to each lab group and tell the students that these will help them in today's lesson. Show the Three-Story Intellect model (Figure 5.1) and explain that students will gather, process and apply information about classifying in a lab called "Create a Creature."

➤ Working the Crew

Using lab groups of three members each, assign and define the roles:

Researcher:	Finds the information in the text.
Recorder:	Charts the information.
Illustrator:	Draws, diagrams, and labels the creature with the designated attributes.

To gather information, distribute a copy of the blank Create-A-Creature matrix to each lab group. Using the text, have student groups complete the matrix by choosing possible variables. A completed one might look like the chart on the next page.

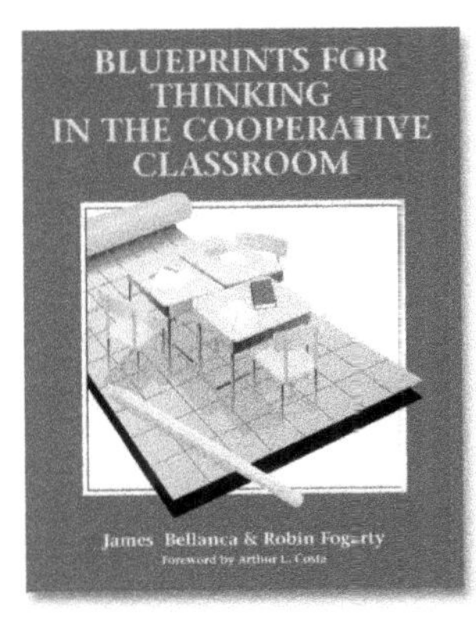

Lesson courtesy of Bob Kapheim, retired biology teacher, York High School, Elmhurst, IL. Adapted from *Blueprints for Thinking in the Cooperative Classroom* by James Bellanca and Robin Fogarty, pp. 66–67 and 456–57.

Create a Creature

	A	B	C	D	E	F
	BODY SYMMETRY	**SEGMENTATION**	**FORM OF LOCOMOTION**	**SENSORY ORGANS**	**SUPPORT STRUCTURES**	**BODY COVERING**
1	bi-lateral	none	none	eyes, ears, & nostrils	bony skeleton	skin-hair
2	radial	2 body segments	2 or 4 walking legs	paired antennae	cartilaginous skeleton	scales
3	bi-lateral	3 body segments	legs & wings	compound eye & antennae	exoskeleton	skin-hair
4	bi-lateral	multiple segments	6 or 8 legs	tentacles	soft bodied	feathers
5	radial	2 body segments	fins	eyes, ears & nostrils	shell hinged	scales
6	bi-lateral	none	multiple walking legs	compound eye & antennae	shell carried	skin-hair

Once the grids are complete, have students roll the die. For each roll, have them circle the corresponding squares in each column of the grid. For example, for the first column the toss might be 4. Students would circle the fourth item in first column (bilateral). For the second column, if the toss is 2, circle the second item (2 body segments).

	A	B	C	D	E	F
	BODY SYMMETRY	**SEGMENTATION**	**FORM OF LOCOMOTION**	**SENSORY ORGANS**	**SUPPORT STRUCTURES**	**BODY COVERING**
1	bi-lateral	none	none	eyes, ears, & nostrils	bony skeleton	skin-hair
2	radial	2 body segments	2 or 4 walking legs	paired antennae	cartilaginous skeleton	scales
3	bi-lateral	3 body segments	legs & wings	compound eye & antennae	exoskeleton	skin-hair
4	bi-lateral	multiple segments	6 or 8 legs	tentacles	soft bodied	feathers
5	radial	2 body segments	fins	eyes, ears & nostrils	shell hinged	scales
6	bi-lateral	none	multiple walking legs	compound eye & antennae	shell carried	skin-hair

Three-Story Intellect

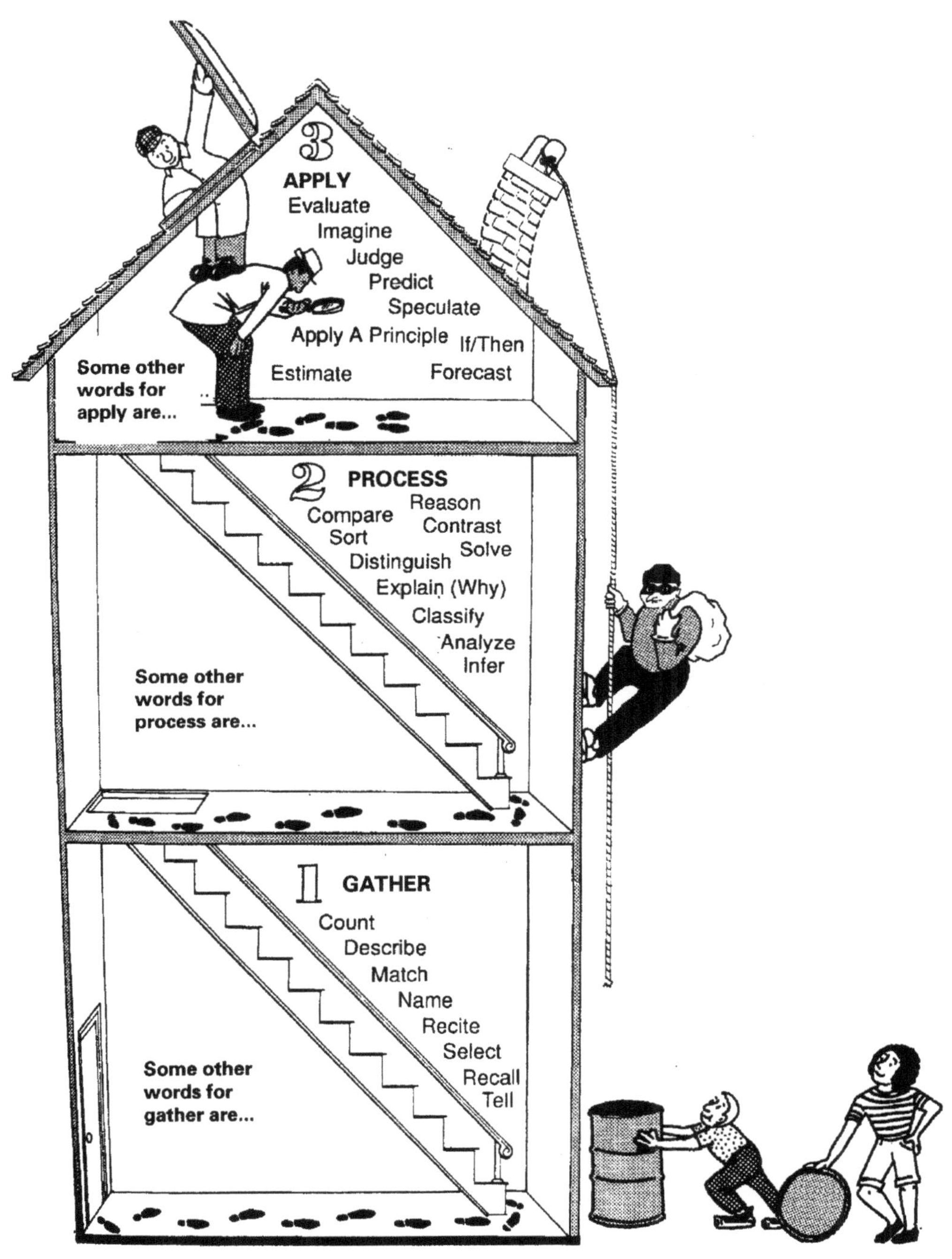
3
APPLY
Evaluate
Imagine
Judge
Predict
Speculate
Apply A Principle
If/Then
Estimate
Forecast
Some other words for apply are...
2
PROCESS
Reason
Compare
Contrast
Sort
Solve
Distinguish
Explain (Why)
Classify
Analyze
Infer
Some other words for process are...
1
GATHER
Count
Describe
Match
Name
Recite
Select
Recall
Tell
Some other words for gather are...

Figure 5.1

Create a Creature

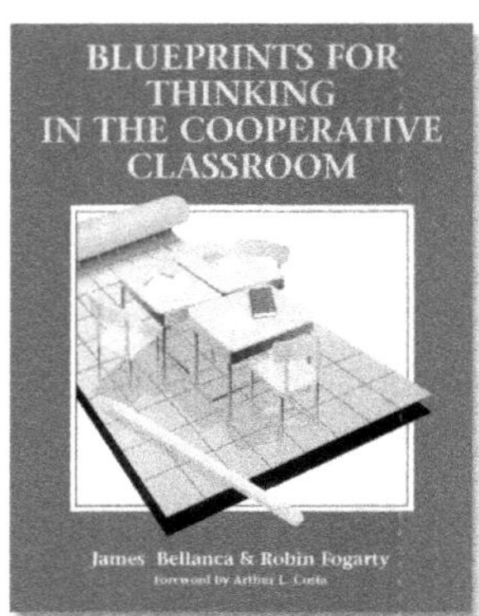

Continue with the tosses until all columns have a circled item.

To process the information, have students predict what they might do next. Invariably, students will figure out that the next step is to synthesize the various elements by creating a creature designed by the circled items.

> **CREATE A CREATURE**
>
> Directions:
> 1. Illustrate the new creature.
> 2. Label the diagram with all the designated attributes.
> 3. Name the creature appropriately.
> 4. Have all group members sign the sheet.
> 5. Display the creatures on the bulletin board.

To apply the information during the next lab period, have student groups select a creature other than their own. Using the labeled attributes on the diagram and referencing the text for the classification procedure, the lab groups should classify the creature according to formal scientific methodology. Once the creatures are classified in the appropriate manner, have the groups return the creature diagrams to the originators.

PMI

What I liked **P**luses (+)	
What I didn't like **M**inuses (–)	
Questions or thoughts **I**ntriguing (?)	

Figure 5.2

Reflecting on the Design

For affective processing, use a PMI (Figure 5.2) to talk about the pluses and minuses they felt about the lesson.

For processing the social skills, have students complete the following stem:

Taking turns is both good and bad because . . . .

For processing at the cognitive level, have students share their classifications.

For processing at the metacognitive level, have students complete a log entry on the lab technique using the following lead-in:

What if . . . ?

Create a Creature

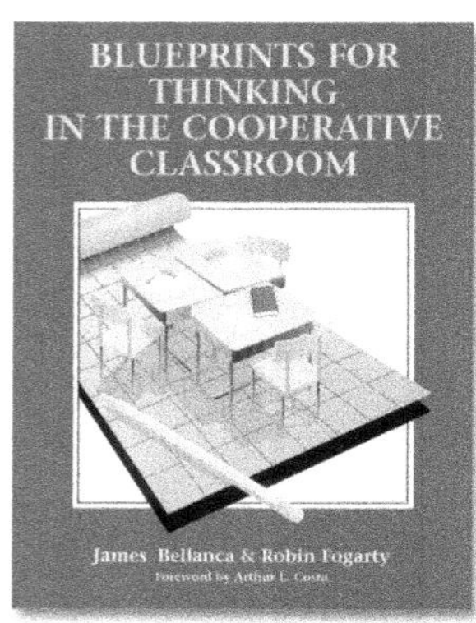

REFERENCES

Bellanca, J. 1989. *Team stars.* Palatine, IL: IRI/SkyLight Training and Publishing.

———. 1990a. *The cooperative think tank.* Palatine, IL: IRI/SkyLight Training and Publishing.

———. 1990b. *Keep them thinking: Level III.* Palatine, IL: IRI/SkyLight Training and Publishing.

Bellanca, J., and R. Fogarty. 1986. *Catch them thinking: A handbook of classroom strategies.* Palatine, IL: IRI/SkyLight Training and Publishing.

Circles of Learning (16 mm film). 1983. Edina, MN: Interaction Book Company.

Costa, A. L. 1991. *The school as a home for the mind.* Palatine, IL: IRI/SkyLight Training and Publishing.

de Bono, E. 1967. *New think.* New York: Basic Books.

———. 1973. *Lateral thinking: Creativity step by step.* New York: Harper and Row.

———. 1976. *Teaching thinking.* New York: Penguin Books.

Feuerstein, R. 1980. *Instrumental Enrichment.* Baltimore, MD: University Park Press.

Fogarty, R. 1989. *From training to transfer: The role of creativity in the adult learner.* Doctoral dissertation, Loyola University of Chicago.

———. 1990. *Keep them thinking: Level II.* Palatine, IL: IRI/SkyLight Training and Publishing.

Fogarty, R., and J. Bellanca 1986a. *Planning for thinking: A guidebook for instructional leaders.* Palatine, IL: IRI Group.

———. 1986b. *Teach them thinking.* Palatine, IL: IRI/SkyLight Training and Publishing.

———. 1989. *Patterns for thinking—Patterns for transfer.* Palatine, IL: IRI/SkyLight Training and Publishing.

Fogarty, R., and J. Haack 1986a. *The thinking log.* Palatine, IL: IRI/SkyLight Training and Publishing.

———. 1986b. *The thinking/writing connection.* Palatine, IL: IRI/SkyLight Training and Publishing.

Fogarty, R., and K. Opeka. 1988. *Start them thinking.* Palatine, IL: IRI/SkyLight Training and Publishing.

Gardner, H. 1983. *Frames of mind: The theory of multiple intelligences.* New York: Basic Books.

Glasser, W. 1986. *Control theory in the classroom.* New York: Harper & Row.

Johnson, D. W., and R. Johnson. 1986. *Circles of learning: Cooperation in the classroom.* Alexandria, VA: Association for Supervision and Curriculum Development.

———. 1987a. *Joining together: Group theory and group skills* (third edition). Englewood Cliffs, NJ: Prentice-Hall.

———. 1987b. *Learning together & alone: Cooperative, competitive & individualistic learning.* Englewood Cliffs, NJ: Prentice-Hall.

Marcus, S.A., and P. McDonald. 1990. *Tools for the cooperative classroom.* Palatine, IL: IRI/SkyLight Training and Publishing.

Ogle, D. 1986. K-W-L: A teaching model that develops active reading of expository text. *The Reading Teacher.* 6: 564–570.

Opeka, K. 1990. *Keep them thinking: Level I.* Palatine, IL: IRI/SkyLight Training and Publishing.

Schmuck, R., and P. Schmuck. 1983. *Group processes in the classroom.* Dubuque, Iowa: Wm. C. Brown.

Sharan, S. 1980. Cooperative learning in small groups: Recent methods and effects on achievement, attitudes, and ethnic relations. *Review of Educational Research.* 50: 241–271.

Sharan, S., and Y. Sharan. 1976. *Small-group teaching.* Englewood Cliffs, NJ: Educational Technology Publications.

Slavin, R. E. 1983. *Cooperative learning.* New York: Longman.

Swartz, R. J., and D. N. Perkins. 1989. *Teaching thinking: Issues and approaches.* Pacific Grove, CA: Midwest Publications.

von Oech, R. 1983. *A whack on the side of the head.* New York: Warner Books.

———. 1986. *A kick in the seat of the pants.* New York: Harper & Row.

SELECTION 7

African and Asian Elephants

A Middle School Lesson

by **James Bellanca and Robin Fogarty**

Setting Up the Scaffolding

Tell students to form groups of three with the following roles:

Recorder: Writes on chart.
Reporter: Reports results.
Leader: Talks about group.

Explain that this lesson has a double focus:

1. Learning how to compare and contrast, and
2. Using a Venn diagram as a graphic organizer to make thinking visible.

Show a Venn diagram model that illustrates the organizer's usefulness in listing similarities and differences.

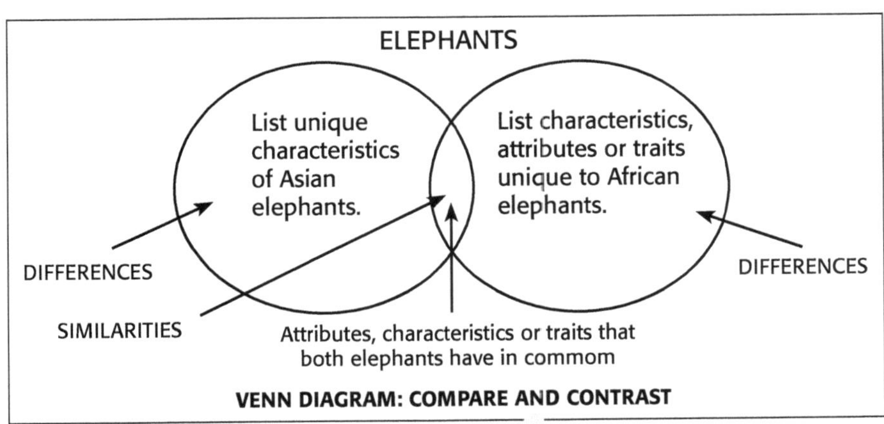

Adapted from *Blueprints for Thinking in the Cooperative Classroom* by James Bellanca and Robin Fogarty, pp. 112–15 and 349–55. © 1991 by IRI/SkyLight Training and Publishing, Inc.

African and Asian Elephants

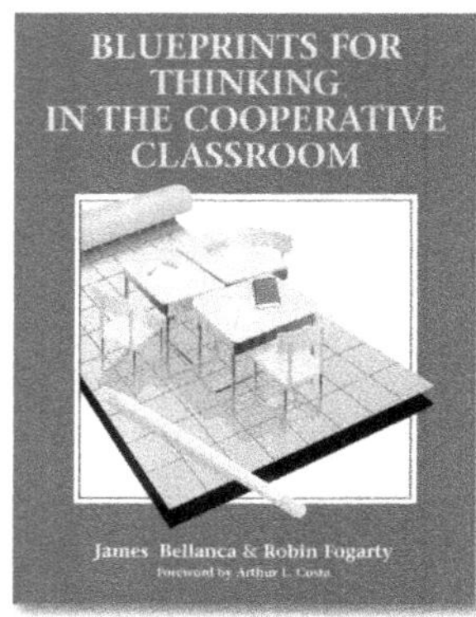

Working the Crew

Once students understand how to use the Venn diagram to delineate similarities and differences, have each reader get some large poster paper, a marking pen and a copy of the article "African & Asian Elephants."

African and Asian Elephants

Elephants are the largest of all land animals, and they are among the strangest-looking animals in the world, with their long trunks, big ears and pointed tusks. There are two basic kinds of elephants—African elephants and Asian (or Indian) elephants. It is rather easy to tell one kind from another.

Asian elephants have smaller ears than African elephants. They have a high forehead with two rather large "bumps" on it. The back of the Asian elephant bends up in the middle, and usually only the males have tusks.

African elephants have very large ears. Their foreheads don't have big bumps on them. The back of an African elephant bends down in the middle, and both the males and females have tusks.

African elephants are larger than Asian elephants, and the males of both kinds are larger than the females. The average Asian male is about 9 feet tall (2.74 meters) at the shoulder and weighs about 10,000 pounds (4,535 kilograms). African males average about 10 feet tall (3 meters) and weigh about 12,000 pounds (5,443 kilograms).

However, some elephants grow much larger than this. The largest African male on record was more than 12 ½ feet tall (3.66 meters) and weighed about 22,000 pounds (9,979 kilograms). The single elephant weighed as much as 150 average-sized people.

Male elephants are called bulls, and females are called cows. Young elephants are called calves. When an elephant calf is born, it is already a big animal. It is about three feet tall (1 meter) and weighs about 200 pounds (90 kilograms). Baby elephants are covered with hair, but as they grow they lose most of it.

Elephants can live a very long time. Asian elephants may live as long as 80 years, and African elephants may live for 60 years.

Figure 7.1

Instruct students to read the piece and have the recorders jot down the attributes of each type of elephant in the appropriate section of the Venn diagram.

Once students have analyzed the characteristics, ask the groups to draw some conclusions about the likenesses and differences of the elephants. Sample the ideas as a class.

Reflecting on the Design

For affective processing, ask students to perform a PMI evaluation of the Venn diagram, telling what they like and what they don't like.

VENN DIAGRAMS

P(+)	
M(–)	
I(?)	

To process the social skills, have students compare good teamwork and poor teamwork.

To process at the cognitive level, have students use the completed Venn diagrams to formulate fat and skinny questions about other mammals.

African and Asian Elephants

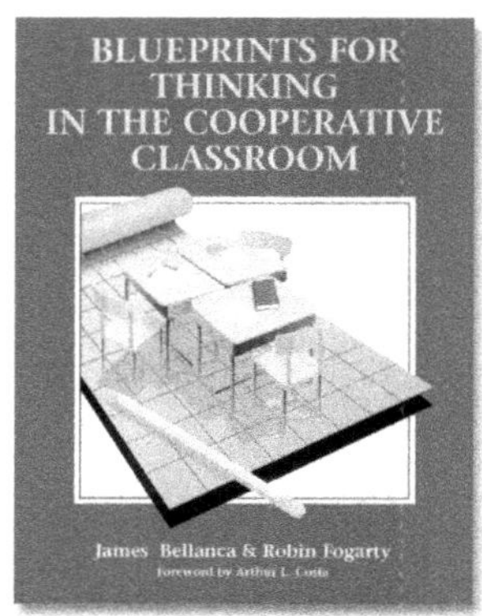

FAT	**Skinny**
Write three FAT questions about __ that will get FAT answers.	Write three SKINNY questions about __ that will get SKINNY answers.
1.	1.
2.	2.
3.	3.

Finally, to help students metacognitively reflect on other uses of the Venn diagram, have students:

1. Make a human Venn diagram by having students actually move in and out of large Venn diagrams of yarn that are "drawn" on the floor.

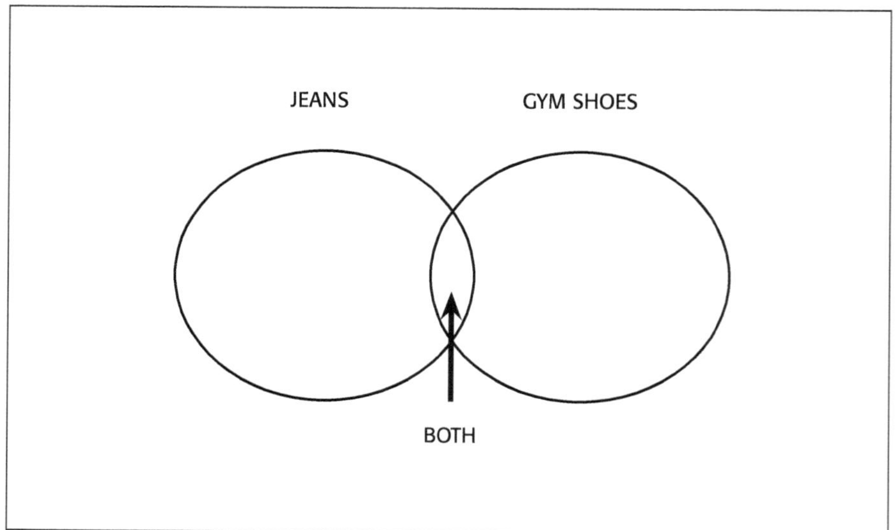

2. With a partner, design a use for Venn diagrams in math, science, literature and social studies.

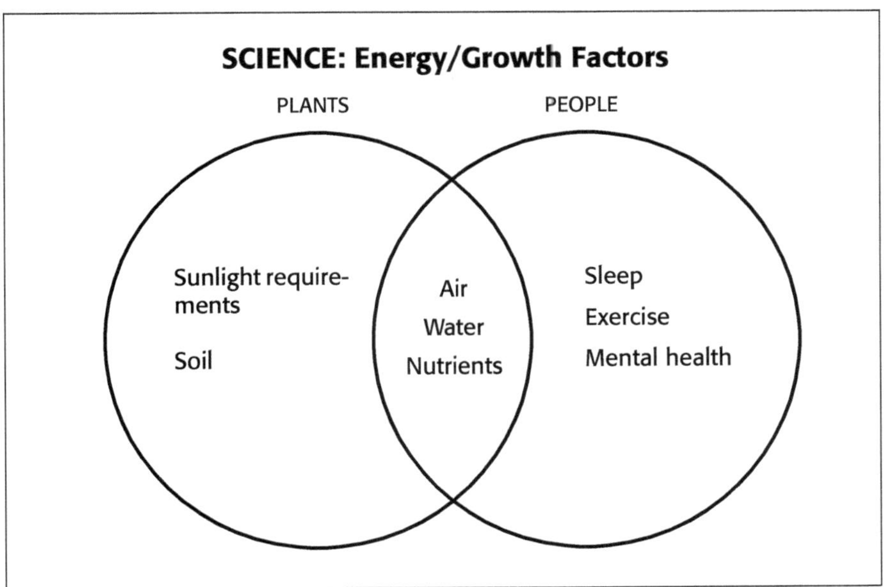

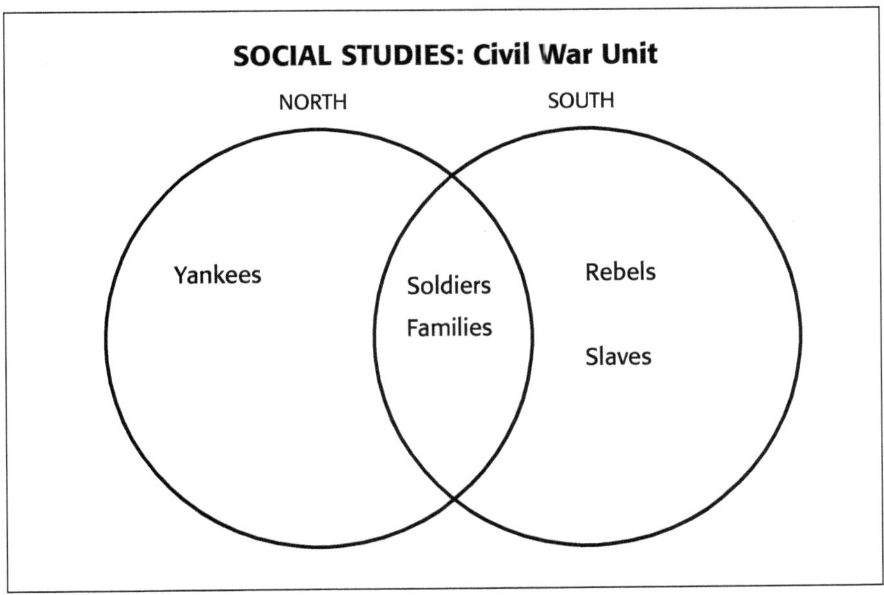

African and Asian Elephants

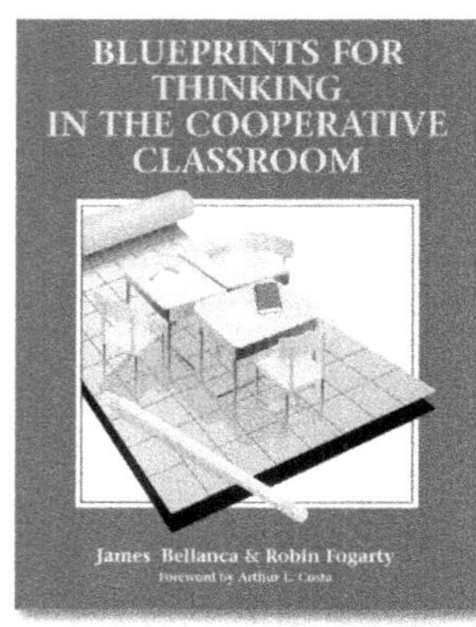

REFERENCES

Bellanca, J. 1989. *Team stars.* Palatine, IL: IRI/SkyLight Training and Publishing.

———. 1990a. *The cooperative think tank.* Palatine, IL: IRI/SkyLight Training and Publishing.

———. 1990b. *Keep them thinking: Level III.* Palatine, IL: IRI/SkyLight Training and Publishing.

Bellanca, J., and R. Fogarty. 1986. *Catch them thinking: A handbook of classroom strategies.* Palatine, IL: IRI/SkyLight Training and Publishing.

Circles of Learning (16 mm film). 1983. Edina, MN: Interaction Book Company.

Costa, A. L. 1991. *The school as a home for the mind.* Palatine, IL: IRI/SkyLight Training and Publishing.

de Bono, E. 1967. *New think.* New York: Basic Books.

———. 1973. *Lateral thinking: Creativity step by step.* New York: Harper and Row.

———. 1976. *Teaching thinking.* New York: Penguin Books.

Feuerstein, R. 1980. *Instrumental Enrichment.* Baltimore, MD: University Park Press.

Fogarty, R. 1989. *From training to transfer: The role of creativity in the adult learner.* Doctoral dissertation, Loyola University of Chicago.

———. 1990. *Keep them thinking: Level II.* Palatine, IL: IRI/SkyLight Training and Publishing.

Fogarty, R., and J. Bellanca 1986a. *Planning for thinking: A guidebook for instructional leaders.* Palatine, IL: IRI Group.

———. 1986b. *Teach them thinking.* Palatine, IL: IRI/SkyLight Training and Publishing.

———. 1989. *Patterns for thinking—Patterns for transfer.* Palatine, IL: IRI/SkyLight Training and Publishing.

Fogarty, R., and J. Haack 1986a. *The thinking log.* Palatine, IL: IRI/SkyLight Training and Publishing.

———. 1986b. *The thinking/writing connection.* Palatine, IL: IRI/SkyLight Training and Publishing.

Fogarty, R., and K. Opeka 1988. *Start them thinking.* Palatine, IL: IRI/SkyLight Training and Publishing.

Gardner, H. 1983. *Frames of mind: The theory of multiple intelligences.* New York: Basic Books.

Glasser, W. 1986. *Control theory in the classroom.* New York: Harper & Row.

Johnson, D. W., and R. Johnson 1986. *Circles of learning: Cooperation in the classroom.* Alexandria, VA: Association for Supervision and Curriculum Development.

———. 1987a. *Joining together: Group theory and group skills* (third edition). Englewood Cliffs, NJ: Prentice-Hall.

———. 1987b. *Learning together & alone: Cooperative, competitive & individualistic learning*. Englewood Cliffs, NJ: Prentice-Hall.

Marcus, S. A., and P. McDonald. 1990. *Tools for the cooperative classroom*. Palatine, IL: SkyLight Training and Publishing.

Ogle, D. 1986. K-W-L: A teaching model that develops active reading of expository text. *The Reading Teacher*. 6: 564–570.

Opeka, K. 1990. *Keep them thinking: Level I*. Palatine, IL: IRI/SkyLight Training and Publishing.

Schmuck, R., and P. Schmuck. 1983. *Group processes in the classroom*. Dubuque, Iowa: Wm. C. Brown.

Sharan, S. 1980. Cooperative learning in small groups: Recent methods and effects on achievement, attitudes, and ethnic relations. *Review of Educational Research*. 50: 241–271.

Sharan, S., and Y. Sharan. 1976. *Small-group teaching*. Englewood Cliffs, NJ: Educational Technology Publications.

Slavin, R. E. 1983. *Cooperative learning*. New York: Longman.

Swartz, R. J., and D. N. Perkins. 1989. *Teaching thinking: Issues and approaches*. Pacific Grove, CA: Midwest Publications.

von Oech, R. 1983. *A whack on the side of the head*. New York: Warner Books.

———. 1986. *A kick in the seat of the pants*. New York: Harper & Row.

SELECTION 8

Challenge

by **Eleanor Reneé Rodriguez and James Bellanca**

When someone is taught the joy of learning, it becomes a lifelong process that never stops, a process that creates a logical individual. That is the challenge and joy of teaching.
—Marva Collins

Researchers who try to understand what makes an effective teacher seldom seem to follow Marva Collins's advice about the joy of learning. Instead, they seem devoted to the behaviorist model and hold instead that the effective teacher has a pocketful of motivational tricks and techniques, the effectiveness of which can be easily measured. According to author Alfie Kohn, these techniques fall into two categories: rewards and punishments. Rewards are good grades, gold stars, praise, and warm fuzzies; punishments are low grades, criticism, time out or detention, and the forbidding "call home."

Kohn, Feuerstein, and Herzberg build on the tradition that prefers intrinsic motivation. In the mediation of challenge, the mediator creates conditions and opportunities for students to achieve. These opportunities allow for the development of intrinsic motivation for completion of tasks that evoke feelings of interest, excitement, and determination, even though tasks may appear difficult. With support, encouragement, and mediation for challenge, students discover potentials previously unknown.

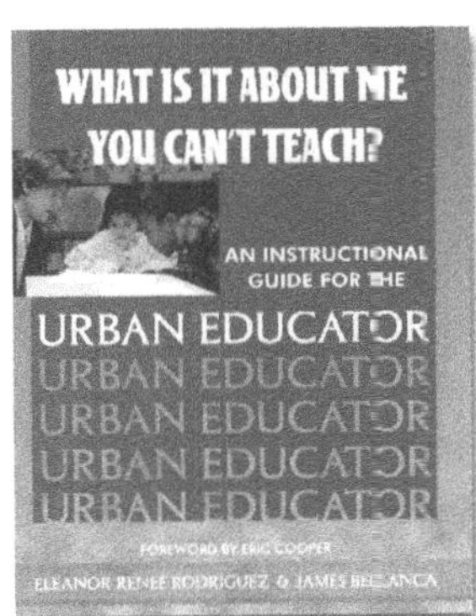

Adapted from *What is It About Me You Can't Teach?: An Instructional Guide for the Urban Educator* by Eleanor Reneé Rodriguez and James Bellanca, pp. 167–70, 176–81, and 199–201. © 1997 by IRI/SkyLight Training and Publishing, Inc.

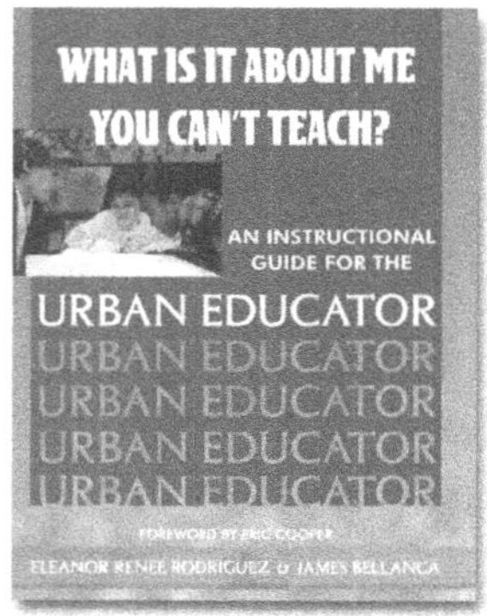

The Mediation of Challenge

Consider students in two different elementary mathematics classrooms. In one, the teacher hands out a worksheet with fifty-four number problems. She tells the students what to do and then sits down at her desk. If a student has a question, he lines up to the right of the teacher's desk and waits his turn. In the other classroom, the teacher sits her students in groups of three. She gives each group a cup of dry corn and a cup of marbles. She asks each group to take out three pieces of corn and four marbles from the cups. The group has to agree quickly on the number of "pieces" they have. She repeats the process several times. Each time the problem becomes more difficult. The children become more excited with each new challenge. When all the corn and marbles are on the tables, she asks them to explain what they learned about adding the pieces. After their talk, she gives them the first numbers to add. Once again, as they succeed, she ups the ante with a more difficult problem.

When a teacher or parent mediates challenge as in the second example, the students experience in their academics what novice skiers experience on the mountainside. First, there is the tension of the bunny hill. After the instructor coaches the skiers down the hill without a fall or picks up and restarts those who do fall, the novices return to the course on their own. As their confidence grows, the skiers tire: gone is the novelty of the initial challenge. Now they are sure and ready for the green runs. Once these are mastered, the skiers are ready for the tougher blue runs and, ultimately, for the double black diamond run. Do these students receive stickers and stars for each new triumph? No—their reward is the internal excitement and pleasure that comes with conquering fears, taking risks, and pushing one's limits.

Creating Challenges

What does the mediator do to create the challenges? First, she models an open and excited attitude about taking on the tougher word problem. As the student's body language and oral expression say "Oh my gosh, I will never do that," the mediator encourages, "I know this is tough, but I also know what you can do. Together we can do this."

Second, the mediator prepares a sequence of increasingly challenging and complex tasks. She charts the way for the students and shows them how they will conquer the "bunny hill" to get ready for the tougher runs. And she gives them a novel perspective: instead of the boring, repetitive worksheets that get "done" and filed, the mediator provides hands-on, activity-based situations that grow in difficulty, which the students see they will be able to conquer one at a time while their confidence grows.

Third, the mediator encourages creativity, curiosity, and originality in performing the tasks. As students master the basic steps, she provides more difficult tasks, and she challenges the students to figure new ways to solve the problem: "Tell me another idea you have"; "What's a different way?" The students try out their methods in search of the best approach.

Fourth, the mediator encourages appropriate risk taking. She pushes the students to use new approaches in the strategies that they want to try. "Will this stretch you? Will this take you out of your comfort zone?"

Fifth, the mediator helps students reflect on the reasons for their successes, identify their best work strategies, and build patterns of thinking into their methods. The mediator communicates her observations of their work with enthusiasm and excitement about her satisfaction with their progress. She places special emphasis on what they have chosen to do and what they have accomplished: "You picked this strategy; you made it work."

Three Things Not to Do

What a parent or teacher does not do may be as important as what he or she does do to mediate challenge. First, the mediator does not rescue students by interfering with or performing the task or answering the question. A mediator who steps in too soon without good wait time and takes over the task is denying students the necessary practice and the opportunity to correct mistakes.

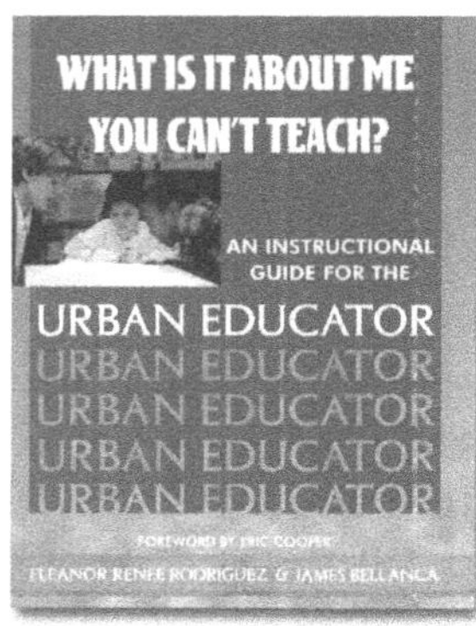

Second, the mediator avoids using extrinsic behavior modification, especially with conditional promises of rewards: "If you do this, then I will give you . . . ." Conditional rewards build a student's dependency on the reward. As the student is satisfied with a small reward, the expectation of a bigger reward soon follows: first, the new pair of shoes; next, an expensive dress—how long before the car keys? Once caught in the extrinsic reward trap, the student loses focus on the fact that she had positive feelings about overcoming an obstacle that she had approached with uncertainty.

Third, the mediator avoids making the task seem insurmountable. Using the ski analogy, the mediator doesn't take the novice to the tip of the black diamond slope and say, "Ski down, I know you can do it." Risk that appears overwhelming is only discouraging.

Problem-Solving Stories

PRIMARY SCHOOL LESSON

Problem
How to read a story from a problem focus.

Focus Intelligence
Verbal/Linguistic

Supporting Intelligences
All

Checking Prior Knowledge

Post the problem-solving observation chart for the children to review the listed behaviors. Select a strong reader to read each behavior and lead the class in a choral reading review. Indicate that you will use the chart again as you observe them practicing the behaviors during the group work for this lesson.

Structuring the Task

1. Select a story on video. (You may use this same lesson outline for several problem-solving practice lessons.) Following is a selection of story videos. Be sure to preview each one to determine the spots in the story where you want to stop and have the students discuss the questions. (You may wish to substitute a story that you read to the

class. Use the same questions at the appropriate spot in each story. If you have sufficient readers, before the video or in place of the video, have a reader in each group read the story and stop at the places you indicate so that the groups can discuss the questions.)

Stories Available on Video

- How the Elephant Got His Trunk
- The Tinder Box
- The Emperor's New Clothes
- Sleeping Beauty
- The Staunch Tin Soldier
- Little Tom Thumb
- The Frog Prince
- Tale of the Ugly Duckling
- Hansel and Gretel
- Rumpelstiltskin
- The Boy Who Cried Wolf
- The Ears of King Midas

2. Before you start the video, divide the class into trios. Use cards with colored dots to determine the jobs in each group. The reader will read the questions and the story, if you elect that approach; the recorder will write the answers; the checker will make sure that all members agree with each answer.
3. Give a copy of the problem-solving worksheet to each recorder:

Problem-Solving Worksheet

Names____

The Problem	Ways to Solve the Problem	The Solution

4. Tell students that you will stop the video as soon as the problem or challenge is identified. Review the questions on the problem-solving observation chart that the group will use at this spot. After you have shown the video or told the story, allow five minutes for each group to fill in the first block on their problem-solving worksheet, "the problem."

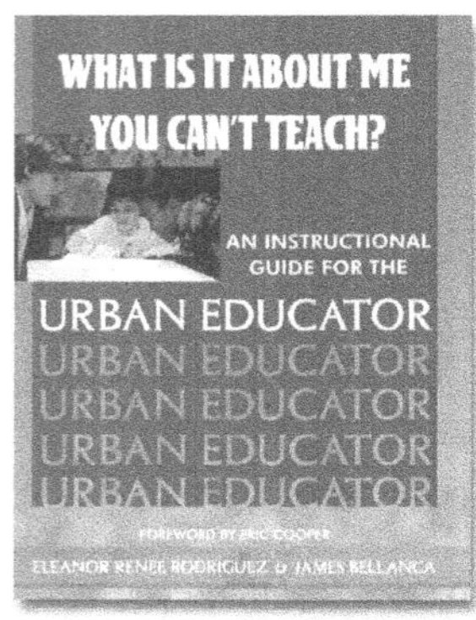

5. Repeat the procedure for each of the remaining two blocks. Tell where you will stop, review the appropriate problem-solving behaviors, and allow five minutes after the video.

Looking Back

Ask for sample responses to each of the blocks. Write the samples on the board and discuss the variations. Encourage the class to agree on a single response. Do not suggest or give an answer. Summarize what each group reports and ask for agreements. Finalize the agreement for each block on the chart before you proceed to the next one. When you are gathering the data from the groups, avoid going back to the same groups.

Bridging Forward

1. Invite the groups to write the following on the back of the problem-solving worksheet: (1) a lesson they learned from how the character(s) in this story solved the problem; (2) what problem-solving behaviors from the chart they used well. Sample the responses to each question. After the groups have shared their answers to the second question, use the chart to give your feedback on the problem-solving behaviors you observed. Post it for the class to see.
2. Chart the students' uses of the problem-solving behaviors so they can see their own progress. You may wish to add an incentive for the class to reach certain milestones. Use of the chart will benefit the students most if you use this same lesson outline with a sequence of stories and mediate for challenge as each story becomes more difficult.

Materials

Problem-solving observation charts, selected video, TV, video player, index cards, colored dots, problem-solving worksheet, masking tape

Variations

1. If video equipment is not available, select a story to read to the class.
2. For "Looking Back," mediate challenge by asking students to discuss (a) the challenges faced by the story characters, (b) how each dealt with the challenge, and (c) what they could learn from the characters about "challenges."

Heritage Heroes

MIDDLE SCHOOL LESSON

Problem

How to benefit from the contributions made to American history by cultural groups represented in the classroom.

Focus Intelligence

Verbal/Linguistic

Supporting Intelligence

Intrapersonal

Checking Prior Knowledge

1. Create one or more webs on a bulletin board labeled "Heritage Heroes." (Make one web for each culture represented in the class.)
2. Invite students to make a name card for each famous person they can identify by name. Place it on the appropriate web. Invite students to tell what they know about the nominees.

Structuring the Task

To the webs already started, add names that were not nominated.

1. Invite each student to select one name from the web. Allow one week for each student to research the person. Have them get the following information:

   a. Who is this person? (important dates and facts)

   b. What contributions did he or she make?

   c. What challenges did he or she overcome?

   d. What lessons can we learn from his or her life?

   Show students how to use index cards to record answers and identify the source of information.
2. Instruct each student to write a five-paragraph essay (one beginning, three middle, one end) that answers the questions. Discuss the indicators of success you will use. Discuss with each student the first draft and correct grammar, spelling, structure, etc.
3. Collect, review, and post the final drafts.
4. Randomly assign three students to a group. The group will identify how the different "heroes" are alike and different in their thinking, beliefs, and attitudes.
5. Give each group time to plan and produce a five-minute meeting of the "heroes" on a TV interview show. The heroes will discuss a

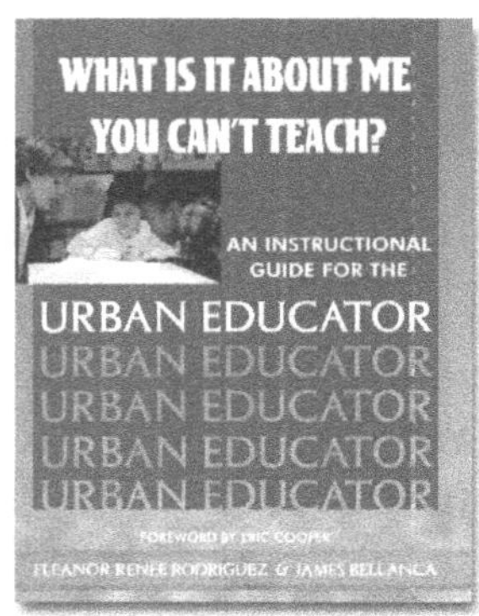

current event. Afterward, the group members will each explain why their characters argued for a certain point. (To allow time for this pageant, play only two to three presentations per day.)

Looking Back

Ask the students to discuss what lessons they learned about facing challenges from the "heroes." How might they apply the same resources in facing their everyday lives?

Bridging Forward

Invite each student to write a letter to his character. The letter will explain what lessons the student learned and how the student will apply that lesson to his own life. Be sure to review the indicators of success before they write.

Assessing Student Performance

1. To what degree does the five-paragraph essay respond to the four questions in a clear and concise manner?
2. To what degree does the group presentation capture the beliefs and ideas of the characters?
3. To what degree does the letter make a significant application of the character's best qualities?

Materials

Bulletin board, tacks or tape, multicolored paper, markers or crayons, index cards

Variations

1. Allow groups of three to do the research on a character.
2. Make a complete pageant with authentic costumes for each character.
3. In place of the essay, assign students to make a collage for each character.
4. In place of the current events discussion, give each group a current social problem to solve from the perspective of the "heroes." Let them enact the solution in a mini-play.

Heritage Heroes

African Americans
Muhammad Ali
Maya Angelou
Louis Armstrong
Arthur Ashe
Marian Anderson
James Baldwin
Benjamin Banneker
Ronald Brown
William Bessie
Mary McLeod Bethune
Gwendolyn Brooks
George W. Carver
Cab Calloway
Dr. William "Bill" Cosby
Countee Cullen
Frederick Douglass
W. E. B. DuBois
Paul L. Dunbar
Charles Drew
Jean-Baptiste DuSable
Medgar Evers
Marcus Garvey
Althea Gibson
Nikki Giovanni
Lorraine Hansbury
Billie Holiday
Langston Hughes
Rev. Dr. Martin Luther King, Jr.
Thurgood Marshall
James Meredith
Garrett Morgan
Jesse Owens
Rosa Parks
Leontyne Price
Joseph Rainey
A. Phillip Randolph
Paul Robeson
Jackie Robinson
Octavia Rogers
Sojourner Truth
Harriet Tubman
Madame C. J. Walker
Ida B. Wells
Roy Wilkins
Carter G. Woodson
Malcolm X
Andrew Young

Other World Figures of African Descent
Aesop
Sonni Ali
Richmond Barthé
Ludwig van Beethoven
Robert Browning
Paul Belloni Du Chaillu
Cleopatra
Samuel Taylor Coleridge
Samuel Crowler
Alfred Dobbs
Alexandre Dumas
Hannibal
H. H. Harrison
Queen Hatshepsut
Richard Hill
Imhotep
Isaac Wallace-Johnson
Lokman
Makeda, Queen of Sheba
Nelson Mandela
Joachim Murat
Allesandro de' Medici
Queen Nzingha
Touissant L'Overture
Aleksander Pushkin
Haile Selassie
Charles Spaulding
Mary Church Terrell
Thutmose III
William Trotten
Desmond Tutu
Zenobia

Hispanic Americans
Lope de Aguirre
Pedro Antonio de Alarcón
Isaac Albéniz
Pedro de Alvarado
Everett Alvarez
Jorge Carrera Andrade
Pío Baroja
Garcia Calderon
Richard E. Cavazos
César Chávez
Roberto Clemente
Fernando De Rojas
Roberto Durán
Carlos Finlay
Fernanco García
Carlos Gomes
Cecilia Gonzalez
Guerrero
Jose Maria deHeredia
Julio Iglesias
Juan Ramón Jiménez
Agustín Lara
Diego Maradona
Ricardo Montalbán
Rita Moreno
Juan Ortega
Manuel Piar
Horacio Rivero
Chi Chi Rodriguez
César Romero
Francisco de Zorrilla Rojas
Arantxa Sanchez-Vicario
George Santayana
Lee Treviño
Fernando Valenzuela
Joseph White

Other World Figures of Hispanic Descent
Vasco Núñez de Balboa
Simón Bolívar
Jorge Luis Borges
Pablo Casals
Salvador Dalí
Plácido Domingo
Benito Juárez
Federico García Lorca
Pablo Neruda
Pelé
Pablo Picasso
Diego Rivera
Andrés Segovia
Fray Junípero Serra
Diego Velázquez
Emiliano Zapata

Native Americans
Dr. Charles Alexander
Bigfoot
Abel Bosum
Joseph Brant
Cochise
Crazy Horse/Tashunkewitko
Dan George
Geronimo
Hurston
Joseph
Naiche
Zora Neale
Quanna Parker
Gregory Perillo
Pontiac
Red Cloud
John Ross
Santana
Sequoya
Sitting Bull
Tecumseh

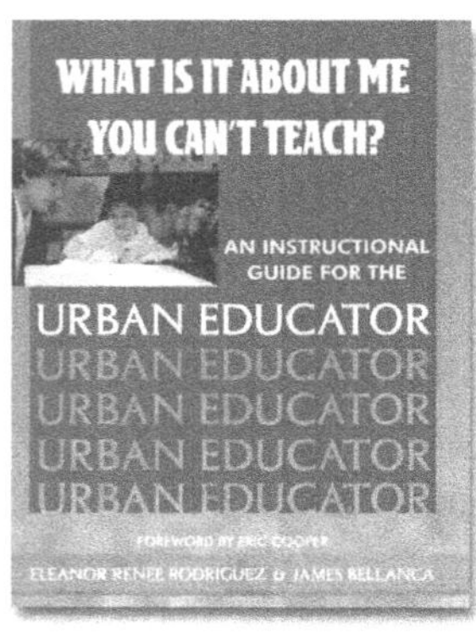

REFERENCES

Anderson, Kamili. 1989. Urban coalition encourages minority youth to "say yes" to math and science. *Black Issues in Higher Education.* 5(21): 6–8.

Anyon, J. 1995. Race, social class, and educational reform in an inner-city school. *Teachers' College Record.* 97(1): 69–94.

Aronson, E. 1978. *The jigsaw classroom.* Beverly Hills, CA: Sage Publications.

Ascher, C. 1993. Changing schools for urban students: The school development program, accelerated schools, and success for all. *Trends and Issues No. 18.* New York: ERIC Clearinghouse on Urban Education.

Atwater, M. M., et al. 1995. A study of urban middle school students with high and low attitudes toward science. *Journal of Research in Science Teaching.* 32(6): 665–77.

Ausubel, D. 1978. *Educational psychology: A cognitive view.* 2nd ed. New York: Holt, Rinehart & Winston.

Ball, A. F. 1995. Text design patterns in the writing of urban African American students: Teaching to the cultural strengths of students in multicultural settings. *Urban Education.* 30(3): 253–89. Englewood Cliffs, NJ: E. T. Press.

Becum, L. C., et. al. 1989. The urban landscape: Education for the twenty-first century. *Journal of Negro Education.* 58(3): 430–41.

Bellanca, J., and R. Fogarty. 1991. *Blueprints for thinking in the cooperative classroom.* Palatine, IL: IRI/SkyLight Training and Publishing.

Ben-Hur, M., ed. 1994. *On Feuerstein's Instrumental Enrichment: A collection.* Palatine, IL: IRI/SkyLight Training and Publishing.

Carter, R. L. 1995. The unending struggle for equal educational opportunity. *Teachers' College Record.* 96(4): 619–26.

Chapman, C. 1993. *If the shoe fits . . .: How to develop multiple intelligences in the classroom.* Palatine, IL: IRI/SkyLight Training and Publishing.

Cooper, E. J., and J. Sherk. 1989. Addressing urban school reform: Issues and alliances. *Journal of Negro Education.* 58(3): 315–31.

Costa, A. L., and R. Garmston. 1985, March. The art of cognitive coaching: Supervision for intelligence teaching. Paper presented at the Annual Conference of the Association for Supervision and Curriculum Development, Chicago, IL.

Dahl, K. L. and P. A. Freppon. 1995. A comparison of innercity children's interpretations of reading and writing instruction in the early grades in skills-based and whole language classrooms. *Reading Research Quarterly.* 30(1): 50–74.

Davis, B. 1995. *How to involve parents in a multicultural school.* Alexandria, VA: Association for Supervision and Curriculum Development.

de Bono, E. 1985. *Six thinking hats.* Boston: Little, Brown.
Feuerstein, R. 1980. *Instrumental Enrichment.* Baltimore: University Park Press.
Flavell, J. 1976. Metacognitive aspects of problem solving. In *The nature of intelligence,* edited by L. B. Resnick. Hillsdale, NJ: Lawrence Erlbaum Associates.
Gardner, H. 1983. *Frames of mind: The theory of multiple intelligences.* New York: Basic Books.
Glasser, W. 1986. *Control theory in the classroom.* New York: Harper & Row.
Gonzales, M. R. 1995, April. Multicultural education in practice: Teacher's social constructions and classroom enactments. Paper presented at the Annual Meeting of the American Educational Research Association, San Francisco, CA.
Harris, H. W., et al. 1995. *Racial and ethnic identity: Psychological development and creative expression.* New York: Routledge.
Johnson, D. W., and R. Johnson. 1986. *Circles of learning: Cooperating in the classroom.* Alexandria, VA: Association for Supervision and Curriculum Development.
Johnson, V. R. 1990. Schools reaching out: Changing the message to "good news." *Equity and Choice.* 6(3): 20–24.
Kagan, S. 1992. *Cooperative learning.* San Juan Capistrano, CA: Resources for Teachers.
Kohn, A. 1993. *Punished by rewards.* New York: Houghton-Mifflin.
Kozol, J. 1991. *Savage inequalities.* New York: Crown.
———. 1992. Inequality and the will to change. *Equity and Choice.* 8(3): 45–47.
Lee, C. D. 1995. A culturally based cognitive apprenticeship: Teaching African American high school students skills in literary interpretation. *Reading Research Quarterly.* 30(4): 608–30.
Luria, A. R. 1976. *Cognitive development: Its cultural and social foundations.* Cambridge, MA: Harvard University Press.
Sharan, S., and Y. Sharan. 1992. *Expanding cooperative learning through group investigation.* New York: Teachers' College Press.
Sharron, H. 1987. *Changing children's minds: Feuerstein's revolution in the teaching of intelligence.* London: Souvenir Press.
Slavin, R. E. 1983. *Cooperative learning.* New York: Longman.

SELECTION 9

The Stock Market

by **Hope Martin**

The National Council of Teachers of Mathematics standards maintain that making connections between mathematics and other curricular areas allow students to (1) understand how mathematics relates to their everyday lives; (2) apply mathematical thinking and problem solving to other disciplines; and (3) understand the role mathematics plays in our culture and society. In the middle grades, students see school mathematics as different from math in the "real world." By connecting math activities to real-world questions, teachers can dispel the notion that school mathematics is useless, and perhaps they will never again have to hear the question, "When are we ever going to use this?"

One area that supports strong interdisciplinary connections is an extended project introducing students to the stock market. The history of the economic growth in the United States shows a country of small, privately owned businesses prior to the 1700s. The industrial revolution brought the growth of businesses, and the need for capital encouraged people to open their businesses to new investment. This was the beginning of public corporations, investments, investors, and the stock market. An examination of the interrelationships between economic growth and history makes a rich study in the social studies classroom.

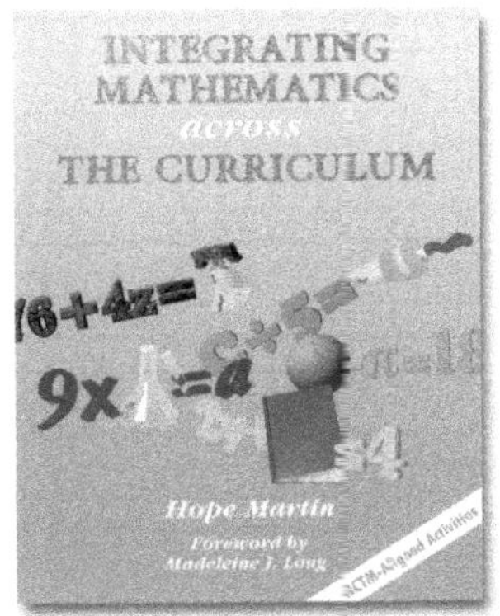

The stock market crash in 1929 and the literature connected with this black day in American history can make exciting connections between history and literature.

Adapted from *Integrating Mathematics Across the Curriculum* by Hope Martin, pp. 93–100, 104–05, 108, 115–17, and 291–92. © 1996 by IRI/SkyLight Training and Publishing, Inc.

The Stock Market

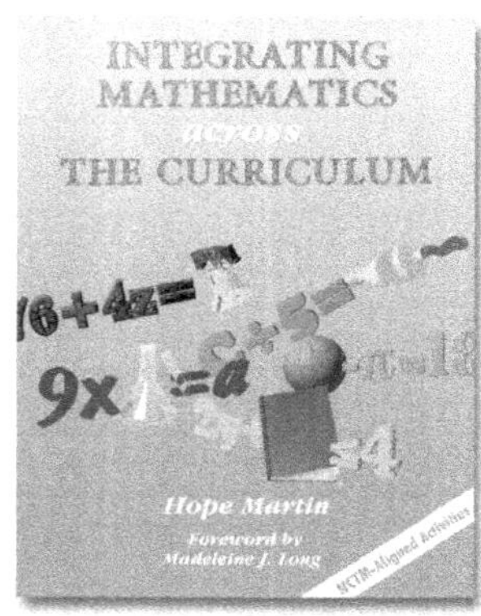

In the mathematics classroom, the stock market project is a wealth of essential middle school studies. Conversion of fractions to decimals, computation, percents, graphs, and integers are just a small part of the mathematics students use to keep track of their "investments" during the course of the project.

Investors look to the stock market for long-range investments. A study of the market shows that over the course of one year, investors can make a profit or lose money, depending on the market. When you extend the time frame to five years of investment, you find that during most five-year periods, investors make money in the stock market! This means that as students invest their "money" they should understand the need for patience. Many stock market projects last for too short a period of time. This project has been designed to begin in October and end in May; students keep track of their investments once a week. You will need eight to ten copies of the financial section of the paper for students to use in the stock market project.

Reading the financial section of the newspaper can be very confusing for youngsters, but there is a wealth of information to be found on these pages. The stock market project begins with a short lesson on reading the financial pages and understanding what the column headings mean.

Once students understand the financial pages, they can be asked to research a stock for a period of two weeks. Have them keep track of the closing price each day, graph its ups and downs, calculate how many shares they can purchase with their share of the money, and interview adults to help them make their decisions. When this lesson is completed, the students can contribute their financial knowledge to their groups.

Place students into groups of four and give them \$10,000 to invest in four different stocks using the "First Week to Buy Stock" sheet. Each student can make his or her recommendation to the group, purchase the stocks, and enter the costs on the sheet. Each of the stocks should be about 25 percent (or \$2,500) of the total. Each student's recommendation should be respected; no one stock should be "loved" more than another! A broken-line graph of the stock's price should be kept each week.

The "Week-to-Week Stock Sheet" is for groups to keep track of stocks once each week. Finally, at the end of the project, students will sell their stocks using the "Final Sale" sheet. How much are the groups worth? Have they made a profit? Did they invest wisely?

Each phase of the stock market project has an explanation page similar to those supplied with the other interdisciplinary experiences. However, the assessment component is different. The two most significant elements of ongoing assessment for this project are student products (the weekly stock sheets) and the observation of students (the accomplishments of the group). Let's examine each of these individually.

The mathematics involved in this project is difficult for most middle school students. It is essential that their weekly calculations be monitored closely to prevent small errors from becoming monumental inaccuracies. Misconceptions and arithmetic problems can be cleared up quickly if they are controlled weekly.

Observing students is another critical factor of assessment. Each student in the group must be held accountable for the material, especially in such a long-range experience. This is best regulated by careful observation to determine if the following are true:

1. Each student has a viable and important role in the deliberations.
2. Each student has a significant task during calculation.
3. The roles of students rotate so each has an opportunity to assume a particular role.

Because these roles are so different, it is important for them to rotate weekly so each student has the opportunity to learn the skills and concepts that are part of that task.

When setting up the groups, roles can be discussed and the importance of rotation emphasized. The roles of students might be the following:

The recorder—Enters the data from the newspaper

The Stock Market

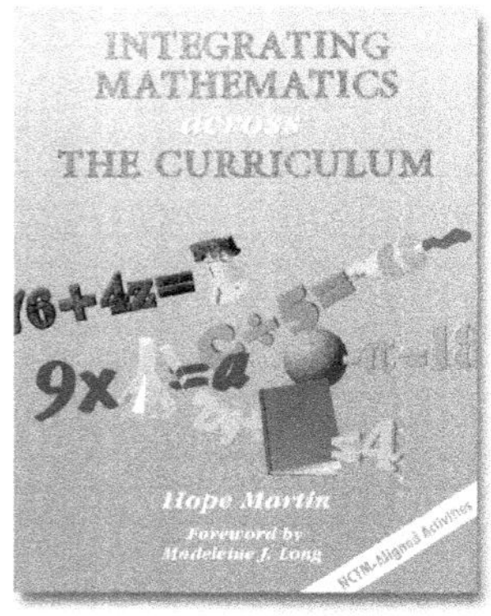

The locator—Finds each of the group's stocks in the paper and determines the closing price

Two computers—Convert the mixed numbers to money (decimals) and complete the Week-to-Week Stock Sheet

Some problems may arise as students work together. Following are a few guidelines that may be helpful for the students to know:

1. You are responsible for your own behavior. You must have respect for and consideration of all members of the class. Every group is working hard to keep track of their stocks; they need to be able to concentrate.
2. You must be willing to help anyone in your group who asks. While working in groups, we are interested in cooperation, not competition. Your group cannot succeed financially unless you work together.
3. You may not ask the teacher for help unless all members of your group have the same question. If you have not discussed a question within the group, the teacher will not work with you.
4. Any member of your group may be called on to explain the thinking or reasoning of the group. It is necessary for everyone to understand each part of the project and what the roles involve!

Investing in the Market

Mathematical Connections
reading a table, converting fractions to decimals, integers
Intelligences
verbal/linguistic, logical/mathematical
Other Curricular Connections
Social Studies: Economics, history

Concepts

Students will do the following:

1. Learn to read information from the financial pages in the newspaper
2. Convert fractions and mixed numbers to decimals
3. Analyze numerical information

Materials Needed

calculators; copies of this section's blacklines; local financial papers

Procedures

Discuss with students what a share of stock is. Be sure they understand that if a person owns a share of stock, he or she owns a piece of the company. If any of the students own stock, have them share their investments with the other students. If they don't, ask if they know of a company that they might like to own a piece of.

Read through the "Deciding on a Stock" blackline. The stocks in the table are actual companies and the students should know of them. Most financial pages have additional information to that presented on the table. The data on the "Deciding on a Stock" blackline is all that will be used by groups in their considerations.

Once students understand how to read these pages, give each student a copy of the "Keeping Track of a Stock" blackline so they can track one stock for a period of at least two weeks. It is important to complete this next phase so students understand how to read the financial pages.

Assessment

1. Student products—Successful completion of blacklines
2. Observation of students

The Stock Market

Deciding on a Stock

Names____

____

Date____

Class ____

What is the stock market and why do people invest their money in it? The stock market is a group of companies who sell shares to the public. If you buy a share of stock in McDonalds, you own a piece of that company! How do you know what company to invest your money in? We can learn more about the financial health of a company by understanding the information found on the financial pages of a newspaper.

Below is a table of stock prices for five companies as they appeared in the *Chicago Tribune.* Only the columns that will be used in this lesson have been copied.

The first column (52-Week High/Low Stock Prices) is the highest price and the lowest price this stock has sold for in the past 365 days, or previous year. The second column is the name of the company in abbreviated form. Sometimes it is hard to understand the abbreviation. Can you tell what these stand for? The third column is the number of shares of stock that were sold the previous day (3565 means 356,500). The fourth, fifth, and sixth columns indicate, respectively, the highest price anyone paid for the stock this day, the lowest price, and what the stock was selling for when the stock market closed at 3:00 p.m. The Net Change column is not how much the stock changed during the day but how much it has changed from the day before. If the last column shows $+\frac{1}{4}$, the stock cost $.25 more today than when it closed yesterday.

52-Week High/Low Stock 365 Day	Stock	Sales in hundreds	High	Low	Close	Net change
$31\frac{3}{8}/22\frac{3}{4}$	AbbtLab	7837	$27\frac{1}{2}$	$27\frac{1}{8}$	$27\frac{1}{2}$	$+\frac{3}{8}$
$61\frac{1}{4}/50\frac{7}{8}$	Amoco	4646	$59\frac{1}{8}$	$58\frac{3}{4}$	59	$+\frac{1}{4}$
$29\frac{1}{4}/16\frac{1}{2}$	CirCty	2067	$23\frac{1}{4}$	$22\frac{1}{2}$	23	$-\frac{1}{8}$
$32\frac{3}{8}/8\frac{1}{4}$	CompUSA	1374	$8\frac{1}{4}$	8	8	$-\frac{1}{4}$
$62\frac{1}{2}/41$	StJoe	83	$59\frac{5}{8}$	$58\frac{3}{4}$	$59\frac{7}{8}$	–

The Dynamics of a Stock

Names_______________________________

____

Date_______________________________

Class _______________________________

Directions: Use the table of stock prices in this packet to answer these questions.

1. Using the 52-week high/low figures, determine the range in prices for each stock:

   a. AbbtLab ____________________
   b. Amoco ____________________
   c. CirCty ____________________
   d. CompUSA ____________________
   e. StJoe ____________________

2. Which of the stocks showed the greatest fluctuation in price during the day shown? (Remember the Net Change column indicates the change in price from the day before.)

   ____

   Explain your answer.

   ____
   ____
   ____
   ____

3. AbbtLab closed at $\$27\frac{1}{2}$, which means that one share cost \$27.50. The equivalent of the fraction $\frac{1}{2}$ is the decimal .50. Convert the high and low prices for the day to dollars and cents (using decimals).

	High	Low
a. AbbtLab	____________	____________
b. Amoco	____________	____________
c. CirCty	____________	____________
d. CompUSA	____________	____________
e. StJoe	____________	____________

The Stock Market

First Week to Buy Stock

Names____________________________________

____

Date_____________________________________

Class ____________________________________

Use this sheet when your group is buying stock. You will also balance your checkbook by filling out the bottom section.

Name of stock	Abbreviation for stock	Cost per share	Number of shares purchased	Total cost for this stock	This cost is what percent of $10,000

Total cost of today's purchases ____________________

Use this section of the sheet to balance your checkbook. By doing this you will have a current record of (1) the amount of money you have invested in stocks, and (2) the amount of money you have not spent (money in the bank).

Balancing the Bank

A. We started with $ ____________________

B. Subtract today's purchases $ ____________________

C. Is there any money not spent? $ ____________________

At the end of this week we have (B + C) $ ____________________

Closing Stock Prices

Names______________________________________

____

Date______________________________________

Class ______________________________________

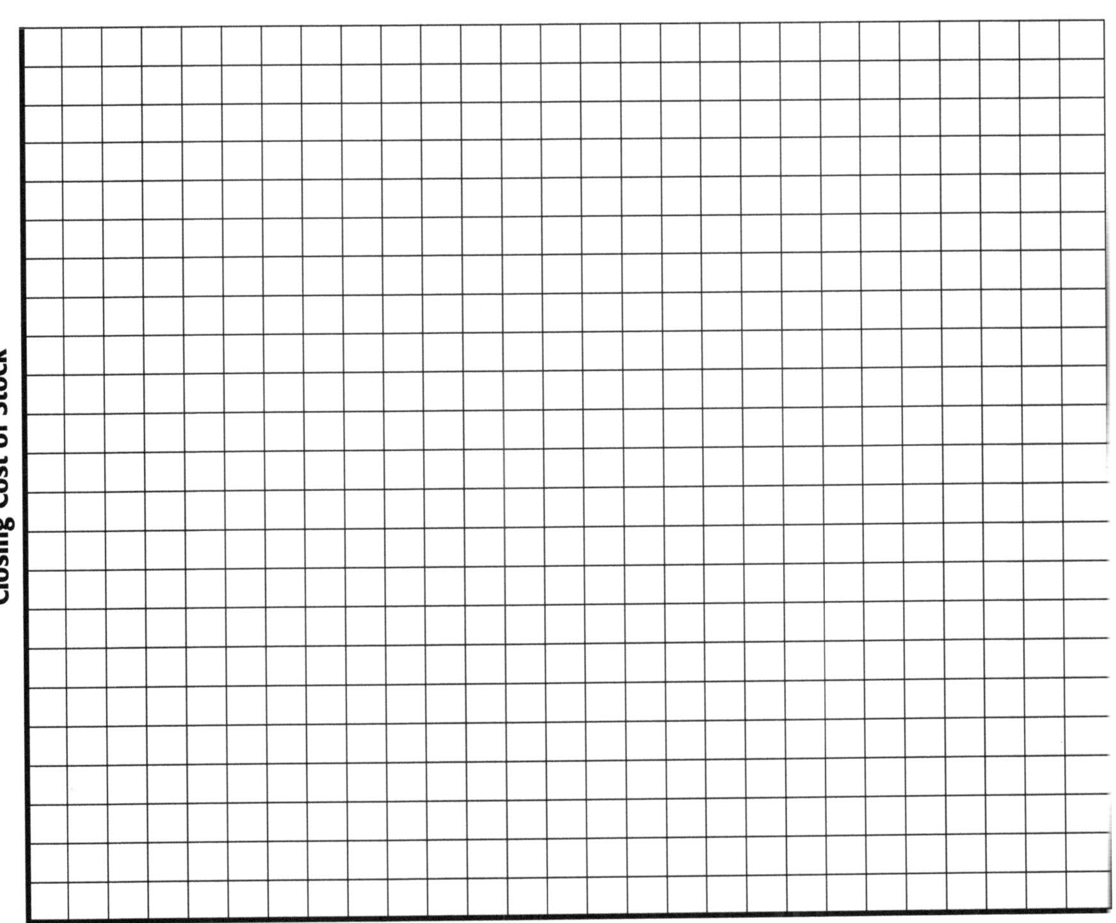

The Stock Market

Week-to-Week Stock Sheet

Names____________________________________

____

Date______________________________________

Class _____________________________________

Week #________ Date of newspaper__________

Use this sheet when your group is keeping track of stocks. You cannot buy or sell stocks using this sheet. Be sure to convert the mixed numbers from the financial column to money (decimals) to make your calculations easier. You will also balance your checkbook by filling out the bottom section.

Abbreviation for stock	Number of shares owned	Closing cost of stock in LAST WEEK'S paper	Closing cost of stock in TODAY'S paper	+ or – (How much?)	Profit (+) or loss (–) multiplied by number of shares

Profit or loss this week (the total of the last column) ____________

Use this section of the sheet to balance your checkbook. By doing this, you will have a current record of the current value of your stock group.

Balancing the Bank

A. Last week our stocks were worth (see last week) $ ________________

B. Profit or loss this week $ ________________

C. This week our group is worth (A ± B) $ ________________

Our Final Sell Week

Mathematical Connections
fractions, decimals, computation, problem solving

Intelligences
logical/mathematical, interpersonal

Other Curricular Connections
Social Studies: Current events, economics
Language Arts: Reading tables

Concepts

Students will do the following:

1. Find and record the closing prices of their stocks in the newspaper for the current week
2. Convert the mixed numbers to decimals and record the price
3. Calculate the value of the stock at the closing price
4. Balance the bank by adding the money received from the sale of their stocks to any money that remains unspent (in the bank)
5. Determine the total value of their group at the end of this project

Materials Needed

calculators (essential); a copy of the financial section of the paper that includes closing stock quotations for each group; a copy of "The Final Sale" blackline for each group

Procedures

At this point, students will be selling all of their stocks to determine the total value of their group at the end of the project. For this reason, they are not concerned with the value of the stock in last week's paper but only with the closing costs for the current week.

For example, if the total value of their sale is $15,200, then the group made a profit of $5,200 (since they began the project with $10,000.) They can compute their percentage of profit:

$$\text{\% of Profit} = \frac{\text{difference (5,200)}}{\text{original money (10,000)}} = 0.52 = 52\%$$

This group did very well in their adventures in the stock market!

The Stock Market

The Final Sale

Names________________________________

____

Date_________________________________

Class ________________________________

Week #________

Date of newspaper_________

Use this sheet when your group is planning to sell all of its stocks at the end of the project. You will also balance your checkbook by filling out the bottom section.

Name of stock	Abbreviation for stock	Closing cost per share	Number of shares to sell	Total money for selling this stock

Total receipt for today's sales ______________

Balancing the Bank

Money from sale of stock $ ____________________

Money left in bank $ ____________________

At the end of this project we have $ ____________________ (total)

Now calculate your percentage of profit by using this simple formula:

$$\text{Our percentage of profit} = \frac{\text{amount of profit}}{\$10{,}000} \times 100$$

Assessment

1. Student products—successful completion of blackline
2. Observation of students

REFERENCES

American Association for the Advancement of Science. 1989. *Project 2061: Science of all Americans.* Washington, DC: AAAS Publications.

Bressler, L., and others. 1993. *The Usborne book of facts and lists.* Tulsa, OK: EDC Publishing.

Fogarty, R. 1991. *The mindful school: How to integrate the curricula.* Palatine, IL: IRI/SkyLight Training and Publishing.

Fogarty, R. 1995. *Think about . . . Block scheduling.* Palatine, IL: IRI/SkyLight Training and Publishing.

Gardner, H. 1983. *Frames of mind.* New York: Basic Books.

Illinois State Board of Education. 1995. *Effective scoring rubrics: A guide to their use and development.* Springfield, IL: author.

Lappan, G., and D. Briars. 1995. How should mathematics be taught? In *Prospects for school mathematics.* Reston, VA: NCTM.

Martin, H. ed. 1996. *Multiple intelligences in the mathematics classroom.* Palatine, IL: IRI/SkyLight Training and Publishing.

Mathematical Sciences Education Board. 1989. *Everybody counts.* Washington, DC: National Academy of Science.

National Council of Teachers of Mathematics. 1989. *Curriculum and evaluation standards for school mathematics.* Reston, VA: author.

Randinelli, T. 1989. On a roll. *Scholastic Math Magazine.* 9(14): 9–11.

World almanac and book of facts. 1992. New York: Pharos Books.

SELECTION 10

Helping Students Become Strategic Readers

by **Bonnie Burns**

Comprehending meaning is the heart and soul of reading, and learning to fully comprehend written text is complex. It is a task so intricate that it takes several years to become a mature reader who can handle simultaneously and almost automatically the multitude of tasks involved in reading comprehension.

Because reading is so automatic for most adults, it is difficult to imagine, much less to imagine teaching, all of the tasks that are involved in comprehension. Yet, take out an old high school or college foreign language text and start reading a passage. You will find yourself consciously, not automatically, using the skills and strategies of reading. You may find yourself reduced to subvocalizing and sounding out words that have slipped from sight vocabulary. You will consciously use context clues, reread, read ahead, skip, come back, read again, remember root words, and problem solve. You will predict and reject and recall situations from your past experience to figure out the meaning. It is a good experience to read in a partially remembered foreign language to see how reading strategies are problem-solving strategies, enabling the reader to construct meaning from the text. But you are an experienced reader, and you know the most important strategy of all: It is supposed to make sense and convey meaning.

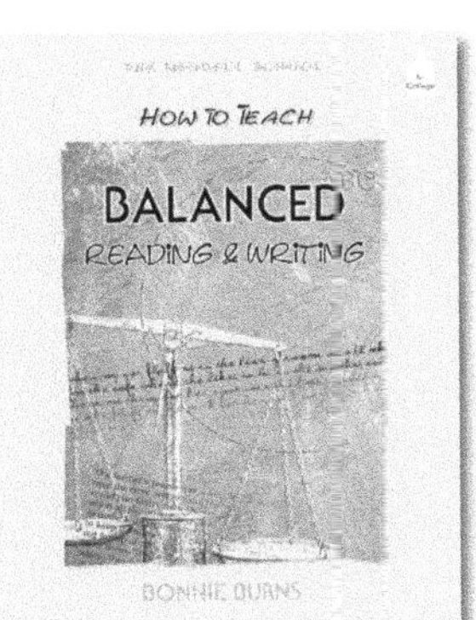

Helping Students Become Strategic Readers

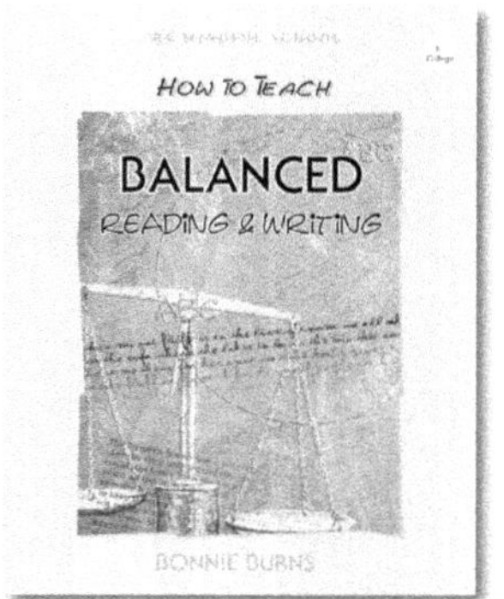

Factors Affecting Comprehension

Comprehension is affected by the ability to recognize words quickly and automatically, the background and knowledge that the reader brings to the task, the familiarity of the reader with the content and vocabulary of the text, the complexity of the style in which the text is written, the ability of the reader to organize information, and the motivation of the reader. All of these components must be orchestrated together for good comprehension. If any component is missing, comprehension will be inhibited.

Fluency and Automaticity in Word Recognition

To comprehend material, students must be able to decode fast enough and automatically enough to keep the content in short-term memory so that meaning can be constructed. If the reader is not fluent and automatic in decoding skills, he forgets the beginning of the sentence by the time he gets to the end. Fluency doesn't ensure comprehension, but comprehension is difficult without fluency. If decoding is not automatic, reading becomes a long and laborious task that requires constant rereading.

Background, Prior Knowledge, and Schema

Another factor that affects comprehension is the reader's prior knowledge. When the reader can recognize nearly every word in the passage but does not have a clue as to the meaning, there is often a mismatch between the reader's and author's schemas. "A schema as we define the term is an organized cognitive structure of related knowledge, ideas, emotions, and actions that has been internalized and that guides and controls a person's use of subsequent information and response to experience" (Goodman and Goodman, 1998, p. 115).

In other words, a schema is composed of personal background knowledge, and it acts as a filing system that has been set up to organize past experiences and interpret future experiences. For example, a restaurant schema includes tablecloths, menus, waiters, price ranges, and favorite dishes, so as we read,

"Elena walked into the restaurant and was escorted to a table," we do not expect that the escort is going to sit down with her. A reader's schema helps him understand new text, make connections, and conjure up pictures while reading. Schemas also include attitudes that will influence judgments about what is read.

It is always an exercise in humility when I read a computer catalog. According to my Mac catalog, "For easy and affordable expansion of your 10Base-T twisted pair network, the DaynaSTAR MiniHub-5 and MiniHub-8 are quick and reliable solutions. Small and lightweight, these hubs have 5 or 8 RJ45 ports, and both include an extra cross over RJ45 port that can be used for hub-to-hub connections without a special cross over cable or connector." (MacWarehouse, 1998, p. 62). I can read every word in the catalog, but I am not familiar with the content. My schema doesn't match the author's. There is even a picture to help me, but I still have no idea. Having no idea what I am reading about is a major block to my comprehension.

When a student's schema matches the author's, it is likely that the text will make more sense, and the student will better comprehend and recall the material. When schema doesn't match, the student is reduced to recalling the information on a rote basis. He cannot make any judgment about the material because it is not really understood. A match between schemas may be through similar background knowledge, or it may be through familiarity with a type of text organization such as narrative structure or the type of organization found in scientific papers.

Lack of matching schema is usually not as severe as mine with the computer catalog, but even small mismatches can produce unexpected results. One of my students who wrote about *Sarah Bishop* (O'Dell, 1980) discussed putting a jacket on a deer because the book said that Sarah had dressed a deer. Another student mentioned that an Indian visitor of Sarah's was sick because the text said he was ill at ease. Another, in a retelling, said that Ulysses poked out the eye of the Cyclops with a spear dipped in oregano because she had read the spear was of seasoned wood. These students formed images based on

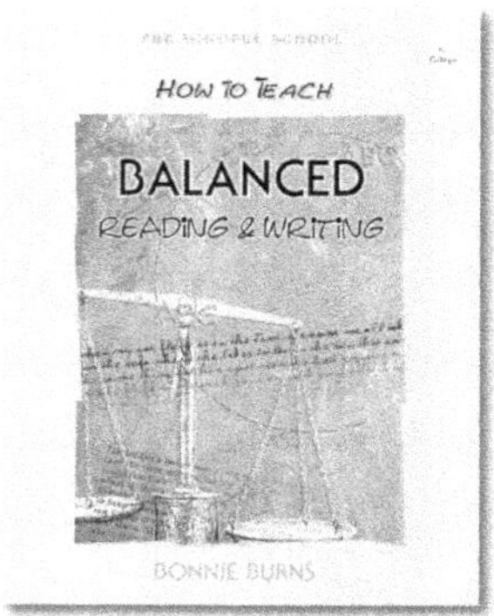

their past knowledge and in remembering the passages swore there were jackets, flu symptoms, and herbs. Some mismatches totally block comprehension, especially if it is an unknown concept, and some mismatches just change the details. Because readers construct meaning based on what they already know and try to integrate new ideas into their systems, the same text can have different interpretations for different readers. Providing background or connections for students increases comprehension.

Difficulty of the Text

The difficulty of the text also affects comprehension. For young students, five unknown words on a single page may mean the book is too difficult for independent reading. Although determining the level of difficulty is often done by counting unknown words, organizational patterns and sentence complexity affect comprehension too. This is especially true in content area textbooks, such as science texts or social studies books.

Determination, Willpower, and Interest

The text, the reader, and an interaction between the two make up the elements of reading. Thus, the attitude and interest of the reader are important factors. "Teachers have long recognized that motivation is at the heart of many of the pervasive problems we face in educating today's children" (Gambrell, 1996, p. 17). The determination of the reader to be a problem-solver when the going gets tough is a factor in comprehension. Students who have an advantage in reading are those who are able to concentrate, see learning as a delightful puzzle to be solved, use a little elbow grease, see a purpose for learning to read, have adult models to imitate, and are risk takers.

High interest can often overcome difficult text. Strong interest can frequently help the reader to transcend his independent and instructional levels of reading (Hunt, 1996–97). Providing motivating situations and interesting content and tasks may be the most challenging and important responsibilities of any teacher.

Capable and Less Capable Readers

The difference between good and poor readers is often seen in the good reader's ability to use a variety of strategies. When one doesn't work, he tries another. Other characteristics of good readers are fluency, the ability to decode rapidly, large vocabularies, the understanding of organizational patterns, the idea that reading is a meaning creating process, and the ability to monitor and use fix-up strategies (Tompkins, 1997).

Less capable readers are more likely to focus on decoding rather than meaning, and as they get older, more likely to focus on a single detail rather than on the whole. They use the same procedures, no matter what the task. When immature readers were asked to read two stories, one just for fun and the other for preparation for a test, they did not adjust their reading strategies. The skilled readers did. "As a result, the immature readers did not remember any more of the story they were supposed to study than the one they were supposed to read for fun" (Anderson et al., 1985, p. 13).

> [Less capable readers] seem reluctant to use unfamiliar strategies or those that require much effort. They do not seem to be motivated or to expect that they will be successful. Less capable readers and writers don't understand or use all the stages of the reading and writing processes effectively. They do not monitor their reading and writing. Or if they do use strategies, they remain dependent on primitive strategies. For example, as they read, less successful readers seldom look ahead or back into the text to clarify misunderstandings or make plans. Or, when they come to an unfamiliar word, they often stop reading unsure of what to do. They may try to sound out an unfamiliar word, but if that is unsuccessful they give up. In contrast capable readers know several strategies, and if one strategy isn't successful they try another (Tompkins, 1997, pp. 136–137).

Helping Students Become Strategic Readers

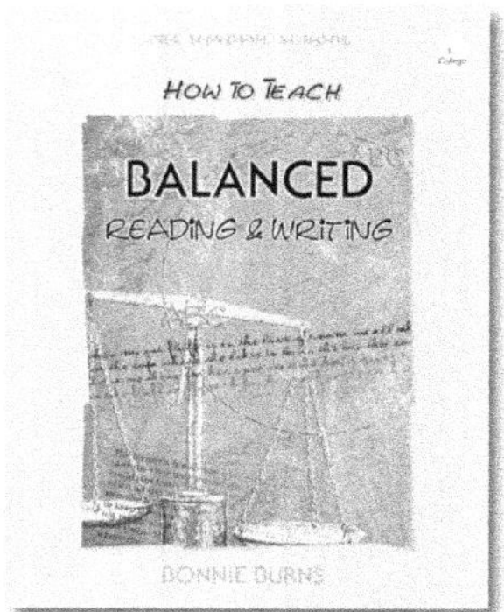

Reading Strategies

Reading strategies are those skills and thinking patterns that help the reader to solve the problems of constructing meaning. Not all strategies are used equally at every level of reading, nor are all strategies used in reading every type of text, but the strategic reader has a variety of techniques at his disposal and can intentionally select which ones to use and can determine when to use them. The proficient reader may not even be aware of using strategies until something goes awry with meaning. It is essential that reading instruction make students aware of strategic reading tactics so they can plan, evaluate, and regulate their own thinking (Tompkins, 1997).

Which strategies do good readers need and use? The first group of strategies includes the basic problem-solving strategies; that is, what good readers do to construct meaning from text. These include:

1. Linking one's background knowledge to the text.
2. Figuring out unknown words.
3. Visualizing.
4. Monitoring comprehension.
5. Predicting and then confirming or rejecting the prediction.
6. Stating main ideas or retelling important information.
7. Organizing ideas into patterns.
8. Using fix-up strategies when the text doesn't make sense.

The second group of strategies includes those that readers use for higher-level thinking:

1. Inferring.
2. Generalizing.
3. Evaluating.

Finally, the third group of strategies involves attitudes and dispositions held by good readers:

1. Understanding that reading is meaningful communication.

2. Desiring to read.
3. Seeing the need to read.
4. Having the willingness to expend considerable time and effort to become proficient.

(The three groups of strategies are derived from the work of Brown, El-Dinary, and Pressley, 1996; May, 1998; and Tompkins, 1997.)

Knowing how and when to use reading strategies requires instruction and the will to learn. Extensive research shows that when teachers explicitly teach strategies, students learn more. In explicit teaching, the teacher models the application of the strategy, carefully explaining to students what is being learned, why it is being learned, when it will be used, and how it will be used (McIntyre, 1996). When strategies are taught using whole text and literature, the approach to teaching comprehension is balanced. The sequence for reading instruction includes the following:

1. Teacher modeling, explanation, and instruction.
2. Guided practice, in which teacher and students share responsibility for constructing meaning, but students gradually assume more independence.
3. Opportunities for discussion among students and with the teacher.
4. Independent practice with feedback and scaffolding.
5. Ample time for practice.
6. Application of the strategies in real reading situations.

Teaching comprehension strategies takes considerable modeling, talking through, and thinking aloud. It requires asking: How did you know that? What clues did you use? What were you thinking about? And, how did you connect that? Learning how to extract meaning is a process that requires active participation and metacognition (thinking about how something is known or came to be understood). If the comprehension strategy is not consciously known, then the student will not be able to transfer that skill to a future application. In other words, the student not only has to be able to do "it," but has to know what

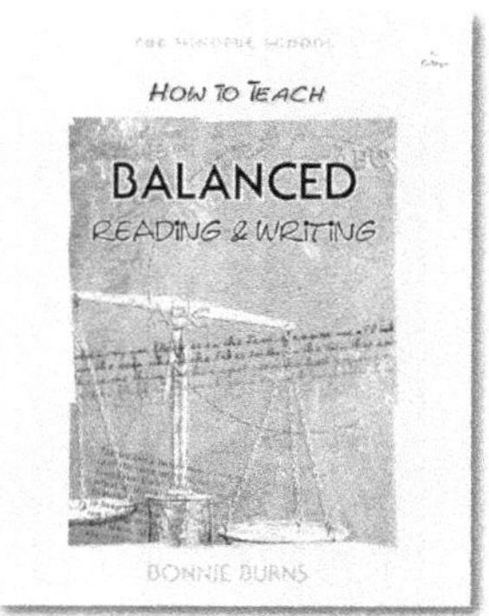

"it" is, and when to do "it" again. Perhaps the most difficult part of teaching strategic reading is remembering that the content of the story is not what is really being taught. It is only the vehicle for learning the process.

Learning how to comprehend is enhanced when there is social interaction. As students hear the teacher explaining how she came to that understanding or listen to other students explaining how they reached a conclusion, they begin to understand the process. Vygotsky is famous for this kind of thinking—that with guided practice and observing the thinking of others, individual students will then be able to do a task by themselves.

Strategies to Teach Prior to Reading the Text

Three types of activities are useful prior to reading the text. They are teaching unfamiliar concepts and content, teaching unfamiliar vocabulary, and providing pictures for visualizing the setting. All enhance comprehension. If the teacher instructs students how to link their own background to new content, how to use context clues, and how to develop images in their own minds, students begin to turn these skills into problem-solving strategies that they will use independently.

Teaching Unfamiliar Concepts and Content

Providing background information, new concepts, synonyms, connections, and simple examples can supply the big picture for readers so that the details fit into a comprehensible whole. People are able to learn the most when they already know 90% of what they are reading. Think of this as having a hook on which to hang new information or a file folder into which new information can be placed. This is obviously important for reading textbooks in which entirely new content is encountered, but it is also important in fiction, especially with stories that are set in other time periods and cultures, or stories that use concepts from an adult realm in which children do not normally participate. Concepts that are unfamiliar to children such as mortgages, organic fertilizers, or patents may need to be pretaught. When the teacher explains these ideas prior to reading, because the author didn't, comprehension is improved.

A teacher needs to carefully consider what content, setting, or concepts may cause a problem. Not everything should be pretaught, only those concepts that will block comprehension of the material.

Linking Background to New Content

Children need to develop the strategy of searching their own schemas when encountering new material. To teach this strategy, the teacher needs to take a slightly different tactic than providing the background. She needs to probe the experiences of the class and help students make their own connections.

To prepare for reading about Hermes in Greek mythology, students were asked to recall where they had seen Hermes' symbols. Their responses included: The winged feet are the symbol of a tire company; the Detroit Red Wings use a logo of a shoe with wings; Hermes is in a Saturn car commercial; his staff is on the Blue Cross logo; and a staff with intertwined snakes is used on the sign at a drugstore. The students' responses helped them realize that the mythological characters were not completely unknown to them, and they could make connections to aid their comprehension and to improve recall.

Prereading discussion is one of the most useful activities for activating prior knowledge or developing concepts. Relating anything to any film is productive, because young students seem to know every movie ever produced. One student will say, "Have you ever seen this movie? Well, it's like that." And, a chorus of now-understanding heads will nod in unison. Calling on every student during a discussion validates everyone's experiences as well as keeping everyone involved. For those who do not wish to or are unable to offer examples of their own, the teacher can offer choice questions such as, "Do you think Tony's story or Kaitlyn's story is the better example? How does her story relate to our discussion?"

Helping Students Become Strategic Readers

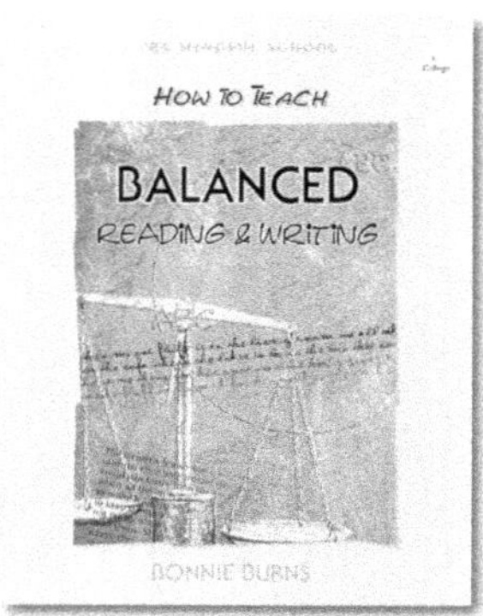

The difficulty with whole class discussion is that it is all verbal interchange and those students with something else on their minds or those who have auditory deficits may still miss the connections. The following activities offer greater opportunity for student participation.

KWL was developed by Donna Ogle (1986). It is a three-part activity in which students describe what they already *know* about a subject, what they *want* to know, and then what they *learned*. It is perfect for nonfiction material, but it can also be used for unfamiliar concepts or settings in fiction. The best use seems to be in small groups in which plenty of discussion and interchange can occur, ensuring more active participation. The *W* can be changed to *T* to represent "*Think* you know for sure" for middle school students who often say they don't want to know anything about the topic.

Used prior to reading, an **anticipation guide** deals on a general level with the issues in an upcoming reading selection. It consists of a list of statements that reflect the underlying issues in the text. The statements are usually written in an ambiguous fashion so there can be both agreement and disagreement, which generally leads to discussion among the students. Each student gets a copy of the anticipation guide. They respond to the statements independently and then develop a set of cooperative answers. The teacher can ask for a consensus, or she can ask for students to check off whether they agree or disagree with a statement after explaining the rationale for their answers. Selected issues can be discussed with the whole class or a poll can be taken to ascertain opinions. "Children who are orphaned are best left in the care of a family member," could be an anticipation guide sentence for an upcoming selection about a child who becomes the responsibility of an uncaring relative.

Unknown Vocabulary Words

It is a great aid to comprehension to understand vocabulary such as *disdainfully*, but if the word can be skipped over without affecting comprehension of the story, then it is not a critical word for preteaching. The greater the importance of a word to understanding the story, the more it needs to be explained and connected prior to reading. *Apprentice* represents a concept, and the relationship between the midwife and the girl in *The Midwife's Apprentice* (Cushman, 1995) might not be understood without knowledge of what apprenticeship entails.

Unknown words can be figured out through the strategy of context clues. Context clues may be at the sentence level or at the story level. Learning how to pick out print clues and meaning clues can be explicitly taught. Reminders, questions, or hints while students are reading whole texts provide scaffolding until using context becomes an independent strategy.

Visualizing the Setting

Unfamiliar settings and times can be easily imagined when the teacher provides pictures. When reading about a story set in Japan, when trying to imagine Kubla Khan's court, when reading about rural Mississippi in the 1930s, it helps the reader to have a picture in her head, so she can see the characters moving through the setting rather than on an empty stage or misplaced in a setting that looks more like her own neighborhood. Clothing, mountain ranges, architecture, and unusual tools and foods come alive. Maps can serve the same purpose. These pictures are not always easy to find, but they are well worth the search.

Visualizing aids memory and deepens comprehension. Zhicheng Zhang (1993, p. 9) claims that visual images are retained longer than verbal recall. "Visual images may effectively transfer large chunks of information to long-term memory and may also act as the most potent device to aid recall of verbal material." The brain's storage capacity for visual information exceeds its capacity for verbal material (Oxford, as cited in Zhang).

Although the teacher may initially supply pictures of the setting, students need to continue envisioning the scene, adding new props as the story progresses. To make visualization a strategy, prompt students to keep imagining and have students share the images that they see. There will be an amazing

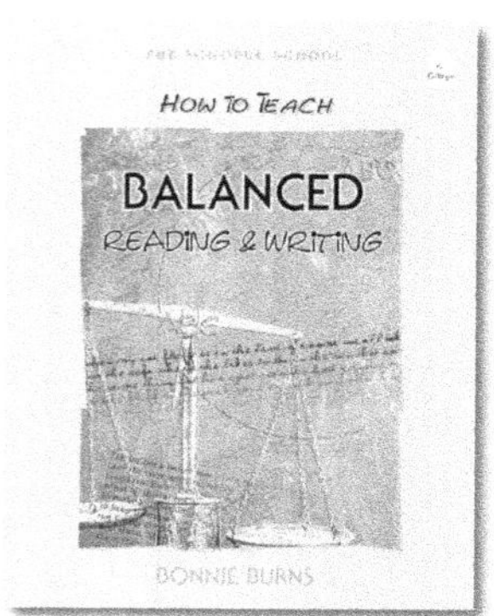

variety. The following example is a response by a sixth grader to "Which scene in the chapter could you visualize the best?" Notice how the writer adds homes that look more like his than the homes of ancient Greece, but there is also no doubt that the writer can imagine Ulysses' longing to reach home as he sees the distant familiar sights.

> In *Keeper of the Winds,* I could visualize Ulysses and his crew almost reaching their hometown. I saw Ulysses' castle on the top of the mountain. I also saw the large red brick houses with the smoke coming out. Along with that I saw people walking on the dirt road. You could see the port with ships lined all around and the mates were working hard on them. In the distance you could see people farming their land.

Drawing scenes also helps students deepen the images as students return to the text to get the details that they want to include. A single scene can be drawn, or a series can be depicted, which helps to firm up the sequence.

Comprehension Skills and Strategies During Reading

Guided reading allows for strategy instruction and constant interchange among teacher and students, but what about providing scaffolding or support during silent reading? Independent reading is perhaps the most difficult time to try to assess reading strategies because the entire complex process is happening silently and without many outward signs. One strategy students must use when reading silently is to monitor their own comprehension.

Monitoring Comprehension

Monitoring comprehension includes paying attention to what one has just read and judging if it is sensible and consistent. M. Grabe and S. Mann (as cited in Anderson et al., 1985) provide an example of consistent and inconsistent paragraphs. Poor readers do not notice the inconsistency because they are not monitoring.

All the people who work on this ship get along very well. The people who make a lot of money and the people who don't make much are still friends. The officers treat me as an equal. We often eat our meals together. I guess we are just one big happy family.

All the people who work on this ship get along very well. The people who make a lot of money and the people who don't make much are still friends. The officers treat me like dirt. We often eat our meals together. I guess we are just one big happy family.

Anderson et al. (1985) in the nationally commissioned report *Becoming a Nation of Readers,* proposes that poor readers do not adequately control the way they read or perhaps they do not see the point of reading and thus do not monitor as they read. Some students are just "doing school" and glide on through the text without constructing meaning—without connecting what passes before their eyes with actually thinking about what they are reading.

To help students develop the strategy of monitoring comprehension, the teacher can use guided reading, which is a read and respond, read and respond technique. During silent reading, she can provide a virtual teacher, that is, a study guide, a set of questions, or specific times to stop and think. These can be thought of as written prompts or reminders, similar to what a teacher might ask during guided reading, so that the student can never go too far without constructing meaning.

Embedded questions are questions that are actually written in the middle of the text and not at the end of the passage. The advantage is that the questions are asked just after the child has read a relatively short passage. If he cannot respond to the question, the reader immediately goes back to what was just read and finds or formulates the answer. Very few texts are written this way, with embedded questions, but no matter. The teacher can alter the text in order to provide guidance. The teacher can accomplish this in two ways, with stop and go questions or with embedded question markers in the text.

With **stop and go questions**, the student reads a question and then reads the text until the answer is found or a clue for a

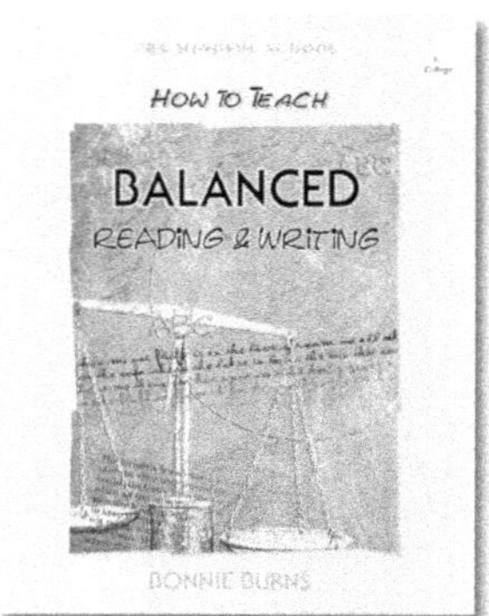

response is encountered. When a student knows the question and reads until encountering the answer, he finds himself reading for a purpose rather than just aimlessly wandering through the text. This aids comprehension considerably. Stop and go questions are the only way to really develop the strategy of making predictions during silent reading.

The questions should be in order and not have page numbers. When page numbers are included, it encourages students to scan or skip pages on which no answers are to be found. If the child reads several pages without finding the answer, he has to use a fix-up strategy such as rereading or reconsidering.

When I've asked students if they prefer the stop and go style, or if they prefer reading straight through and answering questions at the end, it is always about a 50-50 split. However, it is almost always the weakest readers who prefer the stop and go style because it provides a nudge toward continuing to concentrate on the passage and to continually monitor what is being read. Their success rate is improved with support.

A second method to encourage self-monitoring during silent reading is to insert **embedded markers** (in the form of numbers) in the text that match numbered questions, listed on a separate piece of paper. To show students where the embedded numbers go in the text, the teacher can reproduce the text on an overhead transparency. The students then copy the numbers into their own texts where indicated. Or, if a teacher has infinite time, she could insert the numbers into the students' texts herself.

An adaptation from Marguerite Henry's *King of the Wind* (1951, pp. 91–94) provides an example. The story tells of a carter who forces a horse named Sham to pull a load too heavy for one animal up an incline. The cruelty of the act is witnessed by a crowd of onlookers who are silently fearful for Sham. Sham's burden is too great, and he falls to his knees between the shafts of the cart. The carter wants to force the horse to his feet by setting fire to a log braced under Sham's tail. A Quaker named Jethro Coke steps forward and offers a handful of gold coins for the struggling horse. The hard-hearted carter accepts the money. A young boy helps unharness

Sham as the crowd applauds and cheers because the horse's life has been saved.

The teacher embeds numbers throughout a copy of the actual story that correspond to the following steps:

1. Make a prediction.
2. Tell what is happening.
3. Make a prediction.
4. Was your prediction right?
5. Visualize the scene.

However, if students require more scaffolding, the teacher can use **question markers** that are more specific, with the steps written in parentheses following the question:

1. Will Sham make it up the hill? (prediction)
2. Why didn't any of the passersby stop the driver from using his whip? (fact question)
3. What is the Quaker going to do? (prediction)
4. Was your prediction right or wrong? (confirm or reject prediction)
5. Why was there laughter and clapping? Who might have been watching? (visualization and inference)

The teacher can also use both these formats simultaneously, distributing the complete questions to students who need greater prompting, and giving the more independent version to students who are able to read with less prompting. The students might not even notice there are two versions.

As students need less guidance during silent reading to identify strategies or responses in the text, they can determine their own responses. **Say something** and **write something** make excellent bridges. Say something is done with partner reading. As students finish an entire page, each partner must turn to the other and *say something*. *Write something* is a single sentence written at the end of each page and is done independently.

Usually, but not always, the "somethings" are summaries of the plot. This technique also serves to help students monitor their comprehension so they don't get too far before they realize that they have not understood. The more practice that

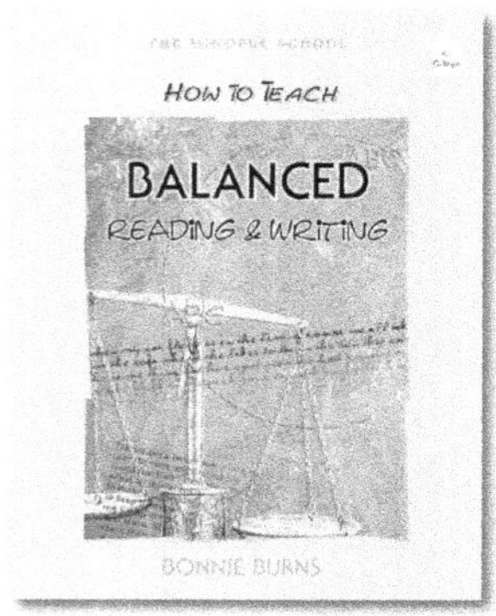

students have in reacting to text rather than just summarizing, the more likely they will respond at the end of the page with a question, a reaction, or an interpretation. For example, from *King of the Wind:*

> p. 38 Agba runs into a camel dealer who recognizes he is a stable boy from the royal stables.
> p. 39 Agba is revived with camel milk with honey. If he liked it, will Sham?
> p. 40 Sham is weak and thin. I bet he gets well, or there will be no story.
> p. 41 Sham loves the camel milk and honey. Agba promises him he will be King of the Wind.

Good readers will have more complex responses, but less mature readers will at least have the literal plot and will be able to fully participate in a guided discussion with higher-level questioning. Write something provides an excellent assessment of comprehension and is easily checked by the teacher. As an added benefit, it makes a good foundation for learning to write a summary.

The teacher can extend this activity by having children compare and evaluate the short summaries. Using children's work as models is often more interesting than teacher modeling. Students can explicitly explain and demonstrate how they came to their answers as well as showing their work.

With **reading logs**, students are free to respond when and with what information they choose, making this activity the most open-ended type of response to reading. Again, the more opportunities students have to work with reacting to text rather than just summarizing, the more likely they will respond with connections, inferences, questions about what will happen, and personal responses. Teachers can encourage higher-level responses by responding to the logs with higher-level answers or by asking students to respond to starter stems, such as, "The most interesting part was . . . ," "This reminds me of another story where . . . ," "The scene that I see most vividly in my mind is . . . ," or "The main character must have been feeling . . . because . . . ."

Predicting and Confirming or Rejecting the Prediction

Predicting is another strategy that good readers use while they are reading. It is a strategy that functions at two levels: predicting the next word or phrase in a sentence or predicting the next event in a story. Good readers predict at the sentence level all the time, which helps with word recognition.

Alex had smooth black hair reaching to his __________. The reader who is predicting is expecting *ears, shoulders, collar, waist* or any noun that could act as a marker for hair length. Successful prediction requires being aware of the meaning (semantic cues) and of regular English sentence patterns (syntactic cues). As the first letter comes into view, *Alex had smooth black hair reaching to his s*__________, the reader also adds graphophonic cues and within a microsecond confirms *shoulders.*

Because good readers make predictions based on what they expect will follow, they sometimes mismatch the text, especially in oral reading, because the brain and eye spans are always ahead of the voice. Good readers, if they have substituted one part of speech for another when reading orally, are able to change the remaining parts of speech in the sentence, maintain the intended meaning, and read the whole sentence in fluent correct English patterns (Weaver, 1998).

A **cloze** exercise is an excellent way to practice predicting using semantic and syntactic cues. Cloze passages (from the word closure) omit every eighth word and substitute a blank. The entire first and last sentences are left intact. Any answer that makes sense is acceptable. Because cloze requires constructing meaning from an incomplete story and feels like a puzzle, students pay very close attention to the content. It is a good exercise for partners because of the social interaction as they discuss choices and help each other notice when a word does not fit with the meaning or with the syntax of the sentence.

When preparing a cloze exercise, do not use a word bank at the bottom of the page except with very young readers, because

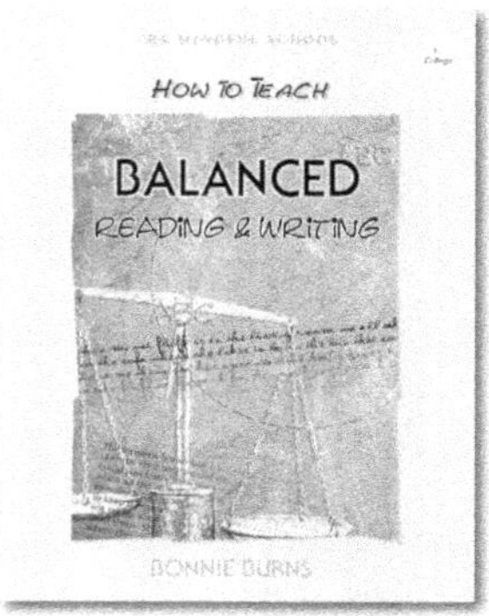

students will be deprived of using several comprehension strategies, and the idea of "one correct answer" is reinforced.

With cloze passages, semantic and syntactic clues are used to fill in the missing words. The reader uses past knowledge and infers time and place. He reads ahead to use all of the context clues that are available, and then he goes back to correct himself after coming across additional information. The reader predicts, confirms, and rejects—all valuable strategies in reading.

The second level of prediction is **predicting at the story level.** A student who predicts is more likely to monitor her own comprehension because she wonders if her prediction is going to be the choice made by the author. Some predicting is more like self-questioning: I wonder why he did that? That seems strange. I bet he doesn't have any friends. Students' prior knowledge may significantly influence what they wonder and predict (Zhang, 1993).

One method for practicing predicting is to reproduce a story and cut it into sections, only distributing one section at a time. Another method is to reproduce the story on an overhead transparency showing only one section at a time. A prediction tree can be used for responses (Figure 10.1).

After reading a section, the student must make a prediction. Being required to write it down ensures that everyone will actually predict, and it encourages more active participation. The probability of the prediction can be discussed as well as which clues were used to draw that conclusion.

Strategies After Reading

Strategies can be taught or practiced before, during, or after reading the selection. Most of the preceding strategies were suitable for before or during reading but could be used at any time. The following reading strategies and teaching activities can be used during guided reading or after reading as students go back and analyze in greater depth what they have read. The reader eventually orchestrates all the strategies for simultaneous use, but explicit teaching of individual strategies helps students identify and apply the strategies.

Prediction Tree

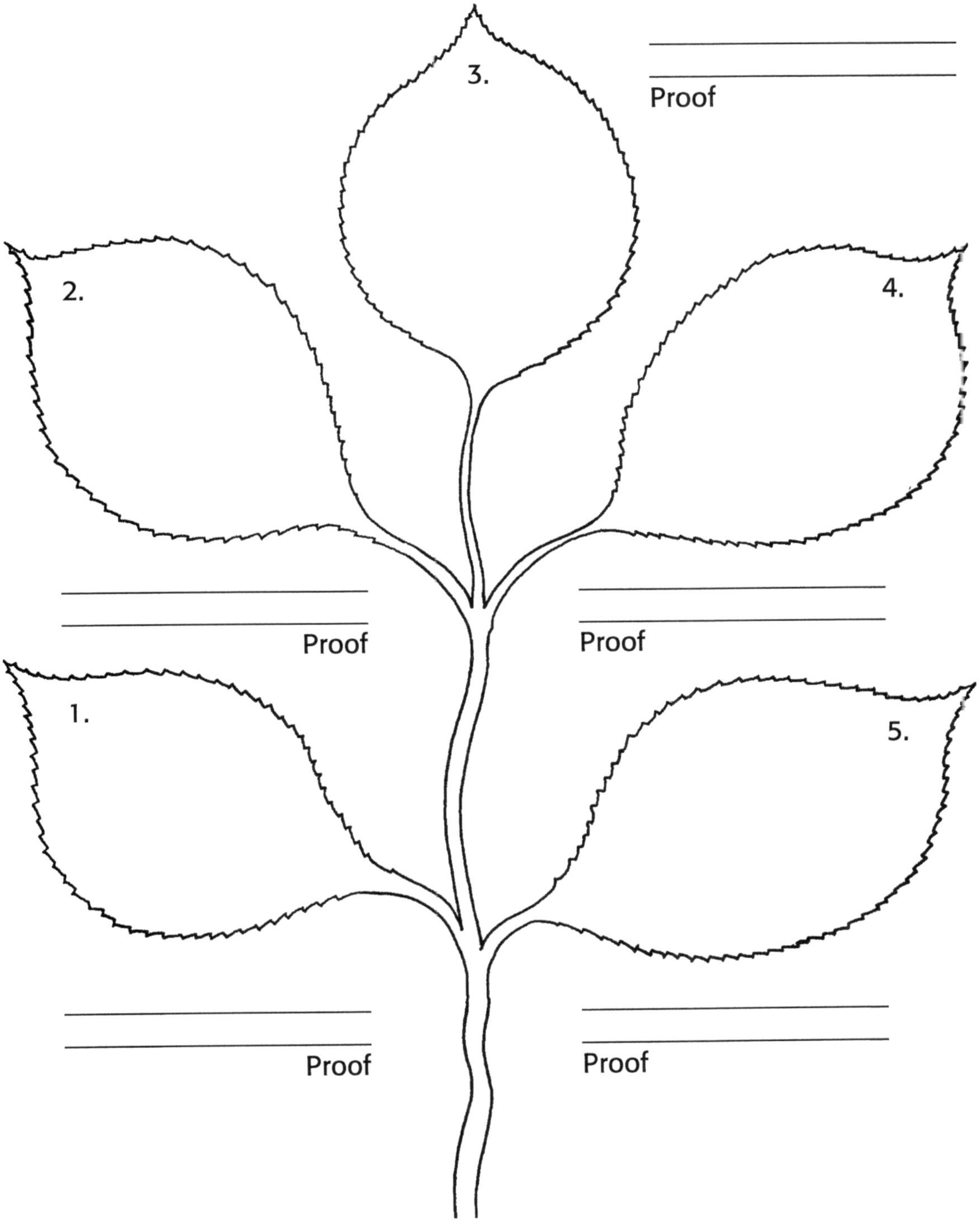

3.

____

____

Proof

2.

4.

____

____

Proof

____

____

Proof

1.

5.

____

____

Proof

____

____

Proof

Figure 10.1

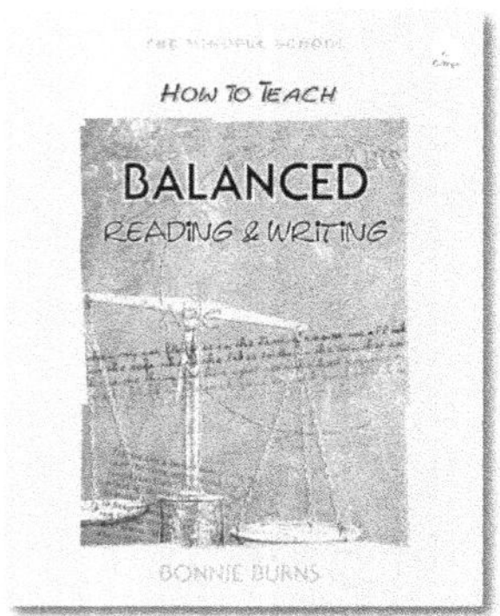

Stating Main Ideas and Retelling Important Information

A strategy that good readers use is to group information according to the main idea or around central events so that the content is easier to remember. This is not so easy to do. Young readers start by retelling the story. Retelling improves comprehension, sense of story structure, and oral language. James Baumann, Helene Hooten, and Patricia White (1996) suggest using a retelling instructional chart, as illustrated in Figure 10.2.

Retelling Instructional Chart

To RETELL part of a story, try . . .

Putting the story into your own words.

Saying the ideas in the order they happened in the story.

Including all the most important events and ideas.

Using the book to help you remember events or ideas.

Figure 10.2

The next step is to state the main idea. Being able to state the main idea is more difficult than retelling because it requires combining, evaluating, and sometimes inferring information. Poor readers have a difficult time relating all the bits of information to each other and deciding what is the main idea. They can tell you several of the details but not combine them into a meaningful whole. To relate the bits of information into a main idea sentence, try this summary format.

Summary Format: Somebody? Wanted? But? So?
Example: *Goldilocks wanted* to see what was in the house, *but* the bears returned and frightened her, *so* she ran away.

The **write something** technique can also provide good practice for identifying main ideas, especially when the "something" is a one-sentence summary less than one written line in length. To make the ideas this short, students must paraphrase, which is another way to manipulate information and improve recall. Whole class processing and evaluation of the "somethings" helps students understand why one piece of information or one event may be more critical than others. Retelling or summarizing the events of a story are important methods for assessing comprehension.

Organizing Ideas into Patterns

Good readers group ideas into organizational patterns such as cause and effect, comparison and contrast, and topic and subtopic. Good readers also sequence story events. When bits of information are tied together into chunks, it helps the reader to see the relationships among the various pieces of information. Good readers summarize and paraphrase in order to group and manipulate the information. This also fosters understanding and memory. Look at the following list for thirty seconds and then try to write it from memory: Oranges, rye bread, pick up blouse at cleaners, compost recycling bags, mustard, drop off pants at the cleaners, spackle, sliced ham.

Most adults who are successful with this experiment categorize or group—grocery story, cleaners, and hardware store. They also count the number of items. Most children try to memorize without a structure. Students need to be taught what the organizational patterns are and how they function.

Story mapping is an enjoyable way to practice **sequencing**. It can be done in a written format, as in Figure 10.3, or in a picture format. In written form, it looks like a simple outline (Routman, 1991, p. 96).

Story Map

Title: ______________________________

Setting: ______________________________

Characters: ______________________________

Problem: ______________________________

  Event 1: ______________________________

  Event 2: ______________________________

Resolution: ______________________________

Figure 10.3

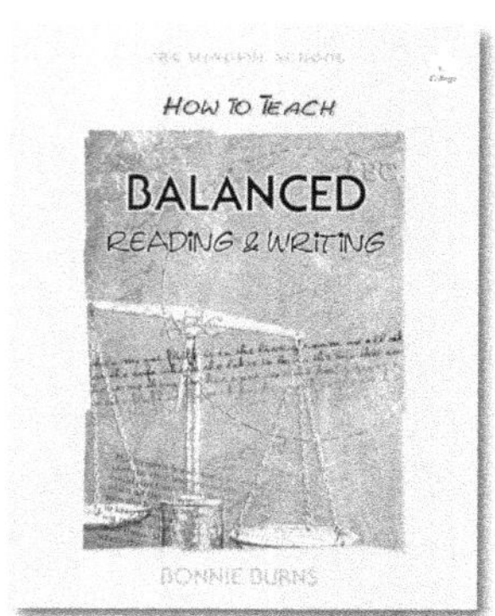

In picture form, the story map can be a series of pictures depicting the major events of the story connected by arrows in a flow chart. Pictures can also be arranged in a tic-tac-toe grid with the first line for the beginning of the story, the middle line for the middle, and the bottom line for the ending. For a whole novel, chapters can be assigned to groups that draw several scenes per chapter. As children visualize the scenes, they also unscramble the sequence and determine cause and effect.

Direct teaching of the elements of literature, or story grammar (opening event, characters, problem, resolution, setting, theme), does not seem to have much effect on comprehension (May, 1998) perhaps because each is being identified as a separate entity without connecting relationships.

The Venn diagram is a perfect vehicle for students to **compare and contrast**. They use it to see the similarities and differences between characters, settings, and even stories. It is a set of overlapping circles with the similarities listed in the overlap.

Cause and effect is a more difficult concept than sequencing or comparing and contrasting, because it often involves inference. It is also a more complex way of thinking for young students. Students who are not accustomed to thinking in this pattern may simply list adjoining events, whether the events have any relationship to each other or not. Once the teacher has directly taught what is meant by cause and effect relationships, most stories and informational texts can be used for practicing this organizational strategy because characters have motivations for their actions or one event dominoes into another.

An effective way for students to become more aware of cause and effect relationships in literature is to use a two-column worksheet that lists cause situations in one column and effects in the other. One side of each pair is left blank so the student fills in either the cause or effect. These questions are at the literal rearranged or inferential levels.

Topic and subtopic is more often found in nonfiction books. Webs or incomplete outlines are effective graphic organizers for helping students become cognizant of which details go with which main ideas. When students use the topic and subtopic organizational pattern in their own writing, it can have a positive impact on reading comprehension (Shanahan, 1997b).

Using Fix-up Strategies When the Text Doesn't Make Sense

Read aloud the following paragraph as an experiment:

The Boat

A man was building a boat in his
cellar. As soon as he had finished
the boot, he tried to take it through the
the cellar door. It would not go though
the door. So he had to take it a part.
He should of planed better.

(Schwartz, 1997, p. 41).

Did you notice the conflicting word and meaning cues in the passage? Did you detect *boot* for *boat,* the double *the, though* for *through, a part* for *apart, should of* for *should've,* and *planed* for *planned?* You probably fixed the errors as you read for meaning.

Good readers who are monitoring their comprehension use fix-up strategies when the text does not make sense, usually because the reader has miscued rather than because the text was incoherent. Corrective action may mean rereading a section, skipping the part or word that is unclear hoping that future information will clarify the problem, or just rethinking. Good readers go back and read more carefully, consider everything they know about the topic or root words, look at the pictures, get help from another source, or ask someone. These behaviors can be more easily seen during oral reading when the reader self-corrects after using a fix-up strategy.

Poor readers aren't aware that the text is not making sense, and when they realize they have a problem, they are unsure of what action to take. Often, they just keep going. Frequent

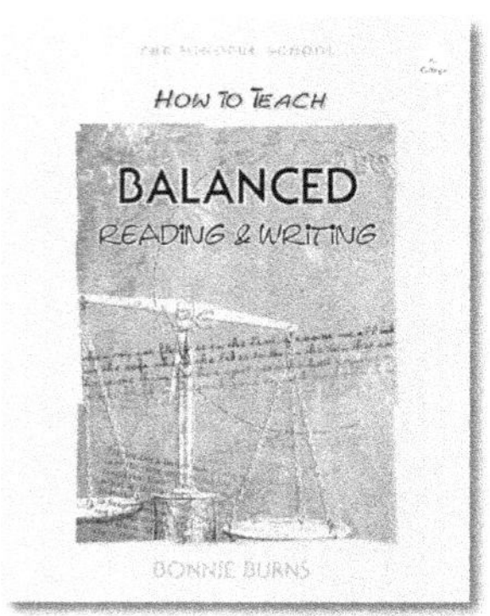

questioning of the reader, through guided reading or the virtual teacher, can help those without fix-up strategies because they need to first realize that they didn't understand. Explicit teaching of fix-up strategies is necessary for these students. The teacher can help students learn to apply fix-up strategies by questioning rather than correcting:

> Student: One of the chefs hailed the other captains.
>
> Teacher: Was he calling them for dinner in the middle of the battle?
>
> Student: (Puzzled, then rereads.) One of the chiefs hailed the other captains.

For those students who want to jump in and correct their classmates, the teacher can ask them to offer a problem-solving clue instead. R. M. Schwartz (1997) suggests posting the following reminder in the classroom to let students know that the ultimate task is to obtain meaning, not get every word correct the first time.

> Readers know that:
> 1. Good readers think about meaning.
> 2. All readers make mistakes.
> 3. Good readers notice and fix some mistakes.

Strategies for Higher-Level Thinking: Inferring, Generalizing, Evaluating

Mature readers go beyond the printed lines: They infer, generalize, and evaluate. Students need to be explicitly taught what an inference is and that good readers are supposed to make inferences while reading. To infer, readers must combine what is in the text with their own knowledge.

Young readers assume that everything that needs to be said has been said by the author, and in order to answer the teacher's questions, they need only to look back to find the relevant section in the text. It comes as a revelation that the author has not directly stated everything that he wishes the reader to know. Good readers use their prior knowledge to fill in the gaps that the author has left. Students who do not think beyond the concrete level benefit greatly from hearing how other students used their own knowledge—knowledge the concrete thinker also possesses—to put together two or more pieces of information to form an inference.

Character motivation seems to be one area in particular that requires making inferences because authors often choose to show motivation through action rather than through direct explanation. When teachers ask, "Why did the character do that?", students appear stymied until the teacher asks, "If you were in that situation, what would you do?" It is as if they think book characters act completely differently than real people do.

Good readers also generalize and evaluate what they read, but they sometimes need help in isolating details. Graphic organizers help to make details visible and separate from the tangle of information in the story.

A graphic organizer that makes the conflict visible is the decision-making chart. Not only must conflicting reasons be identified, but the student must also make a personal choice about the conflict and identify the best reason for the decision. In Figure 10.4, the student must decide if Ulysses should stay with Calypso or continue his journey home.

Graphic organizers help students identify critical information and evaluate decisions. They are excellent bridges between guided reading and independent critical reading.

Decision-Making Chart: Ulysses

Calypso

Should Ulysses Return Home?

Ulysses should stay with Calypso because . . .

1. He would not grow old. (immortal)
2. At home he would live on memories.
3. He would be kicked out of his castle.
4. She'd make him her eternal consort.
5. His home will be wherever Titan's rule.
6. His other son would kill him.

Ulysses should return home because . . .

1. He should see his son.
2. His wife is beng faithful.
3. He could be turned into an animal by Calypso.
4. His things are being taken.
5. He has been gone for 20 years.
6. He has paid for blinding Polyphemous, Poseidon's son.

Your conclusion:

Return home.

Best reason:

His wife is being faithful to him.

Maggie

Figure 10.4

REFERENCES

Anderson, R. C., E. H. Hiebert, J. A. Scott, and I. A. G. Wilkinson. 1985. *Becoming a nation of readers: The report of the commission on reading.* Urbana, IL: Center for the Study of Reading.

Baumann, J., H. Hooten, and P. White. 1996. Teaching skills and strategies with literature. In J. Baltas, and S. Shafer (Eds.), *Scholastic guide to balanced reading* 3–6: 60–70. New York: Scholastic.

Brown, R., P. B. El-Dinary, and M. Pressley. 1996. Balanced comprehension instruction: Transactional strategies instruction. In E. McIntyre and M. Pressley (Eds.), *Balanced instruction: Strategies and skills in whole language,* (pp. 177–92). Norwood, MA: Christopher-Gordon Publishers.

Gambrell, L. 1996. Creating classroom cultures that foster reading motivation. *The Reading Teacher.* 50(1): 14–25.

Goodman, Y., and K. S. Goodman. 1998. To err is human: Learning about language processes by analyzing miscues. In C. Weaver (Ed.), *Reconsidering a balanced approached to reading,* (pp. 101–26). Urbana, IL: National Council of Teachers of English.

Hunt, L. 1996–1997. The effect of self-selection, interest, and motivation upon independent, instructional, and frustrational levels. *The Reading Teacher.* 50(4): 278–82.

MacWarehouse Catalog. 1998. Lakewood, NJ: MacWarehouse.

May, F. 1998. *Reading as communication: To help children write and read* (5th ed.). Upper Saddle River, NJ: Merrill-Prentice Hall.

McIntyre, E. 1996. Strategies and skills in whole language: An introduction to balanced teaching. In E. McIntyre and M. Pressley (Eds.), *Balanced instruction: Strategies and skills in whole language* (pp. 12–20). Norwood, MA: Christopher-Gordon.

Ogle, D. 1986. K-W-L: A teaching model that develops active reading of expository text. *The Reading Teacher.* 39: 564–71.

Routman, R. 1991. *Invitations: Changing as teachers and learners K–12.* Portsmouth, NH: Heinemann Irvin.

Schwartz, R. M. 1997. Self-monitoring in beginning reading. *The Reading Teacher.* 51(1): 40–48.

Shanahan, T. 1997a. Character perspective charting: Helping children to develop a more complete conception of story. *The Reading Teacher.* 50(8): 668–77.

———. 1997b. Reading-writing relationships, thematic units, inquiry learning. . . In pursuit of effective integrated literacy instruction. *The Reading Teacher.* 51(1), 12–19.

Tompkins, G. E. 1997. *Literacy for the 21st century: A balanced approach.* Upper Saddle River, NJ: Merrill-Prentice Hall.

Weaver, C. 1998. Toward a balanced approach to reading. In C. Weaver (Ed.), *Reconsidering a balanced approach to reading,* 11–76. Urbana, IL: National Council of Teachers of English.

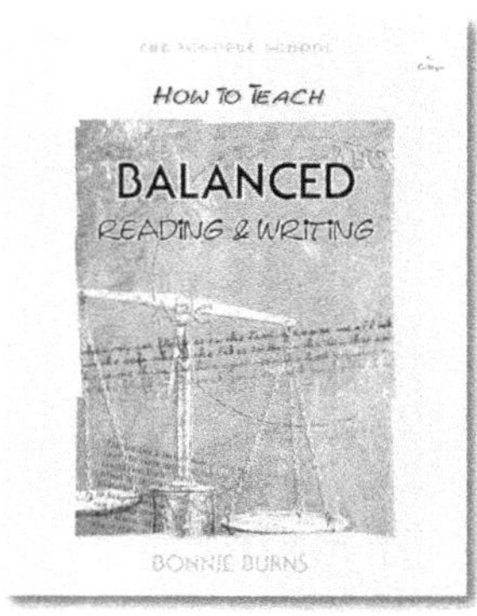

Zhang, Z. 1993. *Literature review on reading strategy research.* Office of Educational Research and Improvement, U. S. Department of Education. (ERIC Document No. ED 366 908).

LITERATURE CITED

Cushman, K. (1995). *The midwife's apprentice.* New York: Harper Trophy.
Evslin, B. (1969). *The adventures of Ulysses.* New York: Scholastic.
Henry, M. (1951). *King of the wind.* Chicago: Rand McNally.
O'Dell, S. (1980). *Sarah Bishop.* New York: Scholastic.
Pinkwater, D. (1977). *The big orange splot.* New York: Scholastic.

Metacognition
Knowing What You Know

by **Evelyn Rothstein and Gerald Lauber**

Once . . . relevant knowledge has been acquired, the skill follows. —E. D. Hirsch Jr.

What Is Metacognition?

Metacognition refers to the conscious awareness of what one knows or doesn't know. It includes both what a person knows deeply and what a person knows on the surface. It also includes what one needs to know in order to achieve his or her goals or objectives. Arthur Costa (1991) includes metacognition as one of the essential characteristics of intelligent human behavior that, together with curiosity and wonderment, motivate people to seek additional knowledge. The concept of metacognition is elaborated upon by David Perkins, who defines four levels of metacognitive learners: tacit learners who are unaware of their knowledge, aware learners who know about some of the kinds of thinking they do, strategic learners who are problem solvers and decision makers, and, finally, reflective learners who "ponder their strategies and revise them" (1992, 102). Teachers generally find that successful or achieving students are aware of what they already know about a particular topic (prior knowledge); they recognize what they have learned that they didn't know before (new knowledge), and they identify what they need to know to meet requirements or standards (expected knowledge).

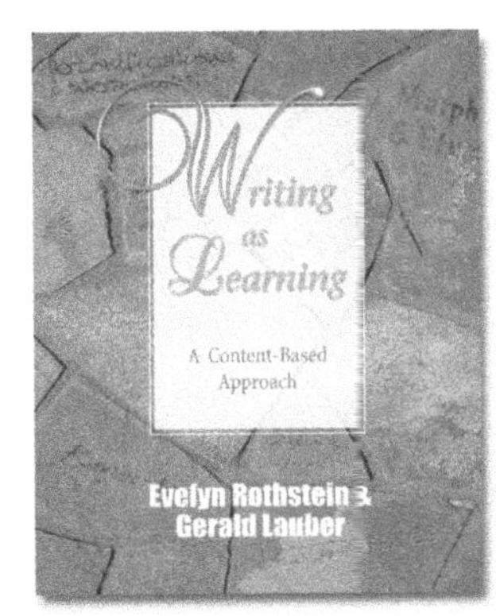

Many teachers use the concepts underlying metacognition when they teach KWL, a procedure developed by Donna Ogle

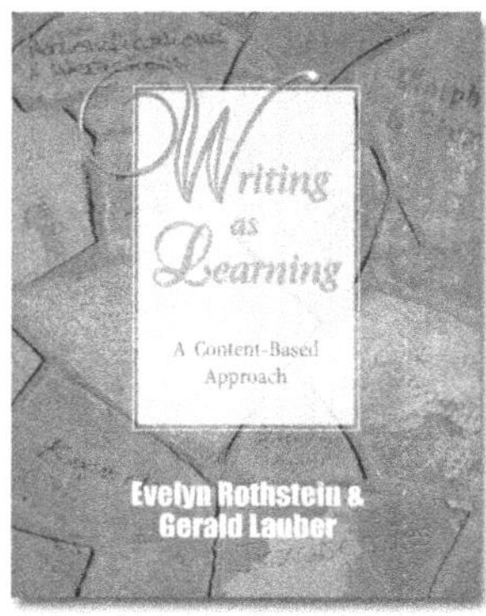

(1986) that asks the student to identify for themselves "what I **k**now," "what I **w**ant to know," and "what I have **l**earned." Through this procedure, the learner can conceptualize or visualize what she or he already understands and then keep track of new understandings that accrue.

Metacognition Through Writing

In this strategy, the students begin by writing what they believe they already know about a specific topic. The purpose of this writing is to develop an awareness of prior knowledge in preparation for adding new knowledge. Metacognition requires reflection on what one has already learned and what one either needs to know or would like to know. When used extensively in every subject and throughout the grades, metacognition (through writing) fosters curiosity to learn more (Costa 1991) and provides strategies for knowing how to learn more (Perkins 1992). Students who use this strategy before, during, and after learning a new topic develop a skill for acquiring and applying knowledge, thereby making the move from tacit learners to reflective learners. Following is a plan for metacognition through writing:

Before starting a new topic, teachers can ask students to write what they believe they already know about that topic, using the sentence starter "I know that I know something about. . . ."

The students complete the statement (e.g., "I know that I know something about the Mississippi River") and then write one, two, or three sentences (depending on grade level and/or ability) that tell what they know. At the conclusion of the writing, the students add, "Now you know something that I know about. . . ."

Here is the prior knowledge statement of a fifth grade student writing in a social studies class.

Metacognition—Prior Knowledge

I know that I know something about the Mississippi River. It is a very long river in the United States. It is in the state of Mississippi. Many steamboats travel on this river. Now you know something that I know about the Mississippi River.

The student then studies the Mississippi River through readings and class discussions, completes a Taxonomy, and Composes with Keywords. The student then writes a Metacognitive Statement to indicate new knowledge, as shown in the following example.

Metacognition—New Knowledge

After reading my social studies book and looking at a map of the United States, I now know more about the Mississippi River than I knew before. I now know that the Mississippi begins in the northern part of the United States at Lake Superior. It touches the states of Minnesota, Wisconsin, Michigan, Iowa, Illinois, Missouri, Kentucky, Tennessee, Arkansas, Mississippi, and Louisiana. It meets the Ohio River in southern Illinois and empties into the Gulf of Mexico in New Orleans. This is some of the important information I know about the Mississippi River.

For the final piece of writing, the student adds his or her recognition of the following knowledge.

Metacognition—Advanced Knowledge

I further know that other rivers besides the Ohio flow into the Mississippi. They are the Missouri, the Red, and the Arkansas Rivers. The Mississippi River is 3,779 kilometers or 2,348 miles long. Many cities are on the river. Some of these cities are St. Paul, Dubuque, Hannibal, St. Louis, Memphis, Vicksburg, Baton Rouge, and New Orleans. Many boats travel on the river today, not only steamboats. Sometimes this river has terrible floods that destroy homes and farms. The last flood was in 1993 and I hope there will be no more for a

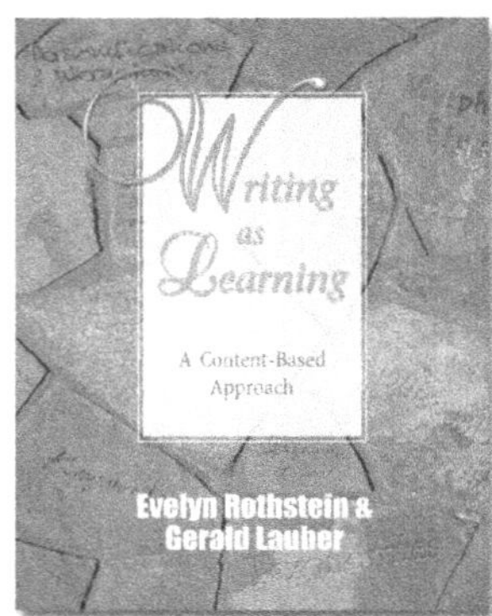

long time. This is my advanced knowledge about the Mississippi River. I now know much more about the Mississippi River than anyone else in my family.

Starting Sentences for Metacognitive Writing

One of the easiest ways to start a metacognitive piece of writing is to use starting sentences. The complexity of the information to be elicited can vary based on the students' level of expertise and knowledge. Starting sentences offer many students—especially beginning writers and writers who have trouble thinking of what to write—a way to get started. Teachers can provide students a list of sample starting sentences or brainstorm starting sentences with students. Lists can be posted in the classroom or copied into students' writing notebooks for reference. Following are several sample starting sentences.

Starting Sentences

- Before I read ________________, I only knew these facts (or this information).
- As I listened (read, watched) _______________, I better understood (realized, learned) _______________.
- After I heard ________________, I remembered (thought about, considered) ________________.
- As a result of reading (hearing, listening to, studying, observing) ________________, I now can ________.

Starters also can be variations of "I know."

- I know that I know a lot about . . .
- I know that I know something about . . .
- I know many things about . . .
- I need to know more about . . .
- I know very little about . . .
- I know nothing about . . .
- I would like to know more about . . .

A fourth grade student used one of the starters to write the following Metacognition paragraph.

> I know that I know something about rivers. Rivers flow but I don't know what makes them flow. I know something about the Hudson River, but I don't anything about other rivers. The Hudson River has a lot of bridges across it. One is called the Tappan Zee Bridge. That is what I know about rivers so far.

Using Taxonomies to Write Metacognitive Statements

As soon as students are able to write, they can compose Metacognitive statements based on the many things they already know about and the new information they are learning. For primary students and students who benefit from visual prompts, teachers can develop a Taxonomy with the students using the sentence "I know that I know something about . . ." and post it in the classroom or have students put it in their Personal Thesaurus notebooks. From these topics, students can write about what they know in their journals or can share information with classmates during a class activity. The topics on the Taxonomy also can be related to materials from readers and other texts, followed by the students writing metacognitive statements on these topics. For example, if the students will be reading about kittens, they first can write what they already know, and then write about "I now know. . . ." Figure 11.1 shows a sample Taxonomy for young students.

Using the "I know that I know something about" Taxonomy, primary students wrote the following metacognitive writings.

> I know about my Mommy. She is good to me. She reads to me. She makes me take a bath. Now you know about my Mommy. —*Kindergarten student*

Taxonomy Sheet

I KNOW THAT I KNOW SOMETHING ABOUT . . .	
A	animals
B	babies
C	carrots
D	daddies
E	eggs
F	friends
G	grandmas and grandpas
H	houses
I	ice cream
J	jump rope
K	kittens
L	lemonade
M	mommies
N	nighttime
O	owls
P	paper
Q	quilts
R	running
S	school
T	television
U	umbrellas
V	voices
W	water
X	x rays
Y	yellow
Z	zoos

Figure 11.1

Metacognition
Knowing What You Know

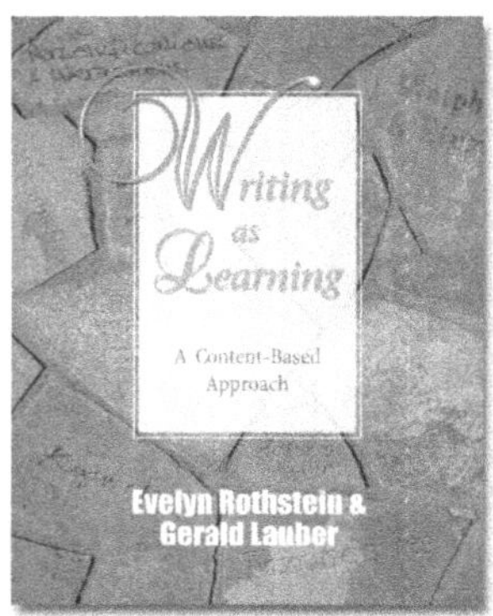

I know that I know something about ice cream. It can be chocolate or vanilla. If you're a grown up it can be something like pistachino (sic) which is green. It comes in a cone or a cup or sometimes on a stick. Now you know something about ice cream. —*First grade student*

My teacher read us Charlotte's Web and now I know what a runt is. It's a baby pig that is too small to live. So sometimes the farmer wants to kill it before it dies by itself. Wilbur was a runt, but Fern saved him from dying. Now I know what a runt pig is. —*Third grade student*

Using Metacognitive Writing to Consolidate Writing with Subject Areas

By the middle grades, students can reinforce their learning by writing metacognitive statements on a daily basis and for a variety of subject areas. The teacher can post a chart or agenda for the day that shows topics students can write about to sum up what they know, have learned, or need to learn.

Assignments may look something like this:

- Mathematics: After you have finished adding fractions with mixed denominators, write a metacognitive statement telling what you now know about fractions.
- Social studies: We will be starting a unit on the Constitution. Write a metacognitive statement telling three ideas that you believe are in the Constitution.
- Science: After you have read the section on "How Plants Make Their Food," write a metacognitive statement telling three new ideas that you learned as a result of your reading.
- Literature: Now that you have read the story of "Arachne and Athena," write a metacognitive statement with this opening "Before I read this story I did not know (or understand). . . . However, I now know (or understand). . . ."

Using Pre- and Post-Metacognition Writing

Students at the middle school or high school level often remember more and have better understanding of topics when they write pre-metacognitive statements, later followed by post-metacognitive statements. While similar to the previously mentioned prior knowledge statements, these differ in that students write two metacognitive statements, which allows them to compare what they knew before the lesson(s) and after the lesson(s). These pre- and post-statements are excellent for students to use in small cooperative groups of three or four where they can discuss what they first thought about the topic and what they have since learned. Better yet is when students in these groups add information they have heard from their classmates to their own writing. This system of pre- and post-writing is far more effective for selecting and reporting knowledge than answering questions from the back of the chapter and then copying the text to satisfy the question. Following are examples of teacher prompts and student responses using metacognition.

American History

Teacher Prompt: Today we will be discussing the Reconstruction Period after the Civil War. Using the Metacognition format, write what you think happened in America during this period of time.

Student's response before teacher's presentation: I know that after the Civil War the former slaves could not find jobs. They had no skills except what they did as slaves which was picking cotton or working in the master's house. The government would have to find a way to help both the slaves and the soldiers who had fought in the war. I think this is why this time was called Reconstruction.

Student's response after teacher's presentation: In today's class discussion, I learned that the southern governments that were in the Civil War passed laws that were called Black Codes. These laws made blacks pay high taxes if they worked at jobs that were not on a farm or plantation. These taxes made blacks go back to where they lived before the war and do the same kind of work. There were many other laws

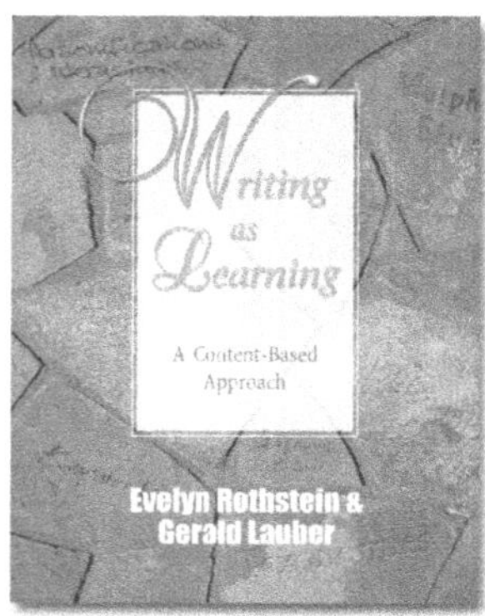

> against blacks. They could not buy land or own guns or even dogs. The worst thing was that their children could be taken from them if their old masters said they were unfit parents. Then the children would practically be slaves again to the masters who had taken them away from their family. I now realize that even though slavery was supposed to end because the North won the Civil War, blacks were not yet free or better off. —*Eleventh grade student*

Combining Strategies: Metacognitve Statement and Composing with Keywords

With the Taxonomy as the "holder" of the terms or vocabulary of a topic, the students have words for writing. Now they must select or draw upon those words that they find meaningful or significant to the topic. The students are becoming cognitive decision makers, making decisions as to what they will write about. Thus, with the words they have selected from the Taxonomy and with the opening metacognitive statement, students have what to say and a format for saying it. This arrangement is especially comfortable for students who ordinarily find writing difficult.

The following example is from a literature class studying Paul Zindel's novel *The Pigman.* Here the students used the strategy Composing with Keywords to write metacognitive statements that expressed their insights on loneliness as it related to the central character in the story, Mr. Pignati. The students first created a Taxonomy of words that describe loneliness (see Figure 11.2).

Next, the students selected three terms from the Taxonomy and wrote what they knew or understood about Mr. Pignati's loneliness. Following is an example written by an eighth grade student.

> The three words of loneliness that help me better understand Mr. Pignati are alienated, ostracized, and unfulfilled. To be alienated means to be unattached to the world, something like an alien. That is how Mr. Pignati feels after his wife dies.

He seems to have very little understanding of what people outside of his world do or feel is correct. Because he can't relate to other people and they can't relate to him, he is ostracized, meaning that no one, except Lorraine and John, want to associate with him. Finally I know that he is unfulfilled in his hopes and dreams. No one appreciates his collection of pigs or can even understand what this collection means to him. I feel sad for Mr. Pignati because I know and feel what loneliness does to destroy a person's sense of worth.

Taxonomy Sheet

ALONE, ALONE, ALL ALONE: THE SAD VOCABULARY OF LONELINESS

A	alone, alienated, abandoned, avoided
B	bored, bereft
C	
D	depressed, detached, disconnected, desolate
E	
F	friendless, forsaken
G	
H	homesick, helpless
I	ignored
J	jilted
K	
L	lonely
M	melancholy
N	
O	ostracized
P	
Q	
R	removed, rejected
S	sad, solemn, solitary, shut-in, shunned
T	tired
U	unfulfilled
V	
W	weary
X	xenophobic
Y	
Z	

Figure 11.2

Linking to the Computer

Metacognitive writing lends itself to using a template that provides a structure for student writers. The template can consist of sentence starters that prompt the writer to reflect on what he or she knows, wants to know, or knows following learning about a specific topic. The teacher can create a template in a word processing program, save it on disk or the computer's hard drive, and make it available to students when they use computers for writing. Charts showing the template can be posted above the computers for easy reference. Following are examples that can be used at different grade levels.

Primary

Metacognition—What Do I Know That I Know?

I know that I know something about ______.
First, I know ______.
I also know ______.
Finally, I know ______.
Now you know something that I know about ______.

Metacognition
Knowing What You Know

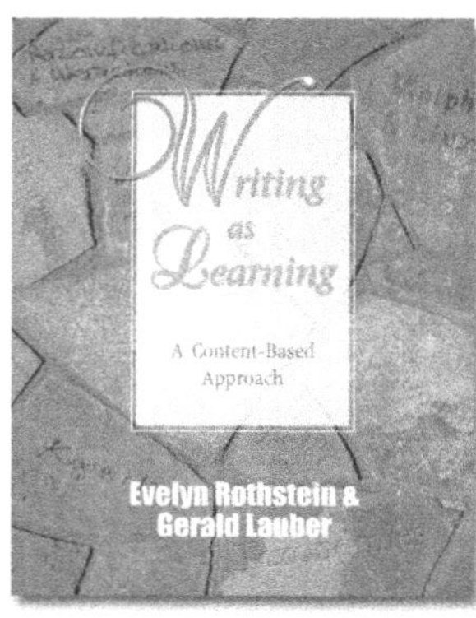

Metacognition—What Would I Like to Know?

I would like to know more about ______.
First, I would like to know why ______.
Then I would like to know where ______.
Last, I would like to know when ______.
These are some of the things I would like to know about ______.

Metacognition—What Do I Need to Know?

I need to know how to ______.
Then I would be able to ______.
I would also be able to ______.
Finally, I could ______.
These are the reasons I need to know how to ______.

Middle School and Secondary Grades

Metacognition—I Know What I Know

In my (subject area) class, I know that I know or under stand several important ideas.
First, I know/understand ______.
In addition, I ______.
Furthermore, I ______.
I am now prepared to ______.

Metacognition—As a Result of . . . I Now . . .

As a result of (reading, studying, listening, discussing), I now (realize, recognize, think about, dream of) ___.
I better understand ______.
Furthermore, I believe ______.
Above all, I ______.
This new (knowledge, discovery, idea, thought) will help me ______.

Metacognition—Present Knowledge to Future Knowledge

In my class, I have been studying (learning) ___________.

When I began this topic, I knew

1) ________________________________

2) ________________________________

3) ________________________________

Over the next few weeks (months), I expect to know

1) ________________________________

2) ________________________________

3) ________________________________

This new knowledge will ______.

As students develop the habit of writing metacognitive statements, they gain a greater sense of ownership of their learning. They have a tangible representation of how much knowledge they started with and how much knowledge they are adding and can add. Metacognitive writing can be compared to setting up one of those charts or "thermometers" that are used to record fund-raising results: "Here is where I began, here is how much I have achieved to date, and here is where I have to go."

REFERENCES

Costa, A. L. 1991. *The school as a home for the mind.* Palatine, IL: IRI/SkyLight Training and Publishing.

Hirsch, E. D. Jr. 1987. *Cultural literacy: What every American needs to know.* Boston: Houghton Mifflin.

Oxford Dictionary of Quotations. 1980. 3rd ed. New York: Oxford University Press.

Ogle, D. 1986. K-W-L: A teaching model that develops active reading of expository text. *The Reading Teacher.* 39: 564–71.

Perkins, D. 1992. *Smart schools.* New York: Free Press.

Zindel, P. 1978. *The pigman.* New York: Harper & Row.

Planning Problem-Based Learning for the Classroom

by **Diane Ronis**

In this chapter, teachers are guided through the actual process of carrying out a problem-based learning experience and are presented with ideas for incorporating problem-based learning into their existing curricula.

Planning for Integrated Learning

The best way for teachers to begin creating a problem-based learning experience is to use a planning outline (see Figure 12.1) that covers all the important aspects of a PBL experience. To better understand planning strategies, teachers may want to begin by applying the questions posed in the outline to a past unit, since the topic will already be familiar. The outline in Figure 12.1 should serve only as a general guide; not every question is applicable to every project.

The following example demonstrates how one teacher used the guidelines given in the outline in Figure 12.1 to prepare a PBL project that met her curriculum needs.

The teacher in this example, Ms. Jones, is a sixth-grade math teacher who is working on a graphing unit with her class and wants to increase her students' understanding of how different graphs can be developed and employed. She decides her topic

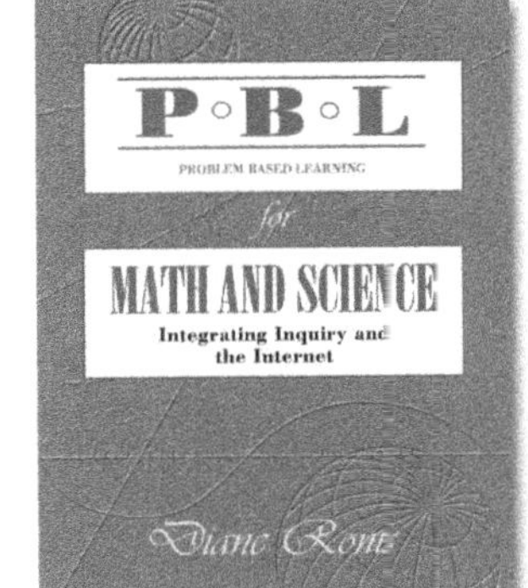

Adapted from *Problem-Based Learning for Math and Science: Integrating Inquiry and the Internet* by Diane Ronis, pp. 97–112 and 169–75.

Planning Problem-Based Learning for the Classroom

Planning Outline

I. CONCEPTS

When contemplating concepts, consider the following:

- On which important math and science concepts should this unit focus?
- In what ways are these concepts defined?
- What might be referred to as the big ideas?

II. PROCESSES

Decide which of the following processes to include (one process or several can be included, depending on the unit):

- Thinking
- Collecting data
- Analyzing data
- Drawing conclusions
- Representing knowledge

III. GENERALIZATIONS

Use the following questions to identify ways in which these concepts can be connected or combined to form the kinds of generalizations mathematicians and scientists accept as true and important.

- Which relationships among these concepts are relevant?
- What are the characteristics, definitions, examples, and/or categories that distinguish each of the concepts?
- What are similarities and/or differences among the concepts?
- What are some of the consequences, causes, effects, and/or predictions that can be made based upon these concepts or processes?
- Under what conditions or in which contexts will these concepts exist or be accomplished?
- Upon what assumptions are these concepts based?

IV. THEORY

Design a way these assumptions can be linked so as to form a theory that is true and important to know.

V. PERFORMANCE TASKS OR PRODUCTS

Decide on the kinds of performance tasks or products students will create to demonstrate their learning (their mastery of the science and math content and processes used). Ask:

- Will students be using the skills and knowledge scientists, engineers, designers, and so forth use in the creation of this performance task or product?
- How does this task or product relate to the developmental needs and interests of the students?
- What are the specific qualities and characteristics that must be contained in the evidence of learning?
- How will production, perception, and reflection be documented?

(continued on next page)

Figure 12.1

VI. ASSESSMENT

Decide how the evidence of learning will be assessed. Ask:

- What kind of authentic and alternative assessment measures will be used?
- What criteria (rubric and benchmarks) will be used for assessing students' products?
- Will the products be the kind that fit the portfolio profile? (Do they conform to the requirements and/or parameters of a portfolio?)

VII. LESSON PLANS

Map out a series of lesson plans for the unit design. Ask:

- What will students do to learn?
- What resources will be used?
- How are these lessons related to students' interests?
- How are these lessons related to students' needs?
- What questions will they ask?

VIII. QUESTIONING STRATEGIES

Decide on the questioning strategies to be employed. Ask:

- What questions should be asked to help students define concepts?
- What questions should be asked to help students link concepts to meaningful generalizations?
- What questions should be asked to help students identify evidence that the generalizations are true?

Figure 12.1 (continued)

will be surveys, and begins creating her problem by determining that the concepts and big ideas important to this topic are measurement gathering, collating, and analyzing the data and representing that data. The processes Ms. Jones wishes to include are collecting data, analyzing data, and drawing conclusions. By asking herself "Which relationships among these concepts are relevant?" and determining that they all involve uses of data, Ms. Jones is able to identify ways in which these concepts can be connected. Ms. Jones decides the performance task will be for students to create graphs that represent the survey data. She wants the graphs to be accurate representations of the data gathered by the students as well as representative of the conclusions drawn from the data. Ms. Jones' task relates to student interest because sixth graders are very interested in learning about the opinions of their peers, which

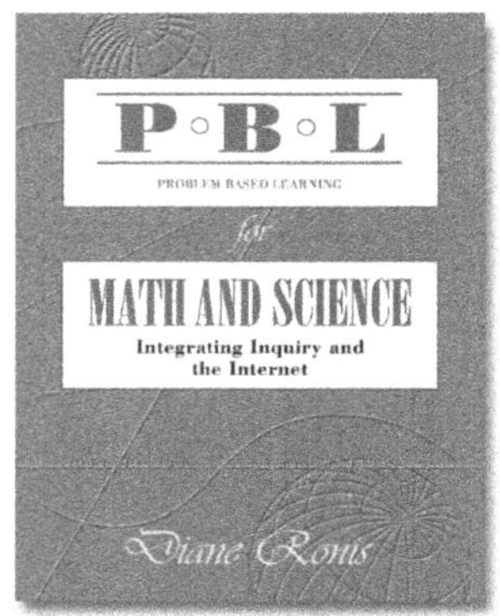

they will discover from the results of the surveys. The specific qualities and characteristics Ms. Jones decides the students should include in their evidence of learning for this unit are accurate data records and accurately constructed graphs that illustrate the conclusions of the survey. Ms. Jones decides to use student activity logs to document students' production, perceptions, and reflection. She also decides to use group and individual reflections for this purpose.

Ms. Jones decides to assess the evidence of learning with a rubric measuring the following characteristics:

- Knowledge of data-recording methods
- Accuracy in data recording
- Accuracy of graph construction and selection
- Clarity of the graph
- Graph creativity and originality
- Teamwork and cooperation

An example of the rubric Ms. Jones developed to assess this project is shown in Figure 12.2.

Guidelines for Implementing a PBL Project

The characteristics, approaches, and aspects of problem-based learning can be combined into guidelines teachers can use as a framework for designing and implementing their own PBL projects. The following steps provide a helpful guide teachers can follow when setting up a PBL project.

Step 1. Teachers begin the PBL process by developing a real-world, open-ended, and messy problem: a problem without a clear-cut solution. This problem should relate to the unit that is being taught in that it should involve the application of the content skills and concepts covered.

Step 2. After teachers have chosen a messy and authentic problem, they need to think of ways in which students can use different research methods and tools in their quest for a solution to the problem. Some research options might include

Rubric for Survey Graph

QUALITY EVALUATED	NOVICE	BASIC	PROFICIENT	ADVANCED
Knowledge of data recording methods	Graph displays no understanding of recording methods	Graph displays partial understanding	Graph displays solid understanding	Graph displays a sophisticated level of understanding
Accuracy in data recording	No evidence of accuracy displayed	Partial accuracy is displayed	Data is recorded accurately	Data is recorded accurately, clearly, and neatly
Accuracy of graph construction and selection	Incorrect graph type used in addition to faulty construction	Correct graph type used but faulty construction	Correct graph choice and construction	Sophisticated use of graphing to represent data
Clarity of graph (Was it easy to understand?)	Graph makes no sense	Graph makes some sense	Graph is easy to understand	Graph clarity allows for sophisticated inferences and extensions to be created
Graph creativity and originality	Little or no creativity displayed	Some creativity evident	Graph displays creativity	Graph is highly creative and innovative
Teamwork and cooperation	Students could not cooperate or work together	Students worked together at times	Students worked together	Students worked together and cooperated at all times

Figure 12.2

conducting research through the Internet, contacting possible sources in the local community, communicating with professionals who work in the field, and so forth.

After teachers have created their project, they can evaluate its effectiveness before presenting it to the class using the evaluation form shown in Figure 12.3. The purpose of this checklist is to help teachers to become "reflective practitioners."

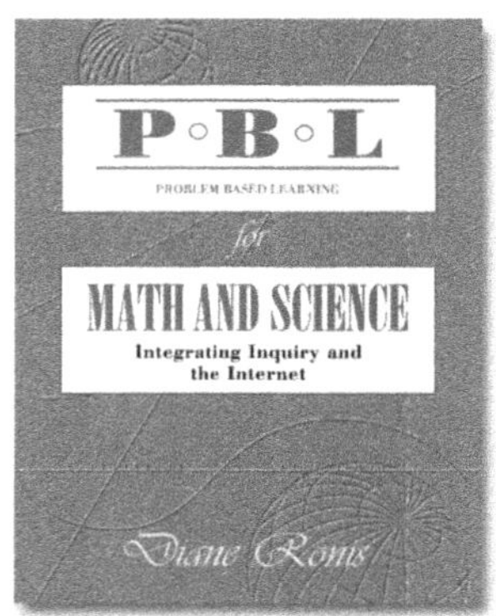

Step 3. Next, teachers should present the problem to their students. Several techniques can be used to do this. One technique is simulation (role-playing) in which students encounter situations similar to those professionals deal with daily. Other techniques are the inquiry contract, in which the parameters of the problem are set up and discussed, and the case study, in which students are presented with the problem and are asked to deal with it as if they were professionally involved. Workshops and study questions are also options. Depending on the technique used, problem presentation can include teachers reading the problem aloud to students or having students read and discuss a written summary outlining the specifics of the problem situation with their partners or teams.

Step 4. After the problem presentation, students can begin their research. Teachers can help students get started by providing them with a list of appropriate Web sites or other research sources that could prove to be a helpful starting point. Once the teacher has set students on their course, students are on their own to conduct their research, plan their strategies, form their hypotheses, and find their solutions. During this time the teacher continually circulates and makes him- or herself available to students, periodically asking questions designed to help keep students on track, but not offering so much information as to lead the inquiry.

Questions to Promote Problem Solving

No matter how well designed a PBL project might be, times may arise during the project when students are unsure of how to start or continue the work needed to reach a solution. In this case, they may look to the teacher for help. While teachers want to avoid providing students with answers or directions, they can use various analytic strategies to encourage students to use problem-solving skills. These strategies include the following:

- Recalling and observing evidence related to the problem

Problem-Based Learning Activity Evaluation Form

General Information

Title and Source: ___

General Description: ___

Standards Addressed

Math: ___

Science: ___

Technology: ___

Approximate Time Frame: ___

Instruction Criteria Continuum	Excellent		Adequate		Weak	Point Total
AFFECT						
• Captures student interest	5	4	3	2	1	
• Has meaning and relevancy	5	4	3	2	1	
CONTENT						
• Is developmentally appropriate	5	4	3	2	1	
• Elicits higher-level thinking skills	5	4	3	2	1	
• Engages students in original and creative thinking	5	4	3	2	1	
• Involves research directly and authentic sources	5	4	3	2	1	
• Elicits student interpretation and conjecture	5	4	3	2	1	
PEDAGOGY						
• Has clear goals and objectives	5	4	3	2	1	
• Has multiple solution possibilities	5	4	3	2	1	
• Elicits the generation of multiple strategies	5	4	3	2	1	
• Promotes inquiry	5	4	3	2	1	
• Elicits student explanations	5	4	3	2	1	

Comments:

Total Project Score: ___

Figure 12.3

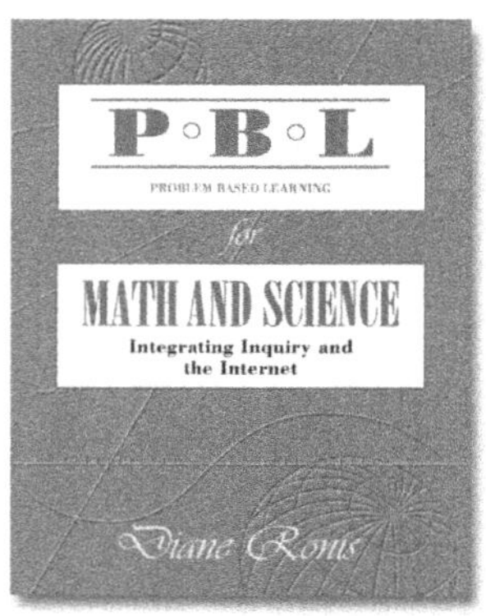

- Comparing and clarifying evidence according to predetermined criteria
- Defining the evidence so that it is clear and unambiguous
- Interpreting the data to explain its meaning and significance
- Generalizing from the evidence to derive a principal or main idea
- Inferring from the evidence to predict and hypothesize beyond the data

Teachers can ask students many types of questions to prompt use of these strategies. When students need help understanding, defining, formulating, or explaining the task they are working on, teachers can ask students questions such as the following:

- What do you need to do in order to complete this task?
- What can you tell me about this task that I don't already know?
- How would you interpret that information?
- Could you explain this information in your own words?
- Is there information that seems to be missing?

Sometimes students may come to a point in their research where they lose focus or move away from a solution path that is valid. To get students back on track, teachers can ask students questions that help them see where their thinking may have gone off course. For example, teachers might ask questions such as:

- How can you determine whether or not your answer makes sense?
- Is there anything you might have overlooked?
- What made you think that was what you should do?
- Does this raise any questions for you?

When teachers ask such questions, they must make sure they are not revealing any part of the solution through the questions. Good questions demonstrate respect for students' thinking and understanding and are designed to include the students' own words. For example, teachers might ask: "Why do you think (students' own words)?" or "What do you mean by (students' own words)?" These types of questions require students to make their thoughts and meanings explicit.

Some of the types of questions teachers can use to foster problem solving include the following:

- **Open-ended questions.** These questions have more than one possible answer and cannot be answered with a simple "yes" or "no." For example: "What are some of the things that happen when . . . ?" or "What other methods have you . . . ?"
- **Divergent questions.** These questions get students thinking about other paths they can take in their thinking and may be answered in a variety of ways. For example: "What completely different result would occur if . . . ?" or "We have all positive . . . . What are some negative . . . ?"
- **Thought-provoking questions.** These questions demand insight and reasoning. They cannot be answered simply and require both logic and reflection. For example: "What have I come to know or come to know differently?" or "What would have to happen or be true in order for . . . ?"
- **Clear questions.** These questions focus on specific phenomena. They cannot be answered with vague generalizations, but rather provide a clear framework for the desired response. For example: "What would happen if . . . ?" or "How would you . . . ?"
- **Focusing questions.** These questions help students to determine outcomes, sequences, similarities and differences, or cause and effect. For example: "What else is different about . . . as opposed to . . . ?"

Teachers can use different types of questions to achieve various purposes during the PBL process. For example, in the scenario described earlier, Ms. Jones decided she would begin the PBL activity by using open-ended questions to get her students thinking about the rationale for surveys. She began with

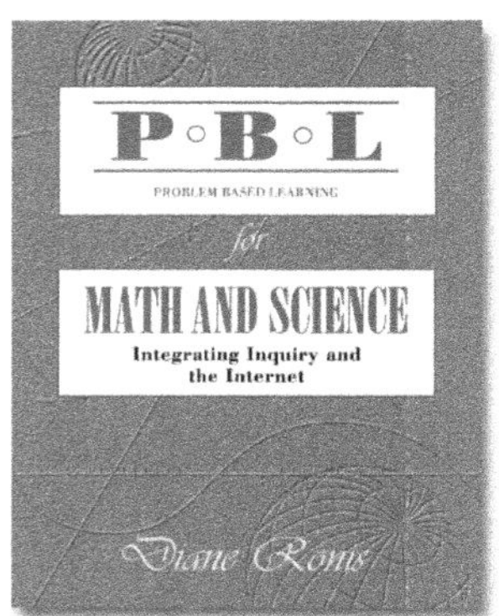

the following question: "What are some methods an ice cream company might use to find out which of their flavors is the most popular?" Later on in the unit she decided to use the following question, which is both divergent and thought-provoking, to help her students think about the validity of their results: "What completely different result would occur if the company decided to survey older ice-cream eaters instead of young ice-cream eaters?" She then used the following focusing questions after her students had completed their research because she wanted them to understand how their results might be used. She asked her students: "If you brought the results of your ice-cream survey to the local store, what effect do you think it might have on the flavors of ice cream they order from their distributor? Why do you think this?"

Figure 12.4 provides a list of specific questions teachers can ask students to facilitate various goals in the problem-solving process.

Encouraging Reflection in Problem Solving

Teachers can ask students the following questions to help students achieve success with the problem-solving process.

Goal: To help students to comprehend the problem

- What must be done for this task? What can you tell me about it?
- Could you explain it in your own words?
- Is there something that is missing or is there something you can eliminate?

Goal: To get students to organize their approach to the problem

- Where could you find the information you will need to solve this?
- What have you tried so far? What steps did you take?
- What did not work?
- Do you have a system? A plan? A strategy?
- Have you tried tables, charts, lists, diagrams, etc.?

Goal: To help students recognize relationships

- What is the relationship of this to that?
- How is it the same? How is it different?
- Can it be broken down into smaller parts? What would those parts be?

Goal: To encourage students to expand their thinking about possible solutions

- Have you tried making a guess?
- Might a different method work as well or better?
- What else have you tried?

Goal: To prompt students to create a hypothesis

- What do you predict will happen?
- How do you feel about your answer?
- What do you think comes next?
- What else would you like to know?

Goal: To encourage students to reflect and self-assess

- What do you need to do next?
- What are your strengths and weaknesses?
- What have you accomplished?
- Was your own group participation appropriate and helpful?

Goal: To prompt students to formulate solutions

- Is that the only possible answer?
- Besides retracing your steps, how can you determine whether or not your answer makes sense?
- Is there anything you might have overlooked?

Goal: To get students to examine results

- What made you think that was what you should do?
- Is there a real-life situation where this might be used?
- Where else could this strategy be useful?
- Can you make a general rule from this?

Figure 12.4

Planning Problem-Based Learning for the Classroom

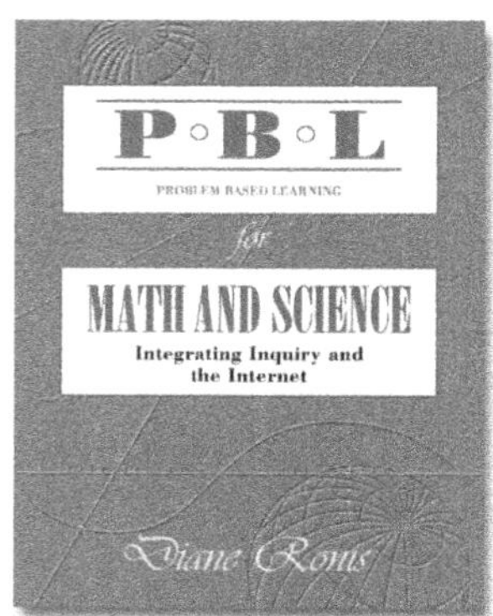

The following inquiry project can be used by teachers to engage students in a problem-based learning experience using the case study technique.

Multilevel Internet Project: The Mississippi Delta Dilemma

The following inquiry project came out of a dilemma faced by a particular geographical area. Teachers might modify this unit by finding a dilemma in their own locale. Teachers can use their own community as a starting point for the creation of a relevant and meaningful problem situation in need of a solution.

This project can be geared to the elementary, middle, or secondary levels depending on the degree of depth and detail the teacher requires for student research as well as the level of mathematics required for the calculations. Teachers can reduce the number of calculations to make the project more suitable for the elementary level by placing the emphasis on the scientific research aspects of this ecological dilemma rather than the mathematical and computational aspects. To do this, teachers could substitute relative math terms such as "a large amount, an amount greater than, an amount less than" and so forth to provide a more generalized view of the problem.

Note: While students are eager to undertake research using the Internet and often do not ask for or require assistance, the pedagogical challenge for educators is to encourage students to critically evaluate the authority of the information source. Teachers can encourage students to do such critical evaluation by reviewing the importance of examining information sources critically. It often helps for teachers to stress the importance of both a source's origin (e.g., whether it is from an academic institution such as a university or another well-known organization such as the government) and its background (information about a source is usually provided on the source's homepage).

Project Standards (Grades 5–8)

I. MATHEMATICS CONTENT STANDARDS

Standard 1: Numbers and Operations

Instructional programs from pre-kindergarten through grade 12 should enable all students to

- understand numbers, ways of representing numbers, relationships among numbers, and number systems;

- understand the meaning of operations and how they relate to each other;
- compute fluently and make reasonable estimates.

Standard 4: Measurement

Instructional programs from pre-kindergarten through grade 12 should enable all students to

- understand attributes, units, and systems of measurement;
- apply a variety of techniques, tools, and formulas for determining measurements.

Standard 5: Data Analysis and Probability

Instructional programs from pre-kindergarten through grade 12 should enable all students to

- formulate questions that can be addressed with data and collect, organize, and display relevant data to answer them;
- select and use appropriate statistical methods to analyze data;
- develop and evaluate inferences and predictions that are based on data.

Standard 6: Problem Solving

Instructional programs from pre-kindergarten through grade 12 should enable all students to

- build new mathematical knowledge through problem solving;
- solve problems that arise in mathematics and in other contexts;
- apply and adapt a wide variety of strategies to solve problems;
- monitor and reflect on the process of mathematical problem solving.

Standard 7: Reasoning and Proof

Instructional programs from pre-kindergarten through grade 12 should enable all students to

- select and use various types of reasoning and methods of proof.

Standard 8: Communication

Instructional programs from pre-kindergarten through grade 12 should enable all students to

- organize and consolidate their mathematical thinking through communication;
- communicate their mathematical thinking coherently and clearly to peers, teachers, and others;
- analyze and evaluate the mathematical thinking and strategies of others.

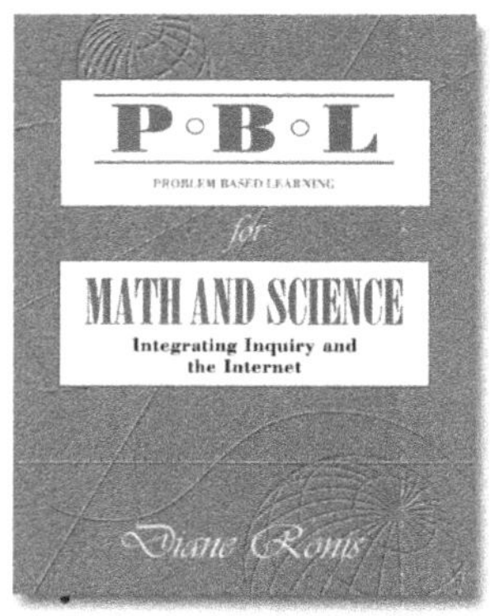

Standard 9: Connections

Instructional programs from pre-kindergarten through grade 12 should enable all students to

- recognize and use connections among mathematical ideas;
- understand how mathematical ideas interconnect and build on one another to produce a coherent whole;
- recognize and apply mathematics in contexts outside of mathematics.

Standard 10: Representation

Instructional programs from pre-kindergarten through grade 12 should enable all students to

- use representations to model and interpret physical, social, and mathematical phenomena.

II. SCIENCE CONTENT STANDARDS (1996)

Content Standard A: Science as Inquiry

Students should develop:

- Abilities necessary to do scientific inquiry
- Understandings about scientific inquiry

Content Standard C: Life Science

Students should develop an understanding of:

- Populations and ecosystems

Content Standard D: Earth and Space

Students should develop an understanding of:

- Energy in the earth system

Content Standard E: Science and Technology

Students should develop:

- Abilities of technological design
- Understandings about science and technology

Content Standard F: Science in Personal and Social Perspective

Students should develop an understanding of:

- Science and technology in local, national, and global challenges

Content Standard G: History and Nature of Science

Students should develop an understanding of:

- Science as a human endeavor
- Nature of scientific knowledge
- Historical perspectives

III. TECHNOLOGY FOUNDATION STANDARDS ([ISTE], [NETS] 1998.)

Basic Operations and Concepts

- Students demonstrate a sound understanding of the nature and operation of technology systems.
- Students are proficient in the use of technology.

Technology Productivity Tools

- Students use technology tools to enhance learning, increase productivity, and promote creativity.
- Students use productivity tools to collaborate in constructing technology-enhanced models, preparing publications, and producing other creative works.

Technology Communications Tools

- Students use telecommunications to collaborate, publish, and interact with peers, experts, and other audiences.
- Students use a variety of media and formats to communicate information and ideas effectively to multiple audiences.

Technology Research Tools

- Students use technology to locate, evaluate, and collect information from a variety of sources.
- Students use technology tools to process data and report results.
- Students evaluate and select new information resources and technological innovations based on the appropriateness to specific tasks.

Technology Problem-Solving and Decision-Making Tools

- Students use technology resources for solving problems and making informed decisions.
- Students employ technology in the development of strategies for solving problems in the real world.

Project Task

An environmental project for the Mississippi Delta area is presented in Figure 12.5. The class is to break into groups to research both the pros and cons of the situation and be ready to present a case in defense of one of the positions (either pro or con).

At the middle level, teachers can copy Figure 12.5 and hand it out to students to read and discuss within their groups. Students should read the information and discuss the pros and cons independently of each other. Once the pros and cons have been discussed among the groups, it is a good idea to have some class discussion about the merits and

(continued on page 182)

Environmental project

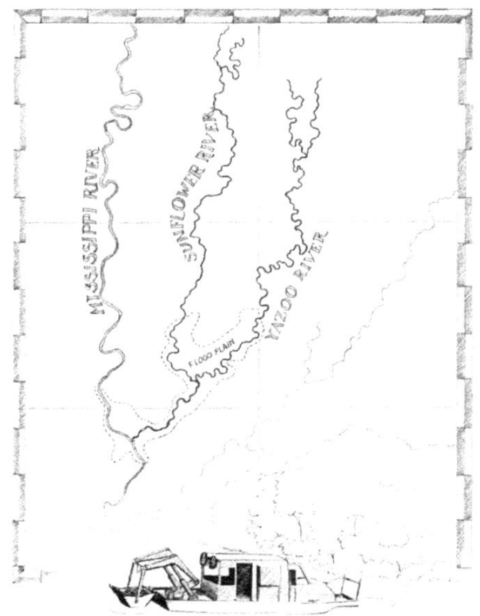

Consider the following after reading the information below:

- What are the two opposing viewpoints presented here?
- How might each position be defended for the plan and against the plan?

Every spring the rising Mississippi River turns the Mississippi Delta area into a vast, forested sea. It is an annual ritual of high water, as local people call it, and it has been going on for thousands of years. Although the water sometimes rises as much as 30 feet and stays at that level for weeks at a time, locals never use the word *flood,* which would imply an unexpected, disastrous event. To them, the yearly high tide is simply part of the natural rhythm of life in the lower Delta.

Today, the land is owned by the U.S. Army Corps of Engineers. It sits at ground zero for a series of plans designed by the Corps to drain and control flooding in the Delta area. The two most notable projects are a $62 million plan to dredge and clear more than 100 miles of the Big Sunflower River to reduce flooding, and the construction of a $150 million backwater pumping plant along Steele Bayou, which would transfer floodwaters from one section of the Delta to another.

While the Army Corps is pushing ahead with the dredging of the Big Sunflower, critics of both plans question whether U.S. taxpayers should have to pay for projects that will benefit only a small number of local landowners while destroying precious natural resources. At stake are thousands of acres of some of the nation's most productive wetlands and bottomland hardwood forests, which include cypress trees more than 1,000 years old, and a languorous river that nurtures what biologists believe is the most dense colony of freshwater mussels on the planet.

In 1963, the Corps bulldozed area woodlands to make way for a system of levees, canals, and pumps that were designed to protect the lower Delta from interior and backwater flooding. The levees were to shut out the Mississippi River backwater, and the pumps were designed to lift water from the interior Delta and discharge it into the Mississippi. The goal was to make more land available for agriculture. The clearing of hundreds of thousands of acres of trees in the 1960s and 1970s—most of which were merely pushed into windrows and burned—was devastating to wildlife. The floods, meanwhile, persisted, and when the price of soybeans fell in the early 1980s, much of the new land created by the Army Corps was abandoned. Today, a wildlife-based economy is emerging in the lower Delta, with resorts offering hunting and fishing excursions as well as nonconsumptive recreational opportunities such as hiking and bird watching. Meanwhile, thousands of acres have been voluntarily reforested or enrolled in federal conservation programs. So why is the U.S. Army Corps of Engineers proceeding with its plans?

The Yazoo pumps and Big Sunflower dredging projects are leftovers from the early 1940s when Congress authorized the most ambitious flood-control program in U.S. history in the Mississippi Delta.

(continued on next page)

Figure 12.5

These projects are linked with upstream flood-control works that have since been completed. Since the overall plan was not finished in the 40s and 50s, the benefits went only to people upriver, and those in the lower Delta were left out.

Many area residents are for the plan, but those who are opposed to it fear that

- Dredging the Big Sunflower River will destroy valuable ecosystems in the river, cause further erosion of the river banks, and waste taxpayer dollars
- The dredging project might increase the current levels of both flooding and erosion (According to Army Corps figures, more than 200,000 acres of cleared land in the backwater area flood on average every five years, and some as often as twice a year.)
- The project represents a threat to mussel beds that are thousands of years old. A biologist with the U.S. Fish and Wildlife Service in Mississippi notes that the mussel beds in the Big Sunflower River represent the most dense accumulation of biomass in the world. As much as 100 pounds of mussels can be found in a square meter of river bottom.

The Corps has altered its plans for the Big Sunflower as a result of negotiations over the past three or four years, but the dredging might still remove an estimated 40 percent of the mussel beds. Tulane University geologist Barry Kohl worries that the project could also release DDT trapped in river sediments, causing more environmental damage downstream. The experts believe that the issue is not whether to have flood control, since some flood control is essential, but where to draw the line.

Last fall, the National Wildlife Federation determined that the line was violated when the Army Corps, in its plans to dredge the Big Sunflower, violated U.S. law. According to the federal Water Resources Development Act, proposed water projects must have only a negligible impact on wildlife and its habitat and local sponsors must share the costs of the project. In the case of the Big Sunflower, the Corps maintains that its plans are exempt from this 1986 law because the project amounts to nothing more than "maintenance" on a portion of the river that was authorized for dredging by Congress in 1944. The National Wildlife Federation (NWF) filed a lawsuit against the U.S. government in November of 1998 to stop the project. The NWF maintains that flooding problems can be addressed with less expensive approaches, such as conservation easements that would give landowners financial incentives to reforest lands.

Such approaches could lessen the need for another controversial flood-control scheme, the Yazoo pump project. This ambitious plan involves building the world's largest pumps, which would lift 10,000 cubic feet of water per second from Steele Bayou and the Big Sunflower into the Yazoo near its meeting point with the Mississippi. The volume is equivalent to the average flow of the Delaware River, and this would be added to the Mississippi's flow during floods.

How many people will benefit from such an expensive project? The Army Corps cannot say for sure, but critics maintain that the number may be as low as a few dozen and that flooding will be reduced, but not eliminated, on these people's land.

As part of its ongoing efforts to protect the nation's wetlands, the National Wildlife Federation (NWF), working with Trial Lawyers for Public Justice (TLPJ), has taken the U.S. Army Corps of Engineers to court to stop the Big Sunflower River dredging project. (TLPJ is a national public-interest law firm.) NWF is also working to persuade the Corps to abandon its Yazoo backwater pumps project.

Figure 12.5 (continued)

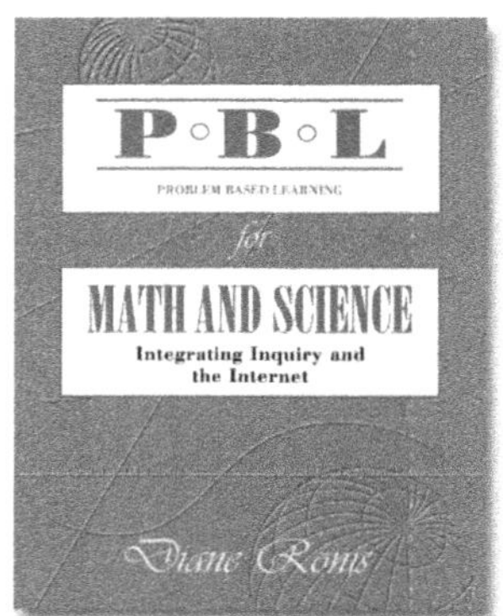

drawbacks regarding the different positions. This also helps to make students aware that issues such as these exist and that different opinions can be valid. After the positions have been discussed and students are familiar with the facts, they can begin conducting their research on both positions via the Internet using the Web sites listed under "Internet Resources."

Internet Resources

http://www.nwf.org/

The National Wildlife Federation's homepage can provide teachers with many additional PBL project ideas dealing with ecology, and also serves as an excellent jumping off point for student Internet research on numerous and varied issues involving ecology and conservation.

http://www.nwf.org/nwf/endangered/news/

The National Wildlife Federation's news page contains direct links to current information and articles dealing with endangered habitats.

http://www.nwf.org/gulfwetlands

Contains information about a National Wildlife Federation program that is working to protect wetlands in the Gulf region and the wildlife found in them.

http://www.tlpj.org

Contains information on Trial Lawyers for Public Justice. Students can look up current cases and peruse related issues and publications.

REFERENCES

Albanese, M. A., and S. Mitchell. 1993. Problem-based learning: A review of literature on its outcomes and implementation issues. *Academic Medicine*. 68(1): 52–81.

Alper, L., D. Findel, S. Fraser, and D. Resek. 1996. Problem-based mathematics not just for the college-bound. *Educational Leadership*. 53(8): 18–21.

Aspy, D. N., C. B. Aspy, and P. N. Quinby. 1993. What doctors can teach teachers about problem-based learning. *Educational Leadership*. 50(7): 22–4.

Boud, D., and G. Feletti. 1991. *The challenge of problem-based learning*. New York: St. Martin's Press.

Casey, M., and E. Tucker. 1994. Problem-centered classrooms. *Phi Delta Kappan*. 10(94): 139–43.

Cheek, D. 1992. *Thinking constructively about science, technology, and society education*. Albany, NY: State University of New York Press.

Clarke, J. 1997. Solving problems. In *Interdisciplinary high school teaching,* edited by J. Clarke and R. M. Agne. Boston: Allyn and Bacon.

Delisle, R. 1997. *How to use problem-based learning in the classroom.* Alexandria, VA: Association for Supervision and Curriculum Development.

Forman, S. L., and L. A. Steen. 1999. *Beyond eighth grade: Functional mathematics for life and work.* Berkeley, CA: National Center for Research in Vocational Education.

Gallagher, S. A., H. Rosenthal, and W. Stepien. 1992. The effects of problem-based learning on problem-solving. *Gifted Child Quarterly.* 36(4): 195–200.

Gallagher, S. A., B. T. Sher, W. J. Stepien, and D. Workman. 1995. Implementing problem-based learning in science classrooms. *School Science and Mathematics.* 95(3): 136–46.

Hendley, V. 1996, October. Let problems drive the learning. *AESS Prism,* 30–36.

International Technology Education Association (ITEA). 1995. *Technology for all Americans: A rationale and structure for the study of technology.* Reston, VA: Instructional Technology Education Association.

Mathematical Sciences Education Board. 1995. *Mathematical preparation of the technical workforce,* Mathematical Sciences Education Board: 5.

Nagel, N. G. 1996. *Learning through real-world problem solving: The power of integrative teaching.* Thousand Oaks, CA: Corwin Press.

National Center for Educational Statistics Third International Mathematics and Science Study. 1998. *Pursuing excellence: A study of U.S. fourth, eighth, and twelfth grade mathematics and science achievement in international context.* Washington, D.C.

National Commission on Excellence in Education. 1983. *A nation at risk: The imperative for educational reform.* U. S. Department of Education.

National Council of Teachers of Mathematics (NCTM). 2000. *Principles and standards for school mathematics.* Reston, VA: NCTM.

National Research Council. 1996. *A sampler of national science education standards.* Washington, D.C.: National Academy Press.

Nelson, G. 1999. Science literacy for all in the 21st century. *Educational Leadership.* 57(2): 14–17.

Norman, G. R., and H. G. Schmidt. 1992. The psychological basis of problem-based learning: A review of the evidence. *Academic Medicine.* 67(9): 557–65.

Perkins, D. 1992. *Smart schools: From training memories to educating minds.* New York: The Free Press.

Ronis, D. 1999. *Brain-compatible mathematics.* Arlington Heights, IL: SkyLight Training and Publishing.

Planning Problem-Based Learning for the Classroom

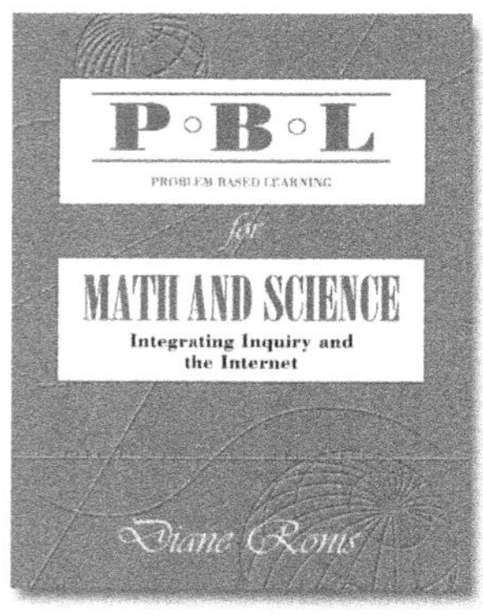

———. 2000. *Brain-compatible assessments.* Arlington Heights, IL: SkyLight Training and Publishing.

Savery, J. R., and T. M. Duffy. 1995. Problem-based learning: An instructional model and its constructivist framework. *Educational Technology.* 35(5): 31–35.

Stepien, W. J., and S. A. Gallagher. 1993. Problem-based learning: As authentic as it gets. *Educational Leadership.* 50(7): 25–28.

Stepien, W. J., S. A. Gallagher, and D. Workman. 1993. Problem-based learning for traditional and interdisciplinary classrooms. *Journal for the Education of the Gifted.* 16(4): 338–57.

Vernon, D., and R. Blake. 1993. Does problem-based learning work? A meta-analysis of evaluative research. *Academic Medicine.* 7(4): 550–63.

West, S. A. 1992. Problem-based learning—A viable addition for secondary school science. *School Science Review.* 73(265): 47–55.

SELECTION 13

How to Integrate Virtual Field Trips into the Curriculum

by **Scott Mandel**

The Shape of Society

Mr. Yasinow* wants his students to comprehend the connection between mathematics and the real world. As modern middle school students, they see little practical application for mathematics outside of knowing how to use a calculator and how to balance a checkbook. For students whose parents have a checkbook type program on their home computers, even the latter function is obsolete.

Mr. Yasinow decides that he will take his students on a virtual field trip into the world of geometry. He wants to show them how geometric theories have practical applications within society. He can accomplish this by showing students various forms of architecture that exemplify the use of geometry.

Mr. Yasinow first searches for a number of Internet sites that contain various examples and pictures of buildings. He is looking for those that explicitly incorporate geometric shapes in their design. Since he is well aware that there are a large number of architecturally oriented sites on the Internet, he decides to start his search with YAHOO!,** which normally contains the best of all of the official architectural locations.

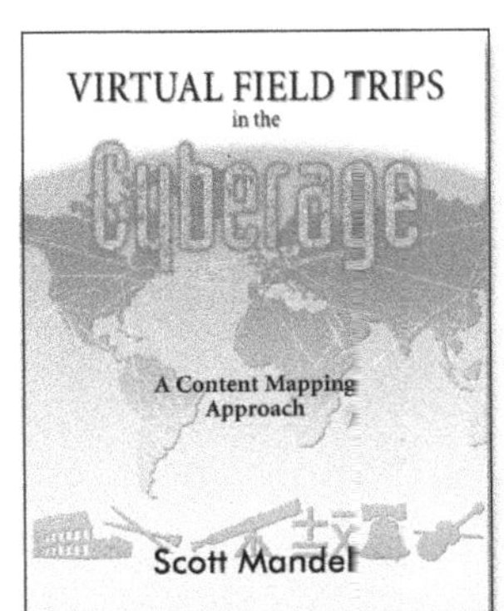

*All names of teachers are fictional.
**Please note: The addresses for the Web sites that appear in capital letters can be found in the Reference section at the end of this excerpt.

Adapted from *Virtual Field Trips in the Cyberage: A Content Mapping Approach* by Scott Mandel, pp. 105–28, 159–61, and 163–64.

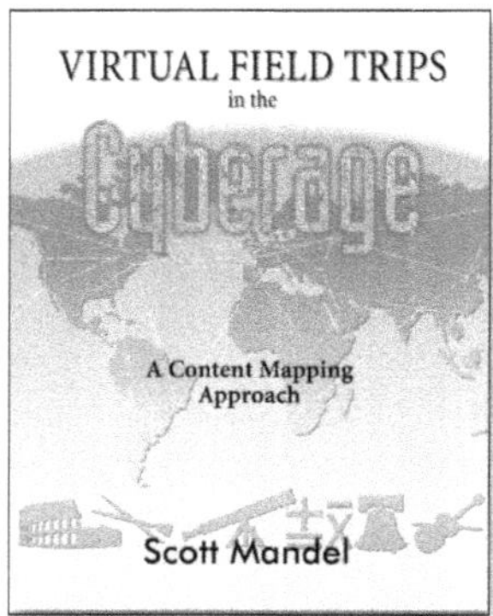

In the YAHOO! index, he first looks at the "Arts & Humanities" category, then follows the links first to "Design Arts," then to "Architecture," and finally to "Buildings and Structures." On that page he discovers over fifty sites concerning the area of architecture. Among them are the following useful sites, each of which contains pictures of structures that incorporate a variety of geometric shapes:

Chicago Cultural Center—architectural showplace for the lively and visual arts, presenting more than 1,000 free programs and exhibitions annually.

Eiffel Tower@ (Please note that YAHOO! uses the notation "@" after a link, rather than a description, when that link is actually a file of various sites, rather than one specific URL.)

Great Pyramid—essay on the oldest structure on earth.

Independence Hall@

Joy of Concrete, The—links to buildings made from concrete.

Poplar Forest—Thomas Jefferson's personal retreat. Explore the octagonal house and learn about the restoration under way and the discoveries of archaeologists.

Rundetaarn, The Round Tower—in Copenhagen, Denmark. King Chr. IV's famous tower. Music, exhibitions, observatory, and more.

Rural Impressions—follow a student across the US on a bike while examining the architectural developments of rural America.

Taj Mahal@

Tower of Pisa@

United States Capitol@

World Federation of Great Towers—association of international monuments working together to foster awareness and develop local and international opportunities for promotion.

Now that he has this extensive list of sites, he puts together a scavenger hunt of the geometrically designed buildings. The students then pair up into teams. Mr. Yasinow gives each team a list of two- and three-dimensional figures to locate, the list of URLs, and an hour of search time. The team that locates and prints out the greatest number of examples wins.

Not only is the experience a huge success, but students use the material that they find as real-life examples within their classwork, particularly in lessons involving area, polygons, surface area, volume, angles, and symmetry. Mr. Yasinow's students discover dozens of examples of geometry in architecture. Ultimately, although reluctantly, they finally admit that mathematics actually is relevant in today's society.

Where to Begin?

This chapter is designed to give teachers some starting points for generating ideas for their own personal virtual field trips. This chapter helps answer the question of how to integrate virtual field trips into curricular subject matter.

The basic goal of this chapter is to spark ideas within teachers' minds. Teachers should not use this chapter as a virtual directory of field trips—where teachers can pick out trips and use them as is. Rather, the material in these pages provides initial ideas to spark teachers' creativity and to steer them toward integrating virtual field trips into their classroom curricula. As teachers scan through these pages, they can think of how to adapt the ideas presented to their own curricula to make the experiences truly personal.

The ideas on these pages are presented in as general a form as possible, while intermingled with some specific examples of how teachers can go about the actual process. The listings are by far not all-inclusive. There are many potential areas within each subject area that the material does not touch on. This chapter focuses on five major curricular areas: language arts, social studies/history, science, mathematics, and the arts.

How to Integrate Virtual Field Trips into the Curriculum

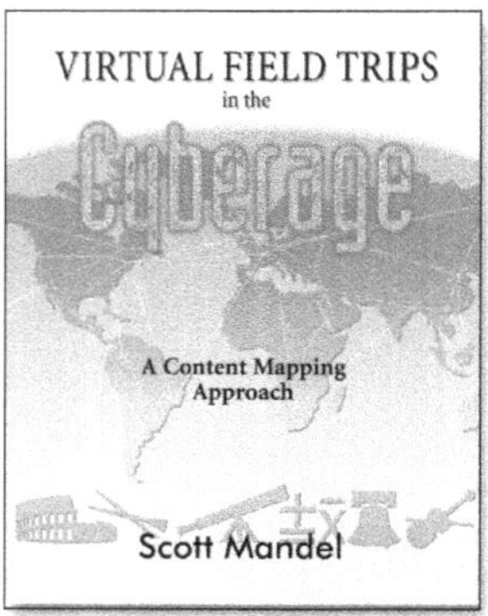

Language Arts

Virtual field trips can greatly expand students' knowledge and experience within the language arts. This section focuses on three basic parts of the language arts curriculum in which virtual field trips have the greatest benefit: literature, authors and poets, and student creative writing.

Literature

Literature is one of the most prolific areas in which to integrate virtual field trips. Within a virtual field trip, teachers can take students into the setting of the novel: either back in time or to a far different location. An online experience can serve as the major resource of supplemental material for a literary work.

Some topics are easily accessible within a virtual field trip, such as taking a trip to the South Pacific as a prelude to reading *Island of the Blue Dolphin* (O'Dell 1990). However, some topics are much more problematic and difficult to create, such as trying to develop a trip to the rural south during the time of *To Kill A Mockingbird* (Lee 1960). Teachers can consider the balance between the benefits of a virtual field trip and the effort needed to locate materials on their topics. The following are a few fundamental considerations to use in making this basic decision:

- Present day locations around the world are very easy to use as a virtual field trip topic.
- Events or locations back in time are more difficult to use as a virtual field trip topic.

Present Day Locations

There are currently picture-laden Internet sites for practically every spot in the world that has electricity. Even a country as small and remote as Nepal, located in the heart of the Himalayas, has 175 different Internet sites registered with YAHOO! Since YAHOO! carries the vast majority of official governmental and large commercial sites dealing with locations around the world, it is the easiest place to start constructing a field trip of this type.

In the YAHOO! index there is a heading titled "Regional." Under that heading, select the most appropriate place: country, region, or U.S. state. This index contains most of the materials and links that teachers will want for their virtual field trips.

Past Events or Locations

Basically, the more well-known or broad an event or time period is, the easier it is to locate material. The key to finding this type of information is to use the social studies collections of sites for the material.

If students are reading *Sarah, Plain and Tall* (Maclachlan 1985) and the teacher wants to locate materials on pioneer life in the 1890s, the easiest place to find this information is the HISTORY/SOCIAL STUDIES WEB SITE FOR K–12 TEACHERS. First going to "American History Sources," then to the "Native Americans and the Frontier West" link, provides dozens of usable sites covering every aspect of pioneer culture imaginable—from the concept of mail-order brides (the main subject of the novel) to examples of the soddies that the pioneers lived in on the plains. The following are two more examples of relevant sites:

Crossing the Frontier
Includes more than 300 images of the American West dating from 1849 to the present that document ". . . changes in the ways we have represented and idealized the vast Western landscape over the last 140 years, from a place of boundless beauty and limitless opportunity . . . to a landscape hemmed in by suburbanization and sometimes tinged with a tragic sense of loss." Under educational resources, the site provides special information on how to use the site information in the classroom. Possible integration topics include: Westward migration and the colliding of cultures in the American West, the growth of Western cities, the history of science and technology in the U. S., the Gold Rush.

How to Integrate Virtual Field Trips into the Curriculum

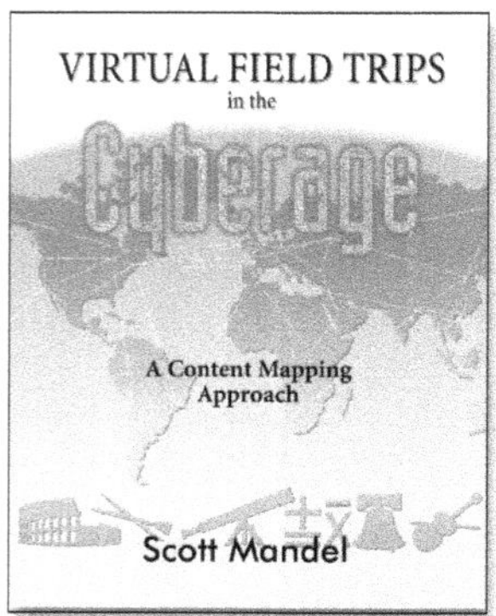

Gallery of the Open Frontier
An image library of photos, paintings, and drawings on American Western history. See the Special Listings Menu—Children on the Frontier, Dams and Canals, Trains and Railroads, Sod Houses and Other Homesteads, Native Americans, Studio Photographs, Schools, Farming, Construction Projects.

While a virtual field trip of this nature is excellent for exemplifying broad cultural and historical events, it is much more difficult for dealing with more narrow issues, such as was mentioned about studying the rural south during the time of *To Kill a Mockingbird*. There is little material either in print or online concerning the narrow topics of racism in the south in the early 1900s or on the southern rural poor before World War II. Generally speaking, if printed curricular material on a subject exists, chances are that teachers can also now find it on the Internet.

Nonetheless, virtual field trips are an invaluable assistance for providing supplemental material for the background and settings of a great many works of literature.

Authors and Poets

Virtual field trips can provide material about the experiences of authors and poets. It is especially beneficial for students to comprehend the writers' environments in which they have lived or currently live that influence their work. This is a particularly important exercise when dealing with an author who is recognizable by the settings of his prose or poetry such as Mark Twain, who wrote about life long ago on the Mississippi River, or Robert Frost, who wrote extensively on life in New England.

If students are doing a lesson on a novel by Mark Twain, understanding the location and lifestyle of the inhabitants of Hannibal, Missouri, greatly adds to students' understanding of the novel. An easy way to accomplish this is with a field trip to Hannibal. Since Hannibal is considered a municipality, YAHOO! is the most logical place to begin.

In the YAHOO! index, teachers can first select the category, "Regional," then "US States," "Missouri," "Cities," and finally

"Hannibal." To learn about life in this area, teachers can select "Community." Under this subheading, teachers can click on "Guides." The following Internet site appears and contains all of the information necessary for a virtual field trip, along with an assortment of additional helpful links:

Hannibal, Missouri—provides historical and current city information as well as in-depth visitor details and guides.

The same basic process works with a study of the environment and community of Robert Frost. Since Frost dealt with an entire region, New England, the search is not quite as straightforward as investigating an individual city. Teachers can, of course, select a typical New England city and use that location as an example. However, teachers may want to investigate the entire region, if at all feasible.

YAHOO! can also assist with this search. By using the category "Regional" once again, teachers can select the subcategory "Regions," then "U.S. Regions," and finally "New England." This page includes categories in all different areas, along with the following specialized Web sites that prove useful for creating a virtual field trip about Robert Frost's environmental inspiration:

Abbington Village—Shop for products "made in New England" and gather information on what to see and do, and where to stay and play in New England.

Explore New England

New England Information Network—Travel, living, and visiting information.

Virtual New England—travel, shops, real estate, and events.

Yankee Web Explorer, The

Of course, teachers can also search on METACRAWLER for "Robert Frost," securing numerous Web sites about the man and his work. Many of these sites may also contain relevant information about the poet. However, if teachers' primary goals are to discover information about the region in which he

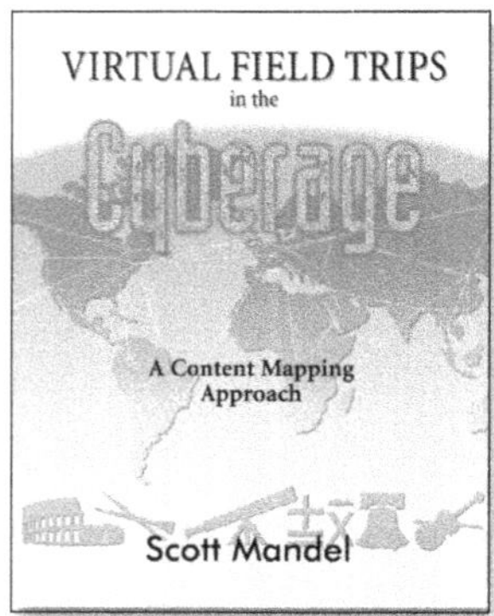

wrote, then a YAHOO! search for New England is the best place to start.

Background information on authors and poets is one way to incorporate virtual Web sites into literature. Unfortunately, this is not quite as helpful when the author is eclectic in setting—when there is no one place or region that really defines the writer. Luckily, many writers now have their own Internet sites that provide a good deal of personal information about that author, including an examination of their writing and thought processes. In this respect, teachers can have the students go on a virtual field trip to a writer's "home" in conjunction with a literature unit. This process works especially well with authors of children's books.

The easiest way to locate information of this nature is to use the CHILDREN'S LITERATURE WEB GUIDE, which teachers can find on the Educational Resources page of the general educational site TEACHERS HELPING TEACHERS. This exercise leads to some remarkable information especially when researching authors who primarily write for children, such as Judy Blume.

By clicking on the "Authors on the Web" link to the CHILDREN'S LITERATURE WEB GUIDE, teachers discover a specialized link to Judy Blume:

Judy Blume's Official Web site—designed for kids

This specialized site contains the following wonderful links for use in a virtual field trip to the author's house:

- A Message from Judy
- Favorite Questions for Judy
- Guest Book
- What's New
- Bio and Photos
- Judy's Books
- Related Links
- Dive in to the Special KIDS Page!!

Judy Blume, as well as other authors and poets, can unexpectedly come alive for younger students.

Student Writing

Older students can turn creative writing and research papers into virtual field trips. They can demonstrate examples of their material by linking appropriate Internet sites into their work. This phenomenon works especially well in some of the newer word processing programs that automatically create hyperlinks to Web sites simply by typing in a URL.

To incorporate such virtual online material into their writing, students can search for sites during a researching session. To start, teachers can show students how to use METACRAWLER, which greatly speeds up the research process since it provides a list of the top sites from all of the major search engines.

If students are writing science fiction stories, they might want to attach one of the links discovered at the NASA Web site into their work. Students can easily enhance an original story of life on Mars with a connection to the "Multi-media gallery" at the NASA Internet site.

Even elementary students can supplement their writing with an Internet experience. If students are studying *The Jungle Book* (Kipling 1894), teachers can help students create an additional story involving Mowgli and the other characters as a supplemental activity. Students can easily integrate a visit to a tiger's habitat into their work by typing in the search term "tiger" into METACRAWLER. The search provides the following excellent site that students can add to their material:

> **Tiger Information Center**
> Excite: The Tiger Information Center is dedicated to providing information to help preserve the remaining five subspecies of tigers. To learn more about tigers, just click on the topic below. If you have more questions, email us. http://www.5tigers.org/ (Excite, Infoseek, WebCrawler)

Older students can implement the same process within a topical research paper. If students are writing formal research papers, they can include links to virtual field trips on various topics, such as a location or a place in time. This is similar to

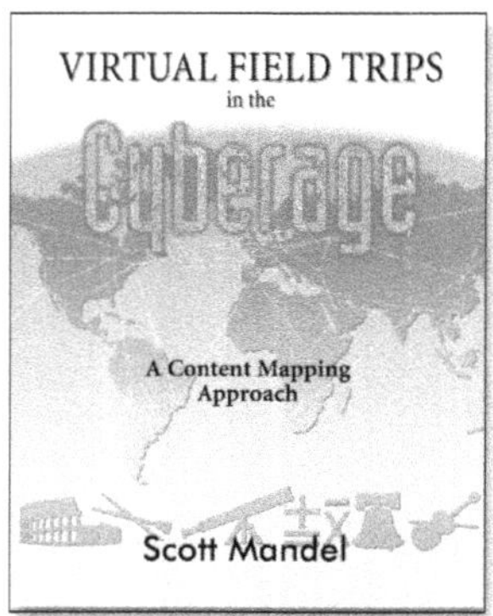

students adding an appendix of additional information to their report.

In any event, there are numerous possibilities for incorporating virtual field trips into language arts, especially in curricular areas involving literature, authors and poets, and student writing.

Social Studies/History

Probably the easiest subject area to implement a virtual field trip is the vast area contained within the social studies/history curricula. The three major topic areas of this part of the curriculum are the studies of the community (elementary grades), United States and world history (upper elementary grades through high school), and the humanities (primarily high school). United States and world history are combined in the following examples since the process of implementing virtual field trips is quite similar between the two (Mandel 1998).

The Community

A virtual field trip to various communities is an extremely easy process to create. The previous example of using YAHOO! to search Hannibal, Missouri, illustrates this process (see language arts). However, often the curriculum involves a study of the school's own particular community or city. A virtual field trip is an excellent way of giving students a personal experience when the school's budget cannot.

In Los Angeles, The Getty Center, a multibillion dollar art museum, recently opened. Although the museum is a fantastic place for all students to visit, most schools cannot afford more than one or two field trips during the school year. Elementary schools may not even consider The Getty Center as a top choice. Luckily, students can experience this museum through a virtual field trip.

Using METACRAWLER and the search term "Getty Center," students immediately find the following link:

Getty, The
Infoseek: The Getty offers opportunities to more fully understand; Yahoo!: through a museum, five institutes and a grant program, the Getty provides opportunities for people to more fully understand, experience, value, and preserve the world's art and cultural heritage.
http://www.getty.edu/ (Infoseek, Yahoo!)

Using this link, along with a subsequent one marked "Online Tour," students are suddenly at the museum looking at many of the exhibits and designs they would see if they were actually there. If teachers have access to projection screen monitors, the experience is even more realistic. Students can actually experience the museum without setting foot in the building.

Using the Internet, teachers can enhance the virtual field trip experience in ways that a real trip to the museum cannot provide. For example, the Getty Center has a beautiful circular garden designed by Robert Irwin, one that is sure to catch students' attention. If teachers want to extend the field trip experience, they can go to the WORLD WIDE ARTS RESOURCES, search for "Irwin," and find additional examples of this artist's work that students can study.

Teachers can implement online community field trips with countless examples in every major city and most small towns, too. In addition, a virtual field trip can help link supplemental material to the curricular experience.

In lower grades, students can study many community-type professions, such as firefighters, police officers, or doctors. Teachers can easily take students on a virtual field trip to visit these people all over the country. Since YAHOO! contains most municipal Internet sites, it is the logical place to start. If teachers search "firefighters" on YAHOO!, they find the overall category of

Health: Public Health and Safety: Fire Protection

If teachers click that link, they find an additional link to the category "Fire Companies," which by itself contains Internet sites for 323 different fire companies around the country.

How to Integrate Virtual Field Trips into the Curriculum

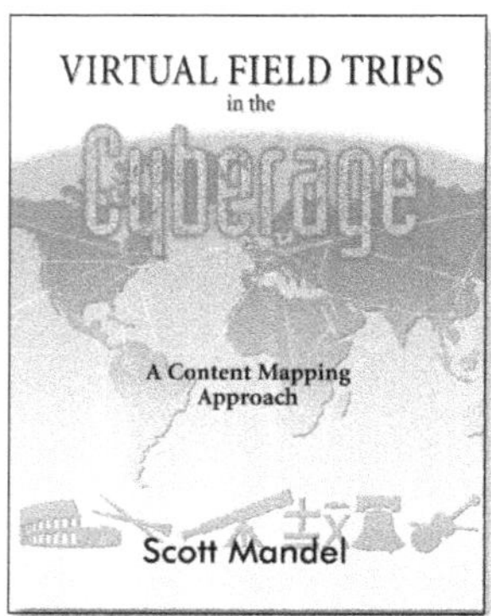

Teachers can easily select one of these fire company sites for their students to visit. On many of these sites, teachers can even personalize the trip by having students correspond with a firefighter through e-mail. Ultimately, this experiential process works with any number of professions that early elementary students study as part of their curricula.

United States and World History

A combination of searches using YAHOO!, METACRAWLER, and general-education and subject-matter Web sites leads teachers to the vast majority of the information and material that is needed to construct virtual field trips into United States and world history. The HISTORY/SOCIAL STUDIES WEB SITE FOR K–12 TEACHERS and the HISTORICAL TEXT ARCHIVE also prove to be two of the most indispensable Internet sites available to teachers constructing virtual field trips.

Complex, multileveled virtual field trips are not the only option for teachers. Teachers can easily create smaller, one- or two-stop virtual field trips to enhance the everyday history curriculum, with minimum effort. There are online possibilities for use in virtually any topic. Here are a number of curricular examples, using the HISTORY/SOCIAL STUDIES WEB SITE FOR K–12 TEACHERS as the source to locate Web sites for the study of various historical topics and time periods:

- Ancient Egypt: Take the students on a tour of Ancient Egypt at THE ANCIENT EGYPTIAN CULTURE EXHIBIT. They can enjoy an experience as they take a virtual field trip of ancient Egyptian daily life, the military, the arts, or architecture of the time.
- The Byzantine Empire: Take the students on a virtual tour of the art and icons of that time and how this work exemplified the religious aspect of the Byzantine Period at the Internet site BYZANTINE RELIGIOUS ICONOGRAPHY AND ICON ART.
- Civil Rights: Take the students to a speech given by Malcolm X at the University of Berkeley in 1963. They

can hear an actual recording of his words at the site AUDIO ONLINE: STREAMED AUDIO FILES, MEDIA RESOURCES CENTER, UCB.

- Holocaust: Take the students on a virtual tour of the ghetto experience, the concentration camps, and other aspects of the Holocaust at A TEACHER'S GUIDE TO THE HOLOCAUST. Also included is a section on the arts, where students can download music from the Holocaust period or take a tour of a gallery of children's art work that was created in the camps.
- The Napoleonic Era: Take the students on a tour of this French leader's life, battles, and an investigation of many additional aspects of his overall history at THE NAPOLEON SERIES: LIFE & TIMES OF NAPOLEON BONEPARTE.
- The Spanish-American War: Take the students on a tour of the battleship Maine, whose sinking was the instigator of the Spanish-American War. Go to the REMEMBER THE MAINE Internet site to see a narrated pictorial history of the ship, event, and the yellow journalism that followed, all of which led the United States into the war.

Teachers do not need a lengthy virtual field trip project to give the students an online experience. Short, one-day trips that require a minimum amount of teacher preparation are readily available in nearly all areas of historical study.

The Humanities

Many teachers describe the humanities as the various topics within social studies that do not fit into the previously discussed areas. This includes topics such as government, cultural studies, and comparative religions to name a few. Most of the non-history-based social studies courses in high school curricula are often placed under the umbrella category of the humanities.

How to Integrate Virtual Field Trips into the Curriculum

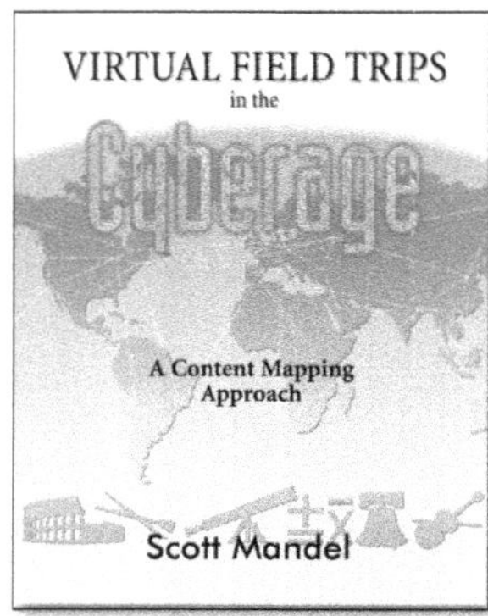

The humanities are an excellent place to integrate virtual field trips. There are numerous places on the Internet where students can expand their knowledge and experiences within the various topic areas. A sampling of examples that deal with the areas of democracy, multicultural studies, and current events follow.

Democracy

Since the curricular area of the humanities is so broad, there is not a model to work from. Students gain a good deal of Internet experience simply from their individual teacher's curriculum, along with the personal creativity of the student. Luckily, there are many places where teachers can turn to find material for these subject areas.

The concept of democracy is an excellent example and one often explicitly found within the secondary curriculum. Students can experience firsthand the democratic process through the use of an Internet site such as THE JEFFERSON PROJECT. This site contains the following goals, information, and links:

> The Jefferson Project is a public service that Net.Capitol, Inc. provides to help stimulate the electronic public discourse. Believing that a democracy requires the broadest possible participation, Net.Capitol maintains this collection of political sites and public fora. In here, you should find everything you need to become an involved member of the American democracy.
>
> - Do-it-yourself Politics—Roll up your sleeves and get active!
> - State Resources—State-by-state listing of local Internet government and political resources.
> - Political Parties—Local and national party sites.
> - Political Humor—Admit it, it's funny.
> - The Left—If you lean this way, go this way.
> - The Right—If you lean this way, go this way.
> - The Issues—What are we arguing about?
> - Government Resources—How does the government use the Internet, and how can you use those resources?

- Political Watchdogs—Who watches the watchmen?
- International Resources—We're not alone.
- Voicebox—Make your voice heard! A public forum for debating our national issues.
- CapWeb Classic—Find your representatives using the search engine that powers Net.Capitol's CapWeb Custom.

An easy virtual field trip that teachers can construct is to have students attend a town hall meeting with representatives from the various political parties in attendance. Teachers can simply link dissimilar positions of different parties, as espoused within the Web site links above. The students can go from one person to another as they learn about the various topics. During presidential election years, students can attend the Democratic or Republican convention by going to those respective parties' Web sites and studying the issues and the candidates, even following the actual itinerary of the convention.

Through various experiences such as those described above, students can get a firsthand working knowledge of how democracy manifests itself within American society.

Multicultural Studies

Multicultural studies are a major focus of the humanities today. Numerous secondary and elementary schools offer or integrate studies of comparative cultures, religions, and regions into the curriculum. Teachers can construct virtual field trips in any of these areas on any level to provide students with a better understanding of the phenomenon.

A popular and basic example is the study of Cinco de Mayo, the Latin American celebration that almost every grade level throughout many regions of the United States observes. Students can easily experience an online celebration of this day while using the Internet.

If teachers type in the term "Cinco de Mayo" into METACRAWLER, they would find the following links and descriptions:

How to Integrate Virtual Field Trips into the Curriculum

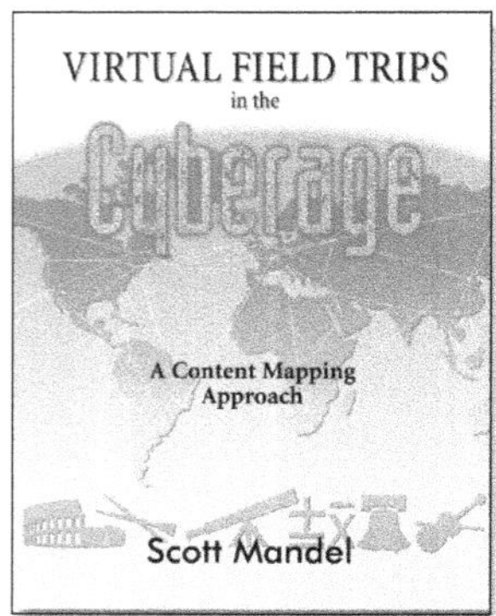

Cinco De Mayo
Excite, WebCrawler: On May 5th my family celebrates Cinco de Mayo. First we go to church, then we have a special dinner with all kinds of different food. We eat enchiladas, tacos, sopa, and my aunt makes a special punch that is delicious. http://intergate.bcsd.k12.ca.us/fremont/h5mayo.htm (Excite, WebCrawler)

NOBLE Web: Cinco de Mayo
NOBLE Web Cinco De Mayo—The story of Cinco de Mayo from Latinonet Cinco de Mayo History— UCLA's Cinco de Mayo
http://www.noble.mass.edu/tty5cin.htm (Lycos)

Infoseek: Cinco de Mayo
Get homework help, parenting tips, events and activities for the kids, holiday fun, and more. http://guide.infoseek.com/Kids . . . ys_and_festivals/Cinco_de_Mayo (Excite)

Cinco de Mayo Fiesta Official Site
V111 Annual Cinco de Mayo Fiesta in Downtown Pasco, WA 1997 FlowerThe Official SiteFlower VIII Cinco de Mayo Fiesta in D. http://www.sired.com/cinco97/ (Lycos)

These are only a few of the offerings. There are many more sites covering a variety of multicultural holidays. Teachers can easily construct a full, multicultural virtual field trip incorporating multiple intelligences using these Internet locations. For example, teachers can create maps of community parks filled with booths and other locations that are linked to sites containing Cinco de Mayo material such as art, music, stories, history of the holiday, and other cultural information.

Teachers can develop similar experiences using material from other religions, cultures, and people around the world to provide students with experiences that they could normally not acquire without physically being at the particular location.

Current Events

Current events is one of the easiest areas from which to construct a virtual field trip experience, and it is a topic found in almost every grade starting with elementary school. Luckily, there are a number of news sites that are extremely useful, especially CNN INTERACTIVE, a site that seems to be designed for student use.

CNN INTERACTIVE contains links for almost every possible area of current events, including most related and side topics to the particular story. Teachers can use these links to create a virtual "news magazine" on a particular current topic or a news broadcast on a variety of selected issues; the possibilities are endless.

Regardless of the topic, teachers can design virtual field trips in every area imaginable within the humanities. Teachers can easily construct curricular lessons to greatly enhance an already very experiential curricular area, directly leading to greater student understanding and appreciation of the various topics.

Science

There is probably no greater number of virtual field trip resources than in the curricular area of the sciences. Previously constructed virtual field trips abound in this subject area, from excursions into rain forest habitats to journeys into the heart of volcanoes to visits to geological excavations.

There is even a special Internet site titled THE VIRTUAL FIELD TRIPS SITE. This site includes probably the best collection of ready-made educationally oriented virtual field trips on the Web. The site currently contains, or has plans to contain, fully constructed virtual field trips in the following curricular areas:

- Beaches
- Bogs
- Construction Sites
- Deserts
- Dinosaurs
- Farms
- Glaciers
- Ponds
- Prairies
- Rain Forests
- Salt Marshes
- Sharks
- Streams
- Tide pools

How to Integrate Virtual Field Trips into the Curriculum

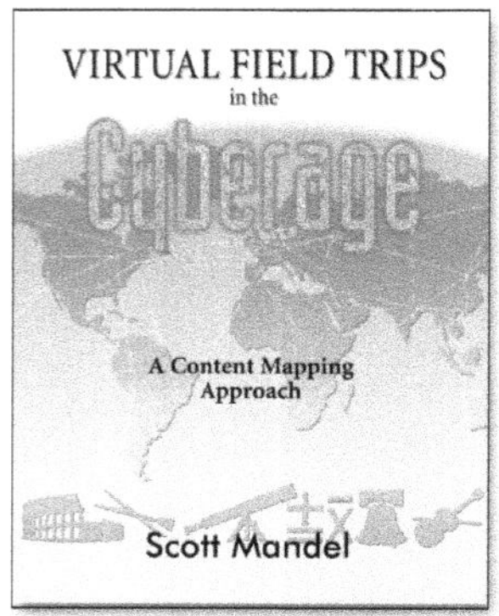

Hurricanes	Urban
Meadows	Volcanoes
Mountains	Whales
Natural Wonders of the World	Woods
Oceans	

Of the twenty-three field trip subject areas listed, at least twenty of them are predominantly science-related, as is the case with the vast majority of virtual field trip sites. Besides this particular Web site, there are numerous other science-related sites on the Internet. Teachers can use these online activities either in their entirety, or they can supplement them with additional material for a more personalized experience for the students.

Unfortunately, the vast majority of these ready-made scientific-based sites involve only a narrow band of topics that primarily fall into four basic categories:

1. Biology Sites: Sites involving individual animal and plant species (such as the tiger example mentioned earlier), collections of animals (such as those found at zoological locations), and ecosystem experiences (such as the rain forest or oceans examples).
2. Space Exploration Sites: Sites involving planetary and galaxy exploration. The best of these sites are connected to NASA.
3. Geology Sites: Sites involving current geological trips around the world, where students can join the geologists. Also included are sites revolving around geological formations, such as volcanoes.
4. Geography Sites: Sites involving various weather phenomenon, such as tornadoes, hurricanes, along with those dealing with specialized climates, such as deserts and the Arctic and Antarctic regions.

Besides these sites, virtual museum experiences are another excellent source of virtual field trips. Again, the majority of these exist within the areas of the sciences. Most major museums such as the SMITHSONIAN INSTITUTE now offer virtual trips through their exhibits. In addition, there are a number of Internet sites that are purely online virtual museums.

One such Internet location is the FRANKLIN INSTITUTE SCIENCE MUSEUM that advertises itself as containing a world of virtual exhibits. The museum has numerous excellent experiential activities for students of all ages and is designed as if the students were walking through the museum itself. Other online activities include the following links and descriptions:

> **Flights of Inspiration** celebrates the 95th anniversary of sustained, powered flight.
>
> Visit the ocean with **Undersea and Oversee.**
>
> Volcanoes erupt, the crust quakes, and rivers rage. **Earthforce** is everywhere.
>
> Be your own neighborhood weather forecaster with **Franklin's Forecast,** an online exhibit about weather forecasting.
>
> Follow the action in one high school biology lab and you'll get the **BioPoint.** Mrs. Mazen's biology class is online, offering both the teacher and student points of view.

All of the above pages include information and activities along with additional links for a complete virtual museum experience on the Internet.

Another example of this type of virtual science experience is a site such as the EXPLORATORIUM. This site provides a new type of virtual field trip every three months dealing with a specific topic. The topic, at the time of printing, is chocolate and includes the following links:

> **Chocolate in the Forest**—A visit to the Amazon, a source for chocolate.
>
> **An "American Invention"**—The Olmecs, the Mayans, and Aztecs.
>
> **Chocolate Invades Europe**—Chocolate conquers the continent.

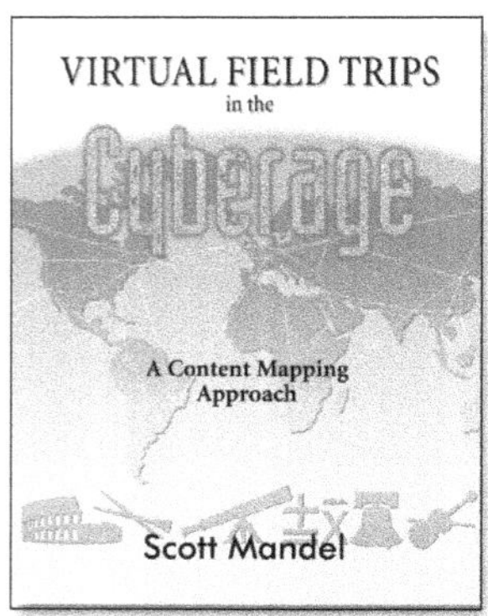

From Bean to Bar—Take a video tour of the Scharffen Berger chocolate factory.

Health Help or Risk—Can chocolate help prevent heart disease?

"Feel Good" Food—More than a food but less than a drug.

Although not entirely science oriented, the site relates the topic in as many ways as possible to science and health. The topics change every three months; so check the site for updates. Links to previous topics include the following:

- Exploring Hair: "Better Hair Through Chemistry"
- Exploring Memories: "Young in Mind"

Unfortunately, there are few ready-made sites available for the curricular areas of chemistry or physics, other than as they relate to the sites above. Still, teachers can create virtual field trips in these areas as they would for any other subject area, using search engines, general educational sites, and subject-matter sites to accumulate appropriate online material. Seeing as there is such an abundance of science-oriented virtual field trips already established on the Internet, it behooves teachers to search the subject at hand as a first step, rather than recreating work already accomplished by others.

Mathematics

There are not many ready-to-use virtual field trips covering the area of mathematics. After all, it is easier to visit a volcano than it is to visit a quadratic equation. Still, there are a number of ways to integrate an Internet virtual experience into the mathematics curriculum (see A Tool or a Fad?). Although peripheral to the mathematics curriculum, two of the easiest possibilities are interviewing mathematicians and creating virtual critical thinking problems. A third option is to have students look at various experiential mathematical sites.

A Tool or a Fad?

Too often in education, we take new innovations and integrate them into every possible facet of the curricula with the reasoning that educational gains of that innovation will automatically be present whenever that innovation is used.

Some curricular areas are more adaptable to them than others. It is quite easy to integrate virtual field trips into the history curriculum on all levels; it is quite a strain to integrate them into the mathematics curriculum on a regular basis.

You need to determine the usefulness of Internet activities toward meeting the goals of the curriculum, rather than simply creating a virtual experience because it is the thing to do.

This is not to say that you cannot integrate virtual field trips into the mathematics curriculum. Although current research stresses that the primary use of the Internet in mathematics is the incorporation of statistic analysis (Drier et al. 1999), a creative math teacher can design excellent ways to bring a virtual field trip experience into the classroom.

In other words, in all subject areas teachers need to first ask the question: *Why* am I planning this specific trip?

Mathematician Interviews

To have students interview a famous mathematician, teachers can create a virtual field trip as described earlier in the language arts examples concerning authors. Teachers link as much personal information and as many examples of the mathematician's work before students "sit down" with the person. Teachers can also construct this online experience as a panel of mathematicians presenting their work and theories.

Virtual Critical-Thinking Problems

Teachers can create virtual critical-thinking problems using almost any subject and grade level. Teachers can make them as simple as linking two pictures of cities, two pictures of trains, and a script describing the trains' speed and distance, along with the obvious question of how soon the two trains would meet.

Teachers can construct mathematical story problems around almost any online scenario, using preexisting or newly created sites. The primary benefit of this endeavor is the built-in motivational factor for getting the students involved with figuring out mathematical problems. Teachers can extend this experience with older students by giving them an Internet site

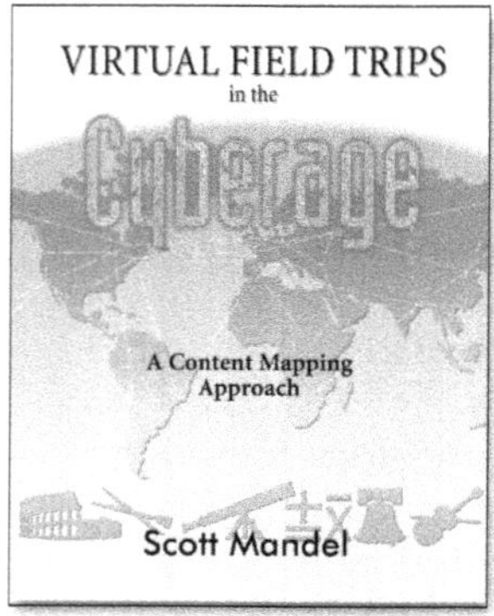

or interesting scenarios and having them develop their own critical thinking problems. There is also a plethora of game and logic mathematics sites, such as INTERACTIVE MATHEMATICS ONLINE or THE MATH FORUM HOME PAGE, in which students can apply, analyze, and evaluate the mathematics concepts associated with the game or puzzle. Teachers can locate these types of sites through most of the general educational Internet sites.

Experiential Mathematical Sites

A final way of creating a virtual experience in the area of mathematics is to incorporate experiential-oriented mathematics sites currently on the Internet into the curriculum. An experiential-oriented site is one where the students become actively engaged in the mathematical simulation. This is in contrast to sites where the student is merely presented with data. Whereas these are not pure virtual field trips, teachers can still use them to create online experiences. One of the best sites in this category is MEGA MATH. This experiential site takes students into various mathematical concepts such as the following topic links:

- The Most Colorful Math of All
- Games on Graphs
- Untangling the Mathematics of Knots
- Algorithms and Ice Cream for All
- Machines that Eat Your Words
- Welcome to the Hotel Infinity
- A Usual Day at Unusual School

Each of these unusual topics contains an additional set of links for the study of each unit. These subtopics include the following:

- Activities
- Background Information
- Big Ideas and Key Concepts
- Evaluation
- For Further Study

- NCTM (National Council of Teachers of Mathematics) Standards
- Prep and Materials
- Vocabulary

Each of these subtopics also contains a narrative and additional links explaining the particular information in greater detail. The material is presented in an interesting and innovative fashion as it strives to give the students an experience with mathematics. Teachers can easily incorporate these areas as a basis for personal virtual field trips.

Besides using the Internet to locate geometric figures in the world, as described in the opening anecdote, there are also experiential sites devoted to the study of geometry. One of these types of Internet locations is THE GEOMETRY CENTER. This site provides interesting experiential material such as the following:

Current Projects—what's hot at the Center

Interactive Web and Java Applications—math you can manipulate

Multimedia Documents—hypertext papers, preprints, forum

Geometry Reference Archive—graphic images, formulas

Downloadable Software—source, binaries, documentation

Video Productions—descriptions, clips, ordering info

Course Materials—lab materials, student work

These are just a few selected examples of experiential mathematical Internet sites and their potential for a mathematics virtual field trip. To see the full range of what is currently out there, teachers can use the normal channels for discovering virtual site material: search engines, general education sites, and subject-matter sites. Teachers' individual curricula and creativity determine how they can incorporate virtual field trips into the classroom.

How to Integrate Virtual Field Trips into the Curriculum

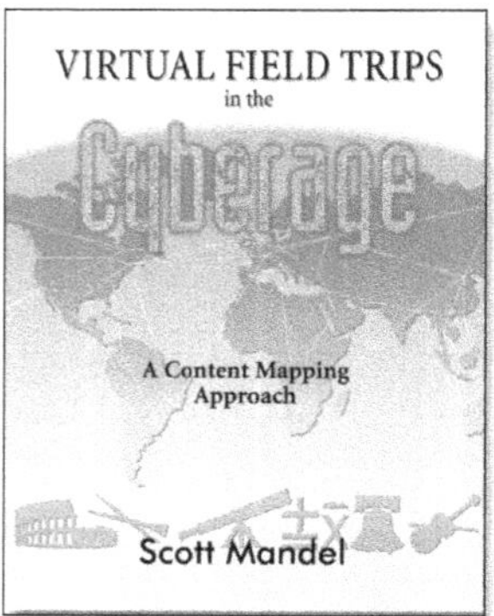

The Arts

Integrating virtual field trips into the arts is almost as easy as integrating them into social studies or language arts. There are already a number of experiential arts-oriented Internet sites online, sites that provide students with actual art experiences as if they were either in a museum or having a hands-on lesson. Locating them is relatively easy. Using them, teachers can develop excellent virtual experiences for their students in the areas of the visual arts and theater.

Visual Arts

The easiest type of visual art-related virtual field trip that teachers can create is a trip to a special exhibit in an art museum. In this type of activity, teachers collect links to paintings by famous artists or of a specific style. Teachers then let students take trips through the exhibits, viewing the various works.

Teachers can begin a virtual field trip of this sort with a visit to the Web site WORLD WIDE ARTS RESOURCES. At this site, teachers can search almost any category even remotely associated with the visual arts. The most valuable aspect of the site is the search index that teachers can use to locate Internet material concerning every major artist in the field today.

If teachers want to put together an exhibit on the famous twentieth century pop art painter Roy Lichtenstein, all they have to do is type in Lichtenstein into this artists search index. They would find a number of links that include numerous references to Lichtenstein's work:

Lichtenstein, Roy
painting, sculpture, pop, American, 20th century.

The Greatest Painters on the Web
Great artists on the web — from Leonardo to Lichtenstein, links featuring the best web sites on: Chagall, Dali, Durer, Gauguin, Kandinsky, Klee, Leonardo, Lichtenstein, Magritte, Michelangelo, Miro, Monet, Picasso, Rembrandt, Renoir, Turner, van Gogh, Warhol

> **Lichtenstein, Roy**
> Roy Lichtenstein born in 1923 in New York. In 1939–40 he studied under Reginald Marsh at the Art Students' League, New York, and 1940–43 and . . .

These links provide teachers with numerous reproductions of his paintings, along with biographical material and articles about his life and fairly recent death. It is surprisingly easy for teachers to integrate this material into a virtual field trip. This search process on the WORLD WIDE ARTS RESOURCES site works for every artist imaginable.

Teachers can also integrate various art-oriented learning activities into the visual art virtual field trip. Teachers around the world have created a variety of sites that provide exceptional ideas and examples for everyday teachers. Teachers can find a collection of these types of sites using a general educational site such as TEACHERS HELPING TEACHERS or KATHY SCHROCK'S GUIDE FOR EDUCATORS.

Theater

Virtual field trips in the area of theater take a little more work than those in the visual arts. In the first place, there is no one all-encompassing Web site in which to locate materials. Also, unlike looking at reproductions of artists' work, it is basically impossible to reproduce a full play or musical on the computer screen. Still, there are a number of avenues that a teacher, using some creativity, can pursue in constructing a virtual field trip for theater students.

Almost every Broadway and off-Broadway play has a number of Internet sites associated with it. These pages fall into two basic categories: official sites created by the producers and theaters themselves and sites established by the many fans of that particular show. Teachers can integrate these different sites into a virtual experience with a little searching and design.

Teachers can integrate material of this sort into both pure theater arts classes, as well as into the general curriculum. Imagine that a teacher is studying early twentieth century American culture and wants to incorporate the award-winning

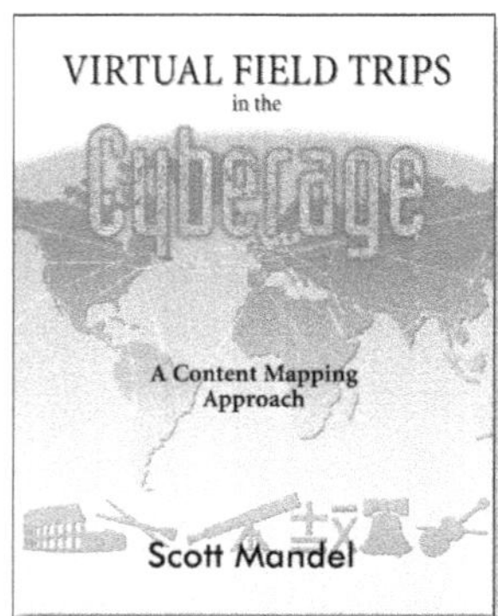

Broadway musical *Ragtime* (McNally et al. 1998) into a virtual class experience. The best place to commence the search for materials is with the use of the search engine METACRAWLER. By typing in the search term *Ragtime,* the teacher receives approximately fifty examples, including the following links and descriptions:

Ragtime
This site is slowly, but surely, moving to www.journey-on.com/ragtime/ and becoming a tribute to the Los Angeles production and cast. http://www.geocities.com/Broadway/Stage/4228/ (AltaVista)

Ragtime: The Musical
Click here to enter the Ragtime: The Musical Home Page. http://members. aol.com/km502/ragtime.htm (AltaVista)

New York Times: The 1998 Tony Award Nominations
Nominees listed with related articles and reviews from the *New York Times.* Free registration required. http://www.nytimes.com/library/theater/tonys-list.html (Infoseek)

Great Performances: Creating Ragtime
Go behind-the-scenes and see the process of bringing *Ragtime* to a new Broadway theater constructed from two pre-existing 42nd Street landmark houses. http://www.pbs.org/wnet/gperf/ragtime/index.html (Yahoo!)

Ragtime
The Immigrant Website. Unofficial site for the Broadway musical. http://www.gemonline.net/fordcenter (Yahoo!)

These sites bring together vast amounts of information about the musical, including a synopsis of the story line, the cast, the songs, and the history of the show, featuring information about its Tony Awards. Teachers can also locate lyrics and photos from the various productions of this show around the country. Teachers can then integrate all of this material into a theater-oriented virtual field trip.

Teachers can easily expand this particular activity using links to the dozens of Internet sites concerning ragtime music, many of which also came up in the METACRAWLER search. These sites contain vast amounts of information about the genre and its musicians, along with a large number of MIDI and other sound files, all of which contain examples of this particular style of music. Using these links, the teacher can develop a full curricular experience.

This is just one example of how teachers can construct virtual field trips in theater. As was outlined earlier with authors in the language arts section, teachers can construct virtual visits with famous playwrights and lyricists such as Stephen Sondheim and Andrew Lloyd Webber. With a little searching, teachers can also insert links on field trip sites that provide online scripts that students can work on together in cooperative groups. All teachers need to create an interesting Internet experience is a little creativity.

REFERENCES

Armstrong, T. 1994. *Multiple intelligences in the classroom.* Alexandria, VA: Association for Supervision and Curriculum Development.

Bigham, V. 1998. *Online education resources.* Englewood Cliffs, NJ: Prentice-Hall.

Buettner, D., and C. deMoll. 1996. Journey into the unknown. *Learning.* 24(4): 36–38.

Checkley, K. 1997. The first seven . . . and the eighth. *Educational Leadership.* 55(1): 8–13.

Cushman, K. 1994. *Catherine, called Birdy.* New York: HarperCollins Publishers.

Drier, H. S., K. M. Dawson, and J. Garofalo. 1999. Not your typical math class. *Educational Leadership.* 56(5): 21–25.

Eisner, E. 1979. *The educational imagination.* New York: Macmillan Publishing.

Fogarty, R. 1997. *Problem-based learning and other curriculum models.* Arlington Heights, IL: IRI/SkyLight Training and Publishing.

Gardner, H. 1993. *Multiple intelligences: The theory in practice.* New York: BasicBooks.

Giagnocano, G. 1996. *Educator's Internet companion.* Classroom Connect.

Goldsworthy, R. 1997. Real-world field trips. *Learning and Leading with Technology.* 24(7): 26–29.

How to Integrate Virtual Field Trips into the Curriculum

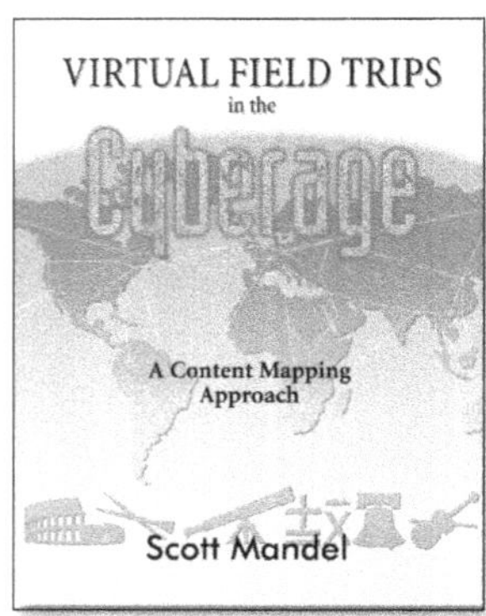

Joyce, B., and M. Weil. 1996. *Models of teaching,* 5th ed. Boston: Allyn and Bacon.

Kipling, R. 1894. *The jungle book.* (Original published date).

Krepel, W.J., and C.R. Duvall. 1981. *Field trips: A guide for planning and conducting educational experiences.* Washington, DC: National Education Association.

Latham, A. 1999. Computers and achievement. *Educational Leadership.* 56(5): 87–88.

Lee, H. 1960. *To kill a mockingbird.* Philadelphia: Lippincott.

Maclachlan, P. 1985. *Sarah plain and tall.* New York: Harper & Row.

McNally, T., S. Flaherty, and L. Ahrens. 1998. *Ragtime—the musical.* Livent (U.S.) Inc.

Mandel, S.M. 1998. *Social studies in the cyberage: Applications with cooperative learning.* Arlington Heights, IL: Skylight Training and Publishing.

Mandel, S.M. 1991. *Responses to cooperative learning processes among elementary-age students.* ERIC Clearinghouse on Elementary and Early Childhood Education, ED 332808.

Millan, D.A. 1995. Field trips: Maximizing the experience. In *Experience and the curriculum.* Dubuque, IA: Kendall/Hunt Publishing Company.

Miller, A. 1953. *The crucible.* New York: Viking Press.

O'Dell, S. 1990. *Island of the blue dolphin.* Boston: Houghton Mifflin.

Rudman, C.L. 1994. A review of the use and implementation of science field trips. *School Science and Mathematics.* 94(3): 138–141.

Slavin, R.E. 1990. *Cooperative learning: Theory, research, and practice.* Englewood Cliffs, NJ: Prentice-Hall.

Tapscott, D. 1999. Educating the net generation. *Educational Leadership.* 56(5): 6–11.

Thomas, L., and D. Knezek. 1999. National educational technology standards. *Educational Leadership.* 56(5): 27.

URLS

ADVENTURE ONLINE
http://www.adventureonline.com

AN AMAZON ADVENTURE
http://jajhs.kana.k12.wv.us/amazon/index.htm

THE AMERICAN CIVIL WAR HOMEPAGE
http://sunsite.utk.edu/civil-war

THE ANCIENT EGYPTIAN CULTURE EXHIBIT
http://EMuseum.mankato.msus.edu/egypt

THE ART TEACHER CONNECTION
http://www.primenet.com/~arted

AUDIO ONLINE: STREAMED AUDIO FILES, MEDIA RESOURCES CENTER, UCB
http://www.lib.berkeley.edu/MRC/audiofiles.html

BYZANTINE RELIGIOUS ICONOGRAPHY AND ICON ART
http://www.csg-i.com/icons

THE CHILDREN'S LITERATURE WEB SITE
http://www.ucalgary.ca/~dkbrown/index.html

CNN INTERACTIVE
http://cnn.com/ALLPOLITICS

CODY'S SCIENCE EDUCATION ZONE!
http://ousdmail.ousd.k12.ca.us/~codypren/CSEZ_Home.htm

DESERT LIFE IN THE AMERICAN SOUTHWEST
http://www.desertusa.com/life.html

EXPLORATORIUM
http://www.exploratorium.edu/exploring/index.html

FRANKLIN INSTITUTE SCIENCE MUSEUM
http://sln.fi.edu/tfi/welcome.html

THE GEOMETRY CENTER
http://www.geom.umn.edu

HAWAIIAN VOLCANO OBSERVATORY
http://wwwhvo.wr.usgs.gov/hazards

HISTORICAL TEXT ARCHIVE
http://www.msstate.edu/Archives/History/USA/usa.html

HISTORY/SOCIAL STUDIES WEB SITE FOR K-12 TEACHERS
http://www.execpc.com/~dboals/boals.html

IMAGINE HAWAII
http://imagine-hawaii.com

INFOSEEK
http://www.infoseek.com

INTERACTIVE MATHEMATICS ONLINE
http://tqd.advanced.org/2647/main.htm

THE JEFFERSON PROJECT
http://www.capweb.net/classic/jefferson/

JUDY BLUME'S OFFICIAL WEB SITE
http://www.judyblume.com

KATHY SCHROCK'S GUIDE FOR EDUCATORS
http://discoveryschool.com/schrockguide

LYCOS
http://www.lycos.com

THE MATH FORUM HOME PAGE
http://forum.swarthmore.edu

MEGA MATH
http://www.c3.lanl.gov/mega-math/menu.html

METACRAWLER
http://www.go2net.com/search.html

How to Integrate Virtual Field Trips into the Curriculum

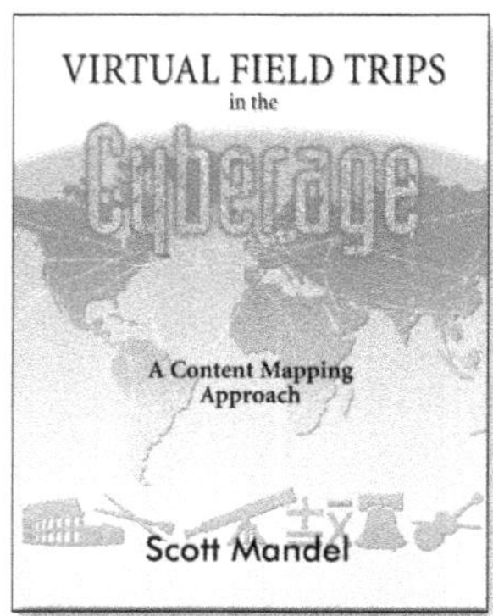

THE NAPOLEON SERIES: LIFE & TIMES OF NAPOLEON BONEPARTE
http://www.ping.be/napoleon.series

NASA
http://www.nasa.gov

A PAGE OF INFORMATION ON ELEPHANTS
http://www.inactive.demon.co.uk/elephant.html

REMEMBER THE MAINE
http://www.smithsonianmag.si.edu/smithsonian/issues98/feb98/maine.html

ROBERT FROST: THREE VOLUMES AND C.
http://www.columbia.edu/acis/bartleby/frost

SMITHSONIAN INSTITUTE
http://www.si.edu

A TEACHER'S GUIDE TO THE HOLOCAUST
http://fcit.coedu.usf.edu/Holocaust

TEACHERS HELPING TEACHERS
http://www.pacificnet.net/~mandel

TIGER INFORMATION CENTER
http://5tigers.org

USA TODAY WEATHER—A TYPICAL NORTHERN HEMISPHERE HURRICANE
http://www.usatoday.com/weather/tg/whurwhat/whurwhat.htm

THE VIRTUAL FIELD TRIPS SITE
http://www.field-guides.com

A VIRTUAL GEOLOGICAL FIELD TRIP TO ICELAND
http://www.casdn.neu.edu/~geology/department/staff/colgan/iceland/welcome.htm

WORLD WIDE ARTS RESOURCES
http://wwar.com

YAHOO!
http://www.yahoo.com

• PART III •

Assessment Tools for Today's Classroom

The Assessment Circle

Assessment, like a circle, has no beginning and no end. Where assessment starts and where it ends are invisible points. The assessment circle includes standards, criteria, rubrics, instructional methods, content, and assessment tools (see Figure III.1).

Standards

Effective and practical assessment of student learning must include standards. Just as there are multiple levels of objectives in the powerful lessons of the curriculum, there are multiple levels of standards. Just as there are multiple tools and strategies that help instruction, there are multiple tools and strategies that help assessment. And just as there are traps and pitfalls in the appropriate use of instructional strategies, there are traps and pitfalls in the appropriate use of assessment.

Sound assessment of student performance begins and ends with standards. A standard can be seen in two ways: as a

The Assessment Circle

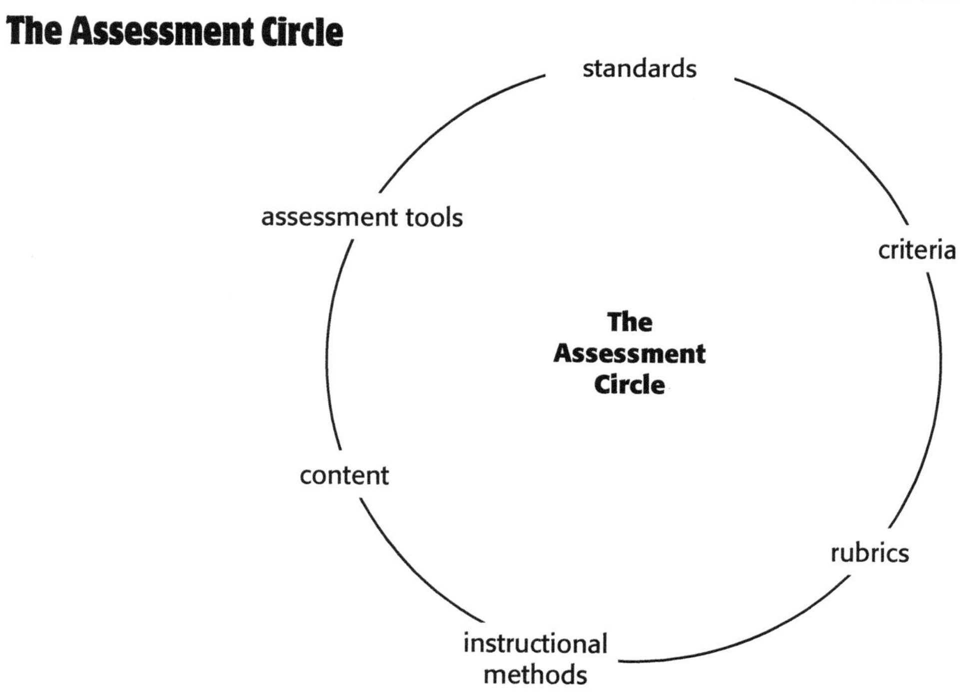

Figure III.1

high-minded, symbolic call to battle or as a unit of measure. In the first sense, a standard bearer leads the charge into battle, holding high the standard as the symbol of strength, inspiration, and core beliefs. The troops follow, charging up the hill, following the standard bearer. In the second sense, a standard is a crafted unit of measure that is perfectly made and carefully stored away. When necessary, the standard is brought out to measure new ideas and items against it.

In education, the second definition of standard is most popular. This popularity stems from the total quality movement in business. As reform voices from business, industry, and government searched for ways to make education more accountable, they imposed their own way of measuring success and failure. Mathematics and science educators have led the way in adopting the vocabulary of the standards approach to their quantitative disciplines. However, when the curriculum moves from quantitative disciplines into the more qualitative and less numerically measurable disciplines (such as language arts, fine arts, and music), this highly structured definition of standards is more difficult to apply. When educators look upon standards as parading a flag, they find it easier to put sensible standards into place.

Sensible standards start by defining what students must know and do at various stages of the curriculum.

Sensible standards start by defining what students must know and do at various stages of the curriculum. For example, the geography standards for middle school can require that students know the five uses of maps, globes, and other geographic tools. These students should also be able to do certain things, such as use a map or globe to identify five countries in each hemisphere and estimate temperatures in each country according to their latitudes. Teachers can assess what additional learning students need and what grade they will earn by ascertaining students' ability to attain these know and do standards (along with other key know and do standards in the geography curriculum).

Reducing qualitative concepts into precise standards can be more difficult. For example, it is challenging to craft standards for determining the quality of a literacy research paper or ascertaining students' ability to "analyze the characteristics of three literary heroes from English literature." In these cases, using the standard as a flag rather than a unit of measure may make more practical sense. In fact, from a teaching point-of-view, seeing standards as flags which the students are expected to follow or to seize and carry into the heat of battle is a more empowering tool.

In order to plan instruction and effective assessments of students' learning, the teacher must define standards and criteria; she must spell out what is most important for the students to know and do. For example, a geometry teacher will identify six to twelve concepts that students must know by the end of the year. The teacher must determine the key attributes of these concepts and choose a variety of instructional strategies that will promote understanding of the concepts by students who learn in different ways. As she proceeds step-by-step in the concept development, she will introduce the operations and procedures that help students apply their understanding. With all three elements—concepts, procedures, and operations—students will gain the knowledge needed to solve geometry problems. Students will know the concepts, procedures, and operations, and they will do the problem solving by using the concepts, procedures, and operations skillfully. When the teacher maps out the concepts, operations, and procedures for herself, she creates a road map for students to follow.

When the teacher maps out the concepts, operations, and procedures, she creates a road map for students to follow.

Criteria

After the teacher has defined standards and concepts, she next formulates criteria (sometimes known as performance benchmarks). For example, the geometry teacher might be teaching the concept of triangles. The criteria for the triangle unit denote what the students must know and do in this unit (see Figure III.2). Each criterium sets the level of learning challenge. Note how the assessment provides a "three-story" challenge: know, use, and transfer. This leveling enables the teacher to spell out what is most essential for all students to master (know), what is important for most to master (use), and what is challenging for the most motivated students (transfer).

Triangle Unit

WHAT IS A TRIANGLE?

Criteria

Concepts
- Understands concept and distinguishes attributes by type
- Uses concepts in problem solving
- Can transfer concepts to new problems

Procedures
- Knows procedures
- Uses procedures in problem solving
- Can transfer procedures to new problems

Operations
- Knows operations
- Uses operations in problem solving
- Can transfer operations in problem solving

Figure III.2

Rubric

If there is any one tool in the assessment field that helps teachers help students most, it is the rubric. However, rubrics must not become burdensome. They cannot be used indiscriminately for every bit of information dissemination that can be jammed into a course of study. Rubrics are helpful when they are used as learning guides or road maps that help students find their way through mountains of information. When rubrics are used this way, the points in the assessment circle move closer together and it becomes easier for teachers to organize standards-based instruction.

When it comes time to grade the students' performance and report progress to the parents, the rubric can ease the teacher's task. For the triangle unit, the teacher can report three subgrades (for concepts, procedures, and operations) and benchmark each student's progress (see Figure III.3). The teacher can use the rubric for determining grades by using the point system. An A grade for basic knowledge requires 8–9 points; B requires 6–7; C requires 5. No grades are given below 5. Any student who does not achieve at least five points can stay in the unit with alternative learning tasks until he demonstrates sufficient knowledge on the assessment tools.

Rubrics are helpful when they are used as road maps that help students find their way through mountains of information.

Rubric for Triangle Unit

Criteria	*Not Yet* (0)	*Some Confusion* (1)	*In the Grasp* (2)	*Sure Grip* (3)
Concepts	Does not understand concept	Understands concept and distinguishes attributes by type	Uses concepts in problem solving	Can transfer concepts to new problems
Procedures	Does not know procedures	Knows procedures	Uses procedures in problem solving	Can transfer procedures to new problems
Operations	Does not know operations	Knows operations	Uses operations in problem solving	Can transfer operations to new problems

Figure III.3

Instructional Methods

After the teacher establishes criteria and a rubric, she can plan her instruction. The three-story approach, used in creating criteria and the rubric, allows her to more easily differentiate instruction. For the fastest and deepest learners, she can provide opportunities to spend considerable time with transfer problems of varying degrees of difficulty. For the students who need the most time to understand the basic concepts, she can allow time to spend learning the attributes of a triangle and how these attributes make one type of triangle different from the others.

Content

The content standards, the ones that are aligned with state and district standardized tests, guide the teacher in teaching what students must know for the test. In high stakes states where promotion is dependent on test scores, students absolutely must reach the knowledge standards. Students pursuing higher education must attain proficiency in the process standards, those that deal with problem solving and transfer.

Assessment Tools

Assessment tools vary for differing situations. The teacher can use standardized or teacher-made tests as well as a variety of assessment strategies ranging from journals, projects, essays, demonstrations, and other artifacts. The teacher can use assessment tools that allow students to demonstrate their abilities to transfer their understanding into a variety of situations.

How will the teacher, parents, and student know that the student has achieved a certain level of mastery? The teacher selects assessment tools for each criteria. The teacher also determines a score or grade for each level of mastery for each criterion. For instance, the geometry teacher may create an attribute knowledge test. On the test, students must correctly identify all attributes of the triangle and selected distinguishing attributes of three out of five of the different types of triangles in order to fall in the "sure grip" category.

Assessment tools allow students to demonstrate their abilities to transfer their understanding into a variety of situations.

Using a rubric in conjunction with an assessment tool has four important advantages. First, it helps the teacher, student, and parents focus on what is most important in the content of a unit. Everyone knows from the start of the unit what is important for the student to learn. Second, it helps the teacher differentiate instruction. All students start the unit together. At key points, perhaps at the end of each week, the teacher assesses for basic level knowledge. Those who pass move to the next level or they can choose to remain in a level until they earn at least a B. Third, the teacher can easily mark student progress to the standard. Fourth, at the end of each week, parents can know easily where the student is on the road map for the unit.

The adage, "what goes around comes around," describes well the assessment circle. The excerpts selected for Part III illustrate in more depth how each of the elements in the cycle work, alternative tools to use, and appropriate use of each. The first excerpt, "Introducing Authentic Assessment," by Kay Burke discusses standardized and teacher-made tests, authentic assessment, portfolios, accountability testing, and balanced assessment. The second excerpt, "Designing and Using the Standards-Based Curriculum," by Daniel M. Perna and James R. Davis explains how to design district criterion standards from state standards. Issues such as creating a writing team, challenging the textbook dilemma, and using criterion-referenced tests are discussed. The third excerpt, "Guidelines for Grading," by Ken O'Connor, explains the underlying perceptions of grading and discusses grading practices, issues, and guidelines. It gives teachers the opportunity to examine their own grading perspectives and procedures through case studies and reflection. The fourth excerpt, "Creating a Multiple Intelligences Portfolio" by James Bellanca, Carolyn Chapman, and Elizabeth Swartz explains how to create portfolios that are organized, selective, representative, and that promote insight. Examples are provided for all levels of instruction. The fifth excerpt, "Electronic Portfolios," by R.W. Burniske describes how to create and manage electronic portfolios. Examples from the author's classroom are included for insight into the process.

It is important to remember the interdependence of assessment, curriculum, and instruction in creating a classroom that is filled with powerful learning.

The excerpts view assessment from a practical vantage point—they are easy to use, valid, reliable, and effectively communicate to parents and students how well the student is progressing in understanding content, problem solving, and transferring knowledge across the curriculum and into real life. Included are discussions of terms such as *standards, benchmarks, rubrics, grades, tests,* and *portfolios.* Although it is possible to separate each of the elements and tools from the other and to study them as independent items, it is most important to remember the interdependence of assessment, curriculum, and instruction in creating a classroom that is filled with powerful learning for each and every child.

REFERENCES

Ash, L. E. 2000. *Electronic student portfolios.* Arlington Heights, IL: SkyLight Training and Publishing.

Bellanca, J., C. Chapman, and B. Swartz. 1997. *Multiple assessments for multiple intelligences,* 3rd ed. Arlington Heights, IL: IRI/SkyLight Training and Publishing.

Burke, K. 1999. *The mindful school: How to assess authentic learning,* 3rd ed. Arlington Heights, IL: SkyLight Training and Publishing.

Burke, K., R. Fogarty, and S. Belgrad. 1994. *The mindful school: The portfolio connection.* Palatine, IL: IRI/SkyLight Training and Publishing.

Burniske, R. W. 2000. *Literacy in the cyberage: Composing ourselves online.* Arlington Heights, IL: SkyLight Training and Publishing.

Fogarty, R. 1998. *Balanced assessment*. Arlington Heights, IL: SkyLight Training and Publishing.

———. 1999. *How to raise test scores*. Arlington Heights, IL: SkyLight Training and Publishing.

O'Connor, K. 1999. *The mindful school: How to grade for learning*. Arlington Heights, IL: SkyLight Training and Publishing.

Perna, D. M., and J. R. Davis. 2000. *Aligning standards and curriculum for classroom success*. Arlington Heights, IL: SkyLight Training and Publishing.

Wiggins, G. and J. McTighe. 1998. *Understanding by design*. Alexandria, VA: Association for Supervision and Curriculum Development.

SELECTION 14

Introducing Authentic Assessment

by **Kay Burke**

Our history is thin when it comes to standard setting and assessment. We know how to design basic skills testing; how to use test data to rank, rather than improve, schools and to sort, rather than educate, children. We have rarely developed productive, rather than reductive or punitive, assessment and accountability systems—despite the fact that our students are among the most tested in the world.

—Wolf, LeMahieu, and Eresh, 1992, p. 9

For many years, the area of assessment has been relegated to a secondary role in the educational process. Many educators feel it has been ignored, misused, and totally misunderstood by administrators, teachers, parents, and students. In the last decade, assessment has emerged as one of the major components in the restructured school. One cannot open an educational journal, attend a workshop, or watch the news without reading and hearing about standards-based reform and performance assessment.

The emergence of authentic assessment coincides with an increase in the significance of standardized testing. Almost everyone is aware of the controversy surrounding standardized tests. Charges that standardized tests do not always measure significant learner achievement, do not measure growth and development, and do not accurately reflect what students can and cannot do have been made over and over again. Yet, despite the research and the criticism of standardized tests, policymakers, parents, and the general public base much of

Adapted from *The Mindful School: How to Assess Authentic Learning* by Kay Burke, 3rd ed., pp. ix–x, xx–xxiv, and 197–205.

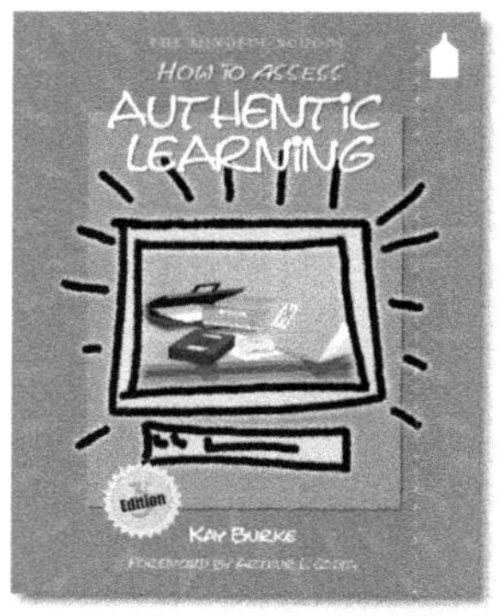

their perception of the educational system on the publication of standardized test scores and the comparisons of the scores in schools, districts, and states.

Standardized and Teacher-Made Tests

Standardized Tests

Despite criticisms that standardized tests do not always assess what students are learning and that they emphasize factual knowledge rather then performance or application, they are still the yardstick that the public and policymakers use to measure educational progress. Standardized tests are viewed by many people as being valid and reliable and, for the most part, the most effective method to compare students, schools, districts, states, and countries.

Most people agree that standardized test scores are used to determine many important educational decisions. Some states are using high stakes standardized tests to track students, to award diplomas, to reward classroom teachers with bonuses, if their students perform well, and to fire teachers and school administrators whose students perform poorly.

Teacher-Made Tests

Even though the press and the public focus on standardized test scores, most educators know that with the exception of placement decisions, bonuses, and probations doled out by some legislatures, teacher-made tests play a much bigger role in the day-to-day assessment process. Students receive grades from teachers. Unfortunately, many teachers do not have adequate training in preparing, evaluating, and using teacher-made tests effectively or in assessing student achievement and achievement of students.

Brandt (1992) states that "Educators who have long protested the misuse of standardized tests must concede that most of the tests students take are devised by teachers, and that some of those are even worse than the published ones" (p. 7).

Some Definitions of Authentic Assessment

Many terms or phrases are used when discussing the alternatives to conventional objective or multiple-choice testing. Alternative assessment, authentic assessment, and performance-based assessment are sometimes used synonymously "to mean variants of performance assessments that require students to generate rather than choose a response" (Herman, Aschbacher, and Winters, 1992, p. 2). Stefonek has gathered the following definitions and phrases from experts in the field to describe authentic assessment:

> - Methods that emphasize learning and thinking, especially higher-order thinking skills such as problem-solving strategies (Collins)
> - Tasks that focus on students' ability to produce a quality product or performance (Wiggins)
> - Disciplined inquiry that integrates and produces knowledge, rather than reproduces fragments of information others have discovered (Newmann)
> - Meaningful tasks at which students should learn to excel (Wiggins)
> - Challenges that require knowledge in good use and good judgment (Wiggins)
> - A new type of positive interaction between the assessor and assessee (Wiggins)
> - An examination of differences between trivial school tasks (e.g., giving definitions of biological terms) and more meaningful performance in nonschool settings (e.g., completing a field survey of wildlife) (Newmann)
> - Involvement that demystifies tasks and standards (Wiggins)
>
> (as cited in Stefonek, 1991, p. 1)

Introducing Authentic Assessment

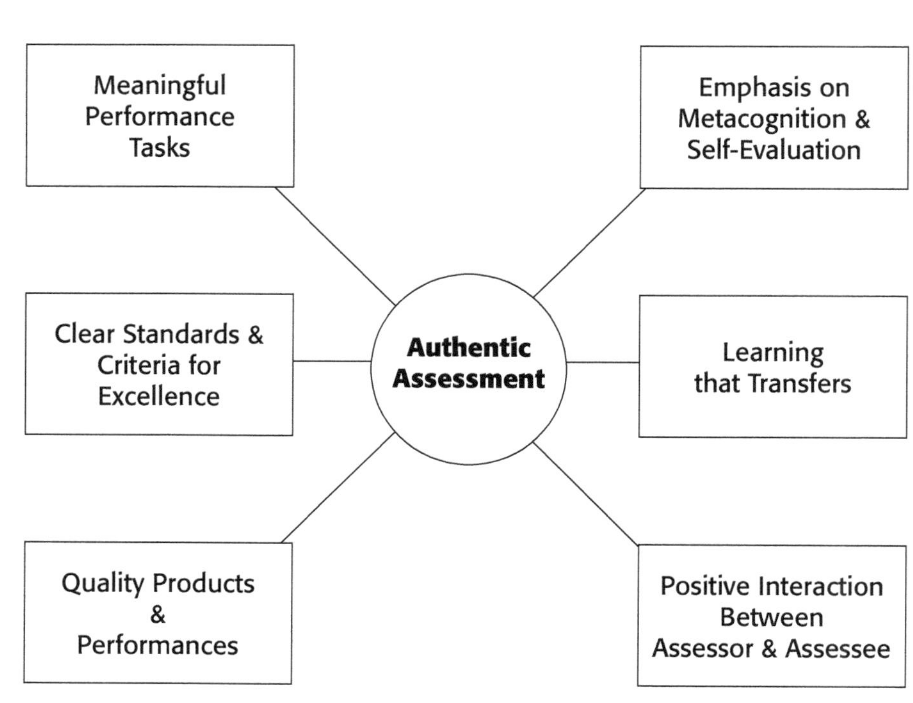

Regardless of the different terminology, most of the various definitions exhibit two central features: "First, all are viewed as *alternatives* to traditional multiple-choice, standardized achievement tests; second, all refer to *direct* examination of student *performance* on significant tasks that are relevant to life outside of school" (Worthen, 1993, p. 445).

Archbald and Newmann describe the term authentic assesment as follows: "A valid assessment system [that] provides information about the particular tasks on which students succeed or fail, but more important, it also presents tasks that are worthwhile, significant, and meaningful—in short, *authentic*" (Archbald & Newmann, 1988, p. 1).

Portfolios

Portfolios are collections of student evidence that show students' growth and development over time. Portfolios allow students to examine their own work and reflect on their learnings. They allow students to analyze their strengths and weaknesses and set both short- and long-term goals. A portfolio can contain both formative and summative evaluations because it is a collection of evidence to show how or if students are meeting goals or standards.

Accountability Testing

In addition to the assessments created and evaluated by teachers in the classroom, many states are implementing large-scale accountability testing that includes traditional standardized tests as well as some of the new performance-based standardized tests created by testing services and agencies.

Cole describes the differences between measurements developed to assess accountability as well as policy goals and measurements designed to assess instruction. (See the following chart.)

Large-Scale Assessment to Serve Accountability and Policy Goals	Classroom Assessment to Support Instruction
1. Formal 2. Objective 3. Time-efficient 4. Cost-effective 5. Widely applicable 6. Centrally processed	1. Informal 2. Teacher-mandated 3. Adapted to local content 4. Locally scored 5. Sensitive to short-term change in students' knowledge 6. Meaningful to students 7. Immediate and detailed feedback 8. Tasks that have instructional value 9. Conducted in a climate of greater trust than standardized tests

(adapted from Cole in Shepard, 1989, p. 7)

Introducing Authentic Assessment

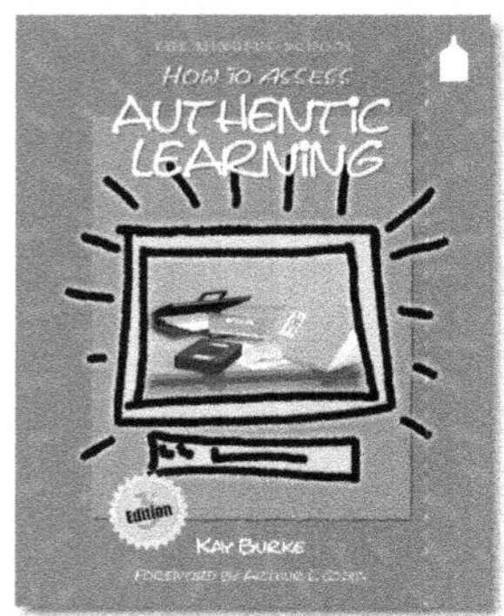

Some experts worry that the new accountability tests may be oversold, and the public will judge the success of teachers and schools solely on the basis of one test! O'Neil states that testing officials must also decide if state assessment programs can use the tests for accountability purposes as well as for improvement of classroom instruction (1992).

Classroom assessments are usually conducted in a climate of greater trust and relaxation than standardized tests. Classroom observations and grades often do not have to meet the same standards of accuracy. "Errors made in judging individual students are less serious and more easily redressed as teachers gather new evidence. Although single-teacher tests are probably less reliable (in a statistical sense) than a one-hour standardized test, accumulation of data gathered about individual pupils in the course of a school year has much more accuracy" (Shepard, 1989, p. 7).

Stiggins wonders why it is necessary to make a choice between traditional and standardized tests and performance assessments. "One of the things that troubles me greatly is that we're setting up performance assessments and paper-and-pencil tests against one another. Each test has a contribution to make. We can't throw away any of the tools at our disposal" (cited in O'Neil, 1992, p. 19). Critics of standardized tests want to throw out the baby with the bath water rather than use all the tools available to assess students fairly, accurately, and authentically.

Balanced Assessment

Assessment should not have to generate an "either or" or a "throw out the baby with the bath water" approach. Most educators agree with Stiggins that we need *all* the tools at our disposal. Shulman (1988) talks about teacher assessment where he suggests educators create "a union of insufficiencies" in which various methods of assessment are combined in such a way that the strengths of one offset the limitations of the other.

Student assessment should follow the same guidelines. No one assessment tool by itself is capable of producing the quality information that is needed to make an accurate judgment of a student's knowledge, skills, understanding of curriculum, motivation, social skills, processing skills and lifelong learning skills. Each single measurement by itself is insufficient to provide a true portrait of the student or learner. If educators combine standardized and teacher-made tests to measure knowledge and content with portfolios to measure process and growth, and performances to measure application, the "union of insufficiencies" will indeed provide a more accurate portrait of the individual learner.

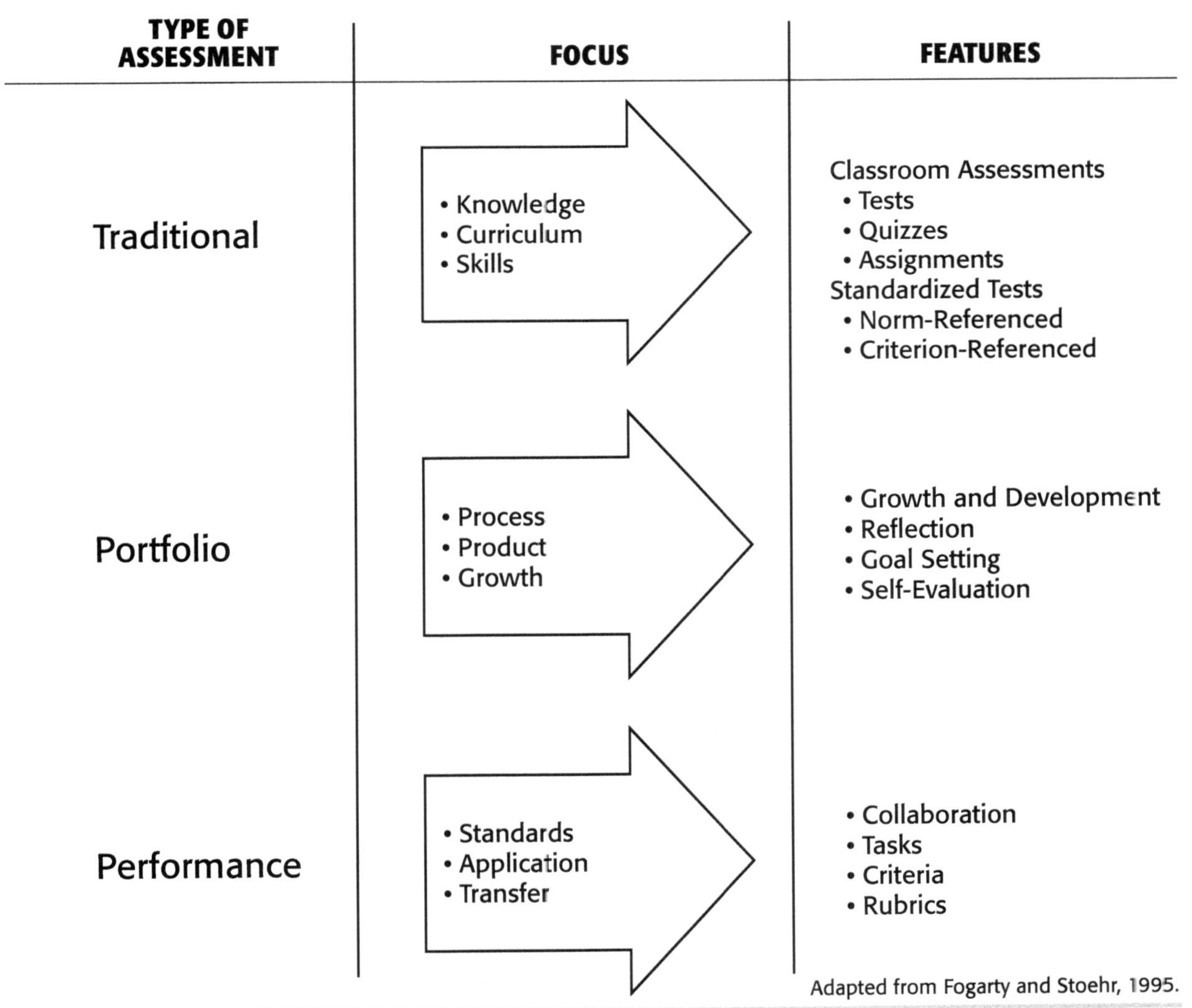

BALANCED ASSESSMENT
TYPE OF ASSESSMENT
FOCUS
FEATURES
Traditional
• Knowledge
• Curriculum
• Skills
Classroom Assessments
• Tests
• Quizzes
• Assignments
Standardized Tests
• Norm-Referenced
• Criterion-Referenced
Portfolio
• Process
• Product
• Growth
• Growth and Development
• Reflection
• Goal Setting
• Self-Evaluation
Performance
• Standards
• Application
• Transfer
• Collaboration
• Tasks
• Criteria
• Rubrics

Adapted from Fogarty and Stoehr, 1995.

Introducing Authentic Assessment

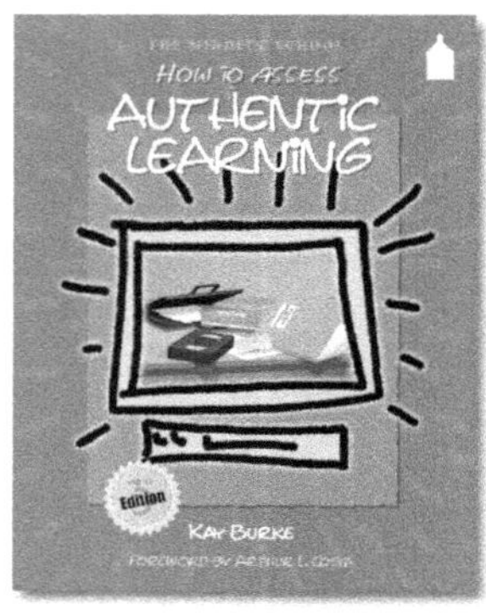

REFERENCES

Archbald, D. A., and F. M. Newmann. 1988. *Beyond standardized testing: Assessing authentic academic achievement in the secondary school.* Madison: University of Wisconsin, National Association of Secondary School Principals.

Brandt, R. 1992, May. Overview: A fresh focus for curriculum. *Educational Leadership,* 7.

Fogarty, R., and J. Stoehr. 1995. *Integrating curricula with multiple intelligences: Teams, themes, and threads.* Palatine, IL: IRI/SkyLight Training and Publishing.

Herman, J. L., P. R. Aschbacher, and L. Winters. 1992. *A practical guide to alternative assessment.* Alexandria, VA: Association for Supervision and Curriculum Development.

Hills, J. R. 1991, March. Apathy concerning grading and testing. *Phi Delta Kappan,* 540–45.

O'Neil, J. 1992, May. Putting performance assessment to the test. *Educational Leadership,* 14–19.

Shepard, L. 1989, April. Why we need better assessments. *Educational Leadership,* 4–9.

Shulman, L. 1988. A union of insufficiencies: Strategies for teacher assessment in a period of reform. *Educational Leadership.* 46: 36–41.

Stefonek, T. 1991. *Alternative assessment: A national perspective: Policy Briefs.* No. 15 and 16. Oak Brook, IL: North Central Regional Educational Laboratory.

Wolf, D. P., P. G. LeMahieu, and J. Eresh. 1992, May. Good measure: Assessment as a tool for educational reform. *Educational Leadership,* 8–13.

Worthen, B. R. 1993, February. Critical issues that will determine the future of alternative assessment. *Phi Delta Kappan,* 444–56.

SELECTION 15

Designing and Using the Standards-Based Curriculum

by **Daniel M. Perna and James R. Davis**

Designing the standards-based curriculum at the district level so that it can be put to meaningful use in the classroom involves the application of some basic tools that simplify the system, but the primary action involved in this work is the thought process. To do the work of aligning curriculum to standards, analytical, interpretive, and creative thinking is required. It follows then that to do this well takes practice. Designing curriculum that is standards-based using criterion standards results in having an articulated list of performance expectations that define how curriculum and instruction are directly tied to standards. In addition, within the criterion standards themselves are the means for evaluating whether or not the standards have been met by students.

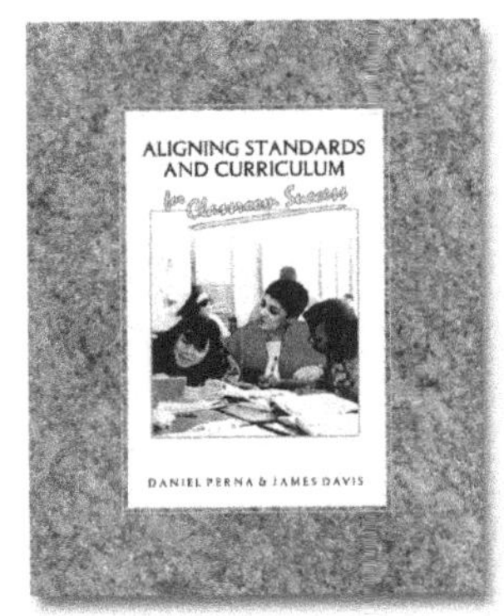

ALIGNING STANDARDS AND CURRICULUM
for Classroom Success
DANIEL PERNA & JAMES DAVIS

The concept of designing criterion standards from state standards is in agreement with the work done by Wiggins and McTighe (1998). In defining a process they call backward design, they recommend identifying desired results as the first step. Because standards are statements that describe the desired results, looking at standards is the first step. In the second step, McTighe and Wiggins contend that there must be a determination of what evidence will be expected to prove that the desired result has been achieved. Criterion standards provide the statements of what the evidence must be. Thirdly,

Designing and Using the Standards-Based Curriculum

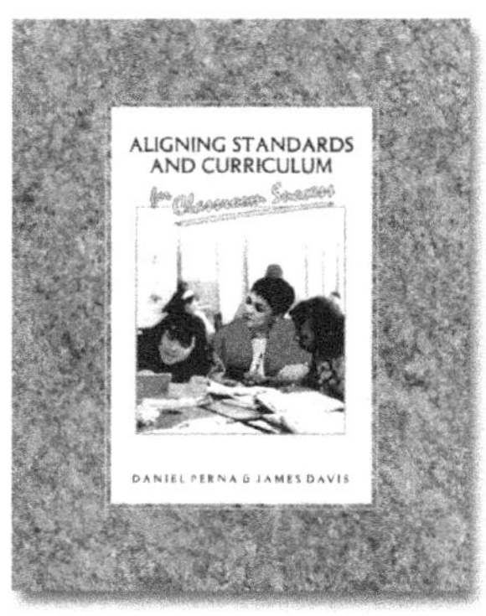

McTighe and Wiggins say that learning experiences and instruction can only be designed after one knows the results and the evidence necessary to support achievement of the results. After criterion standards are composed, teachers must decide how they will teach students to demonstrate completion of the criterion standards. Figure 15.1 expresses the relationship between the graduation standard and the criterion standards.

Satisfying a criterion standard is indicative of a student attaining an element of the graduation standard. The student either can or cannot listen to something and *retell* what was heard. The student either can or cannot *employ* each component of the protocol for group discussion, which is part of attaining the graduation standard. However, achievement of a standard cannot be reliably determined unless students are required to demonstrate in numerous situations, over a period of time, or within the complexity of the general expectations of the curriculum that they can do what the criterion standard asks of them. Criterion standards must be written with enough

Criterion Standards as By-products of Graduation Standards

Pennsylvania *(Standard):* Listen to others
Third grade *(Benchmark):* Listening without interrupting; asking clarifying questions; distinguishing relevant information, ideas, and opinions from those which are relevant; and taking notes when prompted
(All statements below are *criterion standards.*)

1. Employs (*performance verb*) protocol for group discussion.
   a. Utilizes (*performance verb*) rule of one person speaking at a time.
   b. Demonstrates (*performance verb*) allowing all people the opportunity to speak.
   c. Employs (*performance verb*) eye contact with speaker while listening.
   d. Utilizes (*performance verb*) the body signals of listening.
   e. Demonstrates (*performance verb*) proper manners when speaker makes an error.
2. Composes (*performance verb*) questions from the oral presentation.
3. Offers (*performance verb*) questions to the speaker.
4. Retells (*performance verb*) ideas presented by the oral source.
5. Explains (*performance verb*) what was presented by the oral source.
6. Identifies (*performance verb*) reality from fantasy in the oral presentation.
7. Determines (*performance verb*) reality and/or fantasy.
8. Identifies (*performance verb*) facts and opinions.
9. Distinguishes (*performance verb*) facts from opinions.

Figure 15.1

Constructing Criterion Standards Using the Standards Assessment System

Step One: Review and evaluate the state standard and its benchmarks.

Step Two: Determine ways students can demonstrate that they have achieved the standard.

Step Three: Choose a performance verb from the appropriate level with which to begin the criterion standard.

Step Four: Review the criterion standard and determine at what grade level the criterion standards should be achieved.

Figure 15.2

information so that the teachers using the standards know exactly what performances to assess.

Figure 15.2 shows the method by which criterion standards are derived using a process called the Standards Assessment System. With this process, local districts and schools define what local students must do in order to accomplish standards in their school. Educators and members of the community draw upon their own experiences, their knowledge of local curriculum, and their understanding of what students need to know and be able to do in order to meet the state standards.

The number of criterion standards created and their level of specificity is up to those writing the standards. However, it is important to remember that one of the central components of aligning standards is making those standards easier to use in the classroom. Too much of even a good thing circumvents the purpose. A workable example of what students need to do is: "students must employ protocol for group discussion;" instead of: "teach students the steps of the protocol for group discussion." Using [Bloom's Taxonomy] as a tool for writing criterion standards calls attention to what level of Bloom's Taxonomy students are expected to function to meet the criterion standards. Writers of criterion standards decide what level of thinking is required for the student to demonstrate achievement of the standard. They make this decision by determining what basic things a student should be able to do to achieve the standard.

What Bloom's Taxonomy has made evident to educators for many years is that learning is not just the memory and recall of

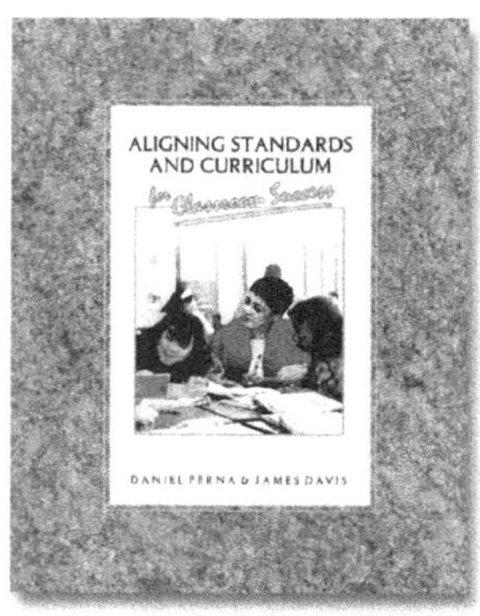

information but that students learn best by exercising the higher levels of thinking. Educators should keep in mind that knowledge, comprehension, extrapolation, and interpretation alone probably will not demonstrate full achievement of a given standard. By thinking about the association of the taxonomy to the completion of standards, it becomes easier to see that by requiring students to perform at all levels, the students will have a greater chance of success in completing the standards and of growing as learners. Educators can check to see if all or most of the levels of the taxonomy are touched upon and to see if the criterion standards constructed range in their level of complexity. If they do not, adjustments can be made.

When each idea about how a student can evidence achievement of a particular state standard has been translated into a criterion standard, educators should then reflect upon the following questions:

- Does the collection of criterion standards as they are now written require students to do more than memory and recall work?
- If a student achieves each of the criterion standards as set forth will that mean that he or she has demonstrated achievement of the state standard?

The performance verb chosen should make what the student must know or be able to do readily apparent. Because learning is a continuum of experience, it makes sense that teachers communicate both horizontally and vertically about what students need to know and be able to do to prepare for the next level of study and for life. Thus, the completion of standards requires a composite view of learning. The development of a standards-based model means that each grade has a part in the achievement of the standards. The groundwork for achieving standards in the twelfth grade begins in kindergarten and even before. Consequently, each grade needs a list of criterion standards to focus with an eye to the future, toward graduation. A grade-by-grade articulation of criterion standards has the potential to dispel the misconception that only teachers at grade levels where testing takes place are responsible to prepare students to meet standards.

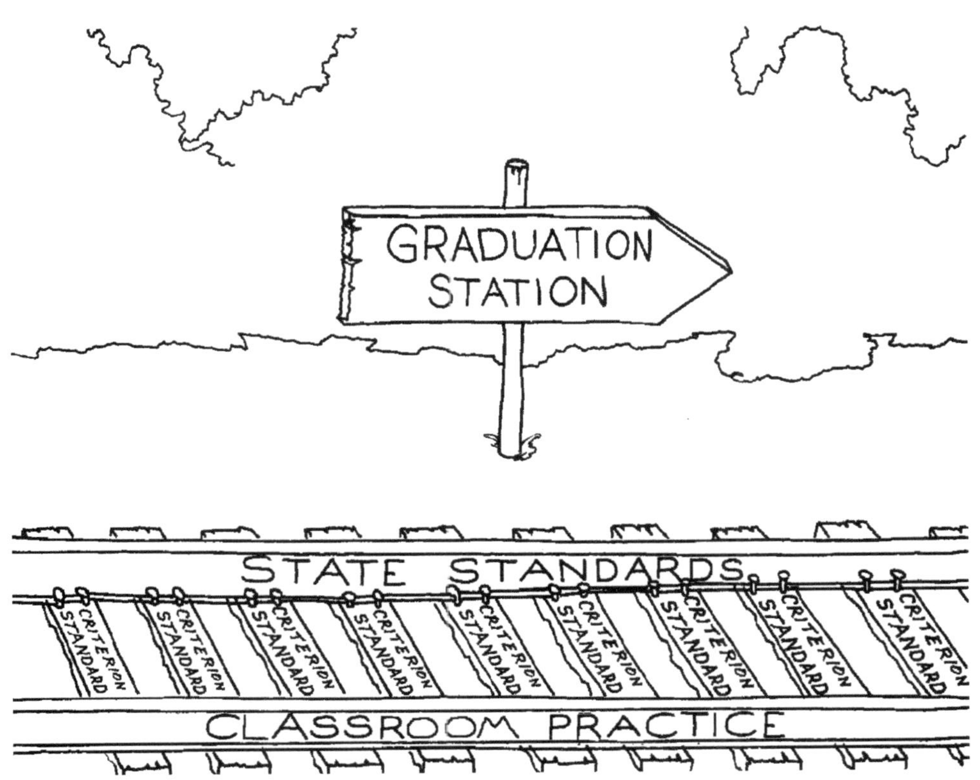

The process of writing criterion standards is about defining the components of learning, and possible demonstrations of that learning are part of achieving the graduation standard. Recognizing that graduation standards require a continuum of performance, educators and non-educators alike can look at criterion standards and see what is expected of a student at each point in his or her education. Criterion standards tie two seemingly divergent concepts together—grades and state standards.

Writing Criterion Standards

While individual teachers can most certainly use the steps in the Standards Assessment System to help derive meaning from state standards documents, criterion standards written as a collaborative process in which all stakeholders take part have the

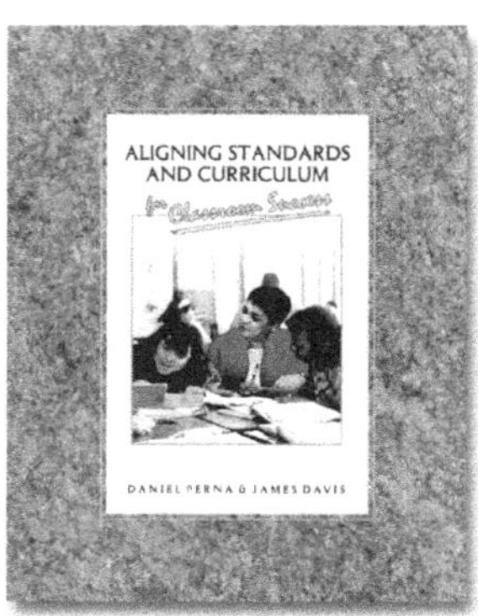

most value and applicability. With this in mind, a team of persons must be formed to write the criterion standards. The objective of the writing team is to produce a document that defines exactly what students are supposed to know and be able to do. It is a framework for the local district's or school's curriculum and provides evidence that the system is teaching to standards. It can be used to gauge student achievement and signal when students are not performing to expectations so that remediation can be undertaken. The result of the writing and design effort will help demonstrate to the community and the state that the persons undertaking this process understand and take seriously the responsibility to prepare students to meet standards. It is crucial for persons serving on the writing team to be cognizant of the fact that the standards have been determined, and it is the team's role to decide how the district, or school, will address the standards.

Building a Team

Selecting teams of individuals to do the writing is very important. Each team must have a writing facilitator, who typically is a teacher, curriculum coordinator, a supervisor of a respective academic department, a principal, or some other designated individual chosen by the administration. The leader's first responsibility is the selection of the group of persons who will write the criterion standards. Inclusive representation is an important consideration. Where the district is relatively small, all faculty members can participate in the process. In large districts, however, it is impractical for all faculty members to be made part of the actual writing process.

Writing teams should include:

- a representative from every grade level and/or academic discipline;
- administrators from each divisional level of the district;
- at least one guidance counselor (social workers and specials teachers may also be included or may consult on the results of the process); and
- one or two parents and/or business persons.

Characteristics of an Effective Writing Team

Characteristics of an effective writing team are the same as those of any effective team. The working dynamic that drives this process requires that team members be cooperative and willing to recognize that debate and challenges to each other's beliefs are not negative. The team members must be able to put aside personal feelings and individual agendas in order to produce the best possible product and compromise with each other. The team must function as one unit, but also be representative of all stakeholders.

It is important for people who have negative feelings about standards to work alongside those who have a more positive view. Those who are neutral on the subject should also be included. All three types are very important to the design process because each must be heard from so that together they create a balanced view and a balanced discussion in arriving at the criterion standards.

The Textbook Dilemma

Traditionally, textbook selection committees had a great deal of influence over what was taught and what students learned, because the materials they selected often became the de facto curriculum. It is not surprising then that some people want to use textbooks as a basis for writing the criterion standards. However, the use of the textbook is the wrong way to develop the criterion standards for the following reasons:

- The developed criterion standards may appear to be an outline of a textbook. This means that the local district uses the text as its curriculum as opposed to having a curriculum that uses the standards as its focus, thereby forfeiting the opportunity the standards system provides to accommodate local priorities.
- Writers likely try very hard to write criterion standards based on an entire text as opposed to focusing the criterion standards on what students must learn and demonstrate in order to show achievement of standards.

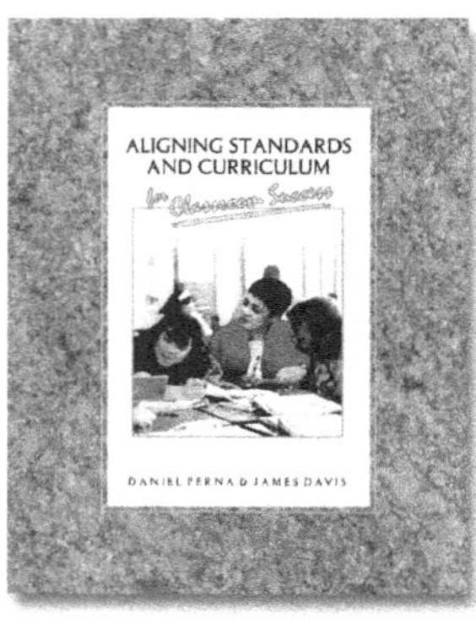

- Participants rely on the text to define criterion standards instead of relying on their experience and expertise.
- Using grade- or level-specific texts hampers both horizontal and vertical efforts at curriculum integration.

Once criterion standards are defined then textbooks can be used to determine if certain concepts are missing or if the text must be mentioned in the process of writing a particular criterion standard. The textbook plays a less significant role as teachers exercise their professional skills and utilize a wide variety of instructional activities aimed at bringing about student success. The same is true with assessment as the assessment process becomes less formal and summative than paper-and-pencil testing. Teachers choose and allow for students to demonstrate proficiency in a wide variety of ways that more adequately allow for individual student differences. Assessment also becomes much more of a process and less of an event. Instruction and assessment becomes ongoing and intertwined. There is no longer a need for instruction to be put on hold while one tests. Articulating criterion standards makes it possible to continually assess while teaching the standards-based curriculum.

Using Criterion Standards

Once graduation standards have been defined in terms of criterion standards they can be used many ways and by many different groups, including:

- analyzing learning expectations using Bloom's Taxonomy,
- planning lessons,
- communicating expectations,
- diagnosing student learning difficulties,
- testing, and
- enhancing teacher performance.

Standards as a Series of Descriptive Statements

Number of standards related to each level of Bloom in Massachusetts standards:

Bloom's Level Taxonomy	Language Arts	Mathematics	Science
Know	43	14	30
Comprehend	1	11	0
Interpret	4	4	15
Extrapolate	1	1	3
Apply	28	55	12
Analyze	20	11	24
Synthesize	10	25	8
Evaluate	1	8	7

Figure 15.3

Analyzing Learning Expectations

Using the relationship of action verbs to the level of learning on Bloom's Taxonomy (Bloom, et al. 1956), each criterion standard is counted as directly relating to one level because of the performance verb that is used. Analysis of the way the criterion standards fit with Bloom's Taxonomy has credibility. An illustration of the results of such an examination is shown in Figure 15.3. This type of analysis can help teachers to see strengths and problems in preparing students for the standards.

In the standards from Massachusetts, for example, analysis of the areas of language arts, mathematics, and science found an emphasis on knowledge and application in language arts, application in mathematics, and knowledge and analysis in science. Figure 15.3 shows the results of this analysis.

The assessment expectations are obviously strong in those categories with high numbers. However, one can note the lack of comprehension, interpretation, and extrapolation expectations in language arts standards. Does this indicate that anything is wrong with Massachusetts' standards? Not necessarily, but the information provides clear-cut data for a group to discuss the situation in terms of standards. Analyzing learner expectations can be done by an individual teacher or a district. Teachers could use this type of analysis to diagnose potential gaps in their own

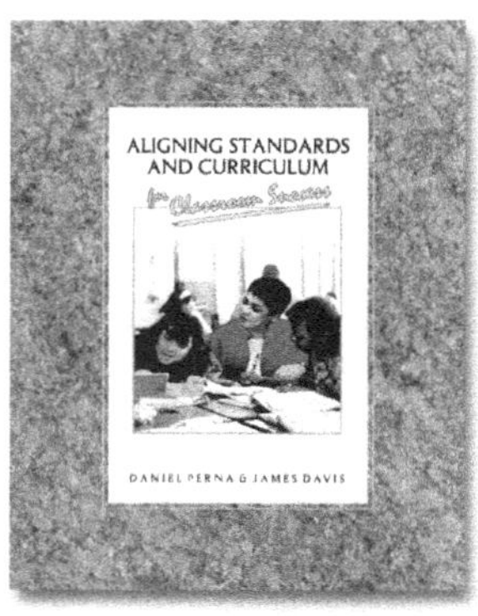

curriculum situation. Only by casting state graduation standards as criterion standards can this process be done.

The Record of Knowledge

Traditional grading systems do not really tell the public what students know and can do. Many attempts have been made to reform traditional grading systems and most have failed because there seems to be a need to give and receive As and Bs or 85s and 90s. Perhaps this happens because these terms or numbers serve to rank students.

The true communication of students' abilities requires a reporting system that is performance- or standards-based and actually tells parents, employers, and colleges what students know and can do. The way this is accomplished is up to the locality, but it may entail portfolios, performance checklists, projects, work samples, and rubrics. By whatever means, the key is to establish a method of communicating what the graduate actually can do. To say that the student received an A or C in mathematics does not really tell much. Using criterion standards as a form of assessment creates a description of what students can do. The example shown in Figure 15.4 of the performance checklist of an eighth-grade science student, shows how criterion standards can be used as the descriptor for assessing what a student can and cannot do. In the example, the teacher assessed students on their abilities to carry out experiments within a laboratory situation. The criterion standards were written as part of the standards-based curriculum. The checklist documents several opportunities for students to take part in laboratory experiences.

Lesson Planning

The established curriculum should be the root of lesson planning. In other words, all instruction should come out of the written curriculum. By using a standards-based curriculum designed with criterion standards, the teacher is able to design lessons directly related to state and local standards.

Communicating Expectations

One of the most obvious ways to use the criterion standards is to publish them for the entire community by placing them on the school's or district's Web page and in print publications such as newsletters, parent handbooks, and curriculum guides, and these can be distributed to parents and business people in addition to teachers and administrators. A district-wide curriculum map is useful in communicating with staff and the public. A glance at a curricular map gives interested parents and other members of the public a basic knowledge of the educational offerings of the district and expectations for students. It should also represent a profile of expectations for graduates and for each grade along the way.

An effort should be made to call parents' attention to the standards and ways that they can use the standards to further their children's learning by monitoring their progress against the articulated criterion standards. In addition, these statements can be used as a tool to further parent/teacher

Performance Checklist: An Alternative to the Traditional Report Card

GRADE 8 ASSESSMENT OF LABORATORY EXPERIENCES

Criteria	*Yes*	*No*
Defines variables.	❏	❏
Defines controls.	❏	❏
Identifies reason for variables.	❏	❏
Identifies reason for controls.	❏	❏
Identifies need to determine why a test must be given.	❏	❏
Identifies inappropriate problems.	❏	❏
Identifies the correct solution to the problems.	❏	❏
Identifies a possible solution but not proper solution.	❏	❏
Utilizes the primary source of information.	❏	❏
Relates need to seek supportive evidence to primary source.	❏	❏
Uses complete sentences in lab reports.	❏	❏

Figure 15.4

communication. When parents and interested community members read them, they know what is expected of students.

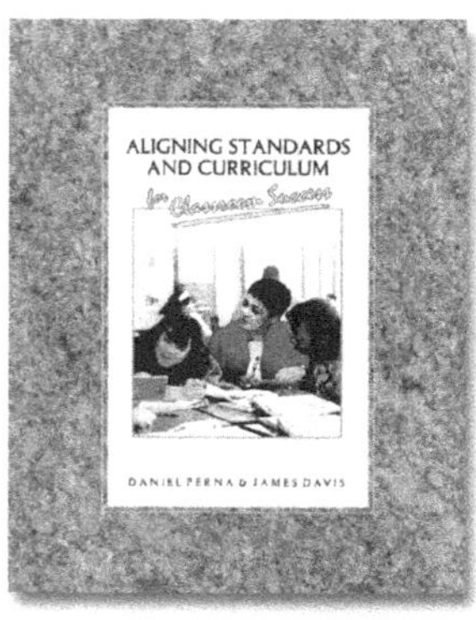

Diagnosing Student Learning Difficulties

By distilling voluminous state standards documents into criterion standards, teachers have a ready checklist to use as a diagnostic tool. Criterion standards itemize what students know and can do, and they make clear what they cannot do. This allows the professional educator to identify potential problems and institute measures to remediate those problems. As diagnostic tools, criterion standards can be used in student conferences, parent conferences, and in discussion or analysis of state-level tests.

Student Conferences

First, the teacher can use the criterion standards in student conferences. If the students are fully aware of what they are supposed to know and be able to do, the teacher can conference by using the statements as a way to discuss with students their strengths and deficiencies. The teacher can literally point to specific criterion standards and tell the child if he or she is meeting the standard.

Parent Conferences

The same thing can be done in parent conferences. In many school districts, teachers use the appropriate criterion standards to inform parents of what their children are doing. The criterion standards are a checklist of items to discuss with the parent, and the teacher points out what the student can do, is getting close to doing, and is not capable of doing. This way, parents have more than a grade to use as a gauge for their children's success.

State-Level Testing

The third way that teachers can use the criterion standards as a diagnostic tool comes while preparing students for state-level testing. If teachers monitor and assess students in accordance with the criterion standards, they have an abundance of evidence that tells them whether students will achieve on the test or not. For example, if the teacher has ascertained that a student knows and can do almost all things on the criterion standard list, then the teacher can be assured that the student will achieve on the assessment test. Conversely, if the teacher has determined that the student shows decided deficiencies, the teacher has a strong case for predicting that the student will have difficulty on the state assessment.

Criterion-Referenced Testing

Criterion-referenced tests are assessment tools that test only those concepts, facts, and ideas (the criteria) that students are informed will be tested. Burke defines criterion-referenced tests as standardized assessments that "are designed to compare a student's test performance to learning tasks or skill levels" (1994, 17). The tests are most often designed by teams of teachers with input from administrators. Districts can use criterion standards they have created to devise criterion-referenced assessments. They can then test the students and gather data to measure the success of the curriculum. Such tests should be devised to assess the achievement of criterion standards exactly as criterion standards were written. Figure 15.5 provides a sample fifth-grade reading test on which the achievement of criterion standards can be assessed.

Standards As a Series of Descriptive Statements

Uses prior knowledge in reading a story.
Writes inferences about the title of the story.
Lists valid reasons why the author wrote the story.
Determines appropriate inferences from the picture.
Predicts a setting correctly.
Employs clues to support inferences of a character's whereabouts.
Infers correctly what a character is doing.
Relates clues to support inference of what a character is doing.
Infers correctly the setting of a character.
Utilizes clues to support the inference of the character's setting.

Figure 15.5

Designing and Using the Standards-Based Curriculum

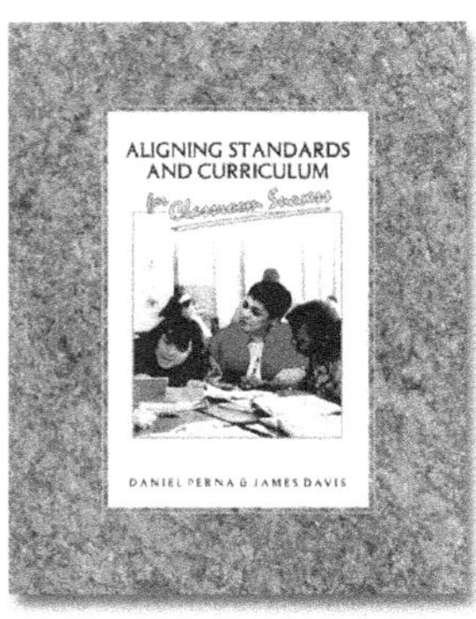

The test provides the means to gather data on each student, but also does something else for the district curriculum. It reports how well the students as a group achieved on the assessment.

An ongoing assessment program in the classroom can be criterion-based if criterion standards are prevalent. Teachers cannot afford the time to stop instruction to conduct assessment activities. When teachers and students enter into the instructional process with an understanding of the standards to be addressed and the procedures for assessment, teachers are encouraged to utilize their professional judgment concerning student's abilities on an ongoing basis. Therefore, criterion-referenced assessment can take place every day.

Teaching to the test is not bad. In fact, if assessments are practical and appropriate, teaching to that assessment is a requirement. Frequently in the past, teachers decided what they were going to teach and then tried to design a test that would measure the success of that instruction. Teachers should instead design the assessment procedures informed by and reflecting criterion standards before instruction occurs. Again, this is in sync with Wiggins and McTighe's (1998) backward planning concept. This procedure allows for student activity on a daily basis to prepare for the test. Consequently, there are no surprises at test time.

By giving students criterion-referenced assessments based on criterion standards, the teacher tests material taught in the curriculum on a regularly sustained basis. In addition, the teacher tests without paper and pencil. The regular activities of the class are used as a means of determining if a student is or is not reaching a criterion standard.

Reporting the results of criterion-referenced assessments must become more narrative in nature. A simple A or B, P or F, or 75 or 90 percent cannot truly communicate what a student knows or can do. Chances are that criterion standards will be scored on a daily basis by handheld computers or card readers as technology increasingly finds its level in the classroom. Students cannot meet a standard half or three-quarters of the way. However, they may be half or three-quarters of the way toward meeting a standard. Rubrics can be designed for grading purposes that give criteria in the categories of "does not meet the standards," "meets the standards," or "exceeds the standards."

Assessment results should be utilized to (1) report progress to students and parents, (2) communicate a student's abilities to subsequent teachers, (3) inform businesses and post-secondary institutions of a given student's abilities, and (4) guide further instruction. Reporting progress to students and parents serves to keep them apprised with respect to where the student stands in the instructional process. Students, teachers, and parents all should have a basic understanding of where the student is at the beginning of the process and where he or she should be at the conclusion of instruction. Given these two landmarks, progress reporting becomes an analysis of the progress the student has made from point A toward point B.

In most cases, students move on to subsequent teachers and/or instructional processes, making the post-assessment from one level become the pre-assessment for the next. This allows the teacher of the next phase to get a clear picture of the student's strengths, weaknesses, and interests, enabling that teacher to plan appropriately. Since the criterion standards are written on a continuum basis from grade to grade and course to course, the teacher knows exactly how to appraise students at the beginning of a particular grade or course. The teacher goes to the criterion standards that should have been achieved and then determines if the student is ready for the next level or phase of instruction.

Testing

With the advent of handheld computers, teachers will be able to keep records of incidental student activities. In this way, assessment will not intrude upon learning. As a student demonstrates performance of one of the criterion standards, the teacher can note and file it electronically. At the end of a

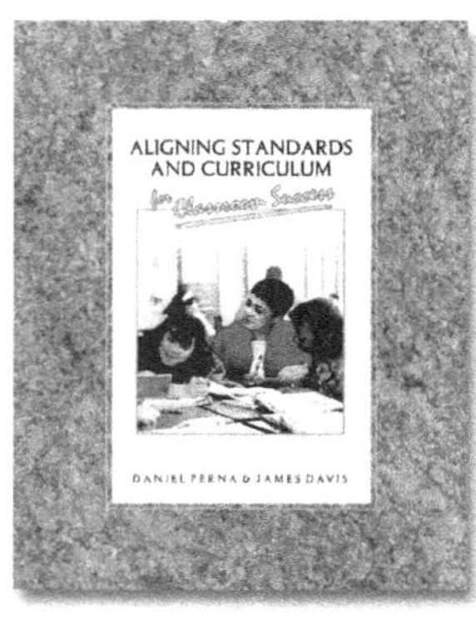

grading period, the teacher can then call up the data and note, for example, that a student effectively performed a criterion standard on five separate occasions.

REFERENCES

Arkansas Department of Education. 1991. *Arkansas curriculum framework*. Little Rock: Arkansas Department of Education.

Bloom, B. S., M. D. Englehart, E. J. Furst, W. H. Hill, and D. R. Krathwohl, eds. 1956. *Taxonomy of educational objectives: Handbook 1, cognitive domain*. New York: Mckay.

Burke, K. 1994. *The mindful school: How to assess authentic learning*. Palatine, IL: IRI/SkyLight Training and Publishing.

Buttram, J. L., and T. Waters. 1997. Improving America's schools through standards-based education. *NASSP Bulletin*.

Daggett, W. R. 1995. Testing and assessment in American schools committing to rigor and relevance. *Conference proceedings: Third annual model schools conference*. Schnectady, NY: International Center for Leadership in Education.

———. 2000. *The curriculum matrix*. Rexford, NY: International Center for Leadership in Education.

Daniels, H., A. Hyde, and S. Zemelman. 1993. *Best practice: New standards for teaching and learning in America's schools*. Portsmouth, NH.

Gagne, R. M., L. J. Briggs, and W. W. Wagner. 1988. *Principals of instructional design*. 3rd ed. New York: Holt, Rinehart, and Wilson.

Gandal, M. 1995. Not all standards are created equal. *Educational Leadership*. Alexandria, VA: Association for Supervision and Curriculum Development.

Gilman, D. A., R. Andrew, and C. D. Rafferty. 1995. Making assessment a meaningful part of instruction. *NASSP Bulletin* 79: 20–24.

Hart, D. 1994. *Authentic assessment: A handbook for educators*. Menlo Park, CA: Addison-Wesley.

International Reading Association and National Council of Teachers of English. 1994. *Standards for the assessment of reading and writing*. Newark, DE: IRA/NCTE Joint Task Force on Assessment, United States of America.

———. 1996. *Standards for the English language arts*. Hillsboro, OR.

Kendall, J. S., and R. J. Marzano. 1995. The McREL Database: A tool for constructing local standards. *Educational Leadership*. Alexandria, VA: Association for Supervision and Curriculum Development.

———. 1996. *Content knowledge: A compendium of standards and benchmarks for K–12 education*. Aurora, CO: Mid-continent Regional Educational Laboratory.

Killion, J. 1999. *Standards provide opportunity for staff development*. Oxford, OH: National Staff Development Council.

Krueger, A. B., and J. T. Sutton. 1997. Do we need new national standards in mathematics and science? *NASSP Bulletin*.

Marzano, R. J., and J. S. Kendall. 1996. *A comprehensive guide to designing standards-based districts, schools, and classrooms*. Alexandria, VA: Association for Supervision and Curriculum Development.

Marzano, R. J., J. McTighe, and D. Pickering. 1993. *Assessing student outcomes: Performance assessment using the dimensions of learning model*. Alexandria, VA: Association for Supervision and Curriculum Development.

Massachusetts Department of Education. 1996a. *Mathematics, curriculum framework*. Malden, MA: Massachusetts Department of Education.

———. 1996b. *English language arts, curriculum framework*. Malden, MA: Massachusetts Department of Education.

———. 1996c. *Science and technology, curriculum framework*. Malden, MA: Massachusetts Department of Education.

McTighe, J. 1995. *Developing performance assessment tasks for the classroom: Templates for designers*. Frederick, MD: Maryland Assessment Consortium.

National Council on Education. Standards and Testing. 1992. *Raising standards for American education*. Washington, DC: U.S. Department of Education.

Perna, D. 1998. *Using trigger verbs to merge curriculum and assessment in a school distict curriculum design*. Dissertation. Ft. Lauderdale, FL: Nova Southeastern University.

Pullin, D. C. 1994. Learning to work: The impact of curriculum and assessment standards on educational opportunity. *Harvard Educational Review*. 64: 31–54.

Schmoker, M., and R. J. Marzano. 1999. Realizing the promise of standards-based education. *Educational Leadership*. 56(6): 17–21.

Shikellamy School District. 1994. *Shikellamy strategic plan*. Sunbury, PA.

———. 1995a. *Communications curriculum draft*. Sunbury, PA.

———. 1995b, September. *Shikellamy board of education minutes*. Sunbury, PA.

———. 1995c. *Science and technology curriculum draft*. Sunbury, PA.

Designing and Using the Standards-Based Curriculum

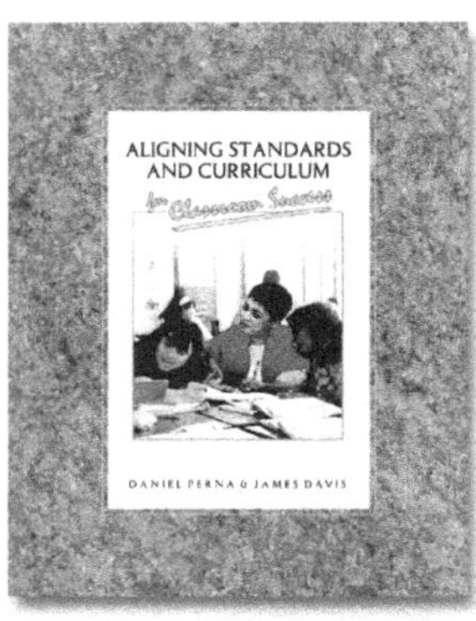

Stiggins, R. 1994. *Student-centered classroom assessment.* Upper Saddle River, NJ: Prentice Hall.

Wiggins, G. 1993. *Assessing student performance: Exploring the purpose and limits of testing.* San Francisco: Jossey-Bass.

———. 1997. Work standards: Why we need standards for instructional and assessment design. *NASSP Bulletin.*

Wiggins, G. and J. McTighe. 1998. *Understanding by design.* Alexandria, VA: Association for Supervision and Curriculum Development.

SELECTION 16

Guidelines for Grading

by **Ken O'Connor**

Why Grade?

REFLECTING ON . . . GRADING PURPOSES

Reflect on why educators grade students and their work. List as many purposes as you can. When you have finished your list, number each purpose in your order of priority (1 for highest priority).

Through such reflection and with discussion with colleagues, you will find that there are many purposes for grading. To understand this fully, it is helpful to consider classifications from two sources. According to Gronlund and Linn in their classic text, *Measurement and Evaluation in Teaching,* there are four general uses for grading:

- *instructional uses,* to clarify learning goals, indicate students' strengths and weaknesses, inform about students' personal-social development, and contribute to student motivation
- *communicative uses,* to inform parents/guardians about the learning program of the school and how well their children are achieving the intended learning goals
- *administrative uses,* to include "determining promotion and graduation, awarding honors, determining

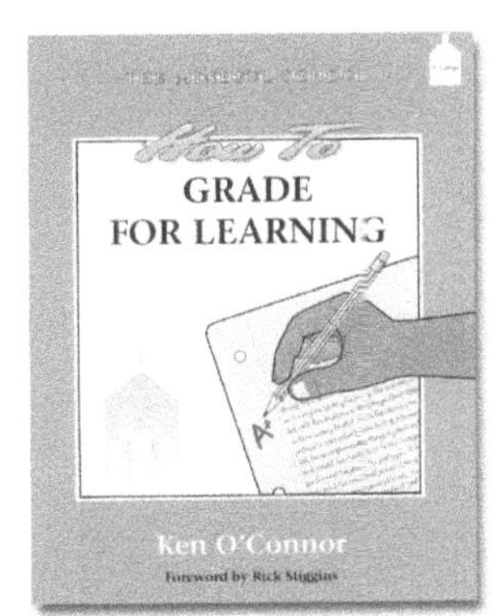

Adapted from *The Mindful School: How to Grade for Learning* by Ken O'Connor, pp. 10–35 and 180–83. © 1999 by SkyLight Training and Publishing Inc.

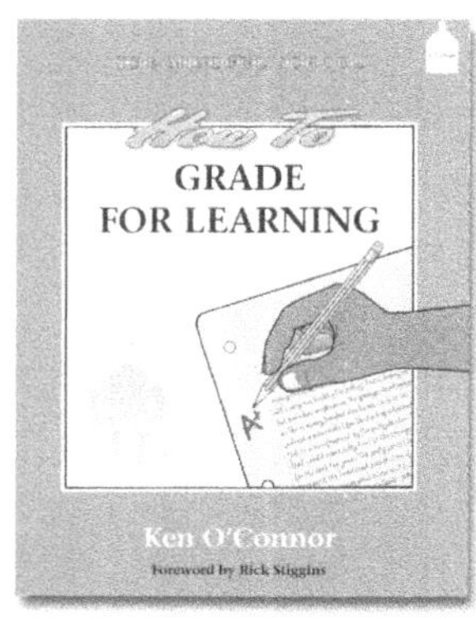

athletic eligibility, and reporting to other schools and prospective employers" (Gronlund and Linn 1990, 429)
- *guidance uses,* to help students make their educational and vocational plans realistically (1990, 428–429)

A second source, Guskey, summarized the purposes of grading as follows:

- *Communicate* the achievement status of students to parents and others.
- *Provide information* that students can use for self-evaluation.
- *Select, identify, or group* students for certain educational paths or programs.
- *Provide incentives* to learn.
- *Evaluate* the effectiveness of instructional programs. (1996, 17)

Both of these classifications were developed relative to the broader, double meaning of grading; when the narrower, single meaning of grading employed in this chapter is used, all of the purposes still apply, although some uses apply more to marks than to grades, for example, self-assessment. Also note that the use of grades, especially traditional grades, for accountability purposes is of very limited value.

It is clear from these two classifications that grades serve many different purposes. Therein lies the basic problem with grades—to serve so many purposes, one letter or number symbol must carry many types of information (achievement, effort, behavior, etc.) in the grade. Putting together such a variety of information makes it very difficult to clearly understand what grades mean. In order to achieve this clarity, a definitive prioritization of the purpose of grades is needed. Bailey and McTighe suggested that "the primary purpose of . . . grades is to *communicate* [emphasis added] student achievement to students, parents, school administrators, post-secondary institutions, and employers" (1996, 120).

Communicating student achievement is the primary purpose of grades. Simply stated, if clear communication does not occur, then none of the other purposes of grades can be effectively carried out. Communication is also the purpose that best fits with what grades are—symbols that summarize performance over a period of time. Communication is most effective when it is clear and concise; grades are certainly concise, and they can be clear communication vehicles if there is shared understanding of how they are determined and, thus, what they mean. Instructional and guidance uses not only need to be based on grades with clear meaning, but also are best served by much more information than is provided by symbols. The administrative uses of grades are really a form of communication and are best served when communication is clear. The other purposes of grades are also best served when communication is the focus—clarity about student achievement enables all the participants in the educational endeavor to do what is needed to support learning and encourage success.

Acknowledging that the primary purpose of grades is communication helps to point teachers in some very clear directions concerning the ingredients of grades and the use of grades at different levels within the school system. Emphasizing communication about achievement means that clarity is needed about what achievement is. This emphasis is reflected in the analysis of grading and the grading guidelines presented in this chapter.

What Are the Underlying Perspectives on Grading?

Seven perspectives, which were developed from a variety of assessment specialists including Stiggins, McTighe, and Guskey, are discussed in the following sections. They provide both a clear indication of the philosophy that underlies the approach to grading advocated in this chapter and a vehicle for addressing some of the myths about grades and some of the criticisms of grading.

Guidelines for Grading

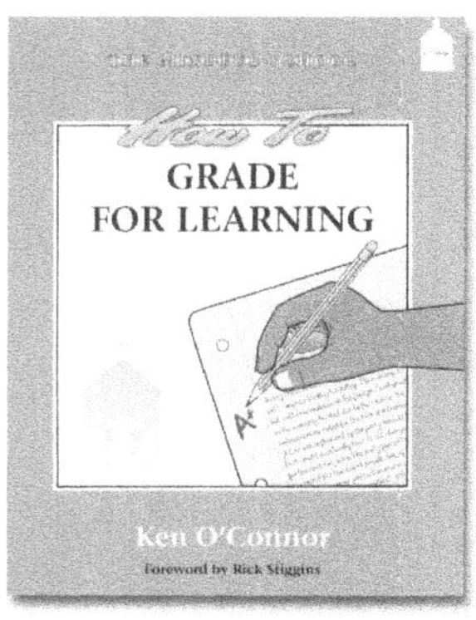

REFLECTING ON . . . THE SEVEN PERSPECTIVES

Without reading any further, what is your reaction to these seven perspectives? Keep a record of your initial reaction as you read the rest of this section.

1. Grading is not essential for learning.
2. Grading is complicated.
3. Grading is subjective and emotional.
4. Grading is inescapable.
5. Grading has a limited research base.
6. Grading has no single best practice.
7. Grading that is faulty damages students—and teachers.

With which perspectives do you agree? Disagree? Which ones are you not sure about?

Perspective One: Grading Is Not Essential for Learning

Although many teachers appear from their actions to believe otherwise, "teachers do not need grades or reporting forms to teach well, and students can and do learn well without them" (Guskey 1996, 16). Proof of this can be found in co-curricular activities, such as teams and clubs, and in interest courses, such as night school craft courses. In each of these situations, excellent teaching and superb learning take place—without grades. The problem in the school system is that, as soon as grades are introduced, teachers, parents, and students emphasize grades rather than learning. Teachers usually say this is because grades motivate. Kohn (1993b) believes very strongly that grades should be abolished because as extrinsic motivators, grades destroy positive motivation, which is intrinsic. Kagan, however, suggested that "if a student is performing a behavior and enjoys it and happens to receive praise or recognition, the recognition will not necessarily erode intrinsic motivation" (1994, 16.8). Brookhart offers another view, saying:

> Cognitive evaluation theory suggests that if students get feedback that helps them make progress, then motivation and

> control should increase. . . . Students will behave because their efforts will cause learning, and because enhancing perceived competence is motivating in and of itself. Students will perceive grades and other assessments which teachers use to provide informational feedback as more soundly based and reliable than grades and other assessments used to provide controlling feedback (1994, 296).

The issue of motivation and learning is of vital importance in this analysis of grading. It is important to acknowledge several facts:

- Teachers need to learn more about motivation so that they can use knowledge rather than perception to guide their practices.
- Students—and parents—have been taught to overvalue grades and, although it will not be easy, if teachers grade better, both may learn to value grades more appropriately.
- Good grades may motivate, but poor grades have no motivational value; in fact, the only grades that do motivate are those that are higher than a student usually receives, or As.
- Educators must emphasize that learners are responsible for learning. It is then clear that the learner must be motivated by the intrinsic interest and the worth of what is being learned, not by the carrot and stick approach that emphasizes gold stars and A's. Kohn (1993b, 212–221) suggested that what matters is the three Cs of motivation: content (things worth knowing), choice (autonomy in the classroom), and collaboration (learning together).

Perspective Two: Grading Is Complicated

Much grading is done in a mechanistic way, using formulas to produce the final grade as merely the result of arithmetic calculations. Teachers and students, therefore, come to believe that grading is simple, but, in fact, it is extremely complicated.

Guidelines for Grading

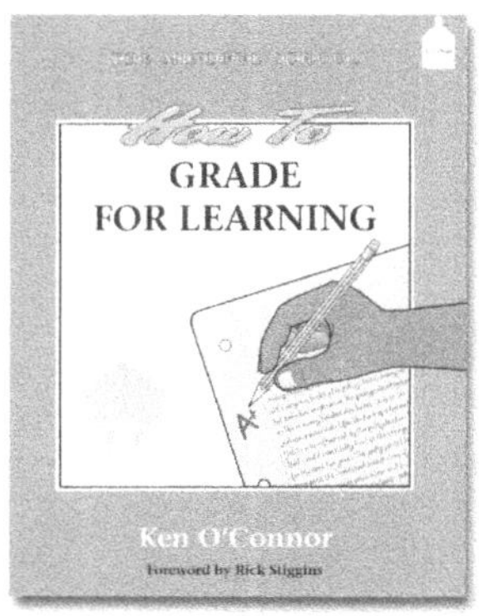

Grades are shorthand, that is, symbols that represent student performance. In order to arrive at grades, hundreds of decisions have been made along the way; the final grade could be very different if any of those choices had been made differently. In particular, the decisions that are made about how the numbers are "crunched," or manipulated, are critical.

Perspective Three: Grading Is Subjective and Emotional

Rather than looking at the volume and complexity of the decisions about calculations, this perspective focuses on decisions about what is included in grades and those about the why of calculations. Because grades are usually the result of at least some numerical calculation, teachers often claim that grades are objective measures of student performance; but, as Kohn said, "What grades offer is spurious precision, a subjective rating masquerading as an objective assessment" (1993b, 201). Grades are as much a matter of values as they are of science because, all along the assessment trail, the teacher has made value judgments about what type of assessment to use, what to include and what not to include in each assessment, how the assessment is scored, the actual scoring of the assessment, and why the scores are to be combined in a particular way to arrive at a final grade. Most of these value judgments are professional ones, and this is exactly as it should be; these are the professional decisions that teachers are trained (and paid) to make. The basic point here is that it should be acknowledged that these are, for the most part, subjective, not objective, judgments.

It should also be acknowledged that, although most teachers' decisions are based on professional judgment, some are based on emotion. Teaching is and, it is hoped, always will be an interpersonal activity. How we feel about the individuals and the groups being assessed sometimes affects our judgment. Again, the point here is not that this is wrong, but that all involved need to acknowledge that giving and receiving grades is not a purely objective act—it has a significant emotional component. The subjective and emotional aspects of grades have implications for how grading is done; grading will contribute to more effective learning when this perspective is acknowledged rather than denied.

Perspective Four: Grading Is Inescapable

There are many criticisms that can be made of grades. Willis (1993, 1, 4, 8) listed these:

- Grades are symbols, but what they represent is unclear.
- Grades sort students rather than help them to succeed.
- Grades give little information about student strengths and weaknesses.
- Grades are arbitrary and subjective.
- Grades undermine new teaching practices.
- Grades demoralize students who learn slower.

Many educators believe that grades should be abolished. Although this might be desirable, it simply is not going to happen in the foreseeable future in most educational jurisdictions. In fact, almost everywhere that schools or school systems have tried to remove grades from report cards, they have been faced with community reaction so strongly negative that educators have been forced to return to traditional grades. A clear example of this was described by Olson (1995) in a blow-by-blow description of what happened in Cranston, Rhode Island, when a parent-teacher committee proposed a report card without traditional grades for elementary schools. The committee prepared for the change very thoroughly, including piloting the new report cards. However, when the new format was adopted, the uproar in the community forced the school system to return to the former reporting methods.

Wiggins stated that "trying to get rid of familiar letter grades . . . gets the matter backwards while leading to needless political battles. . . . Parents have reasons to be suspicious of educators who want to tinker with a 120-year-old system they think they understand—even if we know traditional grades are often of questionable worth" (1996, 142). Getting it backwards means that it is inappropriate to focus on trying to eliminate

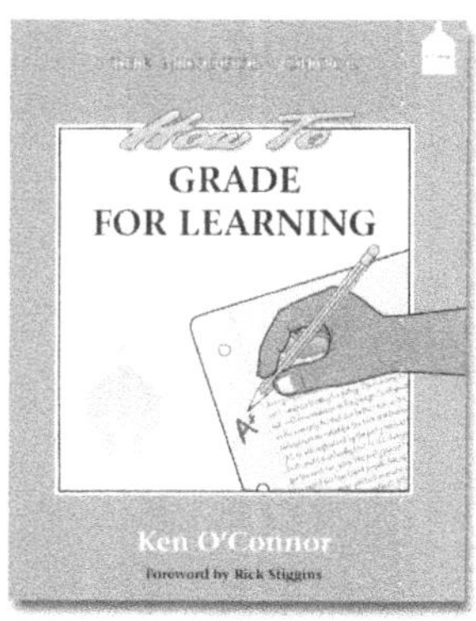

grades; it is more productive to make grades better. Wiggins went on to say that "what critics of grading must understand [is] that the symbol is not the problem; the lack of stable and clear points of reference in using symbols is the problem" (1996, 142).

Wiggins made another basic point: "grades or numbers, like all symbols, offer efficient ways of summarizing" (1996, 142). Although traditional grades may be of questionable worth, they have a long history. It is not worth fighting against this history; rather, it is worth fighting to make grades meaningful and more supportive of learning.

Perspective Five: Grading Has a Limited Research Base

"What a mass and mess it all was." This is how Middleton (quoted in Guskey 1996, 13) described the literature on grading practices—in 1933! Writing in 1995, Reedy said that "since the introduction of percentage grades in public high schools in the early 1900's, grading and grade reporting have recycled rather than evolved" (47). That there has been no real change over a period of almost 100 years probably stems from the fact that there is relatively little pure research on grading practices. Many journal articles and reports have been written on grading, but most of them (as is this chapter) are summaries of previous work and the opinion(s) of the author(s) on how grading should be done. Logical and well-explained as the articles and reports may be, they do not have the weight or authority provided by research. Teachers freely ignore the advice of authors, even those they acknowledge as experts. Stiggins, Frisbie, and Griswold (1989) identified nineteen grading practices that measurement experts agreed were desirable. When they examined the actual practices of a group of teachers, they found that the expert advice was ignored for eleven of these grading practices. Stiggins et al. suggested three reasons for this situation: recommendations may be opinion or philosophical position rather than established fact; recommendations may be unrealistic in actual classroom practice; and recommendations may be outside the knowledge or expertise base of teachers.

Frary, Gross, and Weber came to similar conclusions in their 1992 study and stated that "large proportions of teachers hold opinions and pursue practices contrary to what many measurement specialists would recommend" (2).

Perspective Six: Grading Has No Single Best Practice

The lack of a research base and the fact that every method of grading has advantages and disadvantages means that there is no one way to grade. The private nature of grading and the dramatic inconsistency in approaches within departments in high schools and colleges and between classrooms in elementary schools means that there are major problems that need to be addressed.

This is especially so where grades are "high stakes," that is, when grades serve as more than communication with students and parents. Thus, when grades are the prime or major component of the decision-making process (e.g., for college admission), there needs to be greater consistency, at least within a school and, one hopes, across a school district. Ideally, there will be principles that could be agreed on and that would lead to consistency across many, or even all, educational jurisdictions. That is the basic purpose behind this book—to provide guidelines that all teachers can follow. Because they are guidelines, not rules, teachers may flexibly adapt them to different grade levels and different subjects.

Perspective Seven: Grading That Is Faulty Damages Students—and Teachers

> The flush rose on Alan's face. His hands quivered. "It's not fair," he shouted. "I worked hard. I didn't deserve a B+. This will wreck my chances for Harvard." Mr. Beaster stood silent. As Alan took a breath, Beaster interjected, "Alan," he began, "your grade . . . ." Alan glared. "It's not my grade. I worked for an A. I deserve an A. I need it. This is the last semester. The good colleges will look at my grades. If you don't give me an A, my class rank drops." Again Beaster tried to interrupt, but Alan kept on, nostrils flaring, his face now beet-red,

Guidelines for Grading

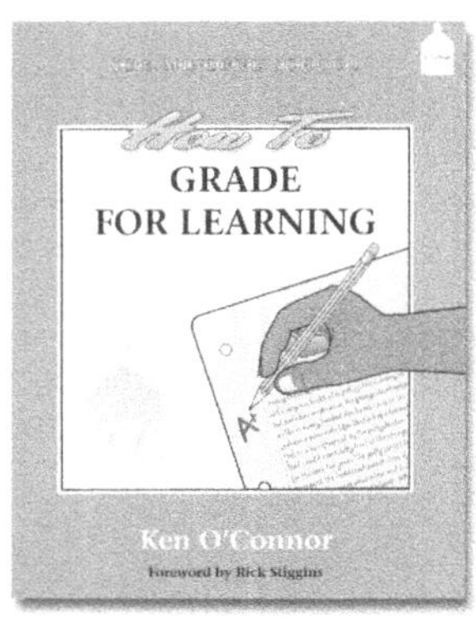

"You're cheating me," he screeched. "You're ruining my life. My father will kill me. There's no way this grade is O.K. If you liked me you would give me an A. You're not fair." "Alan," countered Beaster, "I'm not going to debate this grade with you. If you want to discuss it when you're calm, I'll be glad to." "Bull____ . You'll never change it," Alan pouted as he turned to leave. "You teachers are all alike. You _____ ." (Bellanca 1992, 297)

Carmela stared at the floor. Mrs. Martinez sat beside her. Carmela did not move. "Carmela, what am I going to do with you?" Mrs. Martinez asked. "Your grades are getting worse. You are a bright girl. You should be doing better. You are not a D student." Carmela still did not move. "I do care," she thought, "but it's not so easy. It never has been easy. I've got more to think about than school. School doesn't help me make the dinner or watch my brothers and sisters at night—especially when there is no dinner. And even if I do study, I'm always getting a C or D. So why bother? I can get a C or D without studying." (Bellanca 1992, 297)

These two stories illustrate some of the problems with traditional grading practices. Alan had no concept of what good work was or how his grades were calculated. He had developed the idea that school was only about grades, not learning, and that teachers "gave" good grades to students they liked rather than those who produced quality work. Carmela had different problems; there were too many other things in her life for her to be able to show her ability by producing quality work on demand. Rather than becoming angry, as Alan did, she developed a sense of the inevitable—whatever she did she would get Cs or Ds, so there was no point in trying to improve.

Overemphasis on grades and faulty grading practices have detrimental effects on student achievement, motivation, and self-concept, as can be seen in these examples. Faulty grading also damages the interpersonal relationship on which good teaching and effective learning depend. This problem occurs at least partly because of teachers' dual roles as coach and judge.

Unfortunately, these roles frequently conflict and, as a result, teacher–student relationships are damaged. Many of the problems illustrated by Alan's and Carmela's stories may be at least alleviated and possibly even eliminated if grading practices that support learning and student success are used.

These perspectives on grading contrast with traditional perspectives on grading. Traditional grading is normally seen as being essential for learning ("If I don't give them grades, they won't do the work") and as straightforward and scientific ("The formula says . . .; the calculator shows . . ."). If one followed the first three perspectives to their logical conclusion, a strong case could be made against grading; but the fourth perspective means that, as it is virtually impossible to do away with grades, it is necessary to find ways to do them better. Here, better means to develop grading practices that support learning and encourage student success. Teachers must not see grades as weapons of control, but rather use grading as an exercise in professional judgment to enhance learning. If the seven perspectives are acknowledged by teachers in their dealings with parents, students, and other teachers, grades can become a positive rather than a punitive aspect of educational practice.

REFLECTING ON . . . THE PERSPECTIVES

Now that you have read about each of the perspectives, what do you think?

- With which perspectives do you now agree? Disagree?
- Which perspectives in the list are you now not sure about?
- How did your thinking change from when you first read the list?

Grading Practices, Issues, and Guidelines

This section actively engages readers in analyzing grading practices. It begins with some factual data about grading practices; readers then examine their own beliefs about grading and their own grading practices. Next, seven case studies provide

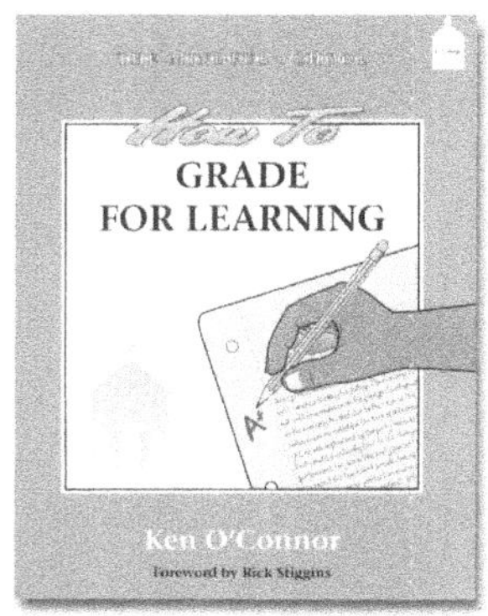

opportunities to analyze grading practices and identify grading issues—the what, how, and why of grading. Readers might keep a list of the issues that they identify to compare with a list provided in the text. Having identified grading issues, one looks for solutions. One solution is practical guidelines that teachers may use in their classrooms and in their gradebooks. A set of eight such guidelines is introduced in this section.

How Is Grading Done?

Robinson and Craver (1989, 26) reported the use of letter and percentage grades at various grade levels in the United States in 1988. Figure 16.1 shows the usage levels for the two most prevalent grading symbol systems: letters and percentages. Unfortunately, there was no comparable report in the 1990s.

This information demonstrates that letter or percentage grades were given to 15% to 20% of kindergarten students; 55% to 70% of students in Grades 1–3; and 80% to 100% of students in Grades 4–12.

There is no reason to believe that the proportions have changed dramatically since Robinson and Craver's 1989 report. We are, therefore, examining an educational practice that is a significant fact of life for most students, parents, and teachers in North America.

Percentage of School Districts Reporting Use of Different Grading Symbols at Different Grade Levels[1]

Grade	Letter	Percentage
Kindergarten	14.8%	4.8%
Grades 1–3	55.4%	15.6%
Grades 4–6	79.2%	20.7%
Grades 7–9	81.9%	26.8%
Grades 10–12	80.2%	28.5%

Data from G. E. Robinson and J. M. Craver, *Assessing and Grading Student Achievement.* (Arlington, Va.: Educational Research Service, 1989), 26.

[1] Percentages may total more than 100% because some districts may use more than one grading symbol system at a grade level.

Figure 16.1

How Do YOU Grade?

Guskey said, "[Grading] practices are not the result of careful thought or sound evidence, . . . Rather, they are used because teachers experienced these practices as students and, having little training or experience with other options, continue their use" (1996, 20). This statement may be unfair to some teachers, but it is certainly true for many, maybe even most, teachers.

REFLECTING ON . . . YOUR GRADING PRACTICES

1. What are your grading practice principles?
2. What are your actual grading practices? Do you grade on the "curve"?
3. What were or are the main influences on your grading principles and practices?
4. How do your grading principles and practices compare with those of other teachers in your school?

One of the best ways to analyze grading practices (and the principles behind them) is to analyze a set of marks and grades and identify the issues that arise from such an analysis. Following are seven case studies that give us the opportunity to analyze grading practices and discover grading issues. See the end of each case study for reflection questions.

CASE STUDY 1: Interim Report Card Grade

Case Study 1 considers the impact of a zero mark on a grade and the possible impact on a student of grade reporting very early in a course/year.

The marks in the chart were given to a student in a senior science class on an interim report card in a school with a semestered block schedule after four weeks of 76-minute classes.

This case study dramatically illustrates the effect of assigning a zero for a missed test. The student has six marks of 90% or higher, two marks in the 80s, and no mark lower than 62.5%; but, the interim grade is lower (58.3%) than the lowest mark! A grade like this could have a devastating effect on students, causing them to give up. This student is achieving well, but the grade suggests otherwise—because of a missed test.

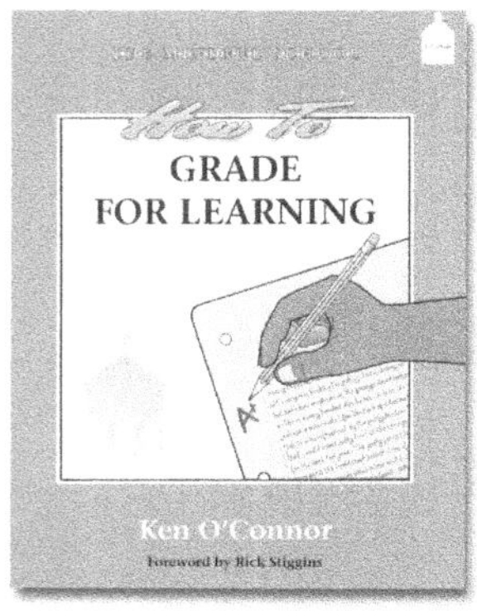

SCORES

Task	Mark/Total Possible	Percentage
Tests (50%)		
Symbols	17/20	85
Matter	0/68 (absent)	0
Reactions	35.5/46	75
Daily Work (25%)		
Assignment	10/10	100
Homework	10/10	100
Homework	9/10	90
Atom Quiz	10/10	100
Moles Quiz	5/8	62.5
Homework	omit/10	omit
Lab Work (25%)		
MP/BP	14.5/15	96.7
Superation	20/24	83.3
Reactions	7/10	70
Periodicity Check	10/10	100

CASE STUDY 1: Reflection

1. What grade would you give the student? Why?
2. The actual grade the student received was 58.3%. What is your reaction to this grade? Was this grade a fair reflection of the student's overall performance?
3. What grading issues arise from this case study?

CASE STUDY 2: Chris Brown's Science Class

Case Study 2 considers the marks and grades of a teacher using a very traditional approach to grading. The student marks have been arranged so that, for most students, there are some obvious problems with their performance and/or the way it is graded.

The marks and grades in the chart are for Chris Brown's science class in Ontario. If you are not a science teacher, put the appropriate items for your subject in place of the lab reports, care of equipment, and so forth. Note carefully the information that is shown below the grade book extract regarding the miscellaneous items, the way absence is dealt with, and the grading scale. Enter to the right of the chart the letter grade each student would get using the grading scale in use in your district/school.

Name	Lab Reports										Total	Tests/Exams			Total	Miscellaneous*						Final Total	Final Grade	
out of	*10*	*10*	*10*	*10*	*10*	*10*	*10*	*10*	*10*	*10*	*100*	*50*	*50*	*100*	*200*	*20*	*20*	*20*	*20*	*20*	*100*	*400*	%	Letter
Robin	6	6	6	6	5	6	6	7	6	6	60	33	39	81	153	15	15	12	0	10	52	265	66	C
Kay	2	3	5	5	6	6	7	8	9	10	61	11	29	86	126	15	13	18	10	10	66	253	63	C
Marg	10	10	A	10	10	10	A	10	A	A	60	50	A	100	150	0	0	0	0	15	15	225	56	D
Dennis	9	8	9	8	9	10	9	10	8	9	89	24	24	49	97	20	17	17	20	20	94	280	70	B
Peter	10	10	9	9	8	8	7	7	6	5	79	45	36	32	113	20	10	15	10	5	60	252	63	C
Lorna	10	10	10	10	10	10	10	10	10	10	100	32	29	59	120	20	20	20	20	20	100	320	80	A
John	8	8	8	7	9	9	8	9	10	8	84	32	30	57	119	20	8	7	0	5	40	243	61	C

A = Absent = 0 (for Lab Reports and Tests/Exams)
*Miscellaneous
1-Attendance; 2-Care of Equipment; 3-Attitude/Participation; 4-Notebook; 5-Reading Reports (4x5 marks)
Letter Grade Legend (in Ontario)
A = 80%–100%; B = 70%–79%; C = 60%–69%; D = 50%–59%; F = 0%–49%
Note: This chart was adapted with permission from workshop material presented by Todd Rogers, University of Alberta.

One A, one B, four Cs, and a D in Ontario—but, did they go to the right students? Marg got the D, but on her achievement alone she probably earned the A. Lorna got the A, but had only a 60% average on tests and exams; is she a weak student who is a teacher's pet—one who receives good marks on the things she can get help on—or is she a very capable student who suffers from severe test anxiety? Kay and Peter both get the same grade but Kay is getting high 80s at the end, whereas Peter is receiving failing marks; is this fair? These are just some of the considerations that arise from an analysis of this case study.

CASE STUDY 2: **Reflection**

1. Do the grades awarded fairly reflect the results from which they were derived for each student?
2. If you indicated "yes," for which students? Why?

3. If you indicated "no," for which students? Why?
4. What grading issues arise from this case study?

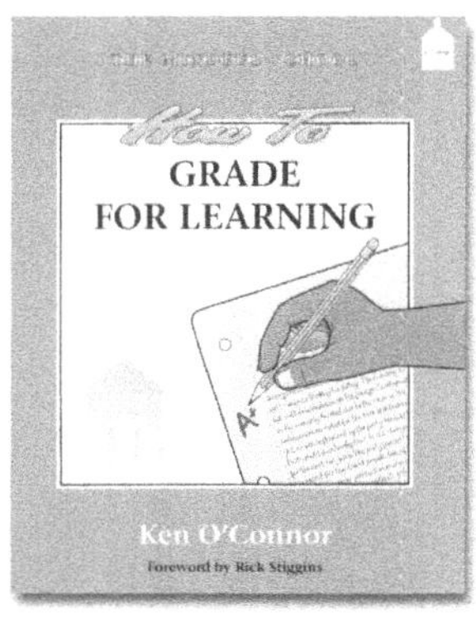

CASE STUDY 3: Hiring a Student

Very often, secondary report cards give little more information than the student's grade and a three or four word comment. Case Study 3 provides an opportunity to analyze how grades are calculated and whether grades provide meaningful information to potential employers, the students themselves, and their parents.

This may appear to be an extreme example, but there have been—and probably still are—many classrooms where this situation exists. This case study illustrates the critical connection between teacher's intent and how grades are actually calculated.

SCENARIO 1
Auto Mechanics

Student #1	Student #2
71%	52%

SCENARIO 2
Weights

Scenario	Practical	Theory	Grade
A (same as scenario)	25%	75%	
Student 1	0/25	71/75	71%
Student 2	25/25	27/75	52%
B	50%	50%	
Student 1	0/50	47/50	47%
Student 2	50/50	18/50	68%
C	75%	25%	
Student 1	0/75	24/25	24%
Student 2	25/75	9/25	84%

CASE STUDY 3: Reflection

1. To which student would you give a job at the local gas station based on the information from Scenario A?
2. Study the additional information in Scenario B. Which student would get the job now?
3. What grading issues arise from this case study?

CASE STUDY 4: **Anita's Grade?**

Number crunching again. Case Study 4 provides many numbers and therefore many possibilities for how grades are calculated.

The teacher of this class bases grades only on unit tests, but believes in multiple assessment opportunities, when it is feasible. Thus on test 2, there are questions on unit 1 and unit 2, on test 3 there are questions on units 1, 2, and 3, and on test 4, there are questions on all four units. This gives students four opportunities to demonstrate their knowledge and skill on unit 1, three opportunities on unit 2, two opportunities on unit 3, but only one opportunity on unit 4. This approach yields many numbers for Anita, as shown in this chart.

TESTS

Unit	Score (percentage)			
1	50/100 (50)	30/50 (60)	30/40 (75)	23/25 (92)
2		30/50 (60)	23/33 (70)	21/25 (84)
3			20/30 (67)	19/25 (76)
4				17/25 (72)
Test Average	50%	60%	71%	81%

Using traditional approaches, there are at least three alternatives for calculating the final grade for Anita:

Alternative A: use the average mark on each test, that is, (50 + 60 + 71 + 81)/4 = 66%

Alternative B: use the final mark on each unit, that is, the marks for each unit on test 4, that is, (92 + 84 + 76 + 72)/4 = 81%

Alternative C: use the mark for the first test on each unit, that is, (50 + 60 + 67 + 72)/4 = 63%

As you can see, these three approaches result in a final grade for Anita that ranges from 63% to 81%, a variation of almost 20%.

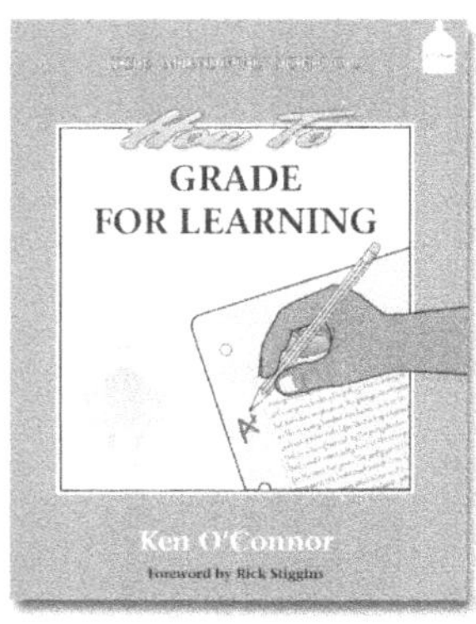

One would hope that the teacher would use alternative B because it is the option that provides multiple opportunities and supports the teacher's intent. However, there are many teachers who would use alternative A, and some who would use alternative C, even though it completely negates the multiple assessment opportunities.

CASE STUDY 4: Reflection

1. Which grade would you give to Anita? Would you use alternative A, B, C, or something else? Why?
2. What grading issues arise from this case study?

CASE STUDY 5: Grading Scales

What does A mean? What does F mean? For 40 and more years, the author, as a student and as a teacher, in Australia and in Canada, has known that an A has been 80% and an F has been less than 50%. Anything different is very hard for me to comprehend. The familiar becomes the norm—but is it right? Case Study 5 shows readers that letter grades, honors, and pass/fail mean very different things in different educational jurisdictions.

The chart on the opposite page shows grading scales used in North America at five different places. You may use the last row to enter the grading scale used in your district/school.

An A can mean anything from 80% to 95%, a failing grade can be anywhere between 49% and 74%. What do these variations mean? For example, is a 49% in Ontario the same as 74% in the district identified by Canady and Hotchkiss as having the highest grade equivalents? There is no way of knowing this without comparing marked student work from both jurisdictions, but the wide variation makes one wonder about the meaning of grades.

CASE STUDY 5: Reflection

1. How do you react to the wide variation in grading scales?

GRADING SCALES
Symbol Conversion

Source	*A*	*B*	*C*	*D*	*F*
Ontario	80–100%	70–79%	60–69%	50–59%	<50%
Ruth Evans*	90–100%	80–89%	70–79%	60–69%	<60%
Rick Werkheiser*	93–100%	85–92%	78–84%	70–77%	<70%
Pam Painter*	95–100%	85–94%	75–84%	65–74%	<65%
R. L. Canady**	95–100%	88–94%	81–87%	75–80%	<75%
Your District					

*From World Wide Web, The School House Teachers' Lounge (Nebraska)
**Reported in R. L. Canady and P. R. Hotchkiss, "It's a Good Score: Just a Bad Grade," *Phi Delta Kappan*, September 1989, 69.

2. What letter grade would Anita (Case Study 4) get if she were in each of these school jurisdictions?
3. What grading issues arise from this case study?

CASE STUDY 6: Grading Inventories

Case Study 6 looks at the recipes teachers use to "cook up" their grades. This case study lets teachers examine how their recipe—or inventory—compares with those of their colleagues.

In most traditional grading situations (see Figure 16.2), teachers have a recipe or inventory for the ingredients in their grades. These usually include some assessment methods and some student behaviors. In addition to the components of grades, such inventories usually include some indication of the relative importance of each component by giving it a (percentage) weight.

There is clearly no right answer or perfect grading inventory, but for those who teach the same grade or course(s) in the same school and, ideally, in the same school district, it would not be unreasonable to expect that there would be some basic similarities or discernible patterns in their grading inventories. If there is not, there is need for serious professional discussion about how grading is carried out.

Guidelines for Grading

Traditional Inventory for Middle School Grading

Evaluation Category	Expected Range
1. Quizzes/Tests/Exams	20–30%
2. Written Assignments creative or explanatory paragraphs, essays, notes, organizers, writing folios, or portfolios	15–25%
3. Oral Presentations or Demonstrations brief or more formal presentations or demonstrations, role-playing, debates, skits, etc.	15–25%
4. Projects/Assignments research tasks, hands-on projects, video- or audiotape productions, analysis of issues, etc.	10–20%
5. Cooperative Group Learning evaluation of the process and skills learned as an individual and as a group member	5–15%
6. Independent Learning individual organizational skills, contributions to class activities and discussions, homework, notebooks	5–15%

Figure 16.2

CASE STUDY 6: Reflection

Use the Grading Inventory chart to identify the grading "recipe" you use. Ask several colleagues in your school to share their inventories. If the categories do not match yours, enter your categories at the bottom.

1. What similarities—or differences—are there between your inventory and those of your colleagues?
2. Why do these differences exist? Should these differences exist?
3. What grading issues arise from this case study?

GRADING INVENTORY

Items Included in Grades	Percentages Allocated			
	Self	Teacher #1	Teacher #2	Teacher #3
Exams				
Tests				
Projects - individual - group				
Demonstrations/Oral Presentations				
Written Assignments - small writing tasks - writing folders or portfolios - essays				
Class Participation and Effort - whole class discussions - group discussions - homework - notebook - attendance, punctuality				
Peer Evaluation				
Self-Evaluation				
(Additional Categories)				

CASE STUDY 7: **Grading Practices That Inhibit Learning**

Canady and Hotchkiss (1989) identified twelve grading practices that inhibit learning, which are shown in Figure 16.3. Many of these are quite common practices that many—or maybe even most—teachers would consider acceptable and normal. The fact that Canady and Hotchkiss labeled them as practices that inhibit learning requires teachers to carefully analyze their own grading practices.

Guidelines for Grading

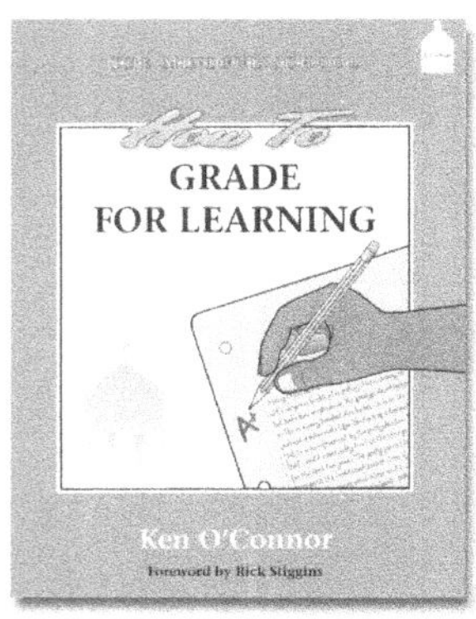

Numbers 2, 3, 4, and 9 in Figure 16.3 were all part of the author's practices when he was a classroom teacher just a few years ago. Most teachers will probably admit that they use at least one-third of the practices listed at least some of the time.

CASE STUDY 7: Reflection

1. Which, if any, of the practices identified by Canady and Hotchkiss in Figure 16.3 as inhibiting learning do you use?
2. What grading issues arise from this case study?

Grading Issues

The case studies have led to the identification of many issues. These grading issues are summarized in this list:

- Ingredients—achievement, ability, effort, attitude/behavior
- Sources of information—paper-and-pencil tests, instructional questions, homework assignments, performance assessments, intuitions, feelings
- Standards—grade distribution
- Weighting and record keeping
- How much data? How recent?
- Student understanding

Although this list is highly generalized, I think it includes all the major grading issues.

REFLECTING ON . . . GRADING ISSUES

1. How does this list of grading issues compare with your list? Which issues that you identified are included?
2. Which issues that you identified are not included?

Now that we have identified these issues, let us look at each more closely.

Grading Practices That Inhibit Learning

1. Inconsistent grading scales	The same performance results in different grades, in different schools or classes.
2. Worshipping averages	Insisting on using all of the math to calculate an average, even when "the average" is not consistent with what the teacher knows about the student's learning.
3. Using zeros indiscriminately	Giving zeros for incomplete work has a devasting effect on averages and often zeros are not even related to learning or achievement but to nonacademic factors like behavior, respect, punctuality, etc.
4. Following the pattern of assign, test, grade, and teach	When teaching occurs after a grade has been assigned, it is too late for the students. They need a lot of teaching and practice that is not graded, although it should be assessed and used to enhance learning before testing takes place.
5. Failing to match testing to teaching	Too many teachers rely on trick questions, new formats, and unfamiliar material. If students are expected to perform skills and produce information for a grade, these should be part of the instruction.
6. Ambushing students	Pop quizzes are more likely to teach students how to cheat on a test than to result in learning. Such tests are often control vehicles designed to get even, not to aid understanding.
7. Suggesting that success is unlikely	Students are not likely to strive for targets that they already know are unattainable to them.
8. Practicing "gotcha" teaching	A nearly foolproof way to inhibit student learning is to keep the outcomes and expectations of their classes secret. Tests become ways of finding out how well students have read their teacher's mind.
9. Grading first efforts	Learning is not a "one-shot" deal. When the products of learning are complex and sophisticated, students need a lot of teaching, practice, and feedback before the product is evaluated.
10. Penalizing students for taking risks	Taking risks is not often rewarded in school. Students need encouragement and support, not low marks, while they try new or more demanding work.
11. Failing to recognize measurement error	Very often grades are reported as objective statistics without attention to weighting factors or the reliability of the scores. In most cases, a composite score may be only a rough estimate of student learning, and sometimes it can be very inaccurate.
12. Establishing inconsistent grading criteria	Criteria for grading in schools and classes often change from day to day, grading period to grading period, and class to class. This lack of consensus makes it difficult for students to understand the rules.

Adapted with permission from R. L. Canady and P. R. Hotchkiss, "It's a Good Score: Just a Bad Grade." *Phi Delta Kappan* (September, 1989): 68–71.

Figure 16.3

Guidelines for Grading

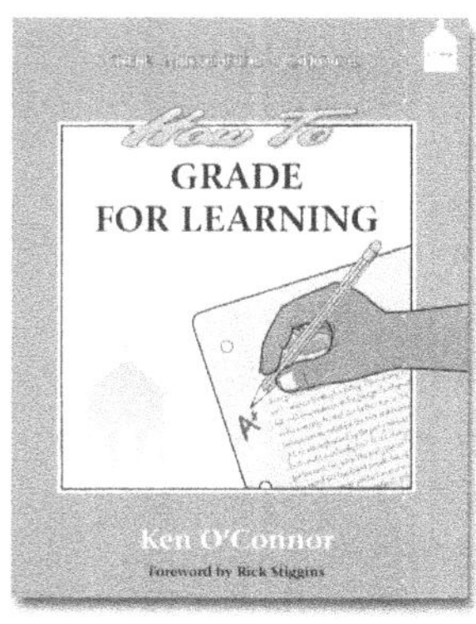

Ingredients

Teachers include and mix many ingredients to arrive at grades. Student characteristics often used in the mix are achievement, ability, effort, attitude, behavior, participation, and attendance. These ingredients are included because grades serve so many purposes. The result is that grades frequently become almost meaningless for their main purpose—communication.

In order to provide effective communication, grades must be clearly understood by the message senders (teachers and schools) and by the message receivers (students, parents, college admissions officers, employers, etc.). "To develop this shared understanding, there must be a consistent and limited basis for what is included in grades; instead of including everything, we must limit the variables or valued attributes that are included in grades" (O'Connor 1995, 94).

Frisbie and Waltman (1992, 38) provided a very helpful way of looking at this issue. They identified a large set of *evaluation* variables, which includes everything (or almost everything) students do in the classroom and the school. This large set of evaluation variables is reduced to a smaller subset of *reporting* variables. The size of this subset depends on what type of reporting to parents is done by each school/district. Care should be taken to ensure that the most highly valued variables are included. The last step is to select a subset of the reporting variables as the *grading* variables. The grading variables should be those things that are the "status indicators at the end of the learning experience" (Frisbie and Waltman 1992, 38).

Guskey (1994, 17) provided another approach to identifying the ingredients in grades. He identified *progress* criteria, for improvement scoring or learning gain; *process* criteria, for work habits, attendance, participation, effort, and so forth; and *product* criteria, for final exams, overall assessments, or other culminating demonstrations of learning.

Frisbie and Waltman's and Guskey's concepts are combined as shown in Figure 16.4. This diagram shows that in Frisbie and Waltman's terms, Guskey's process and progress criteria are the reporting (and evaluation) variables, and the product

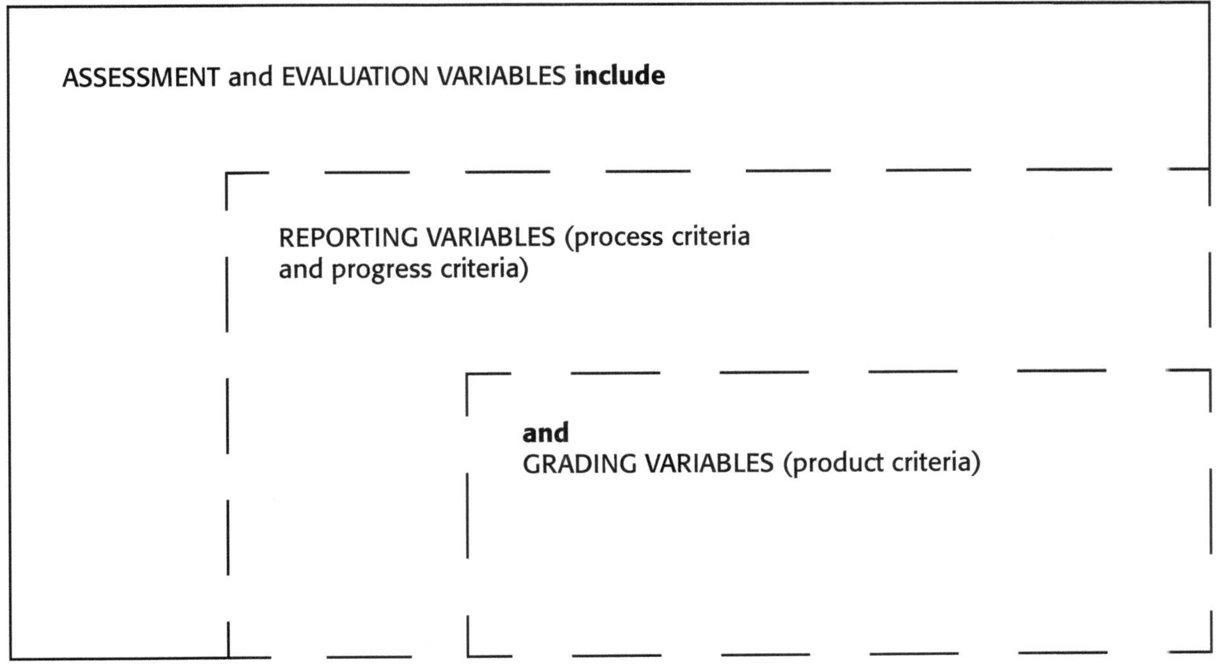

Figure 16.4 Adapted with permission from K. O'Connor "Guidelines for Grading That Support Learning and Student Success." *NASSP Bulletin,* (May, 1995): 24–28, National Association of Secondary School Principals.

criteria are the grading variables. This combination identifies variables that are separated for grading and reporting purposes. The interaction shown in Figure 16.4, however, is rather simplistic, as some process variables may be assessed over time as part of stated learning goals, and, therefore, may legitimately be considered as grading variables. This more complex and more realistic identification of grading and reporting variables is illustrated in Figure 16.5.

Sources of Information

Teachers have many possible sources of information about student achievement. Teachers use a wide variety of assessment methods, but not all sources of information need be included in grades. Decisions about which sources of information to include are based on the reliability and validity of the data and

What Students Do in School

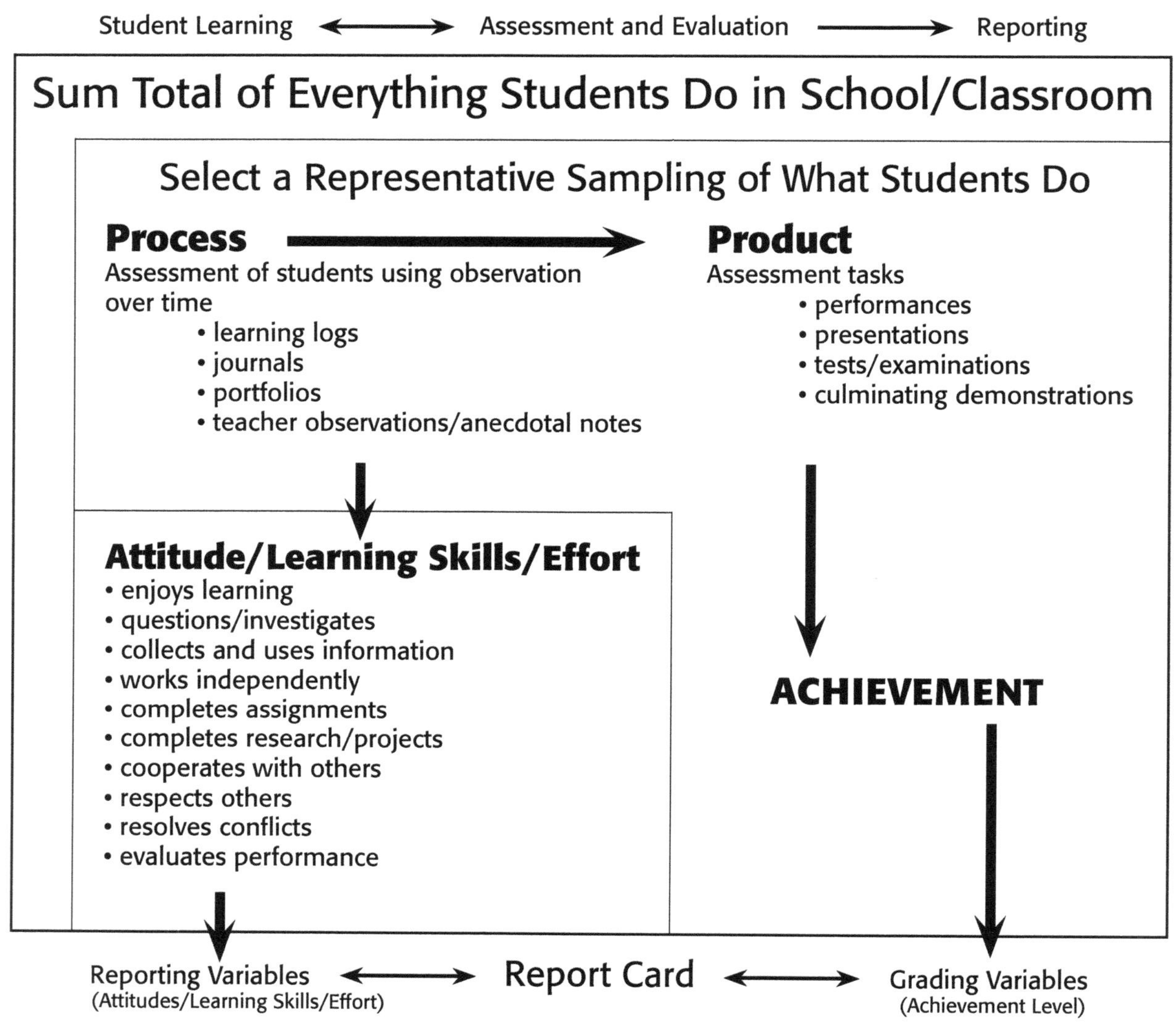

Figure 16.5 Adapted from the work of author (Ken O'Connor) and Damian Cooper, Assessment Consultant, Ontario.

the purpose of the assessment. Teachers make these decisions consciously and carefully.

Standards

In order for grades to have any real meaning, they must be related to some type of standard—norm, criterion, or self-referenced. Traditionally, grades have been *norm-referenced,* that is, they were based on comparing the individual with a group. This frequently involved the use of the bell curve or some modification of the curve.

With the introduction of state and local standards, grades are increasingly based on these standards and so are *criterion-referenced.* Even where there are no published standards, teachers use criterion-referenced standards when they provide their students with rubrics—scoring scales that clearly indicate the criteria for quality work.

Self-referenced standards, which compare students with their own previous performance, can also provide valuable information.

The issue that needs to be considered is which type of standard to use to determine grades and which type to use only in report card comments.

Weighting and Record Keeping

Because there are many ingredients in grades, even if only achievement information is used, teachers have to decide the relative importance of the various components. This is usually done by setting different percentages or weights for each of the various ingredients. This is a key area for subjectivity—that is, carefully thought out and logically justifiable professional judgment. It is an issue because careful thought and logical justification are frequently forgotten.

Record keeping is also important. The complexity of learning goals requires that teachers base grades on complete and accurate tabulated records—on paper, on a computer, or both. It is not justifiable for data that go into a grade to come off the top of a teacher's head at the end of the grading period.

How Much Data? How Recent?

Teachers tend to include everything that they score in student grades. The issue to consider is whether all these data are necessary or appropriate. The amount of data needed is only that which enables confidence that any further information will confirm the previous judgment. Focus should be on the highest

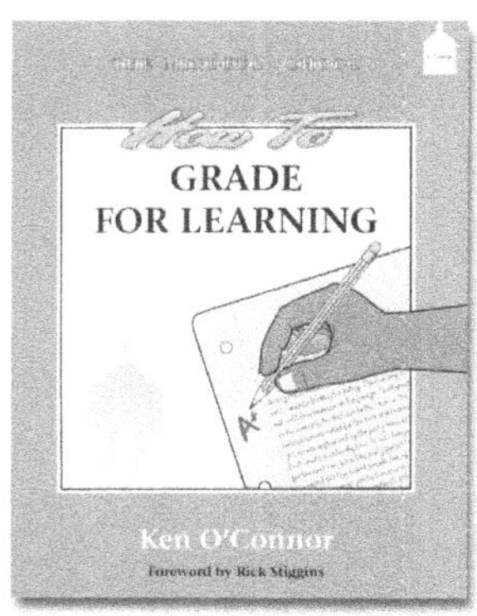

consistent level of performance toward the end of any learning (grading) period because this is the information that tells whether the learning goals have been met.

Student Understanding

Frequently, students do not understand how the grades they received were determined. This occurs because either the grading procedures were not discussed with them or the procedures are too complicated to be understood. The issue is how teachers may best ensure that students understand their grades. If grades are to serve learning, there must be understanding and involvement.

Guidelines for Grading

Grading issues can be addressed in a variety of ways. To avoid the misuse and misinterpretation of grades, a set of grading guidelines that address the practical concerns of teachers is needed.

Traditional grading practices need to change so that grading aligns with and supports current assessment and evaluation philosophy and practices.

The grading guidelines in Figure 16.6 were developed with these principles in mind. Some of them require radical changes in teacher practices, especially at the high school and college levels, and in school and district policies. The guidelines are organized in approximate order of importance to the support of student learning and success and, together, make a consistent group. The order also relates to where most change from traditional grading practices is needed—relatively few teachers using traditional approaches to grading use Guidelines 1, 2, or 3, whereas many (maybe most) teachers already follow Guidelines 7 and 8.

The specific relationships between the grading issues identified and the guidelines are shown in Figure 16.7. Each issue relates primarily to one guideline.

This set of grading guidelines has been modified considerably from those proposed by Gronlund and Linn (1990, 443),

(continued on page 281)

Guidelines for Grading

To Support Learning,
To Encourage Student Success

1. Individual achievement is the only basis for grades.
2. Sample student performance—do not mark everything and do not include all marks in grades.
3. Grade in pencil—keep records so they may be updated easily.
4. Relate grading procedures to learning goals (expectations, standards, etc.).
5. Crunch numbers carefully.
6. Use criterion-referenced (i.e., absolute or preset standards to distribute grades and marks.
7. Use quality assessments and properly record evidence of achievement.
8. Discuss assessment, including grading, with students at the beginning of instruction.

Figure 16.6

Guidelines for Grading

The Relationship Between Grading Issues and the Grading Guidelines

Grading Issue	Guideline
Ingredients	1
Sources of information	2, 4
Standards (grade distribution)	6
Weighting	5
Record keeping	7
How much data?	2
How recent?	3
Student understanding	8

Figure 16.7

but it is important to acknowledge that their list was the starting point. Guidelines such as these are more practical than most guidelines one can find in the literature on grading. They are intended to provide practical guidance to teachers as they decide how to grade students' achievement—and can actually be used by teachers in their grade books or in setting up their computer grading programs. Guidelines also need to have school and/or district policy status, so that students and parents can understand the grading practices used in their classrooms, and so that they can expect grading practices that are consistent among all teachers in each school. Currently, teachers are "all over the book"; these guidelines should at least get teachers in the same chapter and, eventually, on the same page!

REFLECTING ON . . . THE GUIDELINES

1. What is your initial reaction to each of the guidelines for grading in Figure 16.6? Why?
2. Think in terms of what is **P**ositive, what is a **C**oncern, and what is just **I**nteresting (PCI). List your reflections for later reference.

REFERENCES

Bailey, J., and J. McTighe. 1996. Reporting achievement at the secondary level: What and how. In *Communicating student learning: ASCD yearbook 1996,* edited by T. R. Guskey. Alexandria, VA: Association for Supervision and Curriculum Development.

Bellanca, J. 1992. How to grade (if you must). In *If minds matter: A foreword to the future, Vol. 2,* edited by A. L. Costa, J. Bellanca, and R. Fogarty. Palatine, IL: IRI/SkyLight Training and Publishing.

Brookhart, S. M. 1994. Teacher's grading: Theory and practice. *Applied Measurement in Education.* 7(4): 279–301.

Canady, R. L., and P. R. Hotchkiss. 1989, September. It's a good score: Just a bad grade. *Phi Delta Kappan,* 68–71.

Frary, R., J., L. M. Gross, and L. J. Weber. 1992. Testing and grading practices and opinions in the Nineties: 1890s or 1990s. Paper presented at the Annual Meeting of the National Council on Measurement in Education, April 21–23, at San Francisco, California.

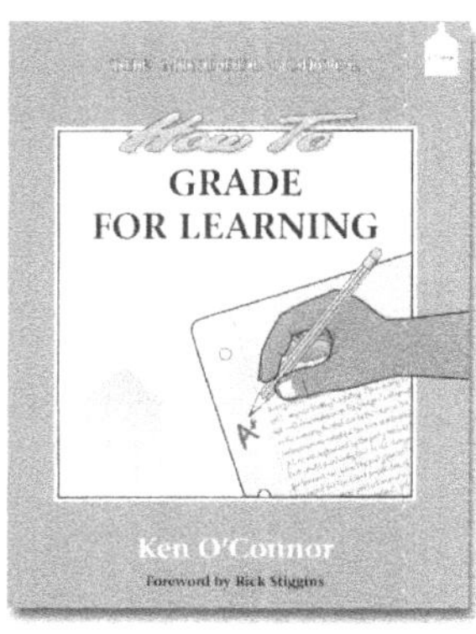

Frisbie, D. A., and K. K. Waltman. 1992, fall. Developing a personal grading plan. *Educational Issues: Measurement and Practice,* 35–42.

Gronlund, N. E., and R. L. Linn. 1990. *Measurement and evaluation in teaching.* 6th ed. New York: Macmillan.

Guskey, T. R. 1993, September 7. *ASCD Update.*

———. 1994, October. Making the grade: What benefits students? *Educational Leadership,* 14–20.

———. 1996. Reporting on student learning: Lessons from the past—prescriptions for the future. In *Communicating student learning: The ASCD yearbook 1996,* edited by T. R. Guskey. Alexandria, VA: Association for Supervision and Curriculum Development.

Kagan, S. 1994. *Cooperative learning.* San Clemente, CA: Kagan Cooperative Learning.

Kohn, A. 1993b. *Punished by rewards: The trouble with gold stars, incentive plans, As, praise and other bribes.* New York: Houghton Mifflin.

McTighe, J. 1996/97, December/January. What happens between assessments. *Educational Leadership,* 6–12.

McTighe, J., and S. Ferrara. 1995, December. Assessing learning in the classroom. *Journal of Quality Learning,* 11–27.

O'Connor, K. 1995, May. Guidelines for grading that support learning and student success. *NASSP Bulletin,* 91–101.

Olson, L. 1995, June 14. Cards on the table. *Education Week.*

Reedy, R. 1995, October. Formative and summative assessment: A possible alternative to the grading-reporting dilemma. *NASSP Bulletin,* 47–51.

Robinson, G. E., and J. E. Craver. 1989. *Assessing and grading student achievement.* Arlington, VA: Educational Research Service.

Stiggins, R. J. 1997. *Student-centered classroom assessment,* 2nd ed. Upper Saddle River, NJ: Merrill/Prentice Hall.

Stiggins, R. J., D. A. Frisbie, and P. A. Griswold. 1989, summer. Inside high school grading practices: Building a research agenda. *Educational Measurement: Issues and Practices,* 5–13.

Stiggins, R. J., and T. Knight. 1997. *But are they really learning?* Portland, OR: Assessment Training Institute.

Wiggins, G. 1996. Honesty and fairness: Toward better grades and reporting. In *Communicating student learning: The ASCD yearbook 1996,* edited by T. R. Guskey. Arlington, VA: Association for Supervision and Curriculum Development.

Willis, S. 1993, September. Are letter grades obsolete? *ASCD Update,* 1, 4, 8.

SELECTION 17

Creating a Multiple Intelligences Portfolio

by **James Bellanca, Carolyn Chapman, and Elizabeth Swartz**

What Is a Portfolio?

A portfolio is a collection of exemplary work. Architects, painters and sculptors, and art students have long used the portfolio for transporting samples of their best work. Today, computer graphic designers, filmmakers, actors, scientists, and stockbrokers use the portfolio to organize the artifacts of their daily work. Whether seeking a patron, applying for a job, preparing for a show, or organizing tax returns, the portfolio is a convenient tool for collecting and carrying samples of what one can do.

The portfolio is first and foremost a collection bin for organizing the artifacts of an individual's work or school life. As an assessment tool, portfolios predate the current grading system. Before letter grades became popular at the turn of the century, the portfolio was the tool that told students and parents how well a student was performing in class. In the one-room schoolhouses of pre-factory school days, children used crates and boxes for storing their slates and samples of the work they did in learning the basic skills or in making a project for social studies or art. During conferences, the teacher or the child would share the child's portfolio of work with the parents.

In the business world, the portfolio is often the tool used in performance reviews. When it is time for the annual

Adapted from *Multiple Assessments for Multiple Intelligences* by James Bellanca, Carolyn Chapman, and Elizabeth Swartz, pp. 203–25 and 241–46.

Creating a Multiple Intelligences Portfolio

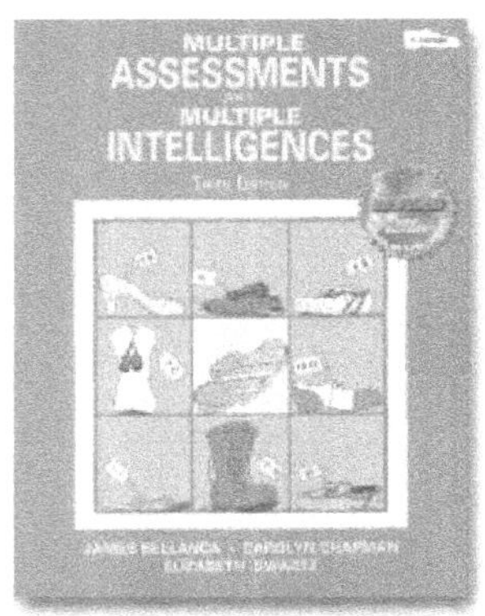

performance review, the manager invites the employee to prepare a self-assessment for the year. The well-organized employee keeps samples of important work done. A novice lawyer may select documents from the two cases he or she won in court. A civil engineer might include photos of the diagrams and blueprints of a construction project he or she supervised. A stockbroker may include charts of his or her clients' stock performance. A graphic artist could include sample video renderings of his or her multimedia ad work. With the best examples as a guide, these employees prepare a written self-evaluation describing what they have accomplished during the year. Before the performance review, the manager considers the portfolio with the employee's self-evaluation as a guide.

If applicants for a job need a way to grab the attention of the personnel director, they might include a miniportfolio with their resumes. When they return for the second interview, they get the upper hand by bringing along a portfolio of their best work. This separates them from the many others seeking the same job.

As teachers elect to teach using the framework of the multiple intelligences, they quickly see how to expand the possible ways they can assess student learning. Instead of relying solely on standardized and teacher-made tests, they see the many uses of observation check lists, essays, journals, logs, exhibits of art work, short stories, demonstrations, model building, interviews, and performances. In order to keep the best of each student's work well organized in classrooms with 20 to 36 primary students or 125 to 150 high schoolers, these teachers use the multiple intelligences portfolio.

A well-constructed portfolio is an excellent, easy-to-use tool for students in the multiple intelligences classroom. To be useful to the teacher, students, and parents who are concerned about performing with quality, the well-constructed portfolio should meet certain standards. What are those standards?

A well-made classroom portfolio, whether in primary, middle, or secondary school, is organized, selective, representative, and promotes insight.

Organized

A quality portfolio is *organized* for easy access. Like a safe deposit box in a bank vault, it comprises the student's most valuable work for the year, indexed and labeled for prompt review. Like a museum, it presents each artist's work so that the viewer focuses on the quality of the artist's achievement.

Paris' Picasso Museum exemplifies the museum as portfolio. When visitors enter the vestibule of the reconstructed mansion, they first see a giant floor plan of the museum. Donated to the French government in lieu of the large estate taxes owed by the Picasso family, the museum is organized according to decades—including the artist's life, times, and artistic periods. Selected pieces of Picasso's pottery, diary, sketches, sculptures, and paintings are arranged chronologically from room to room. In each room, visitors are greeted with a photo display of the major historic events of the decade, photos of Picasso and his family and friends, and a brief essay in English and French that links the artist's life and works of the ten-year period with the social and artistic influences he experienced. A second essay focuses on the major works in the room. This essay describes Picasso's dominant styles of the decade and highlights the best works in the room that represent those styles.

As visitors follow the guided path from room to room and decade to decade, the photo and essay displays reveal the essential themes of Picasso's work. Moving from period to period, visitors can easily grasp the relationships among his works and watch themes and styles develop. From these insights grows a deeper and clearer understanding of Picasso's great and unique contributions to the world of art.

Just as the map in the Picasso museum shows how the museum is organized, an organizational structure that a reader can easily follow sets the first standard for a portfolio. The standard is organization—each student's portfolio has labeled sections arranged in a logical and easily used sequence.

A very helpful aid to organization is the table of contents checklist. This serves as the student's organizing guide, a quick checklist for the teacher, and if grades are needed, a report card.

Creating a Multiple Intelligences Portfolio

PRIMARY EXAMPLE

Targeted Intelligences: Logical/Mathematical, Verbal/Linguistic
Targeted Standard: Problem solving and accuracy

Section A: Problem solving
1. Student goal card for selected intelligence
2. Teacher checklist of observed problem solving in group
3. Student self-checklist for problem-solving step use
4. Student-selected samples of accuracy in math problem solving (2)
5. Student-selected samples of personal problem solving (2)

Selection B: Accuracy
1. Student goal card for selected intelligence
2. Student-selected samples of accurate work in computation (3)
3. Student-selected samples of accurate written work (3)
4. Teacher note about homework

MIDDLE GRADE EXAMPLE

Targeted Intelligences: All
Targeted Standard: Problem Solving

Table of Contents and Teacher Checklist
Section A: *Visual/Spatial*
1. Map of archeological dig site with article and group PMI
2. Photos of group and self in dig
3. Photos of found items in dig
4. Two sketches of dig items found

Section B: *Verbal/Linguistic*
1. Personal KWL about ancient artifacts
2. Poem about trip to dig museum
3. Daily dig journal: focus on problem solving
4. Classroom notes on archeological digs

Section C: *Logical/Mathematical*
1. Measurements of dig site and proportions
2. Calculations of time estimates
3. Teacher checklist of observed problem-solving behavior

Section D: *Interpersonal*
1. Group checklist of group cooperation and problem solving
2. Group notes on contributions to group problem solving
3. Staff award for "most congenial digger"

Section E: *Intrapersonal*
1. My "learning goals for the dig" list
2. Summary evaluation of project portfolio: How we solved our dig problems

Section F: *Musical/Rhythmic*
1. Group song from dig banquet and awards night
2. Sketch of musical instruments from culture

Section G: *Bodily/Kinesthetic*
1. Photo of self digging with pick and ax
2. Group photo of dance replicating culture's ceremonial dance

Section H: *Naturalist*
1. Classification of artifacts.
2. Report on observations of similar attributes of fossils.

SECONDARY EXAMPLE: A UNIT FROM U.S. GOVERNMENT COURSE

Targeted Intelligences: Visual/Spatial, Verbal/Linguistic
Targeted Standard: Complex Thinking—Each student will show the relationships among the branches of national government in resolving a domestic issue of national significance.

Table of Contents and Evaluation Comment Sheet

	Date	A	B	C	D	Comments
Section A: *The Executive Branch*						
1. Research cards						
2. Diagram of responsibilities						
3. Description of role in dispute						
Section B: *The Judicial Branch*						
1. Research cards						
2. Diagram of responsibilities						
3. Description of role in dispute						
Section C: *The Legislative Branch*						
1. Research cards						
2. Diagram of responsibilities						
3. Description of role in dispute						
Section D: *The Connections*						
1. Tree map						
2. Teacher-made final exam						

TECH PREP EXAMPLE: GRAPHIC DESIGN COURSE PORTFOLIO

Targeted Intelligence: Visual/Spatial
Targeted Standard: Precision—The student will use principles of design in building a model home.

Table of Contents and Evaluation Check Sheet

RUBRIC

	A	B	C	D	F	Comments
Section 1: Design Work						
1. Rough sketches and consumer feedback chart						
2. Final floor plan						
3. List of needed materials						
Section 2: Supporting Evidence						
1. Summary of real estate interviews						
2. Photo album of model house under construction						
3. Daily journal						
4. Award ribbon and certificate						
5. Architect evaluations						

TABLE OF CONTENTS EXAMPLE

Name: Vicki Burger Grade: 7

Items in Order	Completed	Points Awarded
Section 1		
1. The Rubric	x	4
2. Journal	x	4
3. Social Studies Concept Map	x	3
4. Short Story	x	2
5. Diorama	x	5
6. Base Group Evaluation	x	3
7. Math Work Sheets	x	4
8. Semester Knowledge Test	x	3
	Total	28
	Score	3.5
	Grade	C+

MAKE YOUR OWN RUBRIC

Targeted Intelligence:

Targeted Standard:

Table of Contents:

— — The Rubric — —

Standard:

THE CRITERIA

High Performance:

Indicators:

Sound Performance:

Indicators:

Adequate Performance:

Indicators:

Not Yet:

Indicators:

Creating a Multiple Intelligences Portfolio

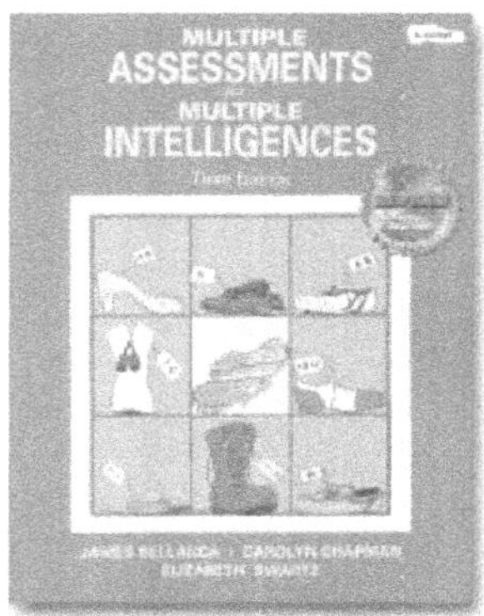

Selective

The second standard for a well-constructed portfolio is selectivity. The selective portfolio is neither a total collection nor a random collection of work. The process of portfolio making requires the student to *select* examples of his or her work that meet the given rubric's standards, criteria, and indicators of success. Sometimes the selection method includes identifying only exemplary or "the best" artifacts. At other times, the selection method may identify the "best," "good," and "not-so-good" examples.

The selection standards and criteria must reflect the seriousness of the learning process. The portfolio is neither a game nor "busy work." If it is used for these purposes, it would be better not to use it at all.

For students to take the portfolio seriously, they must learn to take the responsibility for selecting what is the best of their academic work. Contrast these good and bad examples of portfolio use according to a *selection* scale.

On the selectivity scale, the unacceptable examples should be marked "not yet." First, the unacceptable assessment systems put more emphasis on the teacher's selection than on the students'. If the teachers do the selecting, the students never have the chance to learn through success and failure. The students can go through the motions of putting together a portfolio, but a portfolio that has no significance for them. Second, in both cases, the standards and the criteria for assessment of the portfolio are random and fuzzy. The students are expected to guess their way. While some may guess well and create a meaningful portfolio, history shows that most of their work will be perfunctory.

On the other hand, the acceptable examples show that the teachers are serious about portfolios filled with work that helps students make sound choices. The teachers provide clear instructions and examples. They also give the students ample opportunity to experience success by learning how to assess the best work they do.

Promoting selectivity is best accomplished when the teacher and parents work together to teach students how to select

PRIMARY EXAMPLES

[AN EXAMPLE OF UNACCEPTABLE PORTFOLIO USE]

Each nine weeks, teachers in the Smithton Elementary School invite the children to decorate empty grocery boxes. One day a week, each student is given a box and one hour to decorate it. At the end of the week, the teacher selects one piece of work for the student to date and put into the box. One week, the entry may be a math work sheet; another week, a self-concept activity sheet. Discipline slips are also included.

The principal created the random system as a way to "to raise the children's anxiety" about their daily work and behavior. "They know the box goes home, but they can never guess what will be in it before the teacher picks. When the parents see the box, they get a picture of what the child has done that week."

|-------------------------------|-------------------------------X--|

Promotes Student Selectivity	Allows Student Selection	Not Yet

[AN EXAMPLE OF ACCEPTABLE PORTFOLIO USE]

At the beginning of the school year, teachers at Thomasville Elementary construct a "Guidelines for Your Most Intelligent Work" chart. The students in each class brainstorm lists of indicators of most intelligent work for each of the multiple intelligences. The lists are posted, and each teacher assists the students in preparing the first quarter's goals in the targeted intelligence. Each student writes his or her name on a manila folder and makes symbols to represent three selected goals. Inside the folder, the student puts one symbol in each of three colored dividers. At the end of each week, the student selects one artifact of classroom work that he or she thinks represents "my most intelligent work" for each of the three goals. On Fridays, children sit in the "I-am-smart chair" and share their selections with the class. At the end of the quarter, each student selects "my most intelligent work." The teacher sends the selected work home with the report card.

|--X----------------------------|----------------------------------|

Promotes Student Selectivity	Allows Student Selection	Not Yet

Creating a Multiple Intelligences Portfolio

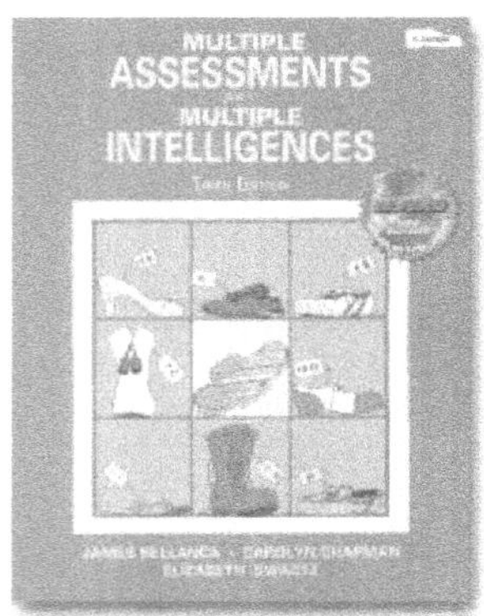

for the portfolio in a "learn-by-doing" mode. In a Georgia elementary school, the leadership team determined that accuracy, problem solving, and transfer of learning would be the exit standards for the eighth grade. Each teacher posted the standards, grade-level criteria, and indicators on the class bulletin board. Each teacher sent the parents a letter that discussed how he or she would use the rubric that year. In explaining "why," each teacher targeted two or three intelligences for special attention in the year's work. The primary teachers spoke about their special emphasis on language development through multiple means of written, oral, and visual tasks. They connected this to an explanation of the importance of developing the verbal/linguistic and visual/spatial intelligences for children of this age.

The middle grade teachers selected a project-based learning approach. Before beginning a project, students in cooperative groups reviewed the three exit standards and developed their own indicators for assessing the project. Each group wrote a letter to the parents. The letters outlined what project the group was doing, why they selected the project, and how they and their parents would evaluate the final work according to the three standards of accuracy, problem solving, and transfer of learning. Note how each of these two groups designed a different project but managed to include a collaborative assessment by students and parents.

SECONDARY EXAMPLES

[AN EXAMPLE OF UNACCEPTABLE PORTFOLIO USE]

In the first week of September, all freshmen are assigned into a counseling group with 250 peers and a counselor. Each receives the following letter from the principal.

Dear Student:

Welcome to New Rapids High School. In the four short years that you will be here, you will want to collect valuable memories of your high school years. As part of your graduation requirement, you must assemble a collection of those memories. We call this your graduation portfolio. By our state law, you cannot graduate without this portfolio.

What you put in the portfolio is up to you. Consider it to be your private yearbook. In past years, students have included pictures of their friends and family, mementos of social events, athletic letters and pins, report cards, and the like.

Sincerely,

Benjamin Thorson

|-----------------------------------|------------------------------------X--|

Promotes Student Selectivity	Allows Student Selection	Not Yet

[AN EXAMPLE OF ACCEPTABLE PORTFOLIO USE]

In the first week of September, all freshmen are introduced to the Centerville High School graduation requirements. This includes a discussion of the grading method for each class with the performance standards that the teacher will use and the creation of a yearly portfolio. In each class, the teacher describes the method the students will use to select samples of their best academic work for the portfolio. For instance, in English classes, the students will select the best test each wrote, the best essay or creative writing piece, and the best journal entry. At the end of each year, their counselor collects the portfolios. At the end of the first semester of the senior year, each senior prepares an overview of his or her three best samples from all classes up to this time and explains why each was selected. In addition, the student proposes a graduation project for the final semester. A faculty committee reviews each portfolio, each plan, and each student's course transcript. Students whose plans are approved may earn a semester's credit for completing and evaluating the senior project.

|--X--------------------------------|---------------------------------------|

Promotes Student Selectivity	Allows Student Selection	Not Yet

Creating a Multiple Intelligences Portfolio

MIDDLE GRADE EXAMPLES

I	II	III
What Construct?	A model of Fort Oglethorpe	Build an energy flow machine
Research:	Books on the history of Georgia	Library articles on energy flow
Standard:	Accuracy	Problem solving
Criteria:	Know facts about building this fort Make a detailed plan Build a precise model to scale	Know theory of energy flow Do math calculations Build machine from scrap materials
Indicators:	90% on history quiz Sketch matches detailed plans in text Connect each object to accuracy	Explain how machine flows energy Vocabulary test at 95% Correct calculations at 100% Machine works Describe problem-solving steps
Intelligences:	Visual/spatial Interpersonal Verbal/linguistic Logical/mathematical	Logical/mathematical Verbal/linguistic Interpersonal Visual/spatial
Time:	14 hours	9 hours

Assessment: Parent review of accuracy. Demonstration to parents with checklists given to teacher.

Representative

The third standard for a well-constructed portfolio, representativeness, gives balance to the selectivity standard. While the selectivity standard enables students to learn how to make meaningful choices about the quality of their work (within guidelines set by the school community), the *representativeness* standard highlights individual development of the intelligences and internal motivation.

A portfolio that is representative provides a *multidimensional* picture of the student's many intelligences. It contains examples of a student's work not only with the traditional emphasis on logical/mathematical and verbal/linguistic work, but also with his or her visual/spatial, musical/rhythmic, interpersonal, intrapersonal, naturalist, and bodily/kinesthetic achievements and potentials. Moreover, the representative portfolio contains assessments of this wider range of work from multiple perspectives. These perspectives may include assessments by the student, his or her peers, other adults, the teacher, and his or her parents.

From the earliest years, the teacher mediates the student's selection of contents for the portfolio. As the student learns how to organize the portfolio and then select "best works," he or she also learns to make sure the portfolio has a balance of materials. The multiple intelligences provide an ideal framework for inviting the student to investigate the widest range of possible abilities. The framework prevents the student from retreating into a narrow and limited "doing what I like to do." With the representative standard, the teacher can challenge the student to move out of comfort zones and into discomfort zones. Following the pathway to maximum development of an intelligence, the teacher can encourage the student to travel from the "encounter" stage to the "embrace" stage in as many of the intelligences as possible.

"E" ASING ON DOWN THE ROAD

Encounter

Employ

Educate

Embrace

(Chapman, 1993, p. 8)

Creating a Multiple Intelligences Portfolio

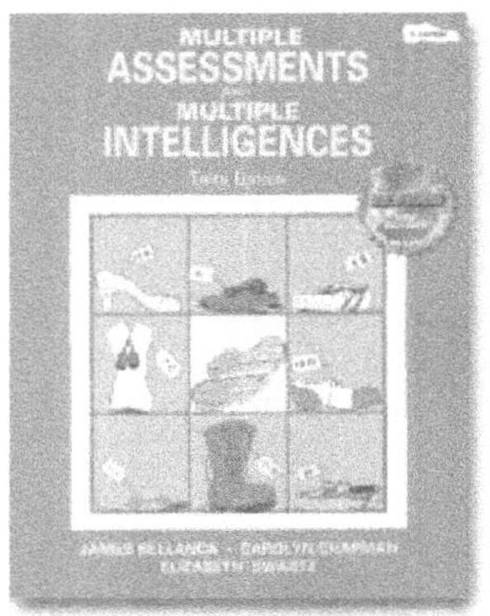

By organizing the exit portfolio according to the multiple intelligences, each student can include a journey assessment sheet similar to the examples adapted from *If the Shoe Fits...: How to Develop Multiple Intelligences in the Classroom* (Chapman, 1993, p 8). With the rubrics completed, the teacher and the student may make periodic entries to assess progress over many semesters along the way. By making the journey rubric the divider in the portfolio, each year the teacher, parent, and student can review the student's progress and refer to "best work" artifacts collected each year for each intelligence.

Each year brings a new representative assessment of the student's performances. In the final year, the teacher facilitates a final portrait. This portrait highlights the student's strengths and potential in many dimensions.

PERSONAL STRENGTH SUMMARY

Name ______________________ Class ______________________

Intelligences	Reasons	Comments
____________	____________	____________
____________	____________	____________
____________	____________	____________
____________	____________	____________
____________	____________	____________

Promotes Insight

The final important standard for a well-constructed portfolio is that it *promotes insight*. It is easy to make a portfolio that collects artifacts of activities. It is difficult to select artifacts that facilitate self-knowledge. Educators have continually struggled to find ways to encourage students to learn, to reflect, and to apply their learning to their lives. In today's classrooms many students believe it is the teacher's job to impart information, to motivate, and to entertain. Teachers who attempt to mediate reflective thinking and facilitate the students' search for meaning know from experience that they will meet resistance.

The portfolio that meets the organization, selectivity, and representative standards to a high degree is an important starting point for promoting student insight into the development of his or her many intelligences.

With the rubrics and the artifacts at his or her disposal, the teacher as *cognitive mediator* has a variety of tools for helping students to examine the connecting threads, the challenges, and the promise found in their portfolios.

PRIMARY EXAMPLES

Mirror, Mirror on the Wall

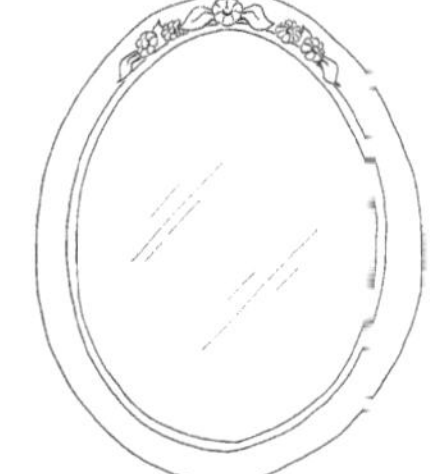

This reflection strategy works well with cooperative groups. Each child receives a copy of the mirror blackline. In turn, each shares his or her best work in each of the intelligences. (As a prompt, the bulletin board names each of the intelligences and shows pictures of people using each.) The other members of the group help the focus child pick out the three best examples for that child. The group helps the child sketch a symbol for each of the three on the mirror blackline. When all are finished, the teacher provides the children with a note to take home. He or she role-plays what will happen when the child shows the mirror to his or her parent(s) and tells about the examples on his or her mirror.

KWL—An Adaptation from Donna Ogle's Prereading Strategy (Ogle, 1986)

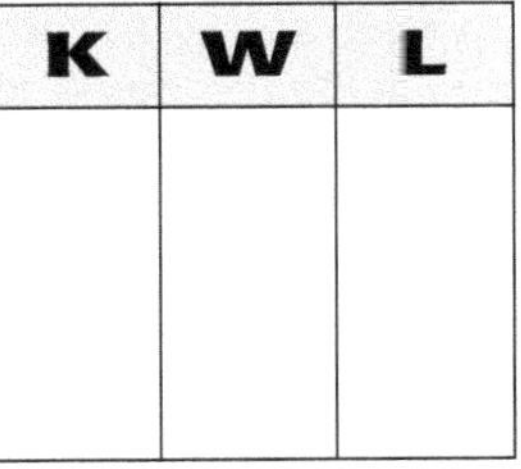

K	W	L

All children are given a copy of the KWL chart. In the K column, the teacher asks them to write what they "know" about their intelligences, and in the W column, what they "want" to improve in their intelligences. The teacher next helps the children select the most important "want" and make that a goal for the next grading period. The chart is put into the portfolio until the end of the grading period. At this time, the children fill in the "learned" (L) column to tell what they learned about their intelligences.

Footsteps

Before starting a new lesson in a targeted intelligence, the teacher helps the students cut out three to five footprints. On the reverse side of each cutout, the student writes his or her name. The teacher tells the students that after the project is finished, the class will brainstorm all the things people did well in completing the task. Then each student will select what he or she did well and write one example on each footprint. After signing his or her footprints, each student tacks them on the "easing down the road to intelligence" bulletin board.

Creating a Multiple Intelligences Portfolio

MIDDLE GRADES EXAMPLES

Snapshot Sequence

At the end of the marking period, the teacher gives each student twelve to eighteen index cards. Each student selects his or her strongest intelligence. Reviewing the artifacts in the portfolio, the student writes words or draws images that represent how he or she has "walked the road" for this intelligence. As cues, the teacher can use an overhead to show the generic road, and the students can refer to the rubrics and their artifacts to help sequence the cards from "encounter" to "embrace." The students can name their roads and glue the cards to poster board for display. Finally, the teacher may invite several students to explain their snapshot sequences before each places it into his or her portfolio.

Video Interview

At the end of a year, students select those items from their portfolios that represent their best development in each intelligence. Next, they will use a ranking ladder to rank-order their level of development among the intelligences. They then prepare a reason for each of the placements. When ready, they participate with a team in an interview. In round robin style, each team member (a) works the camera, (b) interviews, and (c) is interviewed. The team may imitate any television interview show. The interviewer asks: "What intelligence did you most improve this year? Why do you think so?" He or she repeats the questions for the three top-ranked intelligences. The interviewee may show artifacts, the rank ladder, etc. Each interview concludes with the question: "And which intelligence do you want to most improve?" After the students take their videos home and share them with their families, they place them in their respective portfolios.

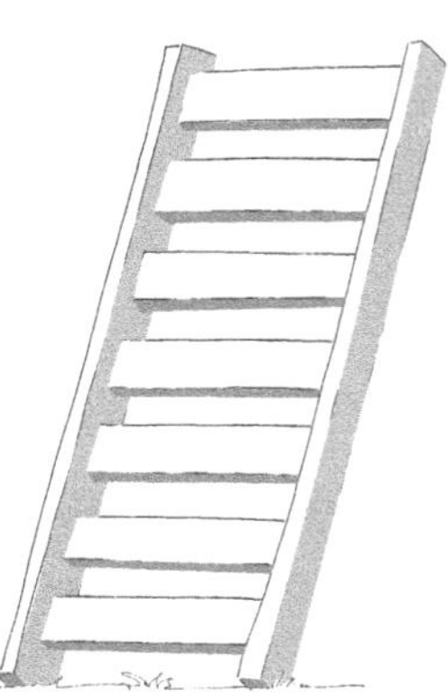

On Target

At the end of a project, each student labels the central circle of the target with the name of the target intelligences. Other intelligences are featured in the outer circles. Under or near each label, the student gives a number rating (1= low, 5= high) to indicate how well he or she did in using this intelligence in the project. On lines at the bottom, the student lists reasons for his or her central choice before placing the target in the portfolio.

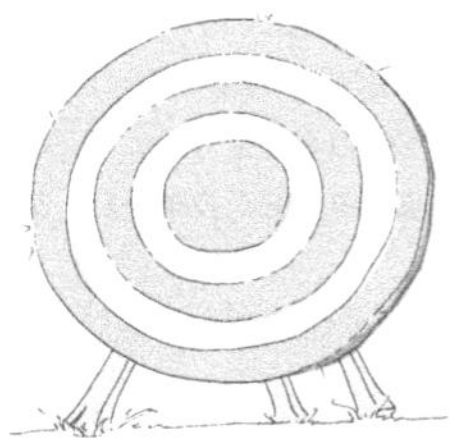

Reasons____________

____

____

SECONDARY EXAMPLES

Bar Graph/Pair Share

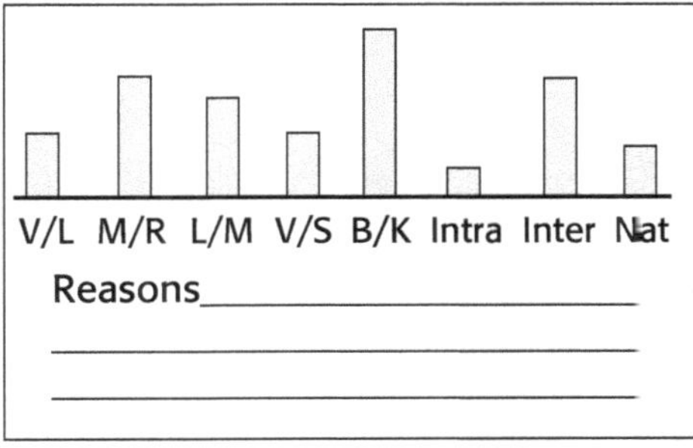

At the end of a marking period, each student reviews his or her portfolio for the course. The teacher provides a blank bar graph. Each student lists the intelligences he or she targeted for improvement in the marking period and graphs the amount of improvement achieved. At the bottom of the graph, he or she indicates reasons for the intelligence with the most improvement. After the graph is done, each student pairs with a partner and shares the graph and reasons before putting the graph in the portfolio.

Goal Review

Before starting a lesson, unit, or project, the teacher asks each student to select one intelligence that he or she wishes to develop. On an index card or in his or her journal, the student lists reasons for this selection. After all have completed their notes, the teacher pairs each student with a partner. Each person in the pair takes turns, asking the following sequence of questions shown on the overhead or in a handout:

What is the intelligence you selected?
Why did you decide to work on this intelligence?
What will be your standard?
How will you know that you are making the improvements you want?

At the end of the lesson, the same pairs get together to discuss these questions:

What was the intelligence you selected?
What was your goal?
What did you do well in reaching that goal?
What would you do differently if given the same chance again?
How pleased are you with what you accomplished?

At the conclusion of the interview, each student uses a note card or journal to summarize what was accomplished with the intelligence goal. The pairs may share the summaries before placing them in the portfolio.

Checklist

After reviewing the rubric for a lesson or project, the teacher gives each student a blank copy of the checklist. Each enters five indicators for the project standard on the checklist. Midway through the unit, each student checks progress made to that date. At the end of the lesson, each student checks and dates the final assessment.

If using the checklist for an entire marking period, the students enter standards on it. At three-week intervals, the students review progress, date the entries, and return the checklist to the portfolio.

Name ______________ Date ____________
Intelligence __________ Goal ____________

	Date
1. ______________________	__________
2. ______________________	__________
3. ______________________	__________
4. ______________________	__________
5. ______________________	__________

Creating a Multiple Intelligences Portfolio

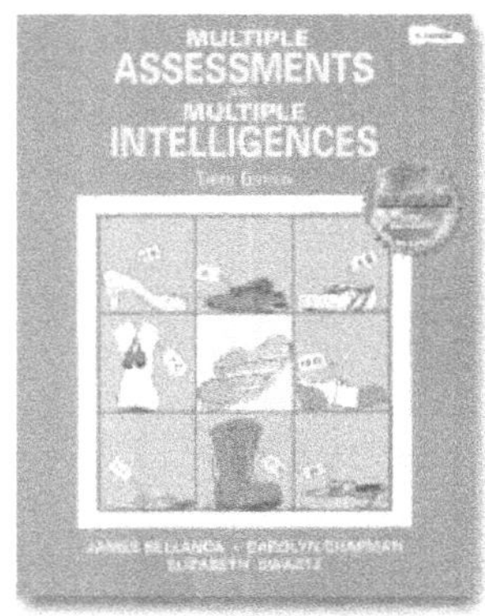

To assist students with judgments about their own work and development, it is best for the teacher to go beyond the facilitating role. The facilitating teacher supplies assessment formats similar to the preceding examples and gives instructions, models, and encouragement to the students. Beyond the facilitating role is the mediating role (Feuerstein et al., 1980; Fogarty, 1994.) The mediating teacher gives the students the opportunity to talk aloud about their judgments and to help them think more clearly about the specifics of their assessments. The mediator does not lecture, make comments, encourage, discourage, or react to the student's thoughts. The mediator asks precise questions that challenge the student to think more clearly about his or her own judgments.

Mediating questions work best in a climate where students listen to each other, respect individual responses, and avoid making verbal or nonverbal comments that would discourage another student's public expression of ideas. They also work best when the teacher-mediator explains to the students what he or she is doing and why for each mediating question and how he or she will wait for the responses. Some of the questions or phrases that help mediate a student's insight are open-ended and invitational in tone.

EXAMPLES OF MEDIATING QUESTIONS

1. I would appreciate it if you could tell us what you did in this project.
2. I would like you to tell us why you selected. . . .
3. I wonder what else you might have to say about. . . .
4. I am not clear about what you mean by. . . . Could you give me an example?
5. You sound (feeling) about_____? Am I right?
6. Why do you think_____?
7. How pleased are you about_____?
8. What pleases you most about_____?
9. How would you do it differently?
10. What help do you need?

MEDIATING QUESTIONS IN ACTION

In Mary Nelson's second grade class, the students used the logical/mathematical strategy for estimating the number of blocks in a wall they would construct. After the measurements were recorded by the groups, Mary gathered all the groups around her rocking chair. First, she praised them for the intensity of their cooperative problem solving. Next, she told them that they were going to review what they had done and the thinking that the task took.

"First I want us to remember our rules for 'think aloud' time." Mary said.

Many hands poked the air. "Francisco, what is one rule?"

"Listen to each other," answered Francisco.

"Sue Ellen?"

"Don't make fun or laugh," said the tiny redhead.

"And George, what will you add?"

George looked blank, "I forgot."

"That's all right, George. Maria?" asked Ms. Nelson softly.

"Don't interrupt."

"That's fine, Maria. And what do you think that big word 'interrupt' means?"

Maria was silent. Ms. Nelson waited. George squirmed.

"It means don't talk when someone else is talking."

"Wonderful, and are there any more ideas?" Mary Nelson looked slowly over her classroom. There were no hands. "Fine," she said. "Let's all remember those rules."

Tommy's hand shot up. "Can I go to the bathroom?"

"Yes," the teacher said. "You may go at any time during the discussion without asking. Just remember to move without distracting us."

Tommy scooted away.

"Now, let's go to my questions about your projects. I don't want to know your answers yet. But I will. I first want to ask the reporter from each group to tell me how you solved the problem."

Tim volunteered. "We all did our jobs. First, we measured our blocks to see how big they were. Then Tommy and Beth measured the room. After that, we took one block and a ruler. We moved the block and counted how many times we moved it. The last thing we did was multiply by three."

Ms. Nelson called on three more groups to describe how they had solved the problem. After she determined there were no new variations, she asked the calculator in each group to tell the class what was the hardest part of the task. This question was followed by a question asking the recorder to tell what was learned about problem solving. When several students struggled, Ms. Nelson coached them. Finally, she came to the application question. "Who is going to tell me how this problem solving will help you learn mathematics?"

Having returned from the bathroom, Tommy raised his hand. "I can help my dad. He is a carpenter."

Ms. Nelson waited a minute. Tommy was silent. "How will this math help you?" she asked.

"Because he has to measure. Sometimes he can't measure. He has to estimate like we did."

"And how are you as an estimator, Tommy."

"I did a good job."

"How so?" asked Ms. Nelson.

"We estimated how many blocks we would need for the wall. After that, we measured the room again. I bet our answer is just right."

Creating a Multiple Intelligences Portfolio

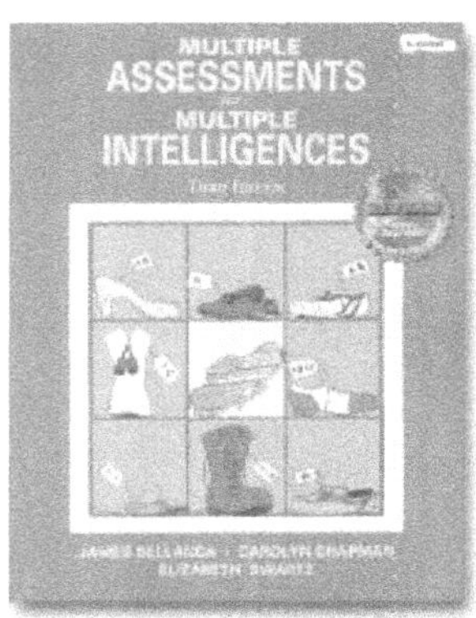

In most instances, these launch questions ask the student to describe what he or she did. After that, the mediator seeks to extend the student's thoughts, to clarify, and to facilitate analysis and synthesis by asking the most appropriate, noninterrupting follow-up questions for the situation. At the end of the mediation, the mediator reviews the questions asked.

The mediation role is appropriate for helping even the youngest students gain insight. Through skillful questions, students are helped to reflect on how they learned and how to apply what they learned to other situations.

While it is important that the student organize a portfolio to select representative work, it is as important that the collection provide insight into his or her learning styles in the various intelligences, his or her strengths and weaknesses, and his or her learning potential. Each section of the portfolio should include an ample representation of self-assessments to go along with teacher observations and checklists.

In the yearly portfolio, the balance created by the collection of the observations of others, the assessments of best performances, and the self-reflections paints a rich multidimensional portrait, a portrait of the student as a young learner with multiple intelligences.

REFERENCES

Bellanca, J. A. 1992b. How to grade (if you must). In A. L. Costa, J. A. Bellanca, and R. Fogarty (Eds.), *If minds matter: A foreword to the future, Volume II* p. 297–311. Palatine, IL: IRI/SkyLight Training and Publishing.

Bellanca, J., and R. Fogarty 1991. *Blueprints for thinking in the cooperative classroom* (2nd ed.). Palatine, IL: IRI/SkyLight Training and Publishing.

Blythe, T., and H. Gardner. 1990, April. A school for all intelligences. *Educational Leadership.* 47(7): 33–37.

Brandt, R. 1992a, May. On performance assessment: A conversation with Grant Wiggins. *Educational Leadership,* p. 35–37.

Burke, K. A. 1993. *The mindful school: How to assess authentic learning.* Arlington Heights, IL: IRI/SkyLight Training and Publishing.

Burke, K., R. Fogarty, and S. Belgrad. 1994. *The mindful school: The portfolio connection.* Palatine, IL: IRI/SkyLight Training and Publishing.

Campbell, L. 1992. *Teaching and learning through multiple intelligences.* Seattle: New Horizons for Learning.

Chapman, C. 1993. *If the shoe fits...: How to develop multiple intelligences in the classroom.* Palatine, IL: IRI/SkyLight Training and Publishing.

Costa, A., J. Bellanca, and R. Fogarty. 1992. *If minds matter: A foreword to the future (Vol. 2).* Palatine, IL: IRI/SkyLight Training and Publishing.

de Bono, E. 1985. *Six thinking hats.* Boston: Little, Brown.

Feuerstein, R., Y. Rand, M. Hoffman, and R. Miller. 1980. *Instrumental enrichment: An intervention program for cognitive modifiability.* Baltimore: University Park Press.

Fogarty, R. 1994. *The mindful school: How to teach for metacognitive reflection.* Palatine, IL: IRI/SkyLight Training and Publishing.

———. 1992. Teaching for transfer. In A. L. Costa, J. A. Bellanca, and R. Fogarty (Eds.), *If minds matter: A foreword to the future, Volume I* (p. 211–223). Palatine, IL: IRI/SkyLight Training and Publishing.

Fogarty, R., and J. Bellanca. 1989. *Patterns for thinking: Patterns for transfer.* Palatine, IL: IRI/SkyLight Training and Publishing.

Gardner, H. 1993. *Multiple Intelligences: The theory in practice.* New York: Basic Books.

———. 1983. *Frames of mind.* New York: Basic Books.

Gardner, H., and T. Hatch. 1990. *Multiple intelligences go to school: Educational implications of the theory of multiple intelligences* (Report No. 4). New York: Center for Technology in Education.

Hamm, M., and D. Adams. 1991, May. Portfolio: It's not just for artists anymore. *The Science Teacher,* p. 18–21.

Hansen, J. 1992, May. Literacy portfolios: Helping students know themselves. *Educational Leadership,* p. 66–68.

Knight, P. 1992, May. How I use portfolios in mathematics. *Educational Leadership,* p. 71–72.

Kohn, A. 1992. *No contest: The case against competition* (rev. ed.), Boston: Houghton Mifflin Company.

Ogle, D. 1986. K-W-L: A teaching model that develops active reading of expository text. *The Reading Teacher* 6: 564–570.

Perkins, D., and G. Salomon. 1992. The science and art of transfer. In A. L. Costa, J. A. Bellanca, and R. Fogarty (Eds.), *If minds matter: A foreword to the future, Volume I* (p. 201–209). Palatine, IL: IRI/SkyLight Training and Publishing.

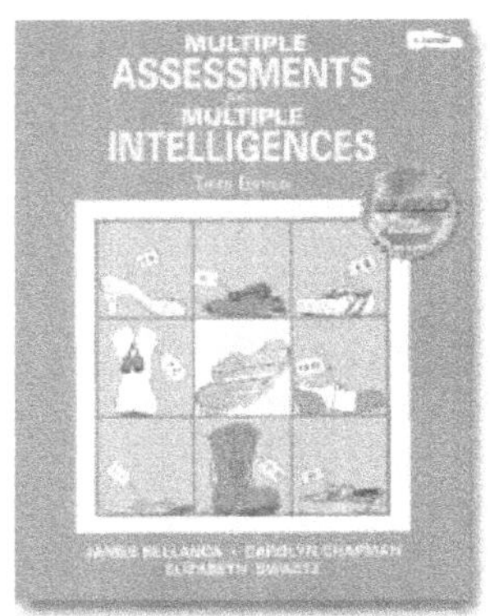

Simon, S. B., and J. A. Bellanca (Eds.). 1976. *Degrading the grading myths: A primer of alternatives to grades and marks.* Washington, D.C.: Association for Supervision and Curriculum Development.

Sternberg, R. J. 1990. *Metaphors of mind: Conceptions of the nature of intelligence.* New York: Viking.

Wolf, D. P. 1989, April. Portfolio assessment: Sampling student work. *Educational Leadership,* p. 35–39.

Creating a Multiple Intelligences Portfolio

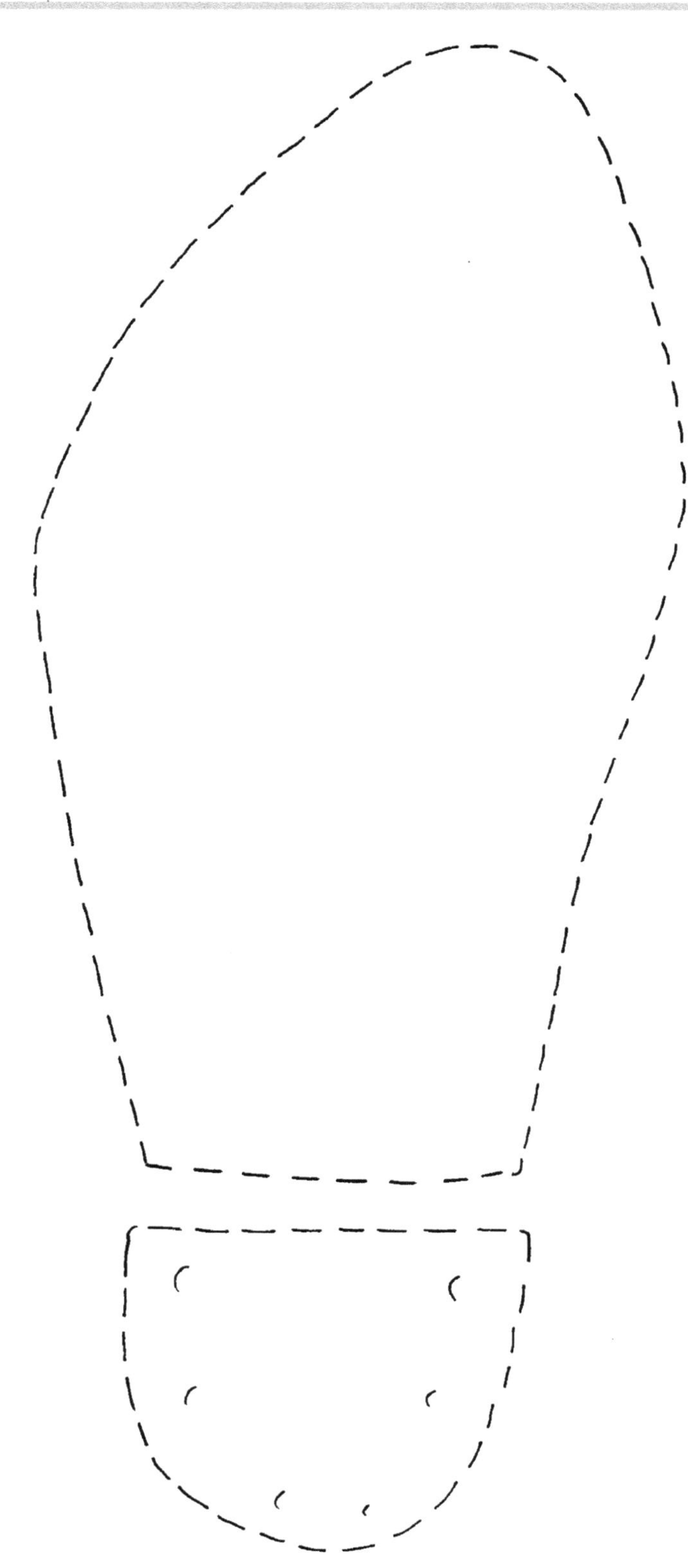

Creating a Multiple Intelligences Portfolio

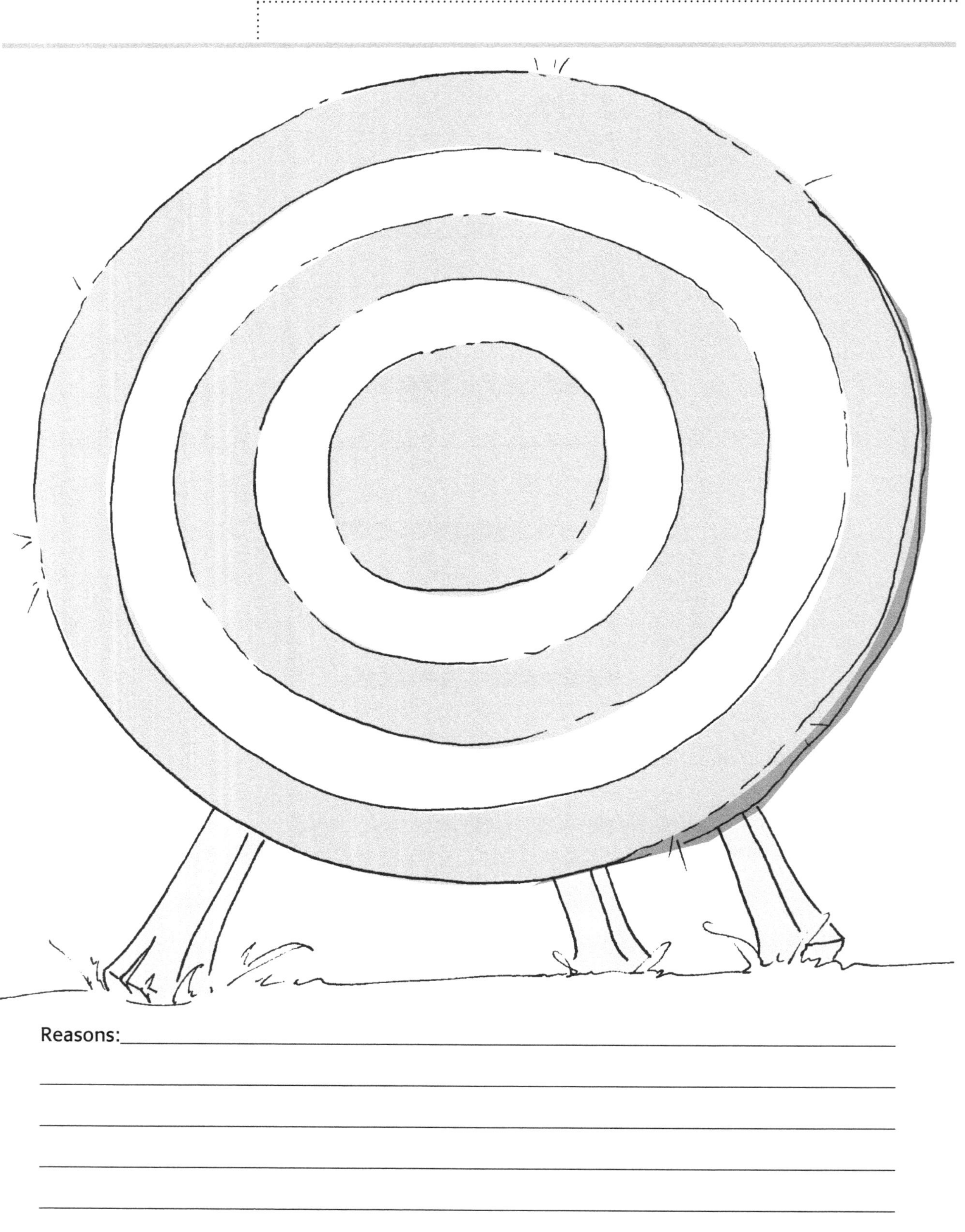

Reasons:____

____

____

____

____

SELECTION 18

Electronic Portfolios

by **R. W. Burniske**

Students need a strategy that encourages reflection upon their research and writing processes as well as a way to collect the disparate pieces of their work. Borrowing from the idea of portfolio assessment with printed materials, teachers can help students through this process by arranging electronic portfolios for a given project. Although this exercise grows out of language arts and humanities instruction, it's applicable to projects in most academic disciplines. It begins with the creation of a simple hypertext template that emphasizes research, reflection, and a process approach to writing. By constructing electronic portfolios, students create a record of their research and writing process, develop HTML skills, and strengthen their evaluative literacy.

What's the appeal of an electronic portfolio? Does this variation accomplish anything that print portfolios couldn't? Certainly, this activity shares a good deal with its print cousin. For one thing, it provides context for student work. How often does a school curriculum encourage students to think in holistic terms, situating disparate learning activities and fragmented disciplines in a larger context? As a result, they often think of learning activities as "busywork" a teacher creates to keep them occupied, rather than as part of a coherent learning process. As much as anything, portfolio assessment tries to overcome this. The electronic portfolio, by extension, will

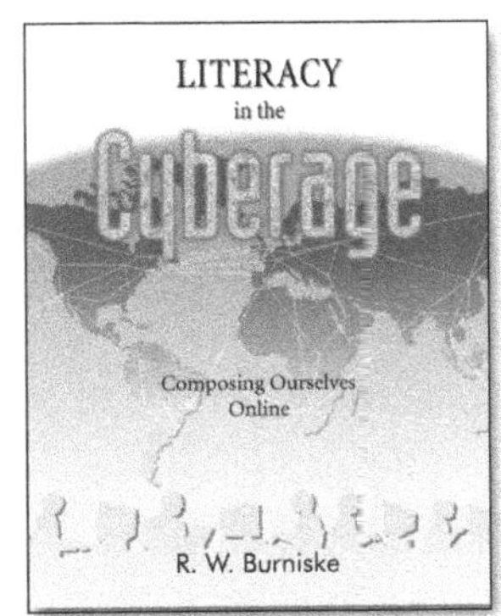

Adapted from *Literacy in the Cyberage: Composing Ourselves Online* by R. W. Burniske, pp. 197–205 and 227–31.

help students think of their work not as an isolated essay or report for a particular teacher or class, but as part of a larger conversation—one that connects them with a community of scholars. The electronic portfolio process distinguishes itself from print variations because the medium allows students to link directly from their composition to online resources. Meanwhile, internal links between the respective portfolio sections encourage a self-conscious and reflective approach to composition.

To illustrate the importance of this type of approach, let's consider a common academic assignment: the research essay. Typically, the process goes something like this: The student chooses a research topic and submits a proposal that the teacher must approve. Then, the student conducts research, taking notes from secondary sources that will help support a particular argument (often a preconceived argument the research will merely reinforce rather than question). Finally, the student outlines an essay, writes a draft or two, and produces a final draft replete with citations and bibliography. Now stop to consider this process. How much time did the student spend reflecting upon it? How much of the process has the teacher seen? How much of it will be reflected by the final draft? How much of the process does the student retain? Does the student see the relationship between that process and the final product? Or has the obsession with that destination blinded the student to the journey?

The answers to these questions will depend largely on the particular students and teacher, but, generally speaking, the final draft of a conventional research paper reveals only a fragment of the process involved in its creation. With a portfolio, however, the final draft is placed within the context of the entire project. The electronic portfolio offers the unique opportunities of hypertext, which allows one to move through the internal links of the portfolio sections as well as depart from it to consider the secondary sources that informed the writer's thinking.

How might one design an electronic portfolio? Figure 18.1 presents the template created for students in *The Rhetoric of Utopia* course.

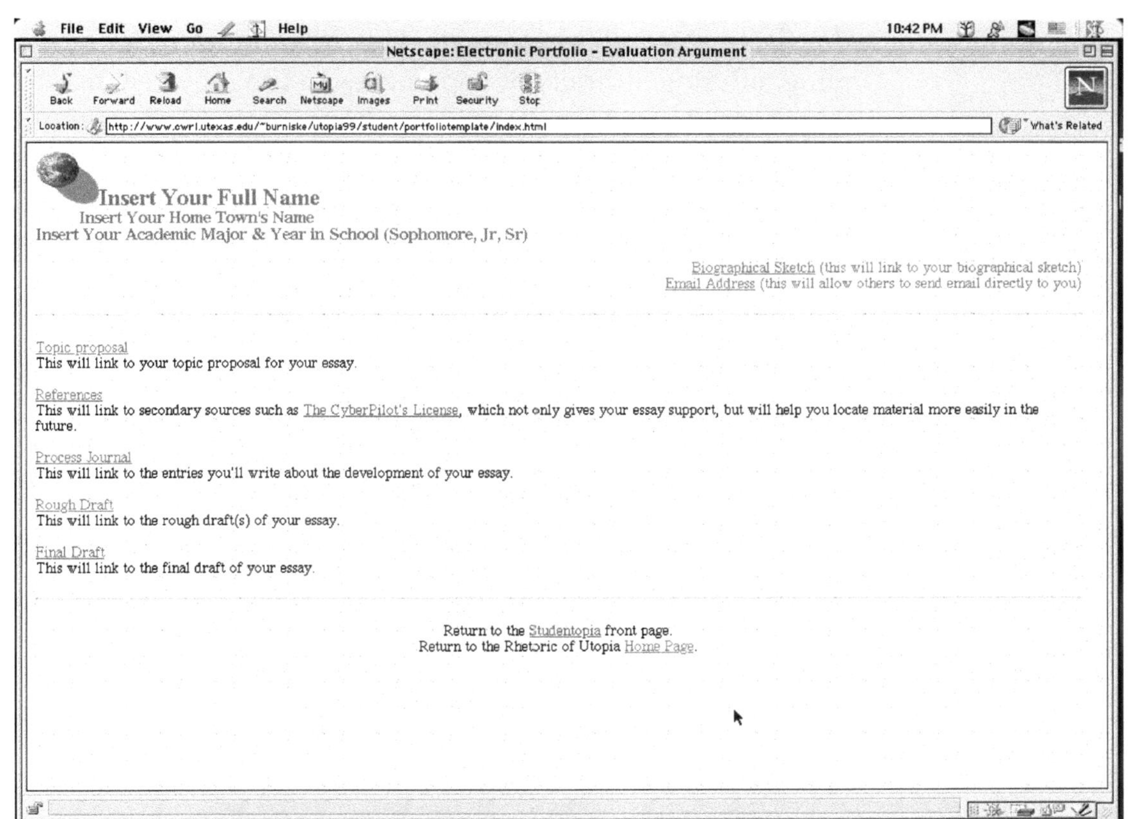

Figure 18.1

In this instance, the teacher established six discrete portfolio sections, though these could certainly be modified depending on the academic discipline and project. From the "index" page of this portfolio, which is shown in Figure 18.1, the reader can follow one of the following internal links:

- Biographical Sketch
- Topic Proposal
- References
- Process Journal
- Rough Draft(s)
- Final Draft

To illustrate each of these sections and discuss their significance within the electronic portfolio, let's look at selected

Electronic Portfolios

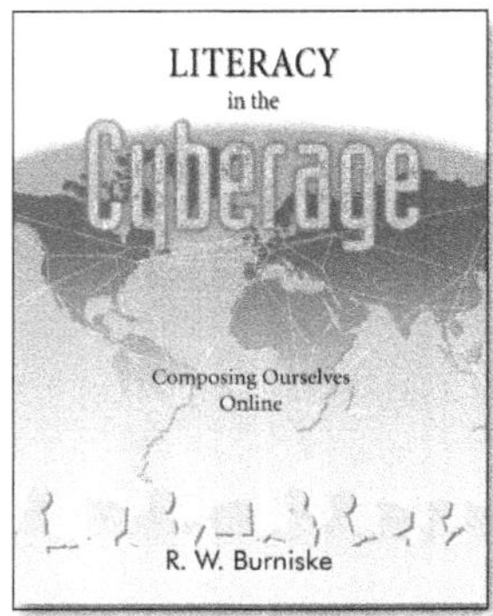

samples rather than follow a particular student's progress through a research assignment. This will allow a wider sampling, offering a variety of approaches to the required tasks. (Note: Readers who prefer to examine an individual portfolio or see more samples should visit the online collections archived in *The Rhetoric of Utopia* course Web site for the Fall 1998 and Spring 1999 semesters: Fall 1998 – http://www.cwrl.utexas.edu~burniske/utopia98/student/index.html; Spring 1999 – http://www.cwrl.utexas.edu/~burniske/utopia99/student/index.html.)

What follows is a brief explanation of the electronic portfolio's respective sections. Although the selected "screenshots" truncate some pages, they illustrate the way in which the respective parts relate to the whole. What's more, they demonstrate how an electronic portfolio, conceived as an online hypertext, may contribute to a student's evaluative literacy.

a. *Biographical sketch.* Every essay or report has a story behind it. The author is the protagonist, drawn to his or her subject because of personal interests or curiosities. This section offers the writer a chance to tell the background to this story. Why did he or she choose this topic? Or, perhaps more accurately, why did this topic choose him or her? It's often best to save this exercise for last, providing one last chance for the student to reflect on the intellectual journey. As Figure 18.2 indicates, pausing to consider the "story" behind an individual's topic selection yields privileged insight. Not only does it help the student and teacher understand the thought process involved in making this decision, but it also reveals the level of personal commitment.

b. *Topic proposal.* All stories have a beginning, middle, and end. The topic proposal is the beginning. Students may decide to change their topic, but unless they write a topic proposal they could delay the decision unnecessarily, procrastinating while they search for the "perfect topic." What they learn from this exercise, more often than not, is that the starting point isn't as important as the subsequent journey. The proposal, nonetheless, helps them overcome inertia at the start of a research project, compelling them to locate sources that will

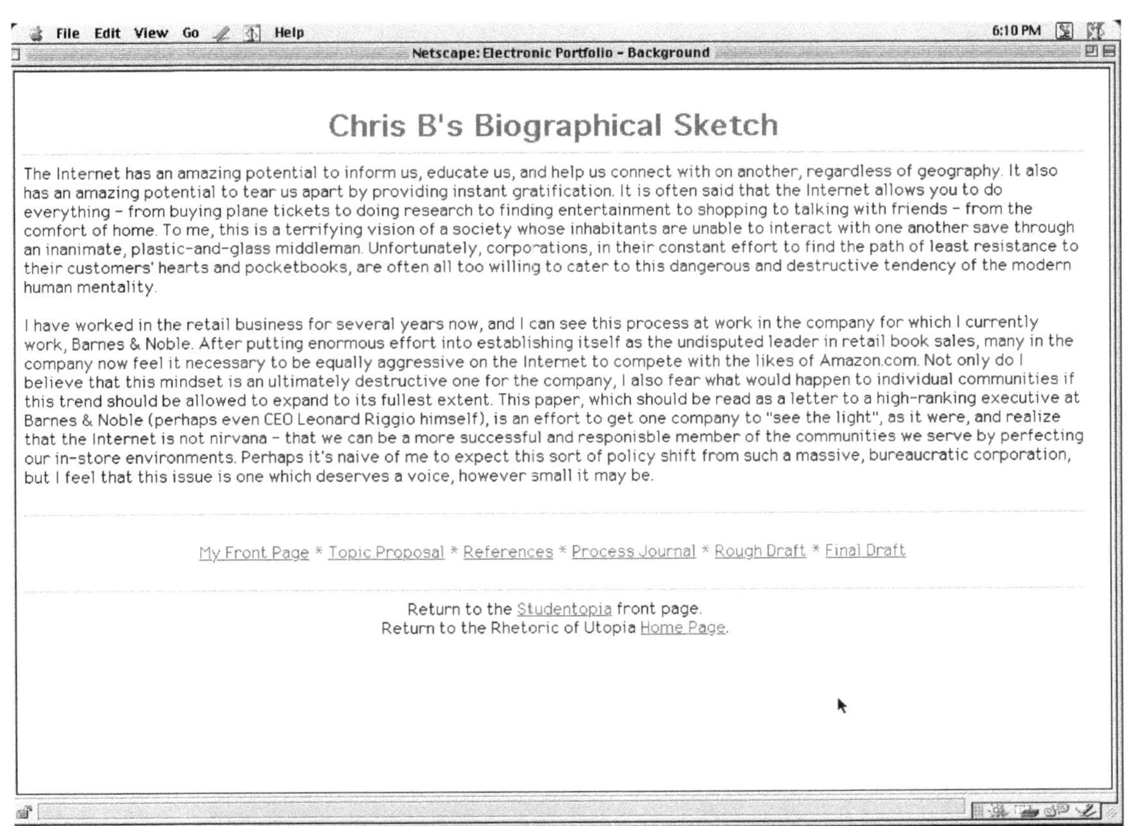
File Edit View Go Help 6:10 PM

Netscape: Electronic Portfolio – Background

Chris B's Biographical Sketch

The Internet has an amazing potential to inform us, educate us, and help us connect with on another, regardless of geography. It also has an amazing potential to tear us apart by providing instant gratification. It is often said that the Internet allows you to do everything – from buying plane tickets to doing research to finding entertainment to shopping to talking with friends – from the comfort of home. To me, this is a terrifying vision of a society whose inhabitants are unable to interact with one another save through an inanimate, plastic-and-glass middleman. Unfortunately, corpo-ations, in their constant effort to find the path of least resistance to their customers' hearts and pocketbooks, are often all too willing to cater to this dangerous and destructive tendency of the modern human mentality.

I have worked in the retail business for several years now, and I can see this process at work in the company for which I currently work, Barnes & Noble. After putting enormous effort into establishing itself as the undisputed leader in retail book sales, many in the company now feel it necessary to be equally aggressive on the Internet to compete with the likes of Amazon.com. Not only do I believe that this mindset is an ultimately destructive one for the company, I also fear what would happen to individual communities if this trend should be allowed to expand to its fullest extent. This paper, which should be read as a letter to a high-ranking executive at Barnes & Noble (perhaps even CEO Leonard Riggio himself), is an effort to get one company to "see the light", as it were, and realize that the Internet is not nirvana – that we can be a more successful and responisble member of the communities we serve by perfecting our in-store environments. Perhaps it's naive of me to expect this sort of policy shift from such a massive, bureaucratic corporation, but I feel that this issue is one which deserves a voice, however small it may be.

My Front Page * Topic Proposal * References * Process Journal * Rough Draft * Final Draft

Return to the Studentopia front page.
Return to the Rhetoric of Utopia Home Page.

Figure 18.2

engage them in discussion of their chosen topic. This piece of the portfolio may help them see where things ran amok, helping them recall the process of topic selection and evaluate its impact upon their performance. In the example depicted in Figure 18.3, students began with a "Why List," before writing a topic proposal indicating their proposed audience and three references that would spur further research.

c. *References.* This is perhaps the most unique feature of an electronic portfolio. Not only does this section allow students to link directly from their in-text citations to full bibliographical references, but in the case of online documents they can provide direct hyperlinks from their final draft to secondary

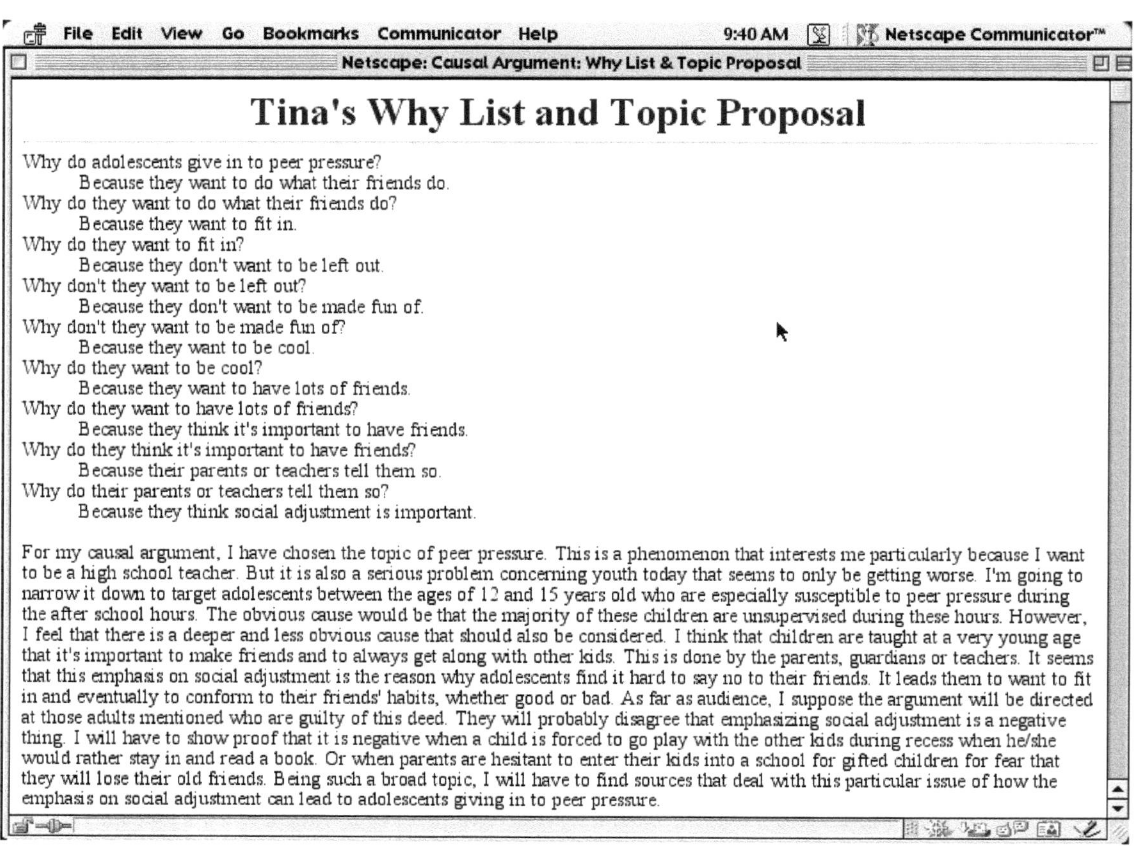

Netscape: Causal Argument: Why List & Topic Proposal

Tina's Why List and Topic Proposal

Why do adolescents give in to peer pressure?
Because they want to do what their friends do.
Why do they want to do what their friends do?
Because they want to fit in.
Why do they want to fit in?
Because they don't want to be left out.
Why don't they want to be left out?
Because they don't want to be made fun of.
Why don't they want to be made fun of?
Because they want to be cool.
Why do they want to be cool?
Because they want to have lots of friends.
Why do they want to have lots of friends?
Because they think it's important to have friends.
Why do they think it's important to have friends?
Because their parents or teachers tell them so.
Why do their parents or teachers tell them so?
Because they think social adjustment is important.

For my causal argument, I have chosen the topic of peer pressure. This is a phenomenon that interests me particularly because I want to be a high school teacher. But it is also a serious problem concerning youth today that seems to only be getting worse. I'm going to narrow it down to target adolescents between the ages of 12 and 15 years old who are especially susceptible to peer pressure during the after school hours. The obvious cause would be that the majority of these children are unsupervised during these hours. However, I feel that there is a deeper and less obvious cause that should also be considered. I think that children are taught at a very young age that it's important to make friends and to always get along with other kids. This is done by the parents, guardians or teachers. It seems that this emphasis on social adjustment is the reason why adolescents find it hard to say no to their friends. It leads them to want to fit in and eventually to conform to their friends' habits, whether good or bad. As far as audience, I suppose the argument will be directed at those adults mentioned who are guilty of this deed. They will probably disagree that emphasizing social adjustment is a negative thing. I will have to show proof that it is negative when a child is forced to go play with the other kids during recess when he/she would rather stay in and read a book. Or when parents are hesitant to enter their kids into a school for gifted children for fear that they will lose their old friends. Being such a broad topic, I will have to find sources that deal with this particular issue of how the emphasis on social adjustment can lead to adolescents giving in to peer pressure.

Figure 18.3

sources. By reinforcing the lessons learned about intellectual property, the reference section compels attention to detail (see Figure 18.4). Unless they're carefully documented, the links from this section to the online references will not work, which obviously damages the author's credibility. Best of all, the reference section places the essay within the context of the larger discussion conducted by the community of scholars the writer has joined. By linking from their own essay to the online resources, the writer allows the reader to see how secondary source material influenced his or her thinking. What's more, the quality of those sources is revealed, calling attention to the fact that the choice of secondary materials affects one's ethos.

d. *Process journal.* This section of the electronic portfolio allows students to demonstrate the process behind their final

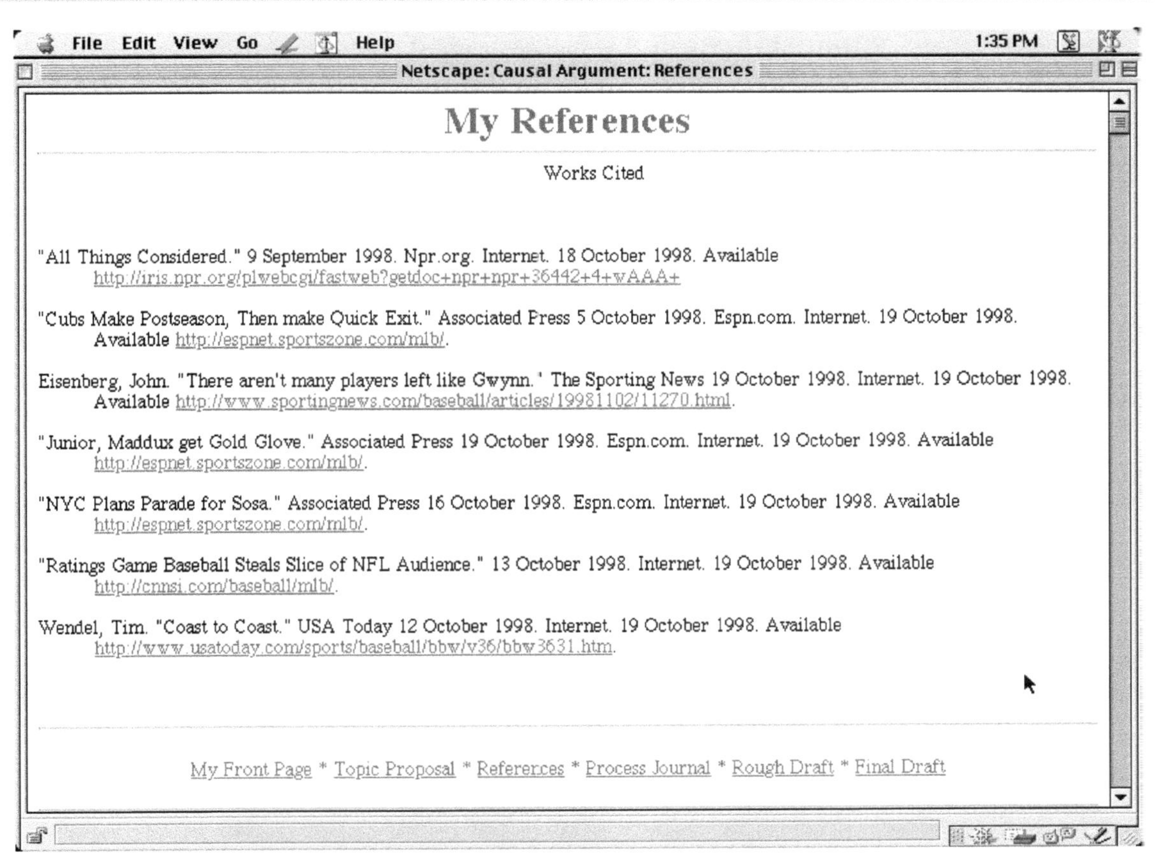

File Edit View Go Help 1:35 PM

Netscape: Causal Argument: References

My References

Works Cited

"All Things Considered." 9 September 1998. Npr.org. Internet. 18 October 1998. Available http://iris.npr.org/plwebcgi/fastweb?getdoc+npr+npr+36442+4+wAAA+

"Cubs Make Postseason, Then make Quick Exit." Associated Press 5 October 1998. Espn.com. Internet. 19 October 1998. Available http://espnet.sportszone.com/mlb/.

Eisenberg, John. "There aren't many players left like Gwynn.' The Sporting News 19 October 1998. Internet. 19 October 1998. Available http://www.sportingnews.com/baseball/articles/19981102/11270.html.

"Junior, Maddux get Gold Glove." Associated Press 19 October 1998. Espn.com. Internet. 19 October 1998. Available http://espnet.sportszone.com/mlb/.

"NYC Plans Parade for Sosa." Associated Press 16 October 1998. Espn.com. Internet. 19 October 1998. Available http://espnet.sportszone.com/mlb/.

"Ratings Game Baseball Steals Slice of NFL Audience." 13 October 1998. Internet. 19 October 1998. Available http://cnnsi.com/baseball/mlb/.

Wendel, Tim. "Coast to Coast." USA Today 12 October 1998. Internet. 19 October 1998. Available http://www.usatoday.com/sports/baseball/bbw/v36/bbw3631.htm.

My Front Page * Topic Proposal * References * Process Journal * Rough Draft * Final Draft

Figure 18.4

product. Teachers may require one or two journal entries per week, but to keep students honest (avoiding the "creative writing" that results from composing entries the night before they're due), it's wise to request that entries be turned in at the end of each week. This will encourage periodic reflection, giving students a better understanding of their own process and what they might do to improve it in the future. In effect, the process journal is the "story behind the story," a behind-the-scenes glimpse of the project's evolution. Raising student awareness in this manner proves remarkably useful, empowering them with a critical literacy that begins with an honest assessment of what went well, what didn't, and what they need to do differently in the future. In just a few brief sentences, the student can speak to the difficulties of settling on a topic;

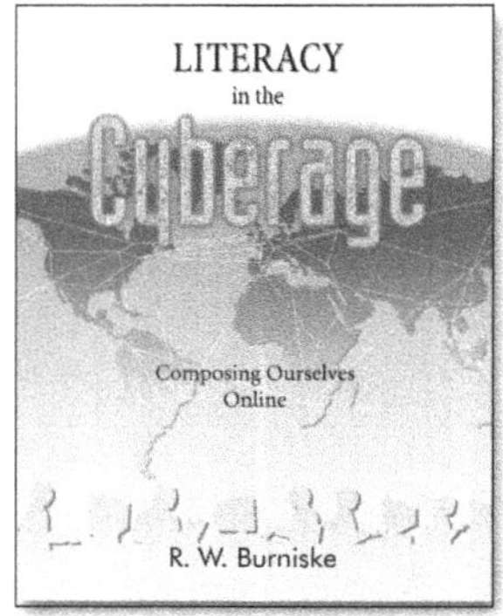

share important research discoveries; describe struggles with initial drafts and revision; reveal the agony and ecstasy of peer review; and speculate on a future course of action. Indeed, all of this appears in the process journal depicted in Figure 18.5, which consists of two brief entries per week over a three-week period.

e. *Rough drafts and peer reviews.* This section offers a detailed portrait of the composition process, including peer reviews. Once students learn how to create copies of an HTML document (which takes one keystroke at the computer), they can link to multiple rough drafts and peer reviews. With their own drafts and peer reviews on display in this section, the depth of the students' commitment to the writing process and to peer review is quickly revealed. As the sample in Figure 18.6

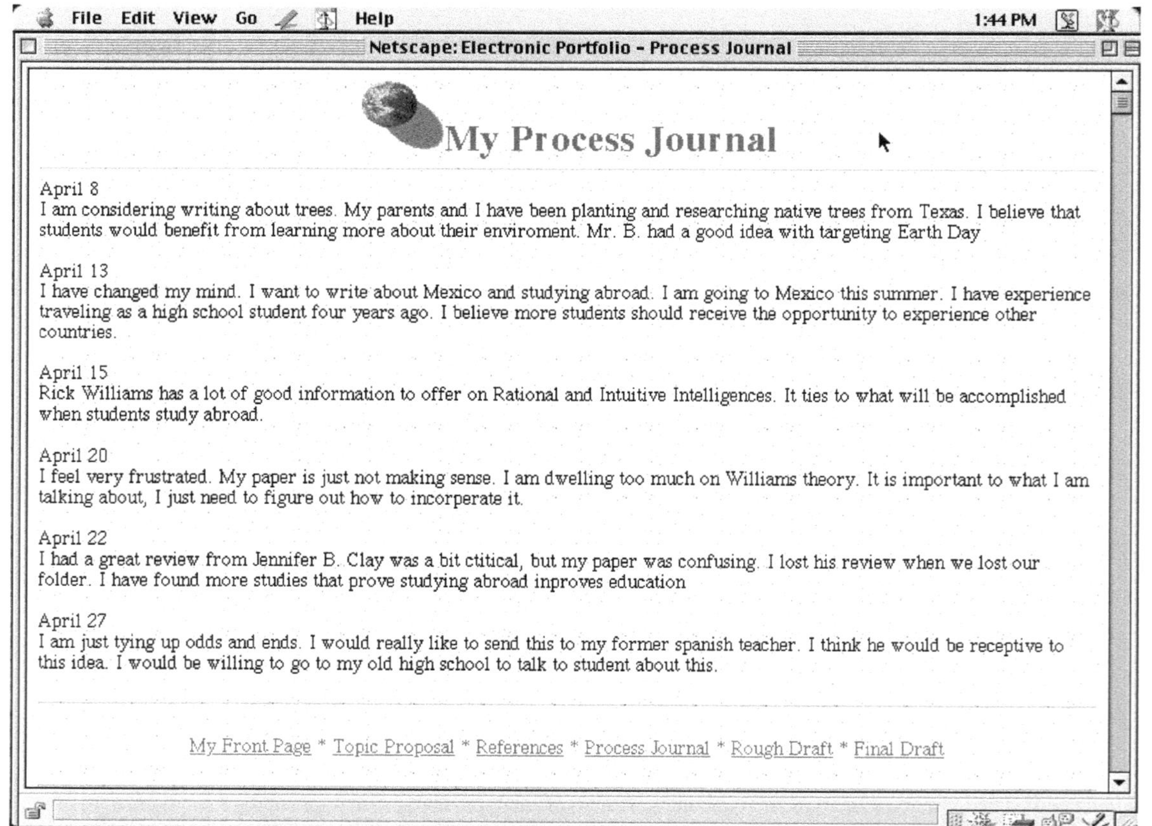

My Process Journal

April 8
I am considering writing about trees. My parents and I have been planting and researching native trees from Texas. I believe that students would benefit from learning more about their enviroment. Mr. B. had a good idea with targeting Earth Day

April 13
I have changed my mind. I want to write about Mexico and studying abroad. I am going to Mexico this summer. I have experience traveling as a high school student four years ago. I believe more students should receive the opportunity to experience other countries.

April 15
Rick Williams has a lot of good information to offer on Rational and Intuitive Intelligences. It ties to what will be accomplished when students study abroad.

April 20
I feel very frustrated. My paper is just not making sense. I am dwelling too much on Williams theory. It is important to what I am talking about, I just need to figure out how to incorperate it.

April 22
I had a great review from Jennifer B. Clay was a bit ctitical, but my paper was confusing. I lost his review when we lost our folder. I have found more studies that prove studying abroad inproves education

April 27
I am just tying up odds and ends. I would really like to send this to my former spanish teacher. I think he would be receptive to this idea. I would be willing to go to my old high school to talk to student about this.

My Front Page * Topic Proposal * References * Process Journal * Rough Draft * Final Draft

Figure 18.5

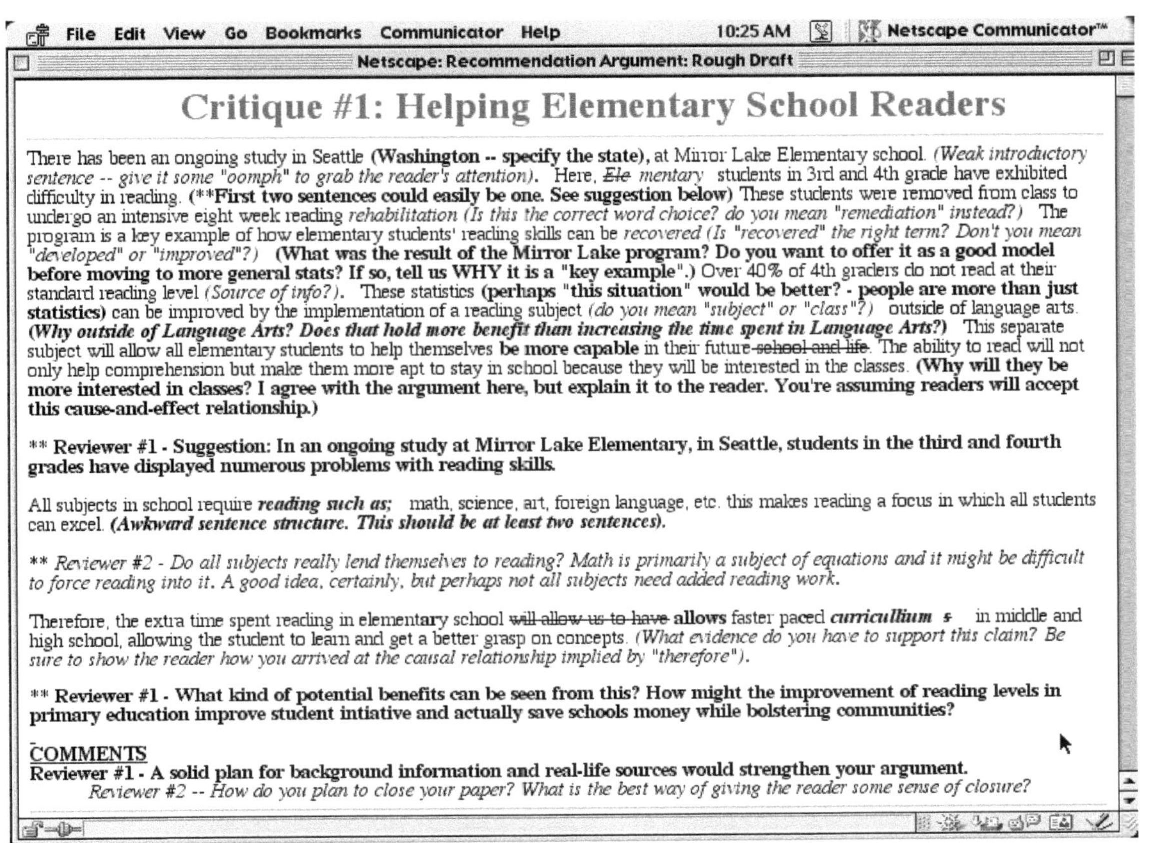

File Edit View Go Bookmarks Communicator Help 10:25 AM Netscape Communicator™

Netscape: Recommendation Argument: Rough Draft

Critique #1: Helping Elementary School Readers

There has been an ongoing study in Seattle **(Washington -- specify the state),** at Mirror Lake Elementary school. *(Weak introductory sentence -- give it some "oomph" to grab the reader's attention).* Here, ~~Ele~~ *mentary* students in 3rd and 4th grade have exhibited difficulty in reading. **(**First two sentences could easily be one. See suggestion below)** These students were removed from class to undergo an intensive eight week reading *rehabilitation (Is this the correct word choice? do you mean "remediation" instead?)* The program is a key example of how elementary students' reading skills can be *recovered (Is "recovered" the right term? Don't you mean "developed" or "improved"?)* **(What was the result of the Mirror Lake program? Do you want to offer it as a good model before moving to more general stats? If so, tell us WHY it is a "key example".)** Over 40% of 4th graders do not read at their standard reading level *(Source of info?).* These statistics **(perhaps "this situation" would be better? - people are more than just statistics)** can be improved by the implementation of a reading subject *(do you mean "subject" or "class"?)* outside of language arts. ***(Why outside of Language Arts? Does that hold more benefit than increasing the time spent in Language Arts?)*** This separate subject will allow all elementary students to help themselves **be more capable** in their future ~~school and life~~. The ability to read will not only help comprehension but make them more apt to stay in school because they will be interested in the classes. **(Why will they be more interested in classes? I agree with the argument here, but explain it to the reader. You're assuming readers will accept this cause-and-effect relationship.)**

** **Reviewer #1 - Suggestion: In an ongoing study at Mirror Lake Elementary, in Seattle, students in the third and fourth grades have displayed numerous problems with reading skills.**

All subjects in school require ***reading such as;*** math, science, art, foreign language, etc. this makes reading a focus in which all students can excel. ***(Awkward sentence structure. This should be at least two sentences).***

** *Reviewer #2 - Do all subjects really lend themselves to reading? Math is primarily a subject of equations and it might be difficult to force reading into it. A good idea, certainly, but perhaps not all subjects need added reading work.*

Therefore, the extra time spent reading in elementary school ~~will allow us to have~~ **allows** faster paced ***curricullium*** ~~s~~ in middle and high school, allowing the student to learn and get a better grasp on concepts. *(What evidence do you have to support this claim? Be sure to show the reader how you arrived at the causal relationship implied by "therefore").*

** **Reviewer #1 - What kind of potential benefits can be seen from this? How might the improvement of reading levels in primary education improve student intiative and actually save schools money while bolstering communities?**

COMMENTS
Reviewer #1 - A solid plan for background information and real-life sources would strengthen your argument.
Reviewer #2 -- How do you plan to close your paper? What is the best way of giving the reader some sense of closure?

Figure 18.6

indicates, peer review sessions that provide time for two reviewers to mark the text using a hypertext editor often produce remarkably thorough commentaries. As a result, hardly a word escapes scrutiny, making the rough drafts an essential part of the portfolio, as well as a key to the students' development of evaluative literacy skills.

f. *Final draft.* This, of course, is the ending, but it should not be considered an isolated piece. The internal links at the foot of the document allow the reader to trace the evolution of this finished "product" back through its rough drafts and peer reviews, its process journal and topic proposal, right to the origins described in the biographical sketch. With all this background information, the reader gains insight into the trials and tribulations involved in this intellectual odyssey. Embedded

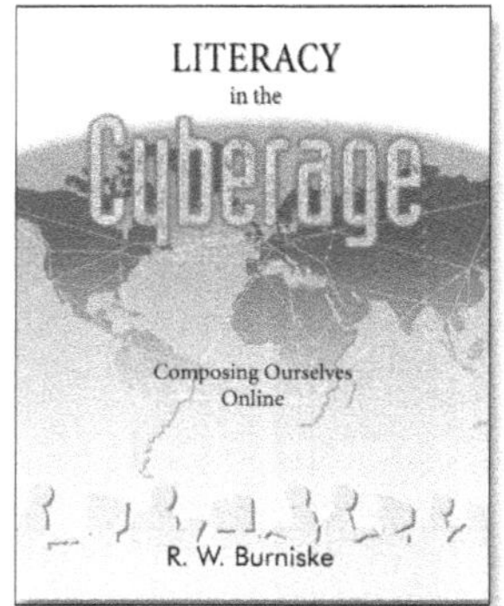

within the text of the final draft are hyperlinks to the references, which will take the reader directly to secondary sources. For example, the underlined in-text citations in Figure 18.7 may provide a hyperlink to the complete bibliography located in the References section of the electronic portfolio, or take the reader directly to the online secondary sources.

Portfolio assessment requires a reorientation, shifting students and teachers away from simplistic grading schemes and standardized tests toward holistic evaluation. Also, it asks students to become self-conscious, paying attention to not only what they learn, but also how they learn it. There are a number of benefits to this, including a change in classroom dynamics. Once students become aware of their learning style, acquire a deeper understanding of their writing process, and realize that

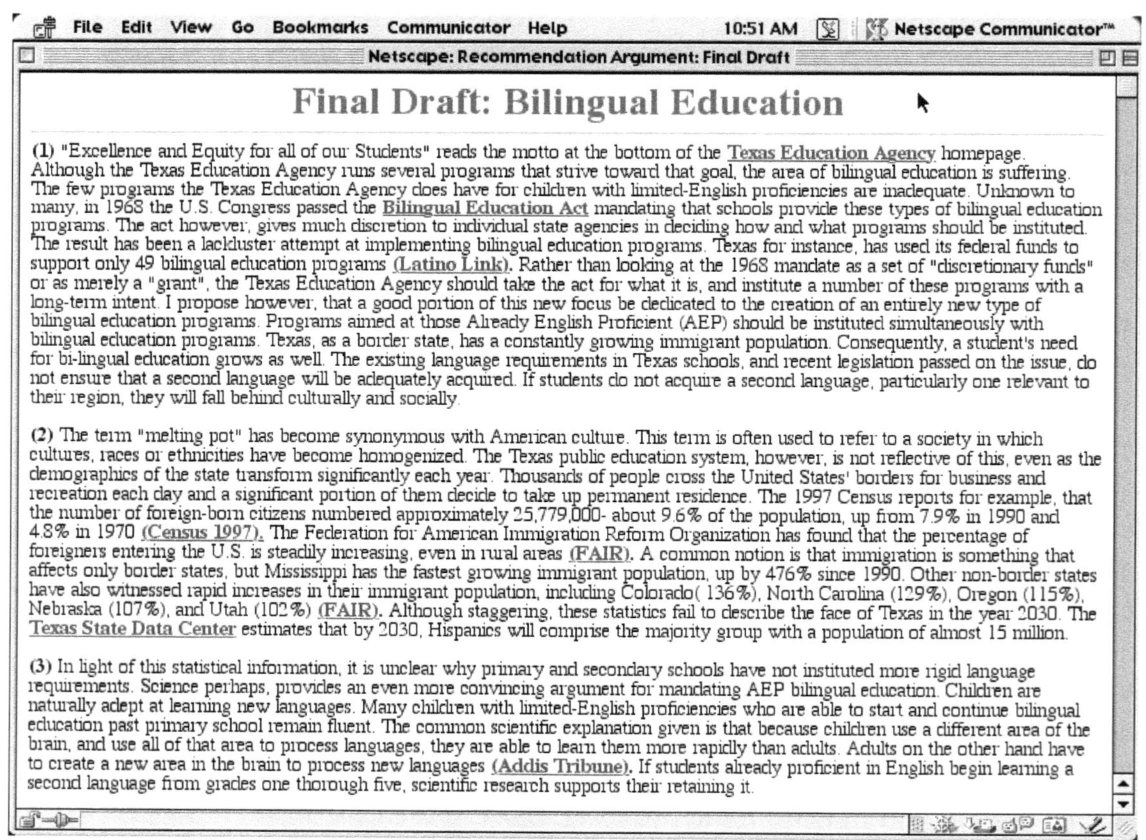

Final Draft: Bilingual Education

(1) "Excellence and Equity for all of our Students" reads the motto at the bottom of the Texas Education Agency homepage. Although the Texas Education Agency runs several programs that strive toward that goal, the area of bilingual education is suffering. The few programs the Texas Education Agency does have for children with limited-English proficiencies are inadequate. Unknown to many, in 1968 the U.S. Congress passed the Bilingual Education Act mandating that schools provide these types of bilingual education programs. The act however, gives much discretion to individual state agencies in deciding how and what programs should be instituted. The result has been a lackluster attempt at implementing bilingual education programs. Texas for instance, has used its federal funds to support only 49 bilingual education programs (Latino Link). Rather than looking at the 1968 mandate as a set of "discretionary funds" or as merely a "grant", the Texas Education Agency should take the act for what it is, and institute a number of these programs with a long-term intent. I propose however, that a good portion of this new focus be dedicated to the creation of an entirely new type of bilingual education programs. Programs aimed at those Already English Proficient (AEP) should be instituted simultaneously with bilingual education programs. Texas, as a border state, has a constantly growing immigrant population. Consequently, a student's need for bi-lingual education grows as well. The existing language requirements in Texas schools, and recent legislation passed on the issue, do not ensure that a second language will be adequately acquired. If students do not acquire a second language, particularly one relevant to their region, they will fall behind culturally and socially.

(2) The term "melting pot" has become synonymous with American culture. This term is often used to refer to a society in which cultures, races or ethnicities have become homogenized. The Texas public education system, however, is not reflective of this, even as the demographics of the state transform significantly each year. Thousands of people cross the United States' borders for business and recreation each day and a significant portion of them decide to take up permanent residence. The 1997 Census reports for example, that the number of foreign-born citizens numbered approximately 25,779,000- about 9.6% of the population, up from 7.9% in 1990 and 4.8% in 1970 (Census 1997). The Federation for American Immigration Reform Organization has found that the percentage of foreigners entering the U.S. is steadily increasing, even in rural areas (FAIR). A common notion is that immigration is something that affects only border states, but Mississippi has the fastest growing immigrant population, up by 476% since 1990. Other non-border states have also witnessed rapid increases in their immigrant population, including Colorado(136%), North Carolina (129%), Oregon (115%), Nebraska (107%), and Utah (102%) (FAIR). Although staggering, these statistics fail to describe the face of Texas in the year 2030. The Texas State Data Center estimates that by 2030, Hispanics will comprise the majority group with a population of almost 15 million.

(3) In light of this statistical information, it is unclear why primary and secondary schools have not instituted more rigid language requirements. Science perhaps, provides an even more convincing argument for mandating AEP bilingual education. Children are naturally adept at learning new languages. Many children with limited-English proficiencies who are able to start and continue bilingual education past primary school remain fluent. The common scientific explanation given is that because children use a different area of the brain, and use all of that area to process languages, they are able to learn them more rapidly than adults. Adults on the other hand have to create a new area in the brain to process new languages (Addis Tribune). If students already proficient in English begin learning a second language from grades one thorough five, scientific research supports their retaining it.

Figure 18.7

they play a role in their own evaluation, they're more likely to view the teacher as an ally in the learning process rather than as an adversary in the "grading game."

REFERENCES

Anderson, D., B. Bret, and W. Paredes-Holt. 1998. *Connections: A guide to on-line writing*. Boston: Allyn and Bacon.

Bolter, J. D. 1991. *Writing space: The computer, hypertext, and the history of writing*. Hillsdale, NJ: Lawrence Erlbaum.

Brewer, B., H. Davis, and P. Jeutonne. 1997. *Electronic discourse: Linquistic individuals in virtual space*. Albany: State University of New York Press.

Bump, J. 1990. Radical changes in class discussions using networked computers. *Computers and Humanities*. 24: 49–65.

Burniske, R. W. 1998. The shadow play: How the integration of technology annihilates debate in our schools. *Phi Delta Kappan*. 80(2): 155–57.

———. 1999. Computer illiteracy: Vice or virtue? *AFT On Campus*. 18(5): 18.

Burniske, R. W., and L. Monke. Forthcoming. *Breaking down the digital walls: Learning to teach in a post-modem world*. Albany: State University of New York Press.

Classroom Connect. December 1994–January 1995. Acceptable use policies: Defining what's allowed online and what's not. *Classroom Connect Newsletter*. Available online: <http://www.wentworth.com/classroom/aup.htm>

Costanzo, W. 1994. Reading, writing and thinking in an age of electronic literacy. In *Literacy and computers: The complications of teaching and learning with technology*, edited by C. L. Selfe and S. Hilligoss. New York: Modern Language Association.

Edgar, C., and S. N. Wood, eds. 1996. *The nearness of you: Students and teachers writing on-line*. New York: Teachers and Writers Collaborative.

Gibaldi, J. 1999. *MLA handbook for writers of research papers*. 5th ed. New York: Modern Language Association.

Gilster, P. 1997. *Digital literacy*. New York: John Wiley.

Haas, C. 1996. *Writing technology: Studies on the materiality of literacy*. Mahwah, NJ: Lawrence Erlbaum.

Harris, J. 1998. *Virtual architecture: Designing and directing curriculum-based telecomputing*. Eugene, OR: IFTE Publications.

Hirsch, E. D. 1987. *Cultural literacy: What every American needs to know*. Boston: Houghton Mifflin.

Electronic Portfolios

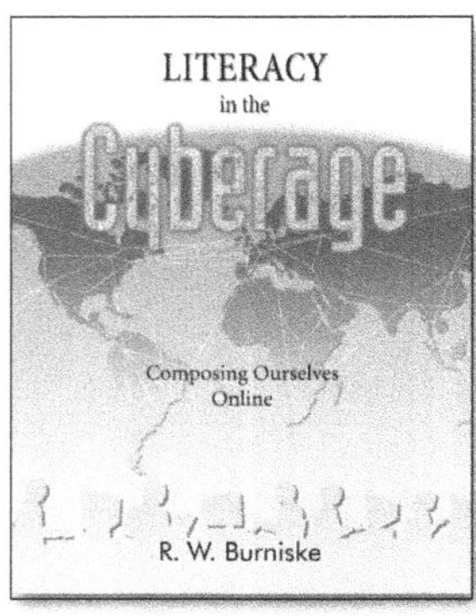

Kelly, K. 1996. The electronic hive. Embrace it. In *Computerization and controversy: Value conflicts and social choices,* 2nd ed., edited by R. Kling. San Diego, CA: Academic Press.

Kling, R., ed. 1996. *Computerization and controversy: Value conflicts and social choices.* 2nd ed. San Diego, CA: Academic Press.

Landauer, T. K. 1996. *The trouble with computers.* Cambridge, MA: MIT Press.

Lanham, R. 1994. *The electronic word: Democracy, technology and the arts.* Chicago: University of Chicago Press.

Lave, J., and E. Wenger. 1991. Situated learning: Legitimate, peripheral participation. In *Learning in doing: Cognitive and computational perspectives,* edited by J. F. B. Roy Pea. Cambridge: Cambridge University Press.

Miller, S. E. 1996. *Civilizing cyberspace: Policy, power and the information superhighway.* New York: Addison-Wesley.

Ong, W. 1982. *Orality and literacy: The technologizing of the word.* London: Methuen.

Rheingold, H. 1993. *The virtual community: Homesteading on the electronic frontier.* NewYork: Addison-Wesley.

Rogers, A. 1998. *Global literacy in a Gutenberg culture.* Available online: http://lrs.ed.uiuc.edu/Guidelines/Global-Literacy-Rogers.html

Selfe, C. L. 1998. *Technology and literacy: A story about the perils of not paying attention.* Available online: http://www.ncte.org/forums/selfe/

Selfe, C. L., and S. Hilligoss, eds. 1994. *Literacy and computers: The complications of teaching and learning with technology.* New York: Modern Language Association.

Snyder, I., ed. 1998. *Page to screen: Taking literacy into the electronic era.* New York: Routledge.

Syverson, M. A. 1998. *Beyond portfolios: The online learning record.* Available online: http://www.cwrl.utexas.edu/~syverson/olr/

Talbott, S. L. 1995. *The future does not compute: Transcending the machines in our midst.* Sebastopol, CA: O'Reilly & Associates.

Tuman, M., ed. 1992a. *Literacy online: The promise (and peril) of reading and writing with computers.* Pittsburg, PA: University of Pittsburgh Press.

———. 1992b. *Word perfect: Literacy in the computer age.* London: Falmer Press.

Tyner, K. R. 1998. *Literacy in a digital world: Teaching and learning in the age of information.* Mahwah, NJ: Lawrence Erlbaum.

Warschauer, M. 1999. *Electronic literacies: Language, culture, and power in online education.* Mahwah, NJ: Lawrence Erlbaum.

Willinsky, J. 1990. *The new literacy: Redefining reading and writing in the schools.* New York: Routledge.

Recommended Reading List

INTRODUCTION: THOSE WHO CAN, TEACH WELL

School Leadership

Jenlink, P. M. 1995. *Systemic change: Touchstones for the future school.* Palatine, IL:: IRI/SkyLight Training and Publishing.

Renzulli, J. S. 2001. *Enriching curriculum for all students.* Arlington Heights, IL: SkyLight Training and Publishing.

Sweeny, B. W. 2001. *Leading the teacher induction and mentoring program.* Arlington Heights, IL: SkyLight Training and Publishing.

Williams, R. B. 1997. *Twelve roles of facilitators for school change.* Arlington Heights, IL: IRI/SkyLight Training and Publishing.

Professional Development

Barbknecht, A. and C. W. Kieffer. 2001. *Peer coaching: The learning team approach.* Arlington Heights, IL: SkyLight Training and Publishing.

Fullan, M., ed. 1997. *The challenge of school change: A collection of articles.* Arlington Heights, IL: SkyLight Training and Publishing.

Pitton, D. E. 2000. *Mentoring novice teachers: Fostering a dialogue process.* Arlington Heights, IL: SkyLight Training and Publishing.

PART I: COGNITIVE TOOLS FOR TEACHING

Classroom Management

Bosch, K. 1999. *Planning classroom management for change.* Arlington Heights, IL: SkyLight Training and Publishing.

Burke, K., ed. 1995. *Managing the interactive classroom: A collection of articles.* Arlington Heights, IL: IRI/SkyLight Training and Publishing.

———. 2000. *What to do with the kid who . . . : Developing cooperation, self-discipline, and responsibility in the classroom.* Arlington Heights, IL: SkyLight Training and Publishing.

———. 2001. *Tips for managing your classroom.* Arlington Heights, IL: SkyLight Training and Publishing.

Costa, A. L., J. Bellanca, and R. Fogarty. 1992a. *If minds matter: A foreword to the future. Vol. 1: Rationale for change.* Palatine, IL: IRI/SkyLight Training and Publishing.

———. 1992b. *If minds matter: A foreword to the future. Vol. 2: Designs for change.* Palatine, IL: IRI/SkyLight Training and Publishing.

Fogarty, R. 1992. *The mindful school: How to Teach for Transfer.* Palatine, IL: IRI/SkyLight Training and Publishing.

———. 1994. *The mindful school: How to teach for metacognitive reflection.* Palatine, IL: IRI/SkyLight Training and Publishing.

Groeber, J. and T. S. Hansell. 1999. *101 tools for thriving in the classroom.* Arlington Heights, IL: SkyLight Training and Publishing.

Lewkowicz, A. B. 1999. *Teaching emotional intelligence: Making informed choices.* Arlington Heights, IL: SkyLight Training and Publishing.

Skowron, J. 2001. *Powerful lesson planning models: The art of 1000 decisions.* Arlington Heights, IL: SkyLight Training and Publishing.

Multiple Intelligences

Chapman, C. 1993. *If the shoe fits . . .: How to develop multiple intelligences in the classroom.* Palatine, IL: IRI/SkyLight Training and Publishing.

Chapman, C. and L. Freeman. 1996. *Multiple intelligences centers and projects.* Arlington Heights, IL: IRI/SkyLight Training and Publishing.

Lazear, D. 1999a. *Eight ways of knowing: Teaching for multiple intelligences,* 3d ed. Arlington Heights, IL: SkyLight Training and Publishing.

———. 1999b. *Eight ways of teaching: The artistry of teaching with multiple intelligences,* 3d ed. Arlington Heights, IL: SkyLight Training and Publishing.

The Brain and Learning

Fogarty, R.1997. *Brain-compatible classrooms.* Arlington Heights, IL: IRI/SkyLight Training and Publishing.

Mangan, M. A. 1998. *Brain-compatible science.* Arlington Heights, IL: SkyLight Training and Publishing.

Nelson, K. 2001. *Teaching in the cyberage: Linking the Internet and brain theory.* Arlington Heights, IL: SkyLight Training and Publishing.

Parry, T., and G. Gregory. 1998. *Designing brain-compatible learning.* Arlington Heights, IL: SkyLight Training and Publishing.

Ronis, D. 1999. *Brain-compatible mathematics.* Arlington Heights, IL: SkyLight Training and Publishing.

———. 2000. *Brain-compatible assessments.* Arlington Heights, IL: SkyLight Training and Publishing.

Williams, R.B. and S.E. Dunn. 2000. *Brain-compatible learning for the block.* Arlington Heights, IL: SkyLight Training and Publishing.

PART II: HANDS-ON TOOLS FOR TEACHING

Teaching Strategies

Beamon, G. W. 2001. *Teaching with adolescent learning in mind.* Arlington Heights, IL: SkyLight Training and Publishing Inc.

Bellanca, J. 1990. *The cooperative think tank: Graphic organizers to teach thinking in the cooperative classroom.* Palatine, IL: IRI/SkyLight Training and Publishing, Inc.

Bellanca, J. 1992a. *Active learning handbook for the multiple intelligences classroom.* Palatine, IL: IRI/SkyLight Training and Publishing, Inc.

———. 1992b. *The cooperative think tank II: Graphic organizers to teach thinking in the cooperative classroom.* Palatine, IL: IRI/SkyLight Training and Publishing.

Bellanca, J. and R. Fogarty. 1991. *Blueprints for thinking in the cooperative classroom.* Palatine, IL: IRI/SkyLight Training and Publishing, Inc.

Burke, K. 2000. *What to do with the kid who . . . : Developing cooperation, self-discipline, and responsibility in the classroom.* Arlington Heights, IL: SkyLight Training and Publishing.

Costa, A. L., ed. 1991. *The school as a home for the mind: A collection of articles.* Palatine, IL: IRI/SkyLight Training and Publishing, Inc.

Fogarty, R. 1995. *Best practices for the learner-centered classroom.* Palatine, IL: IRI/SkyLight Training and Publishing.

Rodriguez, E. R. and J. Bellanca. 1997. *What is it about me you can't teach: An instructional guide for the urban educator.* Arlington Heights, IL: IRI/SkyLight Training and Publishing.

Sternberg, R. J., and E. L. Grigorenko. 2000. *Teaching for successful intelligence: To increase student learning and achievement.* Arlington Heights, IL: SkyLight Training and Publishing.

Mathematics, Science, and Social Studies

Berman, S. 1993. *Catch them thinking in science: A handbook of classroom strategies.* Palatine, IL: IRI/SkyLight Training and Publishing.

Depka, E. 2001. *Designing rubrics for mathematics.* Arlington Heights, IL: SkyLight Training and Publishing.

Hammerman, E., and D. Musial. 1995. *Classroom 2061: Activity-based assessments in science integrated with mathematics and language arts.* Palatine, IL: IRI/SkyLight Training and Publishing.

Hickman, M. and E. O. Wigginton. 1999. *Catch them thinking in social studies: A handbook of cooperative learning activities.* Arlington Heights, IL: SkyLight Training and Publishing.

Martin, H. 1996a. *Integrating mathematics across the curriculum.* Arlington Heights: IRI/SkyLight Training and Publishing.

———. 1996b. *Multiple intelligences in the mathematics classroom.* Arlington Heights, IL: IRI/SkyLight Training and Publishing.

———. 2000. *Multiple intelligences and standards-based mathematics.* Arlington Heights, IL: SkyLight Training and Publishing.

Parratore, P. 1998. *Hands-on science for the active learning classroom.* Arlington Heights, IL: SkyLight Training and Publishing.

Literacy

Burniske, R. W. 2000. *Literacy in the cyberage: Composing ourselves online.* Arlington Heights, IL: SkyLight Training and Publishing.

Burns, B. 1999. *The mindful school: How to teach balanced reading and writing.* Arlington Heights, IL: SkyLight Training and Publishing.

English, E.W. 1999. *Gift of literacy for the multiple intelligences classroom.* Arlington Heights, IL: SkyLight Training and Publishing.

Fogarty, R. 2001. *Literacy matters: Strategies every teacher can use.* Arlington Heights, IL: SkyLight Training and Publishing.

Freed, S. A., and L. Moon. 1999. *The multiple intelligences pathways to literacy: Making SMILIE^{2}S.* Arlington Heights: SkyLight Training and Publishing.

Lauber, G., and E. Rothstein. 2000. *Writing as learning: A content-based approach.* Arlington Heights, IL: SkyLight Training and Publishing.

Groeber, J. 1999. *More than 100 tools for literacy in today's classroom.* Arlington Heights, IL: SkyLight Training and Publishing.

Lipton, L., and D. Hubble. 1997. *More than 50 ways to learner-centered literacy.* Arlington Heights, IL: IRI/SkyLight Training and Publishing.

Sejnost, R., and Thiese, S. 2001. *Reading and writing across content areas.* Arlington Heights, IL: SkyLight Training and Publishing.

Starrett, E. V. 2000. *Teaching phonics for balanced reading.* Arlington Heights, IL: SkyLight Training and Publishing.

Whitehead, D. 1998. *Catch them thinking and writing: A handbook of classroom strategies.* Arlington Heights, IL: SkyLight Training and Publishing.

Problem-Based Learning

Barell, J. 1998. *Problem-based learning: An inquiry approach.* Arlington Heights, IL: SkyLight Training and Publishing.

Berman, S. 1997. *Project learning for the multiple intelligences classroom.* Arlington Heights, IL: IRI/SkyLight Training and Publishing.

———. 1999a. *Performance-based learning for the multiple intelligences classroom.* Arlington Heights, IL: SkyLight Training and Publishing.

———. 1999b. *Service learning for the multiple intelligences classroom*. Arlington Heights, IL: IRI/SkyLight Training and Publishing.

Fogarty, R. 1997. *Problem-based learning and other curriculum models for the multiple intelligences classroom*. Arlington Heights, IL: IRI/SkyLight Training and Publishing.

Moye, V. H. 1998. *Problem-based learning in social studies: Cues to culture and change*. Arlington Heights, IL: SkyLight Training and Publishing.

Ronis, D. 2001. *Problem-based learning for math and science: Integrating inquiry and the Internet*. Arlington Heights, IL: SkyLight Training and Publishing.

Technology

Ash, L., J. Luckey, and J. Avis. 1999. *Design teams for school change: A cyberprojects approach*. Arlington Heights, IL: SkyLight Training and Publishing.

Burniske, R.W. 2000. *Literacy in the cyberage: Composing ourselves online*. Arlington Heights, IL: SkyLight Training and Publishing.

Mandel, S. 1998a. *Social studies in the cyberage: Applications with cooperative learning*. Arlington Heights, IL: SkyLight Training and Publishing.

———. 1998b. *Virtual field trips in the cyberage: A content mapping approach*. Arlington Heights, IL: SkyLight Training and Publishing.

Nelson, K. 2001. *Teaching in the cyberage: Linking the Internet and brain theory*. Arlington Heights, IL: SkyLight Training and Publishing.

Treadwell, M. 1999. *Educator's guide to searching the Internet*. Arlington Heights, IL: SkyLight Training and Publishing.

———. 2001. *1001 best Internet sites for educators*, 2d ed. Arlington Heights, IL: SkyLight Training and Publishing.

PART III: ASSESSMENT TOOLS FOR TODAY'S CLASSROOM

Assessment and Standards

Ash, L. E. 2000. *Electronic student portfolios*. Arlington Heights, IL: SkyLight Training and Publishing.

Bellanca, J., C. Chapman, and B. Swartz. 1997. *Multiple assessments for multiple intelligences*, 3d ed. Arlington Heights, IL: IRI/SkyLight Training and Publishing.

Burke, K. 1999. *The mindful school: How to assess authentic learning*, 3d ed. Arlington Heights, IL: SkyLight Training and Publishing.

Burke, K., R. Fogarty, and S. Belgrad. 1994. *The mindful school: The portfolio connection*. Palatine, IL: IRI/SkyLight Training and Publishing.

Burniske, R. W. 2000. *Literacy in the cyberage: Composing ourselves online*. Arlington Heights, IL: SkyLight Training and Publishing.

Fogarty, R. 1998. *Balanced assessment.* Arlington Heights, IL: SkyLight Training and Publishing.

———. 1999. *How to raise test scores.* Arlington Heights, IL: SkyLight Training and Publishing.

O'Connor, K. 1999. *The mindful school: How to grade for learning.* Arlington Heights, IL: SkyLight Training and Publishing.

Perna, D. M., and J. R. Davis. 2000. *Aligning standards and curriculum for classroom success.* Arlington Heights, IL: SkyLight Training and Publishing.

Index

Notes

Notes

The Corwin logo—a raven striding across an open book—represents the union of courage and learning. Corwin is committed to improving education for all learners by publishing books and other professional development resources for those serving the field of PreK–12 education. By providing practical, hands-on materials, Corwin continues to carry out the promise of its motto: **"Helping Educators Do Their Work Better."**

www.ingramcontent.com/pod-product-compliance
Ingram Content Group UK Ltd.
Pitfield, Milton Keynes, MK11 3LW, UK
UKHW050048180526
471099UK00006B/262

* 9 7 8 1 5 7 5 1 7 4 9 2 1 *